EMBLEMATIC STRUCTURES IN RENAISSANCE FRENCH CULTURE

The emblem and the device (or *impresa*, as it was called in Italy) were the most direct and telling manifestations of a mentality that played a significant role in the generation and reception of discourse and art in Western Europe between the late Middle Ages and the mid-eighteenth century. In the history of Western symbolism, the emblematic sign forms a bridge between late medieval allegory and the Romantic metaphor. These intricate combinations of picture and text, where the picture completes the ellipses of an epigrammatic text, and where the text fixes the intention of the pictured signs, provide useful clues to the way pictures in general were read and textual descriptions were visualized in early modern Europe.

Daniel Russell demonstrates how the emblematic forms developed and how they functioned within early modern French culture and society. He also attempts to show how the guiding principles behind the composition of emblems influenced the production of courtly decoration, ceremony, and propaganda, as well as the composition of literary texts as different as Maurice Scève's *Delie*, Montaigne's *Essais*, and Du Bartas's *Sepmaine*.

(University of Toronto Romance Series)

DANIEL RUSSELL is Professor and Chairman in the Department of French and Italian Languages and Literatures, University of Pittsburgh.

DANIEL RUSSELL

Emblematic Structures in Renaissance French Culture

UNIVERSITY OF TORONTO PRESS
Toronto Buffalo London

Toronto Buffalo London

Reprinted in paperback 2014

ISBN 978-0-8020-0616-5 (cloth)
ISBN 978-1-4426-5501-0 (paper)

University of Toronto Romance Series 71

Printed on acid-free paper

Canadian Cataloguing in Publication Data

Russell, Daniel S.
Emblematic structures in Renaissance French culture

(University of Toronto romance series ; 71)
Includes bibliographical references and index.
ISBN 978-0-8020-0616-5 (bound)
ISBN 978-1-4426-5501-0 (pbk.)

1. Emblems – France – History. 2. Emblem books, French – History. I. Title. II. Series.

PN6348.5.R87 1995 704.9'46 C95-930826-1

University of Toronto Press acknowledges the financial assistance to its publishing program of the Canada Council and the Ontario Arts Council.

FOR LILA

Contents

Illustrations and Credits

Acknowledgments

This study developed over a period of twenty years or more, and the debts I have accumulated along the way are numerous and substantial. First, I must acknowledge the courteous and generous support I have always received from the knowledgeable librarians at the major Paris libraries, especially the Bibliothèque Nationale and the Bibliothèque de l'Arsenal; at the Folger Shakespeare Library in Washington, D.C.; and of course at the libraries that I depend on regularly in Pittsburgh, the Carnegie-Mellon University Library and the Hillman and Frick Fine Arts Libraries at the University of Pittsburgh.

At the University of Pittsburgh my work and its publication have been supported in various ways by the Faculty of Arts and Sciences, and its understanding dean, Peter F.M. Koehler; by the West European Studies Program of the University Center for International Studies; and finally by the Central Research Development Fund. Indispensable trips to France and long periods of uninterrupted research and writing have been made possible by generous grants and fellowships from the National Endowment for the Humanities, the Guggenheim Foundation, and the American Philosophical Society. Finally, I would like to thank all the editors at the University of Toronto Press who have made this manuscript into a book: Ron Schoeffel, who got everything started; Anne Forte, who carried on his good work; and Darlene Money, whose expertise, care, and patience have made it a better book, and a more readable one.

But most precious of all were the support, counsel, and helpful readings of good friends and colleagues. Among them, I would like especially to note the emblem scholars Peter M. Daly, John Manning, William S. Heckscher, Pedro Campa, and David Graham, who all gave me such useful and sympathetic readings of my text at various stages in its development. Alison Stones helped me come as close as I will ever be able to an understanding of the history of medieval manuscript illumination. My student Didier Course provided me with one of the most important theoretical insights underpinning my concluding summary. And my friend Marianne Meijer has supported my work with emblems over the years in ways too numerous to detail. To all of them my deepest gratitude.

EMBLEMATIC STRUCTURES IN RENAISSANCE FRENCH CULTURE

Introduction

The emblem was a highly self-conscious enactment of a particular kind of rhetorical image, which lay somewhere between late medieval allegory and the Romantic metaphor as they were understood in the modernist lexicon of rhetoric and poetics. What this study posits as the emblematic image was more extended, and built on more commonly accepted analogies, than the Romantic metaphor, but it rarely extended into a narrative as allegory did, nor did it use the traditional analogies in the previously expected ways. Such images dominated rhetorical discourse between the early sixteenth century and the coming of Romanticism in the middle of the eighteenth century.

But culture's inherent conservatism did not permit the emblematic mode to disappear completely until the late nineteenth century, and we find emblematic images side by side with Romantic 'symbols' throughout the nineteenth century, despite Romanticism's avowed disdain for allegory and the emblem. Contrasting examples demonstrate how the Romantic metaphor or symbol differed from the emblematic image.

With the *Quatre grandes harmonies* of 1830 the Romantic poet Alphonse de Lamartine attempted to show that, for those who know how to see, everything reveals the existence of God. 'Le Chêne' is the second of these meditations, and in it the poet follows the fortunes of a poor acorn buffeted by the forces of nature until it comes to rest upon a barren rock. There, the process of germination, growth, and maturation turns it into a mighty oak, whose perennial strength, having emerged from such humble beginnings, stands in silent testimony to the power and mystery of nature. The oak is a metonym representing nature in its entirety, and as such is never detached from its surroundings in this poem, but serves simply as the focal point for the poet's meditation on God's role and place in nature. The image is presented in a sweeping landscape picture with the oak at its centre, but in interaction with eagles and the wind; further, its leaves that return with each new year contrast with the wheat that is harvested once and for all, and they contrast too with the tower that falls eventually to ruin, or the river that eventually runs dry.

The oak becomes a symbol that, in its complex relations with its surroundings and the symbolic traditions that it evokes, captures metonymically and metaphorically all the mystery of nature in itself, while also standing as a visible reminder of God's omnipresence and omnipotence. The poet carefully avoids stating any explicit *signifié*, even though he does hint at the direction his meditation is taking when he claims the oak builds its root structure because it seems to know that fierce storms await it in the future: 'Il sait que l'ouragan sonore / L'attend au jour ... ou, s'il l'ignore, / Quelqu'un du moins le sait pour lui' (ll. 33–5). This treatment of the oak may be usefully contrasted with the complex simile the poet develops next around the ship image, to illustrate the young oak's work in laying down a stable foundation of roots in preparation for the struggle against those coming storms:

Ainsi quand le jeune navire
Où s'élancent les matelots,
Avant d'affronter son empire,
Veut s'apprivoiser sur les flots,
Laissant filer son vaste câble,
Son ancre va chercher le sable
Jusqu'au fond des vallons mouvants,
Et sur ce fondement mobile
Il balance son mât fragile
Et dort au vain roulis des vents. (ll. 36–45)

The classical periphrasis in lines 38 and 42 underlines the conservative nature of this image as opposed to the modernity of the Romantic symbol that dominates the poem. But 'empire' and 'vallon' are also terms associated with *terra firma*, and the metaphors they thus imply generate the partial analogies that link this complex image to the main theme. The resulting web of metaphors recalls the mechanism of allegory except for the lack of the narrative thread that is ordinarily a prerequisite for allegory. Finally, though, despite a wealth of concrete, descriptive detail, this image is isolated from the surrounding development in the most exemplary manner; it is a seascape dropped down in the middle of a landscape, a neatly framed painting for some nineteenth-century drawing room.

For all these reasons, this image is what I call an emblematic image, one that can be detached from its setting with no loss of meaning to the argument it is illustrating. The shaping of the oak into a symbol of God's power and its manifestation in nature is, on the other hand, the very subject of the poem,[1] and by its metonymic nature would leave a gaping hole in the landscape if it were removed. It has, then, complex relations with its setting, and hence its potential for meaning is infinitely open-ended.

In a manuscript collection of emblems composed around 1680, René de Bruc, marquis de Montplaisir,[2] composed an emblem with the motto *Dritto e incorrotto* around the image of a cedar tree upon a barren peak in Lebanon (fig. 1). Beneath a topical title, 'De la Justice,' the emblem text exhorts the reader to a particular path of conduct in the first five lines:

Ne fais rien par faveur par haine ou par caprice
Rejette les conseils des folles passions
Et sy tu veux que Dieu te soit tousjours propice
Fais que la Charité, la Raison, la Justice
Reglent touttes tes actions.

This development leads the reader into a metaphorical illustration that reveals the relation between theme, motto, and picture in the last four lines:

Ainsy malgré des Ventz la secousse terrible
Dessus le Mont Liban saint et delicieux,
Le Cedre se maintient tousjours Incorruptible
Et porte ses Rameaux tousjours droit vers les cieux.

Nothing of the meaning is lost if the cedar image is dropped; it is pure rhetorical enhancement; the image in this text is a metaphorical illustration of the theme just as the emblem picture is a literal illustration of the textual image. The cedar stands for incorruptible virtue, no more and no less. It possesses none of the richly suggestive semantic indeterminacy of Lamartine's oak symbol.

More than a hundred years earlier, Jean-Antoine de Baïf composed a sonnet for his *Passetems* that uses substantially the same image in substantially the same way, except that in this version the cedar is replaced by a pine tree:

Comme sur le coupeau d'une grand' roche dure
  Un pin enraciné demeure verdoyant,

De la Justice.

Ne fais rien par faueur par haine ou par caprice
Rejette les conseils des folles passions
Et si tu veux que Dieu te soit tousjours propice
Fais que la Charité, la Raison, la Justice
Reglent touttes tes actions

Fig. 1. *Dritto e incorrotto*, René de Bruc, marquis de Montplaisir, *Emblemes et devises chrestiennes et morales*, no. 9.

Soit que le chaud Soleil de l'aesté flamboyant
Ramene la chaleur, ou l'yver la froidure,
Tousjours planté debout, d'un feuillage qui dure,
Garde le bel honneur: & tousjours s'egayant
D'un fruit en ses rameaux sans cesse pommoyant,
Parmy aspres cailloux repousse tout injure.
Ainsi, ô Villeroy, planté non ébranlable
Aux plus hautes grandeurs de la perverse Court,

Où les vices ont cours, te maintiens ferme & stable:
Et maintiens la vertu, qui seule te commande:
Et recherant l'honneur, où fraude regne et court,
Plus vice y est grand, plus ta gloire en est grande.[3]

Here, as in any device, or *impresa*, where a short motto is coupled with a figure to express an individual ideal or project,[4] the image is applied to an individual, but as in De Bruc's more general emblem, the message would be clear without the image. It seems to be superfluous ornamentation. Upon closer inspection, however, it is clear that Baïf's image has the effect of giving new life to the rhetoric of the message; no longer are the expressions 'planté,' 'non ébranlable,' and 'hautes grandeurs' empty metaphors, but Baïf's concrete description, which gives the same independence to the scene evoked as that of an emblem picture, charges, by the very same token, figures from a dead rhetoric with vivid associations upon which the reader can build further associations at will. Hence, the 'hautes grandeurs' become the stony, barren heights so little conducive to rich and verdant growth, and so on. This is how the best emblematic images worked in Renaissance poetry to broaden and enrich the impact of courtly or didactic rhetoric. The emblematic image is a detachable, ornamental image, but by the very fact that it can stand alone, detached from the development it is intended to support and illuminate, it is also independent from that development, and provides an open field for the free association of the reader. It is no longer held captive by its *signifié*, and as if absorbed by it.[5]

Such an image makes room for a more independent and active role for the reader, and reminds us of the parallel development of so-called realistic description. It is a commonplace that, thanks in part to the introduction of the more sophisticated technique of copperplate engraving, emblem illustrations became, with the passage of time, infinitely more elaborate than the schematic woodblock illustrations of the first editions of Alciato's emblems. These illustrations, as for example in the case of many emblems by the Dutch artist Roemer Visscher, also became much more naturalistic. In other collections, the emblematic sign was placed in a landscape that contained elements extraneous to the emblematic development. As a result, discrepancies between emblem picture and emblem text, which increasingly appeared as two independent entities tied together by some clever conceit, began to open a space that invited independent speculation by a reader/viewer.

Description, too, became increasingly detached from the story-line and thesis of the work that it was intended to support in increasingly vague, oblique, and unstated ways. Neoclassical manuals of rhetoric like that of

Dumarsais define description in terms that recall the *ut pictura poesis* metaphor: they speak of its ecphrastic qualities, its 'energy,' the way it produces hypotyposis, and even the impression of a picture. Description, then, was intended to produce effects of presence, and hence, functioned like all illustration, including emblem illustrations, from the late Middle Ages through the age of the emblem. Further, description also fits into the pattern of a narrative the same way an emblematic image does. Just as in an emblematic image as I have defined it,[6] description is framed by formulas such as 'I was standing at a window ...' and it stops the movement of the narrative.

Indeed, it is truly remarkable how many similarities exist between description as Philippe Hamon defines it in his well-known article in *Poétique*[7] and the emblematic image. One can even claim that description in early modern Europe may often be usefully understood as emblematic to the extent that it articulates our understanding of the thing described in particular ways. It is this emblematic image that I propose to isolate and define in this study. The emblem itself, and the related form known as a *devise* or *impresa*, will be important in this investigation primarily to the extent that they are useful in defining the emblematic image more generally, and in providing clues to the formation of a culture that was conditioned by its use. In short, it is my thesis that the emblematic forms should be seen principally as symptoms of a transitional mentality that defines the period between the Middle Ages and the coming of Romanticism in the middle of the eighteenth century, and at least in some measure, governs its rhetoric and its aesthetic response to art.

Over the past decade or so, French emblem books of the sixteenth century have begun to interest scholars to an extent and in ways unheard of since emblems became marginal to the French cultural experience in the period between 1750 and 1850. Emblems were the subject of the first annual meeting of the recently formed Société Française des Seiziémistes; they have been the focus of an *équipe de recherches* at one of the Paris universities; and now a Parisian publisher has introduced a series of reprint editions of emblem books in the Bibliothèque Interuniversitaire de Lille.[8] More important than any of these developments, however, two recent groundbreaking studies by the French art historians, Anne-Marie Lecoq[9] and Paulette Choné,[10] have changed our view of French cultural history of the sixteenth century in ways that are sure to influence future studies of art and literature. Together with the earlier work of Françoise Bardon,[11] these studies have begun to shed new light on sixteenth-century French culture, which should bring renewed interest to the study of emblems and applied emblematics. In particular, they show how important emblems and the mentality that produced them must have been in shaping the dissemination of moral and religious doctrine, as well as the presentation of political propaganda in Renaissance France. As a result, these studies in cultural history and the *histoire des mentalités* have provided many models for the study that follows, even though their authors are art historians, more or less in the tradition of André Chastel, while I am approaching the subject with the tools of a historian and critic of literature.

However much these studies have contributed to our appreciation of the emblem as a powerful force in Renaissance French culture, French emblem studies are still in their infancy, and they are unlikely to move much further toward maturity until the neo-Latinist Claudie Balavoine publishes her eagerly awaited commentaries on Alciato. As is true of emblem studies more generally, it is still somewhat unclear where the study of French emblems might be headed. While the current interest in French emblems can probably be traced to a broader interest in the relation between picture and text that has emerged in the study of French culture over the past ten or fifteen years, it is still not clear what light the study of emblems can bring to bear on the great problems of cultural history. In the past, emblems have provided a mine of information on individual iconographical problems in the study of particular paintings and literary texts, but their broader place and significance in the cultural configuration of the Renaissance is not yet widely understood and appreciated. Emblem books will likely continue to serve scholars as precious reference texts, but the emblem itself as a cultural form peculiar to the Renaissance can, I believe, tell us much more about the period and its approach to art and communication than it has done so far.

Actually, the period of the emblem, the *aetas emblematica*, may be defined as the time between the mid-fifteenth and the early eighteenth centuries, that is, between the late Middle Ages, with its struggles between realism and nominalism, and the coming of Romanticism around the middle of the eighteenth century. The emblematic forms most certainly predate Alciato's variations on Greek Anthology epigrams, and the felicitous name he chose to give to them, by at least fifty years. Likewise, the emblem persisted well into the eighteenth century, even though it no longer embodied or represented any of the forces shaping French culture, and just like most other cultural forms it continued to linger on into the nineteenth century, like a house guest who has overstayed his welcome, well beyond the time of its cultural pertinence, in France at least, and perhaps in other parts of western Europe as well.

This book is intended to support the hypothesis that the emblem is the characteristic symbolic form in European culture during the period I have just defined. It would seem further that the emblem may well provide a bridge between allegory, the dominant symbolic and rhetorical form of late medieval culture, and the new type of metaphor that begins to take shape with European Romanticism. As such, the emblem would, then, be the typical representative of one of the epistemological forms that shaped thought and expression during the period, and when it ceased to exercise such an influence it could only provide decoration or serve as the vehicle for private devotional meditation and the moral instruction of children, as it did, for example, in Victorian England.

For the purposes of this hypothesis, I have adopted a modernist definition of allegory and metaphor as it is presented by Henri Morier in his classic dictionary of poetry and rhetoric.[12] In a broadly accepted tradition conditioned by Romantic practice and theory, Morier sees metaphor as an 'exaltation du sentiment' that powers the passage from a partial to an absolute identification of a real object with an imagined object (672). For Voltaire, metaphor lies in the domain of passion. It is based on a highly personal intuition, and it is characteristic of poetry as it has been defined throughout the modernist period.

Metaphor may, of course, be found at any time, and in any place, but it would seem to be particularly characteristic of the Romantic and post-Romantic mentality in the west. Allegory, too, may appear anywhere, but it is often taken to be typical, as indeed it actually was in many respects, of the European Middle Ages, especially in their decline. The modernist view of allegory, or at least of 'naive allegory' as Morier puts it, saw it as intellectual and abstract. Allegory was understood to begin with an idea, which was then provided with some concrete vehicle for its expression, whereas metaphor is supposed to begin with a meditation, like that of Lamartine, on some object that evokes a multiplicity of values and ideas (79).

But it is important to recall Aristotle's definition of allegory as an *extended* metaphor. This extension severely limits the possibility of multiplying the objects, ideas, or values signified by an allegory because of the need for the different parts of the extension to hold together in some logical or narrative scheme. Medieval allegories were polyvalent, but coherently unified, projections of a world-view that was supposed to be absolutely valid and able to account for all of human experience. Each of these allegories pretended to be the accurate presentation of the world-view, and taken as a varied and at times differing group, they therefore seem to foreshadow the coming period of more general relativity in the way people viewed the world. With the rediscovery of an ancient past that now appeared to be an autonomous other, with the coming of the Reformation, and with the beginning of the scientific revolution, the Renaissance saw the multiplication of competing world-views. These in turn were modified and modulated by the newly developing national cultures. By the time of the Romantic redefinition of Western consciousness and sensibility, the individual had become an important modulating force in his own right for the variation of world-views, and consequently a prime source for poetic symbolism. And then just as with the decline of realism in the late Middle Ages, the decay of Romanticism was characterized by a new allegorism, that of Freudian psychoanalysis.

It is between allegory, with its external guarantees of meaning and authority, and metaphor, whose guarantees are largely interior and subjective, that the emblematic forms must be understood. The emblem was the symptom of an epistemological condition, and it was just as distinct and characteristic of a specific period as allegory or metaphor.

In the study that follows I have tried to show how such an epistemological form might have taken shape in the slow evolution from a medieval to an early modern society in France, and then how that form, which we may know only as an ideal and hypothetical construct, might provide an analytical model for understanding why different cultural manifestations took the shape they did. Among other things, this model should provide a heuristic tool for understanding better how Renaissance imitation worked and to what ends, for understanding better, too, the way formulaic expression became relegated to the status of quotation alongside what has come to be considered original expression.

Nearly half of my study is devoted to the period that stretches from the high Middle Ages to the time just before the publication of Alciato's emblems, when parallel developments with medieval roots and antecedents may have exercised some influence on the final shape of his emblems. In that section, I could be accused of doing what I have often told my students not to do; that is, I write the history of medieval illumination, medieval typology, and medieval allegory in such a way as to show how their evolution may have led to the emergence of the emblem. It was not my intention, however, to argue that they did not prepare other developments as well, nor that they can be reduced to the role of forerunner of other, later developments. If anything, the emblem, in its classic embodiment, simply represents a decadent form of medieval illustration, but a decadent form that prepares and prefigures something new.

C.-F. Menestrier and the other seventeenth-century theorists were unwilling to credit Alciato with the creation of an entirely new genre or art form. Rather, they felt he had simply revived and perfected an ancient form that, in their eyes, was most conspicuously exemplified by productions like the *Tabula Cebetis*, Philostratus' *Imagines*, Horapollo's *Hieroglyphics*, or even Aesop's fables. Renaissance humanists, of course, had already considered these works to be closely related to the emblem form, as is clear from their presentation and format in some sixteenth-century editions.[13] This Renaissance perception of such ancient works no doubt played an important role in forming the theoretical positions of seventeenth-century emblematists. These writers assumed further, and with some justification, that works of this kind had never completely ceased to be produced during the Middle Ages, and such works actually did begin to proliferate during the fourteenth and fifteenth centuries. Although he might have chosen better examples, Menestrier was fundamentally correct in seeing potential emblems in the alchemical compositions of Nicolas Flamel, and in Petrarch's *Triumphs*.[14]

However profitable it may be to argue whether generically definable emblems actually did exist before the composition of Alciato's *emblemata*, it is undeniable that there existed in France a long indigenous tradition of didactic and inspirational book illustration that dated from the Carolingian renaissance of the ninth century and that became increasingly proto-emblematic toward the end of the Middle Ages. At the very least, this tradition could easily have provided models for the intimate reciprocal relationship between picture and text that has always been taken to characterize the emblem form. Furthermore, as late medieval men and women began to develop a growing need to express thought in visual, concrete form, they began to translate moral precepts and ideas of virtue into allegories of ingenious novelty and decadent complexity, which broke with iconographical traditions and foreshadowed the combinations of allegory and rebus soon to be found in Renaissance emblems.[15] Finally, during the first third of the sixteenth century, combinations bearing a remarkable resemblance to Alciato's emblems did in fact begin to appear with increasing frequency in manuscripts and printed books in France.

There is ample evidence that this long tradition was in no way foreign to, or detached from, the development of a distinctly national emblem literature in France. Emblematists drew heavily on materials and models from this tradition throughout the sixteenth century; and even after the religious emblems produced in Flanders, Germany, and Italy between 1570 and 1650 began to influence French emblematics, French artists continued to look to this indigenous tradition for models and motifs. Then, as the tradition was more or less definitively abandoned in the last third of the seventeenth century, emblem literature too began to lose much of its vitality, and the ground was prepared for the steady decline of interest in these forms during the eighteenth century.

My study of the emblem in its earliest incarnations in France is intended to show how the process of authoring these compositions was a joint venture; a poet-humanist may have prepared texts, but probably did not maintain complete control over the finished product, which required the talents of an artist for the woodcuts, a compositor for the paginal distribution of the parts, and whose final effect was probably often orchestrated by a printer/publisher who may have commissioned the work. As a result, the history of the production of emblem books provides interesting insights into the development of the French printing trade in the sixteenth century, especially as it regards the production and use of woodblock illustrations.

The section devoted to a study of the emblem books themselves in sixteenth-century France is divided into three chapters. After a summary history of Alciato's creation of the forms and, in particular, his use of the two main models for the emblem, the Greek Anthology and Horapollo's *Hieroglyphics*, chapter two offers some speculation about the use and dissemination of emblems to the extent that it can be deduced from the examination of surviving copies of early emblem books with the help of some of the more rudimentary principles of physical bibliography. The last chapter in this section is devoted to an analysis of the form of the sixteenth-century French emblem.

The final section of my study explores the implications of the emblem for the analysis of other cultural phenomena from the French Renaissance. When various other kinds of cultural phenomena show structural influences of the emblematic forms, they may be characterized as instances of 'applied emblematics.' I have already begun the exploration of such similarities in a number of articles published over the past ten years,[16] and the examples I present here are, for the most part, ones that have not yet found their way into other published studies. Here I explore the ways emblematics provided the vehicle for different kinds of courtly and religious communication. Indoctrination and propaganda, both positive and negative, was the goal of such communication, and the forms it took, aside from emblem books proper, were royal *entrées*, *jetons*, broadsheet satire, and the like. The impact of emblematics is also visible in the structure of prose and poetry, as well as portraits and other kinds of painting throughout the period of mannerism that Gustav René Hocke has defined as extending from 1520 to 1650 and where the goal of art was to 'combiner des images disparates ou ... découvrir des analogies cachées entre des objets apparamment sans rapport entre eux.'[17] As is clear from the writings of both Hocke and Robert Klein,[18] the emblem is a product of the mannerist, perhaps even more than the baroque, mentality.

Although I have been speaking of emblematic forms, that expression is deceptive. In my earlier study of emblem theory, I suggested that the device is the true emblematic 'form,' and that the emblem is simply the product of a process for assimilating and presenting information.[19] By defining an emblematic process, it may be possible to understand better how the emblematic conditioned the reception of art and the presentation of moral wisdom, political programs, and even amorous declarations. This study is offered as a contribution to that understanding.

PART ONE

MEDIEVAL AND EARLY RENAISSANCE ANTECEDENTS

1

Book Illustration in Medieval France and the Relation between Picture and Text in the Later Middle Ages

Most of the illustrated Greek rolls that have been preserved contain scientific works where the illustrations are embedded in the narrow columns of text in order to elucidate specific techniques or diagram scientific theories and proofs. These illustrations are situated at the exact point in the text to be clarified and, lacking any frame, they sometimes actually seem to merge with the text. As the codex came to replace the roll for all but a few specialized uses in the period between the second and fourth centuries A.D., the columns of text became wider, thus leaving more space for illustration. This space was filled, not by making the illustrations larger, but by the illustration of additional scenes not directly adjacent to the illustrations themselves.[1]

This development opened the way to a new conception of illustration, detached from its justifying text and often serving an ornamental or memorial function rather than an illustrative or explanatory one. In its most extreme manifestation this development yields something like the Rossano Gospels (6th century A.D.) where the text is preceded by a sizeable group of illustrations of the principal scenes of the entire text. As Mary Carruthers has shown concerning a sixth-century manuscript of the Gospels of St Augustine, such 'picture-pages' permitted a diagrammatic arrangement of key scenes to serve as a memory aid for recalling large sections of the text.[2] As a consequence, illustration was no longer embedded in the text, but rather began to lay claim to its own separate space. Nevertheless, even the most highly ornamental illumination never became completely independent of the text; indeed, the purest ornamentation tended to grow out of the text itself. That is, ornament of this sort was often an excrescence of the initial letters and while it did not necessarily support the meaning of the text, it often did signal the articulations and organization of the text and thus served as an aid in reading and recalling the subject-matter and its divisions.[3]

Then, as those religious, and more especially biblical, texts that were most often illustrated in the early Middle Ages began to be read rather than declaimed, there was a tendency to avoid the increasingly illegible decorated letters such as those in the Hiberno-Saxon tradition in favour of something simpler and more closely related to the body of the text. By the end of the Middle Ages, illuminated initials sometimes became the site of truly emblematic compositions, as in BN ms fr. n. a. 22138 (dated 1460–3), where twenty-three of the twenty-five initial letters of this religious and possibly meditational text are turned into rebus-like compositions, or devices associating the text with its owner.[4] The same pressures for legibility also brought a return during the Carolingian period to a more naturalistic style of illustration that would support the process of deciphering a text that accompanies the medieval act of reading. Responding to a southern, classicizing influence, manuscript illustration then began to move away from the decorative patterns of the Hiberno-Saxon tradition and once again toward true 'illustration' in the modern sense; that is, illustration that was imitative, naturalistic, and explanatory rather than purely ornamental *illustratio* in Quintilian's sense (6, 2, 22) of an 'action d'éclairer, de rendre brillant' as in the rhetorical figure of hypotyposis, a kind of striking and animated description.[5]

Nevertheless, such 'illustrations' are still characterized as 'illuminations,' and properly so. It will be most appropriate to understand 'illuminatio' here as that which adds lustre or enlightens (Vulg.; Ps. 89,8; Aug., Serm. 34,5); this was one of the roles illustrations were to play in relation to the text throughout the later Middle Ages, and this meaning continued to adhere to the word 'illustration' well into the Renaissance, as is clear in the title of Du Bellay's *Deffence et illustration de la langue francoyse*.[6] Illustrations were then supposed to be seen as ornaments both in the allegorical sense as defined by Angus Fletcher,[7] and literally, to highlight and enhance a text presented as a luxurious and precious artefact that served as a symbol of God's Word and man's awe-inspired respect of it. To the extent that it was an allegorical 'ornament,' the illustration then began to enter into a closer and more clearly subordinate relationship to the written text than it had previously done in earlier manuscripts illustrated in the Hiberno-Saxon style.[8]

The text was to retain its primary importance throughout the Middle Ages, as the western Church fought the tendency among the faithful to transform images into icons,[9] and refused to let visual art, whether in the form of sculpture or painting, become anything other than *libri laicorum*, following the often misunderstood image of Albert the Great. Indeed, *titulus*–like inscriptions within the pictures seem to have served to legitimate the visual art by labelling figures with their intended identity.[10] It was also during this period, some seven hundred years after the introduction of the codex in western Europe, that scribes and illustrators began to exploit, for the first time, all the formal implications of the manuscript page for narration. As a result, the traditional interconnection between pictures, which had derived from the frieze, began to break up, and miniatures tended thenceforth to become separate compositions once again as they had been in certain early codices such as the Vatican Virgil (Vat. Lat. 3225) or the Rabula Gospels (586 A.D.).

The classicizing Roman tradition in art, so much in evidence during the Carolingian period, lost some of its prominence in France as the influence of the Church increased with the reform of the monasteries beginning in the tenth century. The classical models were then abandoned, since their rather earthy naturalism was ill-suited to the growing need to express and propagate the transcendental truths of the Christian religion; 'with the rejection of classical models came a new Biblical iconography in the typological system which interpreted the scheme of Redemption by means of parallels from the Old and New Testaments. This applied not only to Biblical illustration but to other works which we should think of as secular. All of them, even the Bestiaries, were made to contribute to this central doctrine of the Church.'[11] This system developed mainly in the twelfth century, although it was based on earlier concepts that leave traces in such manuscripts as the famous Stuttgart Psalter (9th–10th century). The justification for such a program can be traced through proverbial paraphrases of Hebrews 10: 1, such as this one by Adam of St Victor: 'Lex est umbra futurorum,' with 'lex' here referring, of course, to the Old Law,[12] understood along the lines of Augustine's threefold division of time: *ante legem, sub lege, sub gratia.*

This new and highly specific subordination of illustration to a particular theological program has implications for the economy of the manuscript illustration that are summarized in this passage from a thirteenth-century guide for manuscript painters:

> C'est pour mettre un frein à la license des peintres et pour les guider dans la décoration des églises où la peinture est admise, qu'on a composé une série de distiques indiquant brièvement le sujet des scènes de l'Ancien Testament et la concordance allégorique de ces sujets avec différents détails du Nouveau Testament. De telles inscriptions ne seront pas nécessaires pour les scènes évangéliques, qui sont familières à tous les fidèles; sur les tableaux de ce dernier genre il suffira d'inscrire les noms des personnages.[13]

This planned integration of text and illustration parallels the development of the use of *tituli* in the *vitraux* of the medieval cathedrals of the twelfth and thirteenth centuries. The *tituli* clearly partake of a tradition dating back to ancient Greece and Rome, where epigrammatic inscriptions were used to comment on works of visual art or to serve as an interlocutor for the mute work of art in a dialogue between the art object and the viewer. Many such epigrams have been preserved in the Greek Anthology, or in the less well-known Roman Anthology. Renaissance humanists rediscovered the Greek Anthology in the fifteenth century, and it served as one of the principal direct sources of inspiration for Alciato's emblems.[14]

Tituli in the margins of manuscripts, as Carruthers (244–5) has noted, summarized sections of a text, and served as mnemonic markers. Within manuscript illustrations *tituli* helped distinguish characters, so that the reader would not confuse, for example, Venus with the Virgin, as Michael Camille has shown in interesting detail.[15] In the cathedrals, *tituli* were integrated into the design of the windows to paraphrase or explain typological scenes according to a specific religious interpretation. These short texts could be made up (this was one of Suger's specialties) or drawn from sermons, from scholarly works of theology, or from the Bible itself. William S. Heckscher and K.-A. Wirth felt that those *vitraux* that attempt to represent and gloss a passage from the Bible are most interesting for the study of emblems, for there the interpretation of the whole creation can be discovered only by reference to both the picture and the biblical verse.[16] But in fact, as Pierre Laurens has shown, the *tituli* used in late antique and early medieval mosaics, stained glass, and the like were often gnomic sayings expanded into rhymed distichs for mnemonic purposes, and were sometimes indistinguishable from the classic epigrams that served as a model for Alciato's emblems.[17]

With the increasing prominence of the specialized three- or fourfold exegetical system during the high Middle Ages, the Bible was increasingly seen to be susceptible to a variety of interpretations at different levels or in different theological contexts, and a picture could be useful in suggesting or isolating for the viewer a particular interpretation of a given biblical verse.[18] One might compare such *vitraux* to sermons in which a priest interprets a biblical passage in such a way as to elucidate, for example, a specific moral teaching; the recollection of such a sermon, or simply of some biblical passage and some point made in a sermon about it, would serve as the point of departure for a personal meditation, especially, but not exclusively, for someone who could not read.[19] For those who could read, the *titulus* containing the pertinent biblical verse would ensure the proper association.

Although elements of typology are already in evidence in the twelfth century, as for example in Suger's windows, it was not until the thirteenth and early fourteenth centuries that this move toward biblical concordances and Christian syncretism produced systematically illustrated works. The sumptuous *Bibles moralisées*, for example, date back only to 1197 at the earliest, and many of them date from the fourteenth and fifteenth centuries.[20] The intimate fusion of text, illustration and decoration that is so prominent in such manuscripts can be traced back to the Carolingian period and the historiated initials of the Corbie psalter or the Drago Sacramentary, although the evolution from decorative to 'historiated' initials really gained momentum only in the twelfth century. By the thirteenth century, miniatures were being combined with the initial in such a way that they, too, were better linked to the text, and visually more closely integrated with it.

In typological biblical concordances, illustrations were designed to demonstrate that the Old Testament was a series of 'figures' or prefigurations of the New Testament; Old Testament people and events were the 'types' for which the New Testament provided the 'antitypes.' When such works were illustrated, textual metaphors were often represented as if they were simply descriptive terms, or the illustrations sometimes contained pictorial cues, as when the faggots on Isaac's shoulders were positioned in the form of a cross.[21] Elsewhere, the illustration commented on the biblical text in a more independent way; the Bible tells us, for example, that Cain slew Abel, without indicating the weapon used. The illustration was obliged to show some weapon, and the artist's choice reflected independent speculation on the means of the crime.[22] Typological symbolism itself was not rigid; sometimes New Testament scenes served as types, and some concordances also used syncretic assimilation to give a Christian interpretation to the ancient symbols of natural history.[23] Menestrier stressed the emblematic quality of all these typological pointers and *rapprochements*, claiming that 'Toutes les figures de l'ancien Testament sont des Emblemes des Mysteres du nouveau.'[24] Indeed, most of these techniques were later used in the early emblem books.

Although the Bible itself, notably in the Pauline readings of the Old Testament, and later St Augustine, suggested the possibility of interpretation through concordance,[25] the flowering of systematic concordances dates mainly from the twelfth and thirteenth centuries. Suger summed up the principle that guided their rather mechanical composition in the following couplet: 'Quod Moyses velat / Christi doctrina revelat.'[26] The earliest large-scale attempts at concordance appear in the *Bibles moralisées*, but the most popular compendia of typological symbolism were probably the illustrated *Biblia pauperum*, composed around the end of the thirteenth century, and the slightly later *Speculum humanae salvationis* of the early fourteenth century – although these are but a very few of the many concordances that circulated at the time. In a book like the *Speculum humanae salvationis* pictures play an important, if not absolutely essential, role because, as Avril Henry puts it, it is 'rather an illustrated text than a series of explained pictures'[27] like the *Bible moralisée* and the *Biblia pauperum*. The pictures are sometimes literal and sometimes allegorical representations of the text illustrated. These pictures are grouped to suggest the typological parallels intended, and the relations between them are often complex or, in some cases, unexpected. Sometimes sets of pictures bring together scenes of only very superficial similarity to engage the viewer in a meditation, we must assume, on the differences between the scenes, and by using more than one type for a single antitype, a variation can be worked on a well-known parallel.[28]

According to Paul Perdrizet, the pictures were probably most essential to the understanding of the text in the *Biblia pauperum*.[29] Yet there circulated unillustrated manuscripts of all these works except the *Bible moralisée*, and the unillustrated versions were presumably destined for the *pauperes*, the poor *clercs* who could not afford illustrated copies, and who did not need illustrations to follow the abbreviated and elliptical exposition, but for whom these books served as a sort of inexpensive theological handbook. When these works were illustrated, the pictures so dominated the paginal space that it is difficult to imagine them to be illustrations in the modern sense; more likely the texts served to summarize the vast biblical text while the pictures provide the spatial metaphors necessary for the diagrammatic organization of the text into a mnemonically effective presentation. In some cases, the illustrations were surely intended to guide the *illiterati* – that is, those who did not read theology or, later, could not read Latin, and schoolboys or the more generally untutored laity[30] – through the text and to serve as a series of landmarks for locating and deciphering specific passages.[31] But in the *Bibles moralisées* and the *Biblia pauperum*, where the text is little more than a labelling appendage to the pictures, the illustrations would also seem to function as memory places intended to recall key scenes from the biblical narrative, or parallels and *rapprochements* remembered from sermons, in such a way as to serve as a starting-point for personal meditation. Illustrations in such cases provide a spatial architecture for an orderly and memorable distribution of the text being illustrated, or recalled.

The books of concordances apparently dominated the production of illustrated manuscripts in the fourteenth and early fifteenth centuries and, as a result, served as an important repository for symbolic motifs and designs. Most art historians agree that fifteenth-century painters and sculptors, estranged from the sources of typological symbolism, depended in large measure on the *Speculum* and the *Biblia pauperum* for models of this type of religious symbolism.[32] So, like emblem books in the sixteenth century, these works served as indispensable manuals for artists in the fifteenth century.

The format of the *Speculum* may have been at least partly responsible for its success; beneath the illustrations, as Adrian and Joyce Wilson have noted, the text follows a rigid, page-governed pattern that made the book especially convenient for scribes and blockmakers to reproduce.[33] We find the same pattern with variations in incunable books like the *Danse macabre* and others, even to the point of reproducing the architectural frames used for the *Speculum* illustrations. The emblem books were perhaps the last kinds of texts to depend for much of their success on this kind of composition determined by the limitations and requirements of the codex page opening.

With the rise of xylography in the late fourteenth and fifteenth centuries, even artists and poor clerics could have had relatively easy access to illustrated copies of the concordances to provide them with visual models for the construction of either real or imaginary pictures of their own. Xylography came into use in the last quarter of the fourteenth century in Rhineland and in the Flemish territories of the dukes of Burgundy, and probably hastened and facilitated the spread of the iconographical habits and compositional patterns of the illustrated manuscript. At first, this process was used to produce isolated religious pictures, commercial tracts, and playing cards. Later, words of explanation were added to pictures, and finally, late in the first half of the fifteenth century, or so it would seem, xylographic books began to appear.[34] These books were usually religious, and often typological; an example is the famous Netherlandish *Biblia pauperum* recently edited by Avril Henry.[35]

These block books served as a transition between the compositional procedures of the late medieval illuminated manuscript and the illustrated book of the age of movable type. Text and illustration were engraved onto blocks used to print single pages or two facing pages of an opening formed by folding a single printed sheet. The blank versos were glued to those of other openings to form gatherings or whole books.[36] Because of limitations imposed by the woodcutter's craft, block book illustrations were often stripped-down versions of their manuscript models, and necessity was turned into a virtue as the designers of illustrations for such books developed a penchant for the conflation or fusing of more than one traditional scene into a single picture. Metonymy was one technique for achieving this goal, and of course, extraneous detail tended to be discarded. Additions were made only when required by the text. One of the effects of this tightness of design is that of closure, or 'claustrophobia' as Henry (32) puts it, as opposed to an impression rather of diffusion and openness conveyed by manuscript illuminations. The use of architectural frames beginning in the late fifteenth century seems to reinforce this impression of closure by emphatically separating the woodcut scene from its surroundings, both metaphorical (what lies beyond the pictured scene) and real (the surrounding text). As the illustration refers more pointedly to the text it illustrates, it also takes its distance from that text in a way that recalls the detachability of the emblem illustration (see below, 239–41), or more generally any emblematic image.

But if we see a move toward the compositional techniques of the emblem in early block book illustrations, we realize, too, that the block book is still closer in some respects to the manuscript than to the printed book. It still lacks the adaptability of movable type, and its illustrations are still tied to an accompanying text in a way that recalls manuscript illumination rather than early book illustration. The block book is more a medium for captioned illustrations than for a truly illustrated text.[37]

Despite a strong moralizing element in most of them, however, emblem books were, at least in the earliest stage of their development between 1530 and 1560, clearly secular and quite different in purpose from the concordances. The first truly secular medieval works to be illustrated appear to have been scientific ones such as Roger of Parma's *Treatise on Surgery* or the Montecassino herbiary (ninth-to-tenth century) now in Florence (Laurenziana). With the exception of certain works from the classical tradition such as those of Virgil and Terence, the *Iliad*, and historical and scientific texts, the first illustrated secular literary texts did not begin to appear in western Europe before the twelfth century. This development corresponds to the increasing lay participation in the production of illustrated manuscripts in the twelfth century that accompanied the development of professional scriptoria to cater to the needs of the new religious orders as they were beginning to build their own monastic libraries.[38]

The earliest bestiaries cannot very well be considered as secular literature in the modern sense of the word because they, like many other kinds of illustrated literature in the high Middle Ages, were so clearly placed in the service of Christian theology and doctrine. But bestiaries do stand somewhere between sacred and profane literature and are particularly useful for understanding the place of the emblem in relation to a tradition of animal symbolism going back to late antiquity, or even to earlier Oriental sources. From a formal point of view, the bestiaries and their progeny are the most important category of medieval works composed of a series of relatively short, independent texts, each of which calls, to a greater or lesser extent, for an elucidating illustration. The early bestiaries were usually versions of the *Physiologus*, which Emmanuel Walberg once characterized as a 'modeste livre d'instruction.' Because of its nature as a largely anonymous and purely utilitarian work – again according to Walberg – the original mystical interpretation of the birds and beasts evolved over the centuries into a principally moral interpretation.[39]

The Greek *Physiologus* appeared in Alexandrian Egypt around the same time, and emerged from the same traditions, as Horapollo's *Hieroglyphics*.[40] So to the extent that emblems are related to the late enigmatic hieroglyphics, they seem to share a common ancestor with the symbolism of the medieval bestiaries, and this relationship simply reveals another link between emblems and the bestiary tradition. In this regard, it is interesting to note that the earliest emblem books resembled bestiaries as Walberg has described them, while aspiring to the mystical authority and grandeur of the hieroglyphics as they were understood by certain fifteenth-century humanists.[41] The apparent paradox of the down-to-earth didacticism of the emblem books coupled with their aspirations to mystical authority and Neoplatonic ideality may in fact be explained by the evolution of the *Physiologus* as Walberg understood it.

Latin versions of the *Physiologus* began to appear as early perhaps as the fourth century A.D. The so-called B version (Bern MS Lat. 233) was the main source of Latin versions in England and France during the Middle Ages, but French vernacular bestiaries, such as those by Philippe de Thaon and Guillaume Le Clerc, are based largely on the B-Is version, which, by integrating Isidore of Seville's *Etymologies* into the *Physiologus*, nearly doubled its size.[42] Florence McCulloch (44) claims that bestiaries were among the usual contents of an English medieval library, and probably of continental ones as well. And, she tells us, the most popular of the French bestiaries was the derivative *Bestiaire d'amour*, with its variant interpretations of traditional lore.

So by the late Middle Ages, the bestiary genre as it had been expanded by the assimilation of pseudo-hieroglyphics, animal fables, and illustrated proverbs possessed several traits that characterized many of the earliest emblems. Each bestiary was composed of a series of short texts, and each of these texts combined description and moralization in a way that recalls the mechanisms of the emblem and encouraged, if it did not actually require, illustration.[43] Some generic homogeneity was ensured by the existence of pattern books for the manufacture of certain bestiaries.[44] In the end, and in part as a result of such homogenizing efforts, the didactic bestiary tradition transmitted a coherent body of animal lore that would provide a sizeable part of the background for the composition of emblems, even into the seventeenth century. A well-known example that comes immediately to mind is Bishop Giovio's device, formed around the castor who emasculates himself and throws his genitals to the pursuing hunters.[45] When Alciato took up this image in *Aere quandoque salutem redimendam* (153), he followed the configuration of secular interpretations tending to the exhortation to prudence that we find in Giovio's device and that goes back to Aesop and Juvenal.[46] This variation will be unexpected and surprise the reader because of his familiarity with the use of the motif in the bestiary tradition, where it dealt with the casting off of sin.

A secular, or profane, side of the bestiary tradition comes into particularly sharp focus with Richard de Fournival's *Bestiaire d'amour*, which dates from the second half of the thirteenth century and tells us a great deal about the appeal of illustrations in such works. Chancellor of a church in Amiens, Fournival composed his popular little pastiche of the nobler, religious bestiaries for his 'tres bele douce amee' with the specific purpose of keeping his memory ever-present in the mind of his beloved. This explicitly stated artistic intention provides the enamoured poet with an opportunity to explain one important use of illustrations in medieval manuscript books. Mimicking the opening sentences of Aristotle's *Metaphysics*, he begins 'Toutes gens desirent par nature a savoir,' and goes on, quite typically, to explain that no one can know everything. In his love for man, however, God has provided him with 'une vertu de force d'ame ki a non memoire. Ceste memoire si a .ij. portes, veir et oir, et a cascune de ces .ij. portes si a une cemin par ou on i puet aler, che sont painture et parole.'[47]

Fournival was not alone at that time in taking such an attitude toward illustration. When Joinville was composing his *Credo* around 1250, he declared that '... poez veoir ci aprés point et escrit les articles de nostre foi par letres et par ymages selonc ce que on puet poindre selonc l'umanité Jhesu Crit et selonc la nostre.'[48] Since this text was being prepared for oral reading, perhaps to someone illiterate, the pictures were added to keep the listener's eyes occupied and reinforce the verbal message: 'Et devant lou malade façons lire le romant qui devise et enseigne les poinz de nostre foi, si que par les eux et les oreilles mete l'on lou cuer dou malade si plain de la verraie cognoissance que li anemis ne la ne aillour ne puisse riens metre ou malade dou sien douquel Diex nous gart a celle jornee de la mort et aillors!' (51). The pictures are intended to insulate the *malade* from any 'malvaise avisions' by filling his mind completely with the spiritually (and physically?) salutary matter at hand.[49] This goal helps explain, I think, why there exist three sets of illustrations for this work, but only one set with the text; we can assume that the sets without a text were for listeners who could not read but would follow the pictures when someone else read to them.

So although either of the two paths to memory is capable of keeping present what is past or absent, Fournival is going to combine pictures and words for a more compelling presentation, one that will ensure the total attention of his beloved whenever she turns to his present:

> ... vous envoi je ces .ij. coses en une. Car je vous envoie en cest escrit et painture et parole, pour che ke, quant je ne serai presens, ke cis escris par sa painture et par sa parole me rende a vostre memoire comme present.
>
> Et je vous monstrerai comment cis escris a painture et parolle. Car il est bien apert k'il a parole, par che ke toute escripture si est faite pour parole monstrer et pour che ke on le lise; et quant on le list, si revient elle a nature de parole. Et d'autre part k'il ait painture si est en apert par chu ke lettre n'est mie, s'on ne le paint.[50]

Here the text is considered to be a locus where painting and the spoken word meet and coalesce in a single entity that is that text. The text is a painting that can be translated into a spoken message through the act of reading.[51] There is but a step from this way of understanding the text to an ideogrammatic conception of painting; Fournival takes this step as he continues his explanation: 'Et meesmement cis escris est de tel sentence k'il painture desire. Car il est de nature de bestes et d'oisaus ke miex sont conissables paintes ke dites.'[52] The word 'painture' here refers, then, both to the written words and to the accompanying illustrations representing the birds and beasts that are more easily recognizable 'paintes ke dites.' Yet the labelling, descriptive text cannot be considered redundant; for some of the drawings are crude, and some of the animals foreign to the Picard countryside, and consequently difficult to identify without some written guide. More important, as Michael Camille tells us, 'we see their illustrations as "general" and not "particular" because the universal schemata for animal depiction which they used copied formulae of a thousand-year-old tradition and put forward animals not as perceived individuals but as concepts.'[53] Only a text can typecast the pictured animal with sufficient precision to attach it, through some name, to a particular symbolic tradition.

Naming itself would also often be insufficient, for the names of birds and animals were not particularly well fixed in the Middle Ages, and consequently needed some description or picture (they needed to be 'paintes') to be meaningful; naming them (*dites*) was not sufficient for the more precise characterization necessary if the bestiary lore was to be based on analogies to specific properties. John V. Fleming has discussed the case of the *pelicanus*, which could be any bird in the wilderness from an egret to a heron. The context of Psalm 101 made the allusion, description, or picture meaningful. So it seems that a picture or a name, standing alone, was an empty vessel that would be largely meaningless unless and until it was informed by some explanatory or descriptive text.[54] Conversely, the picture helps the reader or listener form a visual image of lions or even more uncommon beasts like unicorns; a description alone, as Lessing insisted, can never do that. At the same time, the picture also simulates the impression of presence produced by oral discourse, which was considered in the Middle Ages to be so much more worthy of confidence than written texts.[55] The picture presents an image of the animal that is vivid enough to become a serviceable memory place upon which the lion's ferocity and nobility or the unicorn's chastity could be stored so that the pleasure of seeing non-religious scenes would not necessarily be devoid of edifying resonances.

Such painted animals could presumably serve this function all the better because of the strength of the iconographical traditions that governed their depiction. After an encounter with one of these bestiary animals, the reader will be edified each time he sees it portrayed, perhaps in a tapestry, or a stained-glass window, because the picture will function iconically to bring the symbolized qualities back to the mind of the viewer each time he sees it. This would not happen as automatically or as forcefully if he had simply read about animal symbolism, but on the other hand, it could not happen at all if some text, real or metaphorical, had not identified the animal and recalled its moral significance. Hence, picture and text are intimately, almost necessarily, related here in the way they were still supposed to be in Renaissance emblems.

Yet, this doubling of the text poses a problem of redundancy that seems to surface in Fournival's claim that birds and animals, by their nature, 'miex sont connissables paintes ke dites.' One can recognize a lion in a picture only if one already knows what a lion is; and if one knows from a text or from experience what a lion is, then the picture will presumably be redundant. Much the same problem was to arise again in the early Renaissance with the Neoplatonic notion that truths could be intuited visually in ideogrammatic signs. Edgar Wind objected that a truth can be 'intuited' this way only if it is already known to the beholder.[56] Perhaps the picture functions in such cases as an additional referent, which presents the textual message iconically instead of discursively. That is, since iconicity assumes that the visible image partakes of the reality of the thing it represents, the iconic picture ensures 'presence' of the idea in a way that a text alone could not do. It would then reinforce the message in much the same way as a paraphrase or repetition with minor variations, but in a much more powerful way for a largely illiterate audience. And some kind of repetitive reinforcement of the message was always deemed useful in an oral culture.[57] On the other hand, as we have seen in the case of the 'pelican,' a name does not necessarily evoke a clearly fixed reality of high specificity. Bestiaries must have functioned as dictionaries, where the text elaborated a configuration of traits, physical and allegorical, while the picture provided a consolidating memory place to which the name and its definition could be attached. Whatever the case, the text remains primordial here as it was always supposed to be in medieval illustrated works; the pictures were all iconic perhaps, but they still presupposed at least a hypothetical text describing, or explaining through analogy, the reality in which the picture supposedly participated.

In Fournival's work, bestiary lore is applied consistently to the realm of profane love in a continuous narrative, rather than in short paratactic, and potentially paradigmatic, individual developments, as in other bestiaries. The application is more to love in general than to the specifics of the poet's love for his lady. Two examples will suffice to show how Fournival plays his clever game and turns this religious lore to his own profane ends of demonstrating the psychology of love. The work opens with two comparisons intended to explain why he was writing in prose rather than verse, why 'cis escris n'est mie fais en cantant, mais en contant.' Like the man who is seen first by the wolf, he, the poet, has lost his voice because he was seen first by his lady.[58] This comparison is particularly appropriate, we learn, because the woman in love is like a wolf in three ways: three of the wolf's 'natures' are found in the love of a woman. The wolf, for example, has a neck so stiff that he cannot turn it without turning his whole body (15); likewise, a woman 'ne se poet doner, se toute ensamble non ...' (16). But the author would be afraid to 'sing' even if he could, for fear of singing so sweetly, so beautifully (because of the inspiration of love), that he would die like the proverbial swan (13–14).

Such an amorous orientation of bestiary lore was not by any means an isolated occurrence. The Provençal poet, Rigaut de Berbezieux, working in the circle of Aliénor d'Aquitaine in the second half of the twelfth century, was presumbably the first to use bestiary lore in worldly love poetry;[59] and the model remained alive and popular well into the sixteenth century. Fournival's work inspired a *Réponse au bestiaire* as well as the anonymous thirteenth-century *Arriereban d'Amour*, and Nicole de Margival imitated it in his *Dit de la Panthere d'Amors.* Fournival's work also enjoyed great popularity in Italy, where it inspired several imitations like the *Bestiario toscano* and the *Fiore di virtù.*[60] Closer to the period of our concerns, Pierre Gringore proposed the same kind of amorous bestiary around 1520 in his *Menus Propos des amoureux.* The satirical, moralizing element, which castigates certain aspects of courtly love, is stronger here than in Fournival's work, but Gringore was still using the same swan image where the old swan '... chante / Quant oyt le son de la harpe accordante ...'[61] Like that of Fournival, Gringore's old swan is not the Renaissance poet, but rather the lover who sings more sweetly when he fears that his lady will refuse his love.

Fournival's effort, however, must not be considered only in relation to its posterity; it must also be viewed in the context of the tradition without which it could not exist. It is a parasite of the bestiary tradition, or a palimpsest (hyper-text).[62] It is in this relationship to the other bestiaries that the pictures may play their most important role. As Cesare Segre has noted, this is the first bestiary to use a narrative, discursive form, as opposed to a paratactic, verse format.[63] That is, a sort of story-line about women and love has as its function to guide the reader's expectations about each animal symbol toward an analogy that will produce the particular moral required by the general theme. Consequently, the more standard moralizations one might find in other bestiaries are recalled mainly by the pictures.

When medieval viewers considered the picture of the wolf, for example, they would remember other lore from the *Physiologus* tradition as it was transmitted by the bestiaries; perhaps they would recall that Pierre de Beauvais, Richard's likely source, had called shameless women 'louves' and that he took the wolf's inflexible neck to be a sign that the Devil could turn toward nothing good.[64] Iconographical commonplaces connected the palimpsest, if we can call it that, to the ur-text of a tradition, both here and in other related works. Consequently, around this rather frivolous work, there would automatically gather the memory of all kinds of moral warnings for any reader who knew enough of the bestiary lore to understand and appreciate what Richard was doing – understand the game of pastiche he was playing.

In the fourteenth century, a wider variety of secular works began to appear in illustrated manuscripts. By this time the bestiaries were being expanded into more encyclopaedic works, which combined the animal lore of the *Physiologus* tradition with material from the fable traditions and from the body of medieval exempla. Such illustrated Latin works as the *Dialogus creaturarum*, probably composed by Petrarch's friend Mayno de' Mayneri, or the *Liber creaturarum* dominated this current; numerous manuscripts and editions attest to their popularity well into the sixteenth century.[65] French vernacular works in the same tradition began to appear in the early fourteenth century with *Les Contes moralisées*, composed by the Anglo-Norman Franciscan Nicole Bozon.[66] Barbara Tiemann (34) considers this work to be a prototype of the emblem books; in it, the poet used biblical quotations and fables to develop a moral that was often far from the one a reader would find attached to the same animal in the bestiary tradition. This liberty of moral interpretation tended to make the development less predictable and hence more intriguing for the reader; the potential for surprise continued to be highly valued in such compositions and was to become one of the most important elements in the appeal of the emblem two hundred years later. Furthermore, some of the material from these collections of moralized fables was either put to use by Corrozet and La Perrière in the earliest French emblems, or networked to them through commonplace titles (the system of *loci communes*).[67]

During the fourteenth and fifteenth centuries, there were many illustrated manuscripts of romances, and particularly the *Roman de la Rose*, in part no doubt because the introduction of paper in France in the early fourteenth century made the production of all kinds of manuscripts more feasible from an economic point of view. But the works of greatest interest for our understanding of the development of the emblem are still those that present a series of short, self-contained texts composed with reference to actual or potential illustrations. Most often, texts of this sort have a moralizing function, and it is among this group of works that the earliest true prototypes of the sixteenth-century French emblem are to be found. Christine de Pisan composed one of the first such works, the *Epistre Othea*, in the early fifteenth century.[68] She rationalized her project this way:

Pour ramener a allegorie le propos de mesme matiere appliquerons la saincte escripture a noz diz aledifficacion de lame estant en cestui miserable monde.

Comme par le somme sapience et hault poissance de dieu toute choses soient crees raisonnablement doivent toutes tendre a fin de lui et pour ce que mesme esperit de dieu cree a son ymage est des choses crees le plus noble apres les anges convenable chose est et necessaire que il soit aournez de vertus par quoy il puist estre convoye a la fin pour quoy il est fait ...

but because of the assaults of the Devil that may divert us from our *beatitude*

nous pouons appeller la vie humaine droicte chevalerie comme dit lescripture en pluseurs pars / et comme toutes choses terrestres soyent fallibles devons avoir en continuele memoire le temps future qui est sanz fin. Et pour ce que cest la somme et parfaicte chevalerie et toute aultre soit de nulle comparoison / et dont les victorieulx sont couronnez en gloire prendrons maniere de parler de l'esperit chevalereulx et ce soit fait ala louenge de dieu principaument et au proffit de ceulx qui se delicteront [en] ce present dictie.[69]

The reader is then prepared for an allegorical narrative, but is instead confronted with allegorical fragments having barely any unifying pretext. These are allegorical fragments to be explained as emblems are, and together they form a kind of compendium of moral wisdom, as the early emblem books would also do. This manual, ostensibly devoted to the formation of the perfect Christian knight in a way that recalls the framing pretext of Erasmus' *Enchiridion*, presents its code of chivalry through a series of one hundred illustrated four-part inventions in verse and prose. The illustration or *histoire* is occasionally preceded by a fragment of the letter that ostensibly links the compositions together and is always followed by a verse *texte*. The final two parts are in prose; the *glose* provides a historical explanation of the story and its moral application, while the *allegorie* gives the spiritual or Christian interpretation.[70]

The forty-fifth *histoire*, for example, presents the story of Pasiphaë and the bull (fig. 2); the four-line *texte* identifies the scene and seems to be cautioning against one possible reading of it:

Pourtant se Pasiphe fu fole
Ne vuelles lire a ton escole
Que telles soyent toutes femmes
Car il est maintes vaillans dames. (f. 22^{v})

But this is in fact the moral lesson, for the *glose* reads the bull to be a man 'de vile condicion' who considers all women to be like Pasiphaë; Prudence (= memory) warns the prospective knight not to be like the bull. The *allegorie* interprets the madness of Pasiphaë as the soul that returns to God.[71]

Fig. 2. Pasiphaë and the bull. Christine de Pisan, *Epistre Othea*, 45th *histoire*.

Manuscript fr. 606 at the Bibliothèque Nationale de France is a particularly interesting copy of this work, because we know Christine herself supervised the production of it. Consequently, we can gauge the extent of similarity and difference between this work and emblems *at the level of conception*. Venus, for example, (f. 6^r) is shown seated on a cloud (Christine has already alerted the reader [f. 1^v] that this is the way she represents the gods and goddesses), collecting the hearts of lovers in her outstretched skirt. Such a literal presentation of figurative language is one of the main techniques used later in the century in the illustrated proverbs and then in emblems. The verse *texte* comments this way:

De Venus ne fais ta deesse
ne te chaille de sa promesse
Le poursuivre en est ravaleux
Non honnourable et perilleux

The *glose* presents her as a very beautiful, but not very faithful, queen of Cyprus, while the *allegorie* brings the reader back to Psalm 30 through the theme of vanity. Here as in the *Ovide moralisé*, there are four levels of interpretation: the natural, the physical, the moral, and the spiritual.

This work is interesting for the proto- or palaeo-history of emblems because the relationship between pictures and texts is so close, because the pictures play such an important part, because it is clear that Christine had a very important role in the production of these illustrations, and finally because this work presents us with a long 'publication' history that stretches into print culture, and can thus give us an idea of the evolution in the patterning of text and illustration as France moved from manuscript to print culture. Sandra Hindman has demonstrated quite convincingly that Christine almost certainly provided illuminators with the subjects for the miniatures in some of the important early manuscripts of her work. Hindman marshalls evidence for this control from manuscript instructions to artisans, and from Christine's explicit belief that illuminators were merely artisans.[72]

But there are also many manuscripts over which Christine exercised no control, and of course she did not supervise the production of early printed editions of her work either. Later in the fifteenth century, there is some indication that the manuscript production of her text was moving in directions similar to those that produced sixteenth-century French emblem books. A mid-fifteenth century *remaniement* of the *Epistre* by Jean Miélot, now in the Bibliothèque Royale de Belgique, is a good example of the

Pour tant se pasiphe fu fole
Ne vueilles dire a ton escole
Que telles soyent toutes femmes
Car y sont maintes vaillans dames
. Glose .
Pasiphe fu une royne et dient aucunes
fables quelle fu femme de grant dissolucion et mes
mement que elle ama ung thorel et que mere fu
de minotaurus qui fu moitie homme et moitie
thorel qui est a entendre que elle se acointa dun
homme de vile condicion de qui elle conceut ung homme
qui fu de grande cruaute et de merveilleuse force
Et pour ce quil ot fourme domme et nature de tho
rel en tant quil fu fort et de grant asprete et si

Fig. 3. Pasiphaë and the bull. Christine de Pisan, *Epistre Othea*, 45th *histoire*.

trend. First, we note a regular paginal format, with each large miniature located in the top half of a verso (fig. 3), as was often the case with the first illustrated books printed in movable type.[73] Then, we note that Miélot has expanded the text: 'Pou ce que souuent briefveté rend les materes obscures aux liseurs et afin que les cent gloses dessus escriptes des cent autorités ... soient égales les unes aux autres come sont les quatre lignes de texte desdictes cent auctorités ... a été faitte et composée de nouvel une addition ou declaration ...'[74] These explanations are mosaics of commonplaces from Virgil, Ovid, and Boccaccio's *Genealogy of the Gods*, and they have the effect of truly integrating the illustration into the text. But the concern in adding them may have been primarily material, for Miélot stresses the goal of making the prose sections equal in length, like the four-line verse *textes*. This explicit double intention of regularity and clarification reminds one of the trends in the publication of Alciato's emblems, or later those of Jean-Jacques Boissard, where commentary expands with each new edition.[75]

A comparison of the unexceptional fifteenth-century manuscript copy of Christine's work at Lille with Philippe Le Noir's early sixteenth-century printed version is particularly instructive for the differences it reveals between early French emblem books and what we might take to be ordinary illustrated manuscripts from the late Middle Ages. The printed version differs from the manuscript copy in two ways that also distinguish the paginal format of the earliest French emblem books. First, the Le Noir edition, like the rather exceptional Brussels manuscript, has a regularly repeated format. In the Le Noir edition the illustration is more or less centred at the top of a page, with the verse *texte* directly beneath it. To the left, the *glose* is reproduced in one column, while on the right the *allegorie* is printed in another. Sometimes the *glose* is too long for its column, and it spills over into the empty space beneath the *texte* in the middle column (fig. 4). There is a very strong sense of typographical space and paginal unity that is totally lacking in the Lille manuscript, where we have the impression of a continuous text with embedded pictures as we might expect to find in a roll. This attention to format in the printed edition may bear witness to an increased effort to come to terms with the spatial limitations of the page or of the potential visual unit formed by two facing pages. This heightened awareness appears to have been typical of early print culture and quite obviously is responsible to a considerable degree for the development of the emblem.

But such a motivation for regular paginal organization may not have been explicit or even conscious; indeed, the effect of regular formatting in the context of a page or opening may simply have been the by-product of

Glose.

Texte.

Durtant se pasiphe fut folle
Ne vueilles sire en ton escolle
Que telles soyent toutes femmes
Car il est maintes vaillans dames

Fig. 4. Pasiphaë and the bull. Christine de Pisan, *Epistre Othea*, 45th *histoire*.

another set of motivations. The tendency in printed editions must have been, not unnaturally, to copy the format of the most luxurious and costly manuscripts. These manuscripts were regularly formatted by page or opening, perhaps to permit more than one scribe or illuminator to work on the manuscript at the same time (see above, 23, and note 33). In printing, such an arrangement would simplify production since the compositor would know more readily where to leave a blank space for the illustration.

In the Lille manuscript, on the other hand, there is no evidence of any conscious attempt to achieve an integrated, unifying format for the text and its illustration. Each picture follows hard on the end of the preceding *allegorie*, and it may be situated at the bottom of a page, completely isolated from its *texte* and narrative developments.[76] This isolation of the picture from its text never occurs in Le Noir's edition, and likewise in sixteenth-century emblem books published in France in the middle years of the century, the text and illustration were always made to form some sort of visual unit.[77]

The second difference between the manuscript and the printed version also highlights a characteristic of sixteenth-century print culture. The woodcut illustrations in Le Noir's edition are somewhat simpler than those in the manuscript. The background tower behind Pasiphaë and the bull, for example, disappears in Le Noir's edition, perhaps because of the limitations of the woodcut technique, or perhaps because of some change in fashion. Whatever the reason, this summary presentation without any background décor is particularly reminiscent of the early French emblems produced between 1530 and 1560. The lack of décor in such emblems is striking and often has the effect of cutting off the emblematic scene or motif from surrounding reality and transferring it from narrative to what has been called allegorical space.[78] Even when it does not explicitly transfer the scene to the level of allegory, this isolation of the scene from surrounding reality can stimulate the viewer's curiosity and draw him to the explanatory text, because it strips away any narrative frame together with the iconographical conventions that would make it possible for him to develop some hypothesis about what is going on in the picture without any further explanation.[79]

If this was indeed the case, then it would seem at first glance paradoxical to find the emblem developing in early print culture as an artistic form based on the close relation between illustration and text. In fact, it was just this situation that permitted the emblem to develop and flourish. If the relation between picture and text is close and clear, no explanation is needed, but if the two parts stand in a problematic relation to each other, for whatever reason, the riddle of that relation needs to be explained. Hence, the iconographical denuding of the woodcut illustration was one of the reasons why the emblem was seen to be related to the enigma. So, in the emblematic situation, the text bound itself to the illustration by explaining its relationship to that illustration, by explaining rather the relationship of its point to the pictured scene. Here again, the emblematic effect may have been an unexpected by-product of a craft whose motivation was to approximate the manuscripts it was copying: that is, these stripped-down illustrations were probably, as Robert Brun has theorized,[80] intended to be no more than simple sketches to guide illuminators. But most of these volumes were never illuminated, nor, increasingly, were they intended to be. The emblem was one way to take advantage of the problem thus posed by simple, stock illustrations, and recycled woodblocks that had been designed to be adaptable, in their simplicity, to multiple textual situations.

2

The Allegorical Antecedents

Even though seventeenth-century theoreticians of the emblematic forms claimed that the emblem was allegorical, and that it is distinguished from the metaphorical device by its allegorical character,[1] the emblem almost never developed as an allegory – at least not in the way we understand the term 'allegory' today. An allegory is now commonly understood to be an extended metaphor in which the vehicle, to use I.A. Richards' terminology,[2] is sometimes quite elaborate while the tenor remains unexpressed, but clearly indicated by the components and structure of the vehicle. Naturally, the situation is, in practice, more complicated than this,[3] but generally an allegory represents one thing in the guise of another, perhaps an abstraction in the guise of a concrete personification engaged in some action that confirms or explains the nature of the character, or a moral or religious discourse in the guise of a narrative about a quest or pilgrimage.[4] According to Northrop Frye, 'there must be some narrative base for allegory.'[5]

The vehicle of an emblem, on the other hand, comprises a naked or isolated sign; that is, the sign of the emblem is presented pictorially with no narrative or rhetorical context to guide the viewer, or reader, to the intended interpretation. As a result, the emblem can generally not be considered a total allegory (*tota allegoria*) but at best only a partial one (*permixta apertis allegoria*), that is, an allegory whose message is partly explicit.[6] The emblem may then be compared to a work like the *Ovide moralisé*, where part of the text glosses another part, whose source lies somewhere outside the work in question.[7] Such a work brings analysis into the play of allegory, and indeed it is the increasing importance of analysis in late medieval allegory that prepared its evolution into the emblem. In a more typical allegory like the *Faerie Queene*, there are multiple tenors, but their number is limited by the syntax of narration, by the fabric of the text, and hence they need not be spelled out explicitly. Emblematic images, however, like the two Leslie T. Duer isolated in *The Duchess of Malfi*, are cut off from the surrounding dramatic text and its action, and hence require some explanation. They are as if bracketed or framed by the process of their telling and their decoding.[8]

While Menestrier did claim that an emblem does not necessarily need a text, any emblem does, in reality, include a 'text' of some kind that makes the intended tenor explicit,[9] for an emblem, like allegory, exists as such only if it has a precise, and precisely intended, meaning.[10] The emblem was not an infinitely open Romantic metaphor; it was not even 'polysemous' as Dante claimed an allegory could be, although any particular emblematic image did contain the potentiality for multiple interpretations, and thus could be made, as Jacob Cats showed in an exemplary exercise in his *Silenus Alcibiades* of 1618, into a multiplicity of emblems. But the emblem needed a text to make the intended meaning clear since no network of allegorical interactions provided the syntax to isolate its meaning in a way that would obviate, at least ostensibly, the need for explanation.

That text might simply be a title, or it might be implicit, as when the illustration presents an iconographical commonplace, or is constructed in such a way as to suggest a well-known fable or proverb. Or the picture might be fashioned in such a way that it can be understood as an ideogrammatic presentation of a message. An example would be Gilles Corrozet's emblem 'L'heure de la mort incerteine,' where we see a skull sitting atop a wheel (of fortune); the skull acts as the face of a clock upon which there is an hour hand, but there are no markings with which to tell time.[11] It is only in such cases that the emblem can recall, however remotely, 'total' allegory, but even then the emblem does not permit multiple interpretations as will a truly complex allegory, because the restricted 'space' of the emblem requires tightly organized figures, and this organization has to be directly translated into a text that removes any possible doubt as to the intended sense. We might see an exception in the case of Alciato's two emblems on Cupid the honey thief (112, 113) where a single motif is provided with two or more distinct texts. But even in this case, the second epigram was eventually provided with a separate illustration, thus turning it into an independent emblem.[12]

M.-D. Chenu once defined medieval religious allegory in these terms: 'l'allégorie est la description analytique d'une *idée* à partir des éléments morcelés et abstraits d'une image, dont chaque détail prend signification.'[13] This understanding of allegory will provide a better approach to the emblem than other modern definitions, and following this approach, we shall see how the emblem is in many respects an increasingly fragmented, secularized and decadent form of late medieval allegory.

For the Greeks the material world was 'only a great myth, a thing whose value lies not in itself but in the spiritual meaning which it hides and reveals,'[14] and it was within the context of this world-view that western allegory was born. But at the end of antiquity another approach to allegory surfaced in the attempts by pagan apologists like Euhemerus to rationalize what by then seemed to be absurdities or immoralities in earlier works of the standard cultural canon by Homer, Hesiod, and others. At more or less the same time, Philo Judaeus, St Basil, and St Ambrose were using the same techniques to interpret the Old Testament. These efforts to adapt earlier works to contemporary standards of morality and cultural *vraisemblance* took the form of a sort of allegorical reading, or allegorizing analysis, that imposed an acceptable allegorical unity on the work under study. Euhemerism, as this technique is sometimes called, tended to rethink or re-order works in terms of a new interpretation that was usually quite extraneous to the original work, at least as it appears to modern scholars. So, by the end of antiquity, there were two kinds of allegory: one was perceived by the observer or reader to be inherent in nature or in a given work, while the other was more or less consciously imposed by an interpreter on a particular work or, more likely, on some part of it, and was quite separate from the original intention of that work. In either case, allegory required the same mode of reading; when one or both attitudes are consciously present at the composition of a work, allegory, or *allégorèse* as it is sometimes called, becomes a mode of writing.[15]

The two types of allegory were presumably present in Christian thinking from the very beginnings of Christianity. Some well-articulated understanding of allegory was crucial to the consuming task of biblical exegesis and the puzzle of understanding how God had revealed himself to the world. As a result, the western Middle Ages developed a more elaborate theory of signs than almost any other period or culture. That theory developed out of the writings of St Augustine, and especially his *De doctrina christiana*.[16] A sign, Augustine tells us there, is a thing (*res*) that conveys to us something more than the impression it makes on our senses (II, 1, 1). But there are several kinds of signs, which can be divided into two main groups. In the *signum proprium*, or sign properly speaking, its quality as sign predominates, and its character as a thing is inconsequential: that is the case in language. In the *signum translatum*, its quality as a thing remains as important as its quality as a sign. Augustine also claims there that some things are simply that and signify nothing but themselves.

He takes a slightly different position in *De Trinitate*, where he claims that all created things are signs of their creator. This position parallels that of the Christian Neoplatonists, as represented by Pseudo-Dionysus the Areopagite, who was translated into Latin by John Scotus Erigena in the second half of the ninth century. Erigena, however, extended this principle to see all things in nature as signs of something spiritual and incorporeal. Although this Christian Neoplatonism made the Church uneasy and was eventually condemned in 1225, it was a line of thought that continued to be pursued into the twelfth century, for example, by Hugh of St Victor in his *Didascalion*, and it influenced Bonaventure and Aquinas even into the thirteenth century.

The Venerable Bede, on the other hand, developed Augustine's main position, the one expounded in *De doctrina christiana*, in an attempt to explain biblical symbolism from a rhetorical point of view. Beginning with a study of tropes, and especially allegory, which seems to subsume all other tropes for Bede, the *tropus quo aliud significatur quam dicitur*, he comes back around to the classic distinction between *allegoria in factis* and *allegoria in verbis*.

As early as St Augustine, the distinction was clear between *allegoria in factis* and *allegoria in verbis*.[17] The first kind was external to the text and historical; it presented God's way of prefiguring events to come and served as the basis for the typological understanding of the Bible. The second kind of allegory was understood to be inherent to the text and embedded in its rhetorical structure; since it was not based on an external revealed truth, it was subject to interpretation and provided an opening for imposing a new and Christian allegory upon the Greek curriculum of myths, in order to integrate it more quickly into the Christian educational scheme as a way of making inroads into the educated upper classes of Roman society.[18] This *allegoria in verbis*, or what came to be known somewhat paradoxically as imposed allegory, was a tool of interpretation used to explain away 'invraisemblances doctrinales,' as Todorov calls them, in relation to the ultimate text of Christian doctrine.[19] This kind of interpretation was set in motion by paradigmatic indices, while the Bible, which was understood as embodying an *allegoria in factis*, was to be read by deciphering an intratextual network of syntagmatic indices to produce what would later commonly become known as 'concordances.'[20] It would take a combination of the two to produce full-blown allegories, what Quintilian called *tota allegoria*.

In biblical interpretation, one knows what the outcome will be; it is just a question of discovering how best to reach that end, of seeing how the ultimate meaning may be revealed through an analysis of the elements of the text, and the construction of the relationships between them. In this case, the unity and all-inclusiveness of Christian doctrine serves to control and limit the polysemousness of the text.[21] However, the movement away from the ideal goal of a unitary and monolithic meaning is implicit in the system of typological exegesis with its four levels of meaning – literal or historical, tropological, anagogical, and typological – that had existed in Christendom since its formulation by John Cassian (c. 360–435 A.D.).[22] The principle can be traced back to the Stoics, and it was later developed by Origen and Philo before its eventual assimilation around the year 700 by Bede to the classical grammarians and rhetoricians. This system of interpretation with multiple levels of meaning, however, did not come into general favour in biblical study until the high Middle Ages.[23] The system surely found favour at that time because of its usefulness in the management of an increasingly complex and unwieldy body of typological interpretation. But the end result of such specialization was a tendency toward partial interpretation with a concomitant danger of losing sight of the larger edifice.

With the resulting fragmentation of the work, it was impossible to base an interpretation on syntagmatic indices, and there was a tendency to take as the basic criterion for the pertinence of an interpretation some kind of paradigmatic resemblance with the interpreted sign; it would appear that the conscious theoretical exploitation of resemblance began with Guillaume d'Auvergne in the thirteenth century. In fact, as interpreters dealt increasingly with parts, analogical resemblance became the major basis for the rationalization of an allegorical reading. This dependence on analogy opens up the text to the outside world and brings nature into exegesis, thus reinforcing the anthropomorphism already present in the Bible.[24] So there was, in short, a shift in emphasis from concern with propositional interpretation of the kind that was necessary to decipher the *allegoria in factis* of traditional typological readings of the Bible or other works, to the reading of texts as if their parts were informed by lexical allegory, the *allegoria in verbis*. This shift made it possible to reconcile sections at least of secular or pagan texts with Christian doctrine by substituting elements of dogma for isolated fragments of the letter of a false text. The criterion used in making such substitutions was some kind of resemblance or analogy.[25]

Analogical analysis itself probably began to take on prominence in exegetical practice in the second half of the twelfth century, as Augustine's conception of the sign began to supplant the Dionysian view of symbolism in the western theological perspective on imagery.[26] In practice this meant that 'les actions symboliques, primitivement destinées à re-présenter les mystères, sont traitées comme des "explications," détaillées et intellectualisées.'[27] In the Dionysian conception of the symbol there is no room for analysis, no more than in the mystery to which the symbol initiates the faithful. 'Actions symboliques' understood in the Augustinian sense, on the other hand, are perceived from the perspective of the individual subject; as Augustine said, there can be no sacrament without the human voice (*verbum*). In this understanding, the subject assimilates the sign intellectually, whereas in the earlier conception of symbolism, the subject would be assimilated through the symbol to the higher reality it represented (or re-presented).

This shift in the approach to allegory and allegorical interpretation translates ultimately, as far as secular literature is concerned, into a different conception of the reader as well as a new idea of the author's role, and a different relation between the reader and the text. Julia Kristeva has characterized this shifting attitude toward the symbolic act as a movement from the symbol as the dominant form of figurative expression to the sign. In a move parallel to that of Chenu, Kristeva describes the symbol as 'une pratique sémiotique cosmogonique: ces éléments (les symboles) renvoient à une (des) transcendance(s) universelle(s) irreprésentable(s) et méconnaissable(s); des connexions univoques relient ces transcendances aux unités qui les évoquent; le symbole ne "ressemble" pas à l'objet qu'il symbolise; les deux espaces (symbolisé-symbolisant) sont séparés et incommunicables.' She explains further that 'La sérénité du symbole est relayée par l'ambivalence tendue de la connexion du *signe* qui prétend à une ressemblance et à une identification des éléments qu'elle relie, malgré leur différence radicale qu'elle postule d'abord.' For Kristeva 'le signe est dualiste, hiérarchique et hiérarchisant' like the symbol, but it 'renvoie à des entités moins vastes, plus *concrétisés* que le symbole – ce sont des universaux *réifiés*, devenus *objets* au sens fort du mot ...'[28] Chenu (190) summarizes the difference this way: 'Symbole, allégorie: le symbolisme émane d'une adhésion de notre être, et sa clarté se cache en quelque sorte, au cours de l'expérience spirituelle, à l'intérieur des images elles-mêmes, médiatrices de mystère; d'où leur intensité et leur valeur, même esthétiques. L'allégorie, elle, procède, non de cette coopération esthétique à l'état pur, mais de son exploitation critique, pour en extraire des pensées abstraites et parvenir à un exposé didactique.'

Elsewhere, I have tried to show how this evolving attitude toward the *signifiant* influenced the interpretive approach to secular allegories like the

Anticlaudianus of Alain de Lille.[29] I have suggested, in particular, that *vulgarisations* of works like this one tended to abridge and condense them into their most pictorial elements and emphasize individual analogies at the expense of the global play of relationships and interactions at the level of intratextual propositional allegory. Slowly, the reader's concern for Truth began to be supplanted, at least at the level of individual analogies in secular literature, by a concern with *vraisemblance*, which became the criterion for validity in allegorical analysis, or what Rosamond Tuve has called 'imposed allegory.' This trend in the late Middle Ages parallels that of euhemeristic interpretation of late antiquity, and we may well wonder whether periods of hesitant faith do not, in general, prefer verisimilitude to Truth.[30]

Late medieval writers prized allegory very highly as a rhetorical tool of communication. In her *Livre des fais et bonnes meurs*, Christine de Pisan praised allegorical language for being more understandable, more nearly all-inclusive, and more pleasing than the language of direct address, while Philippe de Mézières chose to write in allegory because it brought fresh appeal to old matter.[31] But how did these writers understand allegory? A glance at their works shows that they had a somewhat different idea of allegory from their predecessors, both medieval and ancient, for it would appear that a radical change in the conception of secular allegory too occurred in the late twelfth and thirteenth centuries.[32] Jean de Meun's continuation of the *Roman de la Rose*, for example, is profoundly different in its conception, as Paul Zumthor has demonstrated, from the original design of Guillaume de Lorris.[33] The paradigmatic act of naming becomes much more prevalent as a means of conjuring personifications, and as in this prototypical case, allegory generally becomes more self-consciously based on previous works. Jean de Meun's allegory is created against the background of, and in reference to, that of Guillaume de Lorris. In fact, the bipartite *Roman de la Rose* can be seen as an epitome and exemplar of the transition to a new approach to the allegorical narrative, if not as an actual model for the works that followed it in the fourteenth and fifteenth centuries, for Jean de Meun was not alone in his enterprise. M.-R. Jung has discussed a similar work, also from the late thirteenth century, Adam de la Bassée's *Ludus super Anticlaudianum*, which is based, as its name suggests, on Alain de Lille's great Latin allegory.[34] Later it was Ovid who was turned to the same purposes in the *Ovide moralisé*, and by the end of the fifteenth century allegory could not exist in France, or so it would appear, without a clear textual *support* of some kind. Naming is very important in this new kind of allegory, since the name within a text is a kind of deictic signal pointing to something outside the text. Names like Icarus or Male-bouche, coming from the pen of a poet like Marot, automatically evoked other works, and thus situated the text at hand within a more or less precise cultural or textual tradition.

Allegory always points beyond itself, but allegory in the early and high Middle Ages pointed, at least ostensibly and theoretically if not always in fact, to a monolithic and all-encompassing truth, the central truth of Christianity that was the driving force at that time behind the epistemology of the Christian world, even in its most secular manifestations. The late Middle Ages was a transitional period when this ultimate reference needed to be mediated by the middle term of a work of authority in order to be operable, or so it would seem, as the organizing principle of a new kind of allegory. The difficulty lay in the lack of room provided for variation by the generally tight structure of the host work. As a result, there was a tendency to work with fragments of the base text, which could more easily be accommodated to the requirements of a new message than the structure taken as a whole – a structure that had usually been elaborated for the expression of a fairly specific, if complex, message, but one very different from the message it was being made to accommodate.

Although allegory could be either a mode of thought or a mode of expression, fragmentation of the kind I have been discussing tended to make it more a mode of expression than a mode of thought. Nowhere is this more evident than in the parallel development of the medieval arts of memory. Scholastics took a renewed interest in the arts of memory during the thirteenth and fourteenth centuries. The memory arts were part of the classical scheme of rhetoric, and they came down to the Middle Ages from antiquity by a complicated process brilliantly reconstructed by Frances Yates. The basic technique of the art of memory as it was practiced in the Middle Ages consisted in choosing highly concrete visual images to serve as 'memory places' upon which ideas could be stored for easy recall in a certain order. Memory, as Mary Carruthers has recently shown,[35] was always understood through complex and highly visual metaphors such as the book, the storehouse, the pigeon coop, or the house. Beginning with St Thomas Aquinas, it was agreed that ideas would be best remembered if they were encoded in unusual, visual similitudes that were sometimes organized as sets of attributes for personifications used to remember lists of vices and virtues. The creation of imagery for such tasks was turned into a devotional lay exercise, and must, thought Frances Yates, have had real influence on literature and the visual arts. She even wondered if this, rather than some tortured, creative imagination, was not responsible for the proliferation of grotesques, and often ridiculous visual imagery, during the period under consideration.[36] But as Carruthers cautions (142), much of the grotesque imagery that appears to be allegorical and thus have a specific iconographic meaning may simply be a 'mnemonic heuristic.'

Toward the end of the Middle Ages, as classical antiquity came to be better known and as its distinctness from medieval culture became clearer, there also developed a conscious program of syncretism that attempted to integrate this attractive, but slightly alien, body of art and literature into the framework of the Christian world-view. Although syncretism has very little in common with the arts of memory, it is interesting to observe that both kinds of intellectual activity used the tools provided by allegory and the mind-set that it fostered. As late medieval scholars and artists tried to accommodate the ancient myths to Christian doctrine and morality, they looked for straightforward analogies, but often found themselves obliged to hang those analogies upon a single similarity or upon a story-line that did not coincide exactly with the biblical story being set as the standard. As a result, there was a tendency to detach the mythological figure from its complex narrative context and set it up in isolation as a single sign for a given idea or quality.[37]

As the pressures created by this use of allegory in the late Middle Ages began to break down the rather homogeneous body of symbolic lore that made the great allegorical narratives possible, there were attempts at another kind of allegorical organization, which might be characterized as ecphrastic, that is, as pictorial and spatial, rather than oral and linear.[38] Gombrich tells us that the predominance of the word in medieval allegory remained unchallenged before the fourteenth century. But the ever-proliferating definitions and distinctions of scholastic teaching made diagrammatic presentation within a pictorial space increasingly useful.[39] As a result, imaginary pictures became a favoured rhetorical device for the presentation of complex ideas in sermons. These pictures would permit the reader to hold the elements of the sermon in mind and keep them organized in relation to each other as the preacher had presented them. In their spatial and visual arrangement such pictures resemble the memory houses that the preachers may have used to help them recall the different parts of their sermon, and in fact they must have functioned as temporary, and ad hoc, memory systems themselves. Indeed, it would appear they were intended to do no more than that; they were certainly not made to be illustrated, for it would, as Saxl and Smalley have demonstrated, be next to impossible to translate most of them into actual pictures.[40]

The use of such devices in preaching recalls Cebes' *Tablet* where moral wisdom was presented in the guise of an explanation of an imaginary set of pictures on the walls of an ancient temple. This work was extremely popular during the Renaissance, and highly influential, at least in theory, in the generic conceptualization of the emblem at that time. And like the *Tablet*, these compositions began to be illustrated in schematic form with the new art of the woodcut. By the turn of the sixteenth century even an artist like Leonardo da Vinci would use such compositions for the exposition of moral truths. But as Gombrich has noted, without an explanatory text to unriddle the representation of all the complicated definitions and distinctions, no iconologist would understand what was happening.[41] Sometimes such illustrations served as visual *argumenta* for a text to follow, and then they were composed of 'pictograms' that can be read rather like a rebus. At least that is how Anne-Marie Lecoq describes one of the illustrations in the anonymous allegory in the *rhétoriqueur* style, the *Livre de la dedicace du temple saint francoys* of 1506;[42] in one of the illustrations in that work we see a personification of France in front of the temple, a scene that can be read rebus-wise as the 'Temple of France,' and whose allegorical sense is then explained in explicit detail by the following text.[43]

The use of such imaginary pictures where allegorical fragments are fitted together, sometimes diagrammatically, into a kind of 'illustration' of doctrine or morality was common in the exposition of philosophical ideas throughout the period, especially in presentations for sermons and in the schools. This organization sometimes suggests, as Huizinga and Mâle have occasionally noted, that the relationship between vehicle and tenor in late medieval allegory was syllogistic. If such was indeed the case, the allegorical, and later the emblematic, syllogism would find its place within the systems of topical or place logic that experienced a great revival in the late Middle Ages. Peter of Spain was the key figure in initiating this revival in the late thirteenth century, and the fashion reached its apogee with the work of Rudolf Agricola in the second half of the fifteenth century.[44]

Brunetto Latini showed how allegorical imagery can provide a vehicle for the communication of logical process or argumentative persuasion. Allegorical analogies or similes could be used in what he calls an *argument voirsemblable*: 'Des choses ki ont aucune semblance prent li parleours son argument en trois manieres, u par ses contraires, u par ses pareilles, u par celes ki sont d'une meisme raison. Par ses contraires fet on son argument en ceste maniere: se li pecheour vont en infier donc li religieus vont en paradis. Par les pareilles ensi: si comme le lieus sans port n'est pas seurs as neis, tot autresi li corages sans foi n'est parmanables as amis, car lieus sans port et coer sans foi sont samblables en muablete, et nef et amis sont samblables en seurete.'[45] The first kind of argument is no doubt one of the antecedents of the paradox, which was such a popular form for moralizing throughout the Renaissance. Emblems, on the other hand, were built almost exclusively on the kind of analogy suggested by the second model. The use of these figurative comparisons, as Brunetto sees it here, has the goal of making a logical exposition more vivid through the use of concrete terms that translate the abstract message into a vivid picture. Once again, we would probably find the motivation for such strategies in the desire to preserve the sense of presence considered so important in persuasion and in guaranteeing good faith, and such strategies must have become increasingly necessary at a time when language was becoming less animate and increasingly text-based.[46]

Allegory would resemble topical logic more closely than traditional Aristotelian logic because topics or places tend to be conceptualized more concretely than categories. Aristotelian categories deal with predicates and qualities like whiteness, while topics or places replace somewhat abstract qualities with concrete objects that embody them. Allegory, or at least static allegory that stands alone and communicates without a *fabula*,[47] handles abstract concepts in the same way: it embodies them in concrete forms. But although medieval allegory bears formal resemblances to logic, it is not logic. At best, allegory is a device used to give more vivid expression to the functioning, and a visual organization to the results, of a logical process. Somewhere between allegory and mnemonics, Thomas Murner's simplified version of Peter of Spain's logic, which was once classified as an emblem book, shows how allegory, logic, and memory arts are all related through the use of concrete signs that stand in some diagrammatic or analogical relation to the idea to be evoked.[48]

In attempting to understand the kind of complicated allegory popular in the late Middle Ages and characteristic of the period, but so unappealing to twentieth-century tastes, other scholars have taken different approaches. Edgar Wind looked to the grotesque, far-fetched imagery it spawned, and tended to see allegory functioning there as a kind of constructive absurdity. That is, the bizarre vehicle of this allegory was, in his opinion, simply a surprisingly new and striking bottle intended make old wine more palatable. In such a system, every image would be offered as comparable to an ugly Socratic silenus vessel full of rare and precious drugs. The intention of allegory then might be to simplify the complicated and give an aura of difficulty to ideas that seemed perhaps too simple or banal to merit careful consideration on their own.[49] But this kind of allegory also responded to a medieval fascination with the grotesque, and even Bernard de Clairvaux consciously used *ridicula monstruositas* in his sermons.[50] Such imagery is simply a decadent exaggeration of the Pseudo-Dionysius' idea that truths must be carried by *dissimila signa*, by incongruous images. As Michael Camille explains it, 'images were fine [for Dionysius] as long as they were only channels that diverted attention away from the materiality of the signifiers and pointed the viewer to its transcendental meaning.'[51]

Wind's characterization is compelling, but it contains a pejorative nuance that obscures the important fact that this kind of allegory participates, no matter how unsuccessfully to our way of thinking, in a more general aesthetic process of the artistic presentation of ideas. The strange, aesthetically unappealing, late-fifteenth century personifications and memory aids are simply variant examples of what Shklovsky called 'defamiliarization.' Shklovsky used this term to describe the new perspective that results from the fresh and inhabitual point of view provided by someone like Montesquieu's Persians in eighteenth-century Paris. Actually, Shklovsky demonstrated this concept in the works of Tolstoy, where the use of the unexpected point of view of a peasant, or even an animal, 'can make the familiar seem strange, so that we see it again.'[52] Obviously, the techniques of late medieval allegory functioned quite differently, but the goals of such allegory must have been similar, not to say identical, to those of 'defamiliarization' thus defined. Such a phenomenon depends on the more or less independent artistic vision of an increasingly self-conscious artist.

Paradoxically, either approach to signifying was possible only if the signifier did not 'dissolve,' to use Chenu's expression, in the signifying process, as ordinary language tends to do. Either the resemblance is guaranteed by the reality of the signifier, or the mystery of the 'ressemblance dissemblable' is apparent in the ugliness of the thing that God chose to imbue with His truth. Just as the letter of Scripture guaranteed its spiritual sense, so the reality of natural signifiers kept tropology from shriveling into pale abstractions. 'En même temps qu'est rendue attention à la lettre de l'Ecriture, est réhabilitée la valeur des choses, dans les divers champs symboliques. Si paradoxal que ce soit, un certain naturalisme assure le contenu du jeu symbolique, et, de soi, son souci d'explication par les causes ne nuit pas à la signification des réalités ultérieurement référeées au transcendant' (182). So the rise of naturalism in late medieval art can be traced to the preoccupation with symbolism, for a certain 'naturalism' is, as Chenu says, 'la condition élémentaire du symbolisme.'

Neither the explanation of allegory as syllogism nor that of allegory as defamiliarization provides any clues as to why certain signs were chosen to signify certain ideas. Traditions certainly played a great role, and many of the symbolic traditions went back through the late classical polymaths and compilers like Isidore of Seville, Martianus Capella, and Rabanus Maurus to the very origins of western culture. Ancient natural history had worked, over the course of many centuries, to associate certain plants and animals with their supposedly dominant moral characteristics in such a way that they became the allegorical signs of these virtues, vices, qualities, and characteristics. George Boas summarized a long tradition in the following hypothesis to explain this habit of the human mind: 'Men believed that they were both above the beasts in the possession of reason and below them in their morals, and the best explanation of this odd situation was that God had made his lower orders to be an example to the higher.'[53] The emblematist Guillaume Gueroult cited this justification for his exposition of bestiary lore in 1550, and this attitude toward the allegory of animals still remained very much alive, or so it would appear, in the seventeenth century.[54] Hence, each plant or animal was more than just a sign; since God had created the birds and animals, 'ausquelz selon la diversité de leur nature il fait souvent estinceller quelque rayon de sa vive splendeur, par une bonté naturelle,' as Gueroult (A2^{r}) put it, each creature was intrinsically linked to the abstract idea represented and became an exemplar as well of the ways in which that idea might become manifest in the reality of particular things. Like typological symbols, then, they participate in an *allegoria in factis*.

Such Renaissance and modern attempts to describe and explain late medieval allegory are interesting for the study of emblem literature because each echoes in some way the understanding of the mechanisms of symbolic relations among theorists and practitioners of the emblematic forms at different times during their history. By the seventeenth century, theorists like Tesauro and Bouhours considered emblematic constructions to be strictly syllogistic, and there is evidence of syllogistic construction in certain sixteenth-century emblems.[55] While no emblematist would call his allegory absurd, he often looked for surprising parallels – indeed he was encouraged to do so by the theorists – which function in ways not unlike Wind's constructive absurdity, or defamiliarization.

Allegory so conceived was usually intended to give thought a concrete visual shape, and attempts to make thought visual during this period are also reflected, in Marshall McLuhan's view, in other intellectual changes taking place at the same time. An early manifestation of allegory-related visualization is evident, he thought, in a disagreement among theologians over the philosophy of interpreting the Bible, a disagreement 'between those who said that the sacred text was a complex unified at the literal level, and those who felt that the levels of meaning should be taken one at a time in a specialist spirit.'[56] McLuhan attributed the desire to separate the various levels of meaning, what he called the 'specialist spirit,' to an attitude of increasingly visual bias because of the tendency toward quantification (here of content – there are *four* levels of meaning) implied by the specialist spirit. The separation of levels of meaning encourages the use of allegorical analogies with an almost quantifiable specificity and set within a clear network of relationships. Allegory with its patterns of relationships can be useful in directing a reader or listener to a certain level of meaning. If, on the other hand, we envisage a text as a 'complex unified at the literal level,' we are more likely to see symbols involving an infinite and undelimited chain of suggestion than the representation of a specific idea in a specific analogy.

While admitting the role of visualization in the rise of medieval allegory, Huizinga attributed this rise primarily to the nature and evolution of medieval philosophy. He felt that the increased dependence on allegory in the fourteenth and fifteenth centuries not only complemented scholastic method, but resulted from the degeneration of medieval realism.[57] In an idealistic philosophical system like medieval realism, the general tends to dominate the particular, with the result that models, examples, and generalities are prized above individual reality. Every object, each man and animal, is seen as the manifestation of a general principle or idea. The general is seen as incarnate in the particular and related to man. To illustrate the mechanisms for applying this philosophy to the analysis of specific situations, Huizinga recalled the example of Foulques de Toulouse, who, when giving alms to an Albigensian heretic, replied to a critic that he was giving alms to the poor woman, not to the heretic. Here, 'poor woman' and 'heretic' could be written with capital letters, since in either case the woman represents a type or idea.[58] Being manifest in the particular, the idea takes on 'real' existence and comes alive through a kind of personification, as in Huizinga's example. The woman plays a role here as in a morality play, but she could clearly play other roles as well, and that possibility may help explain why theatre became such a popular vehicle for the expression of the play of ideas at the end of the Middle Ages.

Within the context of this philosophical position, particular cases are of little importance except in so far as they are seen to provide the vehicle for an idea. It is easy to see how every event in life could become exemplary, could become the allegorical vehicle for the expression of an idea or several ideas. The ultimate guarantee of meaning in such an allegorization of everyday life was a monolithic world-view supported by Christian doctrine and morals, but clearly the process could be used to support a variety of arguments and doctrines. After all, Foulques could have refused to give to the 'heretic' instead of giving to the 'poor woman.' And so, paradoxically, medieval realism carried within itself the seeds of its own trivialization and eventual destruction. And as an instrument of Christian hegemony its results left a great deal to be desired – as events of the fifteenth and sixteenth centuries so vividly attest. Nevertheless, the belief in the 'Book of Nature,' which, in its Renaissance form, must ultimately have derived from late medieval realism, remained lively well into the seventeenth century, even if different readers could, and did, construe it differently. That different readings were increasingly possible is one of the reasons why emblems came into existence: if everyone read and understood the Book the same way, texts explaining the meaning of its pages would be superfluous.

Symbolism can be understood to be a form of thought; allegory, on the other hand, must be considered, at least in the late stages of its characteristic evolution, to be simply a vehicle for the expression of thought. Huizinga has said that 'symbolism is a very profound function of the mind, allegory is a superficial one. It aids symbolic thought to express itself, but endangers it at the same time by substituting a figure for a living idea.'[59] This rather pejorative characterization of allegory is true only in the context of the Romantic and post-Romantic understanding of symbolism; it is also possible to understand allegory as an attempt at the organization of thought into relational patterns in space. Taken this way, allegory is a step in the direction of the diagrammatic – and hence visual – thought of modern science. Nevertheless, it is useful to keep Huizinga's distinction between symbolism and allegory in mind for any investigation of emblem literature, for the emblematists were much more interested in allegorical representation than in symbolic creation. At least in the practice of their craft, the emblem almost always functioned as a rhetorical device rather than a matrix for poetic creation.

In short, allegory had three principal uses in the late Middle Ages. It was used for communication and elucidation; it served in the formation of one type of memory device; and perhaps most important, allegory provided a potential approach to the reading of almost any text. Allegory as a means of communication can be considered as an adjunct to the entire scholastic method, in which human reason was intended to elucidate and communicate rather than prove the truths of the Christian faith. Since writers and artists used allegory so frequently to express ideas, the reading public developed the habit of looking for allegory in texts and pictures. But allegory became a habit of reading for other reasons as well. In the Middle Ages, all art was, in a sense, applied art. The artists saw themselves as craftsmen, because their production had specific practical or decorative functions and was not conceived to exist for its beauty alone. Aesthetics and edification fused in this art, for artistic beauty formed an ornamental paean to that higher beauty of the omnipresent divinity, or later, the sponsoring patron. With its two levels, allegory was the perfect locus for the union of the didactic, or the encomiastic, and the aesthetic, and the slow disjunction of the two in art and art theory hastened the decline of allegory and signalled the approaching end of the medieval world.

When confronted, then, with the developing awareness of the aesthetic greatness of ancient art, medieval exegetes must have experienced an uneasiness, because moral and doctrinal edification of the kind they were looking for was so often entirely lacking in this art. Yet the world-view of medieval men tended to be all-inclusive, and anything that entered their field of consciousness and still remained outside the perimeters of their world-view necessarily posed a threat to their conception of life and of the world. The problem was all the more acute because a growing corpus of ancient texts and artefacts fed a burgeoning cult of antiquity during the fourteenth and fifteenth centuries. So, embarrassed exegetes turned to syncretism, or an allegorical reading of ancient works, in order to reconcile the contemporary admiration for antiquity with a Christian idea of the function of art. The models for syncretism came ultimately, as we have seen, from late antiquity, when allegory had been used as the tool of a system of Christian apologetics that turned mythology into a *philosophia moralis*. Readers at that time conceded the greatness, for example, of Homer's work, but found it, at first reading, unedifying; they simply assumed this could not have been intended and proceeded to impose an allegory upon it.[60] Such readings provided the model for the same kind of exercise at the end of the Middle Ages in what Rosemond Tuve has called 'an effort to turn the whole classical past into another Old Testament, allegorically revealing the New.'[61]

But there was a difference now because, under the influence of Neoplatonism, late medieval scholars broadened allegorical syncretism in the following manner: 'Their attitude is no longer one of rationalization, aimed at explaining away shocking absurdities; it is the attitude of believers and mystics, reverently seeking the depths of meaning within a sacred text.'[62] Actually, the mystical approach of humanists working under the influence of Neoplatonism was little more than a variation on the mysticism of the concordances that had been useful since the twelfth century in integrating Virgil and Aristotle into late medieval Christian culture. In the fifteenth century, as the psychological pressures in favour of syncretic assimilation grew greater, scholars accomplished the difficult integration of unruly Ovid, and the various versions of the *Ovide moralisé* were successful and often reprinted, sometimes with illustrations and an emblematic format, well into the sixteenth century.[63]

The task of the exegetes and commentators was made easier by the emergence of a more self-conscious and potentially independent reader, who could be counted on to do some of the work of assimilation by actively deciding what was useful and then adapting it to his own situation or point of view on the world. Sandra Hindman has noted that Mansion defends his moralization of Ovid with a parable in which a group of Brabantines gather near the Abbey of St Michel after the felling of a large oak. Each takes from the oak what he needs; the burgher takes the trunk to make a beam for the construction of his house, while the mariner takes the curved branches to build his boat, and so on.[64] Hindman believes Mansion invented this parable, but in fact, Jean Miélot had used the same story in the prologue to his translation of the *Speculum humanae salvationis* in 1450.[65] Taken together, these two apologies for readers' or commentators' right to select what they wish from a text and use it allegorically as they wish, thus imposing meaning on the text, testify to a much more active attitude toward the text and its images than might earlier have been common, despite Augustine's invitation to accept multiple readings made *in latitudine caritatis*,[66] and it foreshadows the Renaissance drama of polysemousness, be it played out in Rabelais or in the emblem books.

The techniques of moralizing became such an ingrained habit of reading that even contemporary works were subjected to the imposition of Christian allegories unintended by their authors. The best-known examples of this phenomenon are the allegories imposed upon the *Roman de la Rose* by Jean Molinet in the late fifteenth century and by Clément Marot in the 1520s. Following the example of the *Ovide moralisé*, these poets considered their readings of the great medieval allegory to be 'moralizations.'[67] As Marot says in the prologue to his 1526 edition of the *Rose*, 'Et si celluy aucteur na ainsi son sens reigle et n'est entre soubz le moralle couverture penetrant jusques a la moelle du nouveau sens mistique/touttes fois lon le peult morallement exposer et en diverses sortes.'[68] In one example that reveals an explicit link with the *Metamorphoses* and its moralization, Marot cites the story of Apuleius returning to his human form when he finds the garland of roses, and likens this transformation to man's metamorphosis back from an animal state to the state of grace upon finding the rose of grace. Obviously then, Marot did not see the author as the absolute source of meaning in his work, but neither did he see the work as imbued with any single meaning. There was no longer a source, but rather many, which could be chosen according to the needs and desires of the reader. The age of the emblem had arrived.

Such then was the heritage of allegorical techniques and allegorizing reflexes bequeathed to the sixteenth and seventeenth centuries by the late Middle Ages. This age accustomed to looking for allegory everywhere made imposed allegory an accepted and common critical practice. Imposed allegory may appear today as a mark of some aesthetic depravity as it did to Rosemond Tuve; but it had a philosophical foundation in realism, it helped make syncretism work smoothly, and it did create a climate that encouraged the use of unexpected and untraditional analogies in the allegorical fragments of emblem literature. And analogies of this sort were essential to the emblematic effect of surprise based on unexpected variation.

3

Proto-emblematics in the Fifteenth Century

During the second half of the fifteenth century, the rather complicated textual structure of the kind surrounding the *histoires* in Christine de Pisan's *Epistre Othea* gives way to a much simpler combination of picture and text in the collections of illustrated proverbs, which ateliers, especially in Lyons, were beginning to produce. The union of picture and text is closer here, and more self-consciously essential, because the obvious function of the picture is to literalize the image of a well-known proverb in a concrete illustration that keeps the idea visually present to the audience while the text develops a moral application and sometimes provides an explanation of the puzzling scene presented in a crude or summary picture.[1] So these illustrated proverbs then are probably the earliest directly influential prototypes of the emblem in France, because they present their folk wisdom in the kind of tripartite form that was to become increasingly typical in emblems during the sixteenth century. V.-L. Saulnier even went so far as to discount Italian influence on the origins of the emblem, saying that emblem literature is 'dans la pure tradition proverbiale.'[2]

Whether or not it is positioned thus, the proverb being illustrated can be compared to the emblem's title, and in certain emblems, Corrozet, for example, actually did use proverbs as titles.[3] As in an emblem, the text of these compositions provides a moralizing development on the proverb and an explanation, where necessary, of the illustration. Proverbs lent themselves well to this kind of presentation because they could be applied and interpreted in various ways and tended to resist fixed, univalent interpretations.[4] In the article just cited, Saulnier put it this way: 'le proverbe n'engage aucune doctrine ni système philosophique; il s'installe sur l'arrête où épicurisme et stoïcisme, dogmatisme et scepticisme, paganisme et christianisme se rejoignent; il est interprétable, accommodable en tous sens'

(90). So moralists could usefully bring proverbs to bear on an almost endless range of particular problems and situations, and proverbs could then form the basis for a truly intriguing emblematic development that would be suspenseful, pleasing, and hence, mnemonically effective. It would be suspenseful because, at a time when a naturalistic perception of reality was beginning to take hold, the viewer would wonder how the author/inventor would use the image – that is, whether naturalistically or allegorically; the whole composition would be pleasing to the reader as the author teasingly led him through a short, but maze-like analysis, with considerable descriptive detail, to a satisfying resolution in the proverb at the end of the *huitain*, bringing together the illustration and moral development in a way that could only be partially anticipated.

Equally significant for the development of the emblem form, these compositions lack the religious interpretation or *allegorie* of Christine's *histoires* and retain only the *glose* or moral application of the scene and proverb. This is the pattern, of course, that dominated French emblem books composed through the middle years of the sixteenth century. The first French emblem book to have a predominantly religious orientation was Georgette de Montenay's *Emblesmes ou devises chrestiennes*, and her book was not published until 1571. But even though this book marked the beginning of a period stretching for a century and a half, during which the production of emblems was dominated by religious concerns, the emergence of the emblem form was still one of the signs of a new independence from an epistemology so dominated by religion that nothing could be conceived in complete isolation from the Church and its view of the world.

In the late 1930s, Grace Frank and Dorothy Miner published a facsimile edition and transcription of what is probably the earliest extant manuscript collection of illustrated proverbs. Containing an apparently representative anthology of 182 compositions of this type, the manuscript is now part of the collection of the Walters Art Gallery in Baltimore.[5] Based mainly on a careful study of the costumes, and their failure to find any Italian influence, the editors tentatively date the manuscript more specifically to the period between 1485 and 1490, and because of a multiplicity of scribal and artistic hands, they assumed further that it is the work of an atelier, probably located somewhere in the Lyonnais. Some of these illustrated proverbs are contained in other manuscripts,[6] and they were most likely produced in the same workshop over a period of fifteen or twenty years from a prototype collection that probably changed somewhat with the passage of time.

Since the collection contains no introductory or concluding material, it is tempting to imagine that it is incomplete, and that may indeed be true, but there is little attention to sequencing, and the collection appears to be nothing more than that: an open-ended collection that could be expanded or contracted at will. Lacking as it does any internal coherence or unifying principle, it is very similar to the earliest collections of emblems. Also like the early emblem books, this anthology of illustrated proverbs rises above the level of a simple *recueil factice* because of the formal homogeneity of the individual pieces. Each *huitain* conforms to a single model, ending with a common proverb that draws together text and illustration in the last line or two lines of the poem, and the combination of picture and text is always positioned in the same way.

The poems occasionally begin with expressions like 'Cest exemple moustre ...' (15) or 'Cest homme est soubtil a merveilles' (111), which refer directly to the picture. Such introductory, deictic phrases suggest that the pictures were supposed to form an integral part of the composition, and it is easy to imagine the poet writing with the pictures before his eyes as did certain emblematists like Barthélemy Aneau.[7] But given the general dominance of text over illustration throughout the Middle Ages, and the history of the illustration of medieval works like Philippe de Thaon's bestiary, Joinville's *Credo*, or Christine de Pisan's *Epistre Othea*, it seems more likely that the poet was writing a 'description' to serve ecphrastically as a set of directives to guide the artist in composing his illustrations. The verses then were perhaps prescriptive as much as descriptive.[8]

The illustrations generally translate the imagery of common proverbs as literally as possible; but occasionally, the artist presented instead a particular application of the proverb as it is developed in the *huitain*. The artist would be hard-pressed, for example, to translate the proverb 'Tout n'est pas or ce qui reluit' into a literal illustration for *huitain* 91. So he pictures the exemplary situation used to illustrate this proverb in the first seven lines of the poem:

> Tel fait grant chiere en sa maison
> Qui n'a de quoy couvrir le couste,
> Mais il aime en toute saison
> Estre honnouré, quoy qu'il luy couste.
> Tousjours le plus beau devant boutte
> Pour croistre et augmenter son bruit,
> Mais qui voit sa richesse toute,
> Tout n'est pas or ce qui reluit.[9]

In the picture (fig. 5) one sees a table laden with dishes in the left back-

Fig. 5. 'Tout n'est pas or ce qui reluit.' *Proverbes en rime.*

ground while a man and woman are ostensibly discussing money matters in the centre right foreground. The man seems to be giving orders, while the woman's upraised hands seem to suggest some kind of protest or resistance.

Here the reader's curiosity is maintained until the end, because it is not clearly evident from the picture alone what proverb is being presented. As in an emblem, the context of the picture, that is, its place in *this* collection, tells the reader a proverbial message is visually or ideogrammatically inscribed in the picture, but the viewer is obliged to consult the text in order to be sure what that message is. A proverb like 'A barbe de fol / Apprent on a rere' (8), on the other hand, is easily guessed from an illustration where the man being shaved is wearing a fool's cap. In this case the *huitain* simply explains the meaning of the proverb, and the suspense that characterizes the riddle-like development of *huitain* 91 is completely absent from the composition. Occasionally, the proverb is difficult to identify without the *huitain*, even though it is presented narratively in the

Fig. 6. 'Pierre qui trop rabat.' *Proverbes en rime.*

illustration. For instance, when one sees irregular little circles on a hillside (fig. 6), one may not immediately think of the proverb 'Pierre qui trop rabat / Ne pourroit cueillir mousse' (89), despite the analogical signal created by the jagged rock outcroppings on either side. The text compensates here for the somewhat primitive artistic technique, as it leads the viewer surely to the proverb, which falls, as usual, in the last two lines.

Paul Zumthor saw these texts as variations on a particular sort of quotation, as fragments of 'le texte sapientiel commun.'[10] Thirty collections of French proverbs were compiled in the thirteenth and fourteenth centuries, and the proverbs they contained were often glossed in different ways. One collection compiled in Lisieux around 1440 provides legal glosses, while others gloss them in an amorous sense. When used in a textual development, such a quotation unsettles the reading process just as emblematic images must have done in late sixteenth-century religious poetry (see below, 227–35): '... inséré dans la chaîne linéaire, il ne la rompt pas, puisqu'il possède, en commun avec les éléments qui le précèdent et le suivent, une structure de phrase; mais il arrête le discours, le fixe, et par le jeu de miroir qu'il y instaure, le ramène pour un moment circulairement sur lui-même.' (154) Hence, it is quite common to find such proverbs situated in what Zumthor calls 'sites stratégiques' where they bring about the effect of a 'globalisation thématique' (155). When the proverb is placed at the beginning of a passage, the following text acts to produce a dispersion of the theme, whereas the proverb produces a summarizing *rassemblement* when it comes at the end. Zumthor calls such a proverb an 'epiphonème,' because 'il engendre le texte, en ce qu'il en constitue l'emblème à la manière des figurations disséminées engendrant à la fois l'unité et le sens global du célèbre tableau de Breughel' (158). That is, the proverb generates the text, and also provides its unity, its meaning. In these senses, the proverb functions exactly the way I would propose an emblematic image functions in a poetic text or painting.[11]

It seems likely that the device, which was also developing during the late fourteenth and fifteenth centuries, is closely related to the fifteenth-century passion for proverbs and their ideogrammatic presentation in just the same way that the later device is related to the emblem. Heraldic arms changed from individual to family identifying marks during the first half of the thirteenth century; they had become highly and rigidly coded by the fourteenth century and any individualistic deviation was practically impossible until the middle of the fourteenth century, when the device began to make its appearance.[12] While the proverb was crystallizing the wisdom that characterized French society at large, the device crystallized the hopes and aspirations of the individual or his attitudes toward himself and the world around him. This fundamental difference would distinguish the emblem from the device throughout the sixteenth and seventeenth centuries, and it is tempting to posit an analogous relation between the two fifteenth-century forms that combined pictographic and discursive language to recall some idea or event. By its concision, its enigmatic quality, and its often sententious turn of phrase, the fifteenth-century device, especially in its more Italianate incarnations, seems closely related to the proverb form. One might even think of it as an individualized proverb that has been made to apply to only one person. In France these *devises* were identifying marks that often served as rallying signs to exhort troops or followers through the evocation of an event or a personal feat. Beginning around 1450, for example in the various *devises* of René d'Anjou, an Italian influence made the French *devises* more like the developing Italian *imprese* and closer to the emblematic model.[13]

Being confined to a single manuscript page with a *huitain* placed beneath each illustration, each of the so-called illustrated proverbs in the Walters manuscript forms a distinct visual unit. Printers like Christian Wechel and Denys Janot took great pains to unify picture and text in the same way in the earliest emblem books published in France. Sometimes they even emphasized that unity by putting part or all of the composition within an ornamental frame. While nearly all the collections of illustrated proverbs were presented in some kind of standard, repeated format, two small French collections composed by Pierre Sala in the 1520s go much farther in their use of regular format and ornamental frames to unify text and picture, and in a way that is distinctly reminiscent of the paginal distribution of text and illustration in Guillaume de La Perrière's first French emblem book, *Le Theatre des bons engins*.

The Lyonnais, Pierre Sala (before 1457–1529), is intriguing because his work forms one of the clearest links between the late medieval tradition of the illustrated proverbs or fables and the early French emblem.[14] His rather copious output remained entirely in manuscript until quite recently; it includes prose versions of *Tristan* and *Yvain* as well as a *Livre d'amitié* and three proto-emblematic works. His family property in Ecully made him a neighbour of the Scève family. In the Scève home the young Maurice Scève may have been able to see devices painted on the walls.[15] It is tempting to think that he may also have seen the manuscript collections of illustrated fables that his older neighbour, Pierre Sala, was composing for Louise de Savoye in the 1520s.

Early in the sixteenth century, Sala had already prepared a magnificent manuscript of twelve emblematic 'enigmas' for the lady he later married, Marguerite Bullioud. Sala gave the same reason as Richard de Fournival for combining text and illustration; in the preface, he indicates that 'affin quil vous en souuiengne je vos enuoye ce petit liure ou il y a peincture. et parolle qui sont les deux chemins par ou lon peult entrer dedans la meson de memoyre. car peincture sert a leiul et parolle a loureille et sont de la chose passee comme si elle estoit presente.'[16] The close, and self-conscious, relationship between picture and text seems to be underlined by the portrait of Sala attributed to Jean Perréal that closes the volume because, on the facing page, we see an inscription in mirror writing as if the inscribed text were a mirror of the portrait: 'Reguardez en pytye / votre loyal amy / qui na Jour ne demy / Bien pour votre amytye.'[17] The combination of portrait and mirror writing seems to function as a metaphor suggesting that the whole text is a mirror of the author's condition, or indeed that each composition is a mirror of some aspect of his situation; the combination of portrait and mirroring text then actually enacts the purpose of the manuscript.

Each of the twelve compositions consists of an elegant miniature by the

Fig. 7. 'Et le fou contrefait le saige.' BL Stowe ms 955, f. 9^{v}.

Master of the Clubfeet on the recto, and, on the facing verso, a quatrain. A few of these compositions speak directly to his love or to love in general, but most of them fit rather into the broader purview of the illustrated-proverb genre. One picture, for example, shows a wise man and a fool each painting a likeness of the other (fig. 7). The quatrain explains:

> Le temps est tel. notez ce mot
> Pour bien jouer son personnage
> Le saige contrefait le sot
> Et le fou contrefait le saige.[18]

This manuscript bears no title, but a later (sixteenth-century?) hand indicated on the back of the portrait that these compositions are 'enimes,' and that is the name Parry gave to the collection in his edition of it. Although not completely reliable, this generic classification is interesting because it gives a clue as to why, during the second half of the sixteenth century, emblems and enigmas could be so easily confused that Claude Mignault felt the need to insist heavily on the difference between them: these 'enigmas' do indeed resemble many early emblems.

Still, the two collections of illustrated animal fables Sala composed toward the end of his life resemble emblems even more.[19] The Pierpont Morgan manuscript contains seventeen of these compositions while the British Library collection contains sixteen, of which seven are not contained in the Morgan manuscript; both collections have the same format. The text of these 'emblems' is presented within an oval ornamental border on the right-hand page while the illustration is framed in a similar way on the facing verso. Aside from this new format, which foreshadows that of some emblem books from the middle third of the century, especially La Perrière's ground-breaking *Theatre des bons engins*, Sala's texts follow the model provided by the Walters manuscript, but Sala often holds the reader's interest and curiosity better by providing a variant development for a commonplace proverb that had already found its way into earlier collections. In the Walters collection, for instance, the eternally popular proverb 'Qui trop embrasse peu estraint' (16) is developed this way:

Chascun selon sa qualité
Doit amasser des biens du monde.
S'il en prent trop grant quantité,
A peu de proffit luy redonde.
Se fortune luy baille l'onde,
A tresbuchier il est contraint.
On dit, est aussy je m'y fonde,
Qui trop embrasse, peu estraint.[20]

The illustration merely shows a man struggling to carry more boards than he is able to grasp. Sala, on the other hand, surprises his reader with an unusual variation on the proverb by conflating it with one of Aesop's fables (fig. 8), the kind of variation that did so much to make emblems into popular little riddles:

Le chien passant ung fleuve
en sa gueulle avoyt
Une piece de cher
dont lombre en leauve voit
La cher laisse aller
cuidant atraper lombre
Qui trop cuide embrasser
souvant pert a grant nombre.[21]

Fig. 8. 'Le chien passant ung fleuve.' Pierre Sala, *Fables et emblemes en vers.*

The construction of this *huitain* shows less mastery of the verse form than its fifteenth-century predecessor, but it does follow the same model with the proverb falling, however limply, in the last two lines. Still, the conflation of an Aesop fable with a common proverb marks a clear advance in the direction of the emblematic technique of variation and conflation.

Elsewhere, Sala conflates a fable with religious symbolism in a way that recalls generally the mechanisms of typological symbolism, as in the following poem that ends with an anagogical observation:

Lasne trop charge crie
et demande la mort
Et apres grans trauuaulx
Il meurt de desconfort
Sa peau sert apres mort
dont sa peyne encor dure
La peine des mondains
est denffer la figure[22]

We note the same new structure of presentation, even though the mechanics of its symbolism are very conservative.

As we have already noted, it was relatively common in the late Middle Ages for short-form poems like *huitains* and *septains* to end on a proverb, and proverbs also occasionally provided refrains for ballads and other fixed-form poems. This custom dates back at least to Eustache Deschamps in the fourteenth century, and its practice was sanctioned by the *rhétoriqueurs* in their manuals of poetic technique.[23] This use of common proverbs remained fairly popular in the sixteenth century and was still not disdained by transitional poets like Clément Marot. Marot composed one of his better-known *chants royaux* as a courtly exercise, when François Ier proposed to test Marot's ability to improvise upon a given theme. The theme in this case was René d'Anjou's famous *devise* in the form of a proverb: 'Desbander l'arc ne guerit pas la plaie.' The proverb served as the refrain for his *chant royal* and, shortly thereafter, Gilles Corrozet developed an emblem around the same proverb.[24]

Although some of the collections of illustrated proverbs were probably no more than edifying picture books for the rising urban bourgeoisie, other, similar compositions were made as guides for artisans designing tapestries or stained-glass windows for bourgeois homes. *Rhétoriqueurs* like Jean Molinet and Jean Robertet tried their hand at this kind of verse, but the most extensive collection of poems expressly intended to serve as instructions to artists and artisans is the work of Henri Baude and seems to date from the last quarter of the fifteenth century.[25] Problems of allegiance at court and a long, difficult lawsuit disrupted the life of this satirically inclined magistrate and poet. Like that of so many of his contemporaries, Baude's biography is not very well-known, but he appears to have been a not atypical fifteenth-century man of letters.[26] His instructions to craftsmen are grouped under the title *Dictz moraulx pour faire tapisserie*.[27] These *dits* are developed around either proverbs or mythological commonplaces. Unlike the *huitains* of the illustrated proverbs, Baude's *dits* do not possess a single, standard form. These poems vary in length from two to forty-four lines; and while commonplace proverbial lore is at the centre of each poem's inspiration, the moral point does not necessarily fall, conceit-like, at the end of the poem.

Much more often than in the illustrated proverbs, Baude's poetry has a quasi-dramatic, oral quality, as one or more of the people, animals, or things are made to speak the lines that were probably supposed to be embroidered onto a cartouche in the tapestry, or perhaps on a banderole emerging from the mouth of the speaker, following common practice in medieval manuscripts and tapestries. Each poem is preceded by a short narrative passage in prose, which describes the scene to be pictured, either in a manuscript illustration or in a tapestry. Certain manuscripts showed the scenes sketched out for the potential artisan, and these illustrations followed the descriptive rubrics that preface the poems in the unillustrated versions.[28] The fortieth *dit*, for example, proposes the following scene: 'Ung beau cheval enferme dans ung parc et en sortant par dessus ung paliz, se mect ung pal en la poictrine.' The laconic verses explain the scene described, and even add some details to it:

Le Cheval
J'avoye bien ou pasturer
si je l'eusse sceu endurer.
L'asne hors le parc, qui ne mengeue que chardons
J'ayme mieulx menger des chardons
qu'estre lardé de tels lardons.[29]

Other compositions by Baude are more complicated and, as in the following example, may present as many as three points of view on a single proverbial motif, thus reminding us of the polyvalence of such commonplace lore. Baude worked the following variation on the traditional butterfly-and-candle theme:

et y a deux hommes dont le premier dit:
Maint homme monte sans eschelle
jusques au feu, pour ce qu'il luyt,
comme le papillon de nuict
qui chet, quant il s'est bruslé l'esle.
La chandelle
Chascun vient sans que je l'appelle,
et je brusle ce qui me suit;
qui est pourtant saige me fuit:
la façon de court est ytelle.
Lautre homme
On prent du riche la querelle,
on flate celluy qui a bruyt,
on fait ainsi que se conduict
le papillon a la chandelle.[30]

In the BN manuscript, which dates from the first third of the sixteenth century, the two actors are looking out of windows on opposite sides of a courtyard in which there stands, much larger than life, the candle (fig. 9). The candle's stanza forms an inscription on a cartouche at the bottom while the other verses are on banderoles near the border, suggesting the way the composition might be disposed in a tapestry.[31]

Fig. 9. 'Butterfly-and-candle.' Henri Baude, *Dictz moraulx pour faire tapisserie*, BN ms fr. 24461, f. 47.

This composition is particularly interesting in the context of the present discussion because it looks forward so clearly to the mechanics of the emblems that were to be composed in France some fifty or sixty years later. The candle is completely detached from any narrative context; it is disproportionately large in relation to everything else in the picture and has been placed on a sort of pedestal in a stage-like setting.[32] The text is organized in a not undramatic, dialogue fashion. Finally, each of the interlocutors presents a slightly different metaphorical point of view, or perspective, on the proverbial commonplace; the possibility of different perspectives on a given motif is, as I have argued elsewhere,[33] absolutely essential for the development of the emblem. Presenting, as it does, three perspectives on a single motif, which is set forth in a kind of narrative or even allegorical void, this composition could be considered emblematic of the emblematic process as it was to develop in the middle of the sixteenth century.

This example may be compared to Guillaume Gueroult's treatment in his bestiary version of the same motif:

Voyant le feu de l'ardante chandelle
Le Papillon grandement s'esjouyt,
Lors il se prend à voler droict vers elle,
L'embrasse, estrainct, mais bien peu en jouyt.
Car le feu chaut qui tout ard et consume,
Brusle son corps aussi bien que sa plume,
Voila comment pour aymer folement:
Le povre oyseau meurt miserablement.
   Ainsi, Amans que vifve amour enflamme
A trop aymer la beauté d'une dame,
Dont ne pouvez avoir contentement:
En la voyant joye vous savourez
Et la perdant en vivant vous mourez:
Malle est l'amour qui na fin que tourment.[34]

The emblematist has glossed the proverbial motif in a different register from Baude, but he has done so as Sala perhaps might have done. That is, he seems to be glossing some proverb on the moth and the flame, but the epiphonemic last line forms a rather unexpected sententious variation on the general theme. The complete break between the description and moralization gives the scene described considerable independence in relation to this or any other interpretation. Then the sententious last line, set off as it is by the introductory colon, brings the reader far from the original scene. Coupled with the unusually concrete and detailed description of that scene, this structural arrangement of signifier and signified in virtually separate and distinct spaces actually turns the poem into a real emblem.

Unfortunately, none of the tapestries or stained-glass windows that might have been executed according to Baude's instructions has survived. But if, as his editors believe, such objects were destined for bourgeois households where they would have been subjected to the bustle and wear of everyday life, it is not surprising that no examples have been preserved.[35] Nevertheless, it has recently come to light that wall paintings in the Château de Busset in the Allier were modeled on Baude's *Dictz*. Anti-courtier sentiments dominate in the scenes chosen for this château, and that may provide a further indication of the bourgeois orientation of this and similar collections.[36] In any event, the relation between tapestries and wall paintings was close. As Christian de Mérindol has noted,[37] wall paintings were probably substituted for tapestries in modest residences, and perhaps it is worth speculating that the word 'tapisserie' in Baude's title is merely a euphemism for a variety of decorative media that only seldom did, in fact, include tapestries.

Other clues to the ways this collection functioned in the economy of decoration in early sixteenth-century France may perhaps be found in a very interesting, though hardly attractive, manuscript at Princeton University. According to David B. Lawall's description,[38] it dates from the first half of the sixteenth century, and existed as a collection of individual leaves simply tied together before they were bound in the early seventeenth century. Lawall was certainly correct when he suggested that the collection was likely produced for private use. But what, we may ask, might that private use have been? Manuscript collections of emblems that were intended as moral guidebooks for a given family were usually produced more elegantly than this volume.[39] Given its original physical presentation, this manuscript may well have been a program for decorating a private residence. The rhymed proverbs might be the motifs for tapestries, while the devices could be used on a ceiling or in recurring decorative motifs in wall paintings and the like. And it is interesting to note that at least five of the proverbs are either taken from Henri Baude's collection, or are variations on compositions by Baude (fig. 10). If this manuscript does in fact constitute such a program for decoration, it would mark Baude's collection as a dictionary-like compendium of motifs from which an individual patron might draw selectively in preparing a program for the decoration of his residence.

From a different perspective, it is interesting to note that this collection furnishes one of the first instances – if Lawall was correct in dating it from around 1550 – where we find devices grouped together with proto-emblematic compositions of this kind. In any event, it does provide early

Fig. 10. 'Jalumay ce feu de boys vert.' Henri Baude, *Dictz moraulx pour faire tapisserie*, Princeton ms 92.

evidence of a perceived link between compositions like those of Baude and one kind of truly emblematic composition, thus demonstrating that, from the start, emblematics actually were perceived within, or in relation to, the tradition of illustrated proverbs and other illustrated moralizing literature.

Other kinds of moralizing compositions from the late Middle Ages resemble Baude's *Dictz* to a certain extent in their format and design, and some of these works inspired windows and mortuary sculpture that have survived. Around 1470 or a little earlier, there came into existence, probably in Rouen, according to Emile Mâle,[40] a new set of personified virtues that tended to replace the simple, elegant personifications used in ecclesiastical sculpture in France until at least the late thirteenth century. These

Fig. 11. Four cardinal virtues. BN ms fr. 9186, f. 304.

strange creations were so complicated in the deployment of their attributes that explanations were necessary, apparently even for contemporaries, to understand the coding of these new and rather bizarre personifications. Hence they were often accompanied by explanatory verse texts.

A particularly beautiful illustrated presentation of the four cardinal virtues constructed this way opens one manuscript version of *Le Livre des quatre vertus*, which was traditionally and erroneously attributed to Seneca and was presented here in a French translation by Jean de Courtecuisse.[41] The four virtues are presented on a single page, each within a compartment delineated by an architectural frame; the symbolism of each virtue is explained in a *dizain* painted on a kind of tablet hung from the top of the compartment. This magnificent miniature is followed by a prose explanation of the virtues.[42] Temperance (fig. 11) is perhaps the most bizarre of the four: on her head there sits a clock, she has a bit in her mouth, holds a pair of glasses in one hand, and has spurs on her feet, which are posed on the vanes of a windmill. The clock on her head is the most aesthetically shocking feature to the modern eye, but each of the virtues is similarly coiffed. Emile Mâle (312) believed the artist found his model for such a positioning of the clock as an attribute of Temperance in the ornate helmet crests of the tournament knights, and he takes the presentation of the virtues and vices, each with an attribute in the form of a crest, in Bernard de Lutzenburg's *Sermones de symbolica colluctatione septem vitiorum et virtutem* (Cologne, 1516) as proof that this was the case. Michel Pastoureau claims that *cimiers* like these were the site for the display of the earliest devices, both in the decorative presentation of heraldic arms on a shield surmounted by one of these crested helmets, and in actual crested helmets worn in tournaments.[43]

The distribution of Temperance's other attributes is quite traditional, except that more are used than was normally the case in earlier personifications. This multiplication of attributes, according to E.H. Gombrich, is a by-product of the mania for definition and distinction in the teaching of the Scholastics.[44] Whatever the rationale and origin of these attributes, they are, at first glance, puzzling, and it is fortunate that the *dizain* guides the viewer in deciphering the complexities of this curious and enigmatic composition:

> Qui a l'orloge soy regarde
> En tous ses faictz heure et temps garde.
> Qui porte le frain en sa bouche
> Chose ne dict qui a mal touche.
> Qui lunectes met a ses yeux
> Prez luy regarde sen voir mieux.

Esperons monstrent que cremeur [peur/crainte]
Font estre le josne homme meur.
Au moulin qui le corps soustient
Nulz excez faire n'appartient.[45]

These attributes belong to the category of implements of everyday life, and some of them are quite modern; one cannot but wonder if they did not emerge as attributes of temperance through their role in contemporary proverbs or metaphorical turns of phrase.

An example where this may well be the case is the bed where Justice is sitting. Upon the bed there is a pillow, and the only other attributes are the traditional sword and scales. The bed, of course, is the traditional *lit de justice* (the 'lit à dais, où le roi se plaçait lorsqu'il tenait une séance solennelle du parlement,' according to the *Petit Robert*). While this is not quite a proverb, it is a metaphorical expression that is being dealt with in our composition just as Baude and others dealt with proverbs; that is, the expression is literalized and the two parts, the literal and the figurative, are linked by an analogy that yields an edifying expansion of the image into an incipient allegory. In this kind of poetic accommodation,[46] the poet fits the two parts of the expression together in the last four lines of the *dizain* in such a way as to convey a moral lesson:

Le lit enseigne quen repos
Doibt juge dire son pourpos
Comme est lorlier au lit propice
Est misericorde a justice.

The integration of the pillow represents one of the trends that was to become more common as poets attempted increasingly to set symbolic objects in a naturalistic décor, and then accommodate the other elements of that setting to the symbolic analogy in question. Or one can see the use of the pillow as an allegorical expansion of the metaphor, a logical extension of the literalization of the figurative expression 'lit de justice.'

The use of rebus-like constructions of the kind we have just encountered in the portrayal of Temperance persisted in certain emblem books through the first century of the form's history.[47] Corrozet composed a number of emblems of this sort, and in La Perrière's variation on Venus as the perfect housewife, we see the goddess with her foot posed on a tortoise, just as the Temperance we have been studying has a foot on the windmill (the good wife does not venture far from home); she has a finger before her lips (the good wife does not gossip); in her other hand, she holds the key that represents the perfect custodianship of her husband's goods.[48] The use of multiple attributes, drawn from multiple sources, to form symbolic collages like this one, completely divorced from any naturalistic narrative situation, continued to be one of the prized techniques of the emblematists well into the seventeenth century.[49] But the appeal of such compositions often depended upon a tension between what the reader would perceive as an anomalous grouping and his naturalistic – and hence proto-scientific – expectations. The emblem, then, depended for its effect on a tension between a residue from earlier forms of thinking and a new perception of the world in which a natural order was explored as an entirely self-contained syntagm, much as the theocentrically organized world was understood in the high Middle Ages.

When the 'new iconography' of the virtues, as Mâle calls it, emerged in the third quarter of the fifteenth century, it quickly became fashionable. It was used extensively throughout the first half of the sixteenth century in church windows and mortuary sculpture, as in Michel Colombe's famous tomb in the Nantes cathedral. One of the most striking examples from this tradition of personified virtues is found in the Panégyrique de St Romain windows in the south transept of Rouen Cathedral. The glass was given in 1521, probably by le seigneur de Brametot. Individual virtues accompany the saint in several panels, and in one section, the death of St Romain is portrayed with the saint assisted by the seven theological and cardinal virtues. These virtues have the new attributes; and interestingly, they are not divided in the traditional way. Faith, Justice, Force, and Hope stand together behind the saint, while Prudence, Charity, and Temperance are in the foreground to provide an interesting example of the breakdown of medieval categories and hierarchies in the early years of the sixteenth century.[50] Without such a breakdown in this and other areas of symbolic culture, the development of the emblematic process of fragmentation and variation could never have taken place.[51]

Like the illustrated proverbs, these new virtues are highly concrete translations of the abstract conceptions of virtue into a system of signs composed of homely objects taken mainly from everyday life and often having a place within the matrix of contemporary proverbial wisdom. Compositions of this sort are often found accompanying illustrated proverbs in manuscript anthologies from around the turn of the sixteenth century. In two of the best-known collections of this kind, one encounters, alongside Baude's poetry and assorted personifications reminiscent of the ones we have been considering, illustrated verse paraphrases of Petrarch's *Triumphs*. There, the *Triumphs* are illustrated without the traditional, if apocryphal, chariots; instead, we see a series of female personifications, each bedecked with attributes and posing with a foot triumphantly placed on the condition she has defeated, just as in certain representations of the virtues.[52]

Petrarch's *Triumphs* inspired artists perhaps more than any other single secular work during the fifteenth and early sixteenth centuries; and as Menestrier noted long ago, they had a very real, if limited, influence on the development of emblem literature.[53] Above all, the idea of the triumphal procession provided emblematists with yet another model for developing personifications, as La Perrière did, for example, with Diligence, whose chariot is pulled by ants as she triumphantly lifts a cornucopia and tramples vanquished Famine beneath her feet.[54] Giotto had already imagined triumphal scenes of an allegorical nature before Petrarch began to compose his *Triumphs* in 1356. However, Petrarch's innovation, as Essling and Müntz have noted, consisted in substituting a triumphal procession for a more or less immobile assembly gathered in some solemn sanctuary.[55] This variation on the original structure of the triumph seems to parallel a more general medieval tendency to infuse what M.-R. Jung has called 'static' allegory with some elements of what he calls 'dynamic' allegory, which involves the dynamic interaction of ideas in some narrative or dramatic scene.[56] Even though Petrarch used a chariot only in the first of his six triumphs, contemporary artists began to use chariots in the representation of each triumph.

The liberty artists were prone to take with the Petrarchan text is attributable, again according to Essling and Müntz, to the contemporary passion for symmetry,[57] but it also seems to correspond in interesting ways to the developing fashion of the processional *entrée*. It seems likely, too, that this use of chariots reflects the late medieval inclination, or perhaps even need, to attach abstract ideas – here the idea of triumph itself – to concrete objects around which speculation could then coalesce in the form of actions and attributes. That is, it would appear that these triumphs are obeying the same laws of symbolic exposition as the new personifications of the virtues that were emerging at about the same time.

Throughout the late Middle Ages Petrarch was greatly admired in France, but more as a *philosophus moralis* than as a humanist and love poet, and his *De remediis utriusque fortunae* was better known than the *Rime*.[58] It is precisely within the context of this reputation that the *Triumphs* came to be appreciated in France in the late fifteenth century. During most of the century, this work of Petrarch was known mainly by hearsay and through a set of Latin verse paraphrases that were wrongly considered to form a true synthesis of Petrarch's poems, but which were, in fact, no more than *argumenta* that tended to concentrate on the more pictorial elements of each Triumph, and condense the basic moral lesson that might be learned from it into a short verse text. Here, for example, is the *argumentum* for the Triumph of Fame:

Omnia Mors mordet, sed Morte Fama triumphat
Cetera mordentem sub pede Fama premit
Egregium facinus post mortem suscitat ipsa
Nec sit Letheos inclita Fama lacus.
  Fama vincit Mortem.

Inscia sum Mortis nece ego invenesto sepultos
Expecto sum claris vita secunda viris.[59]

Following a medieval tradition, some anonymous reader had attached these Latin *argumenta* to the work in the early fifteenth century, but during the century they somehow became detached from the poems and began to lead a life of their own.[60]

Even during the last decades of the century when Petrarch's *Triumphs* began to circulate in the magnificent manuscripts Charles VIII and his armies had brought back among the booty from the Italian campaigns, poets did not immediately translate them into French, and they still worked with the Latin *argumenta* even when they knew Petrarch's poems.[61] Such is the case, according to Simone, with Jean Robertet, his son François, and Jean Molinet, all of whom composed French 'triumphs,' which often have very little to do with Petrarch, but which are generally based quite closely on the *argumenta* to produce the type of quasi-static pictorial allegory combined with a concise moralizing analogy that appealed to their audience. Hence, Jean Robertet renders the Triumph of Fame in a *huitain*:

La Mort mort tout, mais Clere Renommée
Sur Mort triumphe et la tient deprimée
Dessoubz ses piedz; mais apres ces effors
Fame suscite les haulx faitz des gens mors,
Qui par vertu ont meritée gloire,
Qu'apres leur mort de leur fait soit memoire.
Inclite Fame n'eust jamais congnoissance
De Letheus, le grant lac d'oubliance.[62]

What Robertet does here is make explicit the notion that only virtue is rewarded by posthumous Fame, a theme merely implied in Petrarch's poem. Further, he condenses Petrarch's long enumeration of famous men and their deeds to a few generalities.

In short, what he has done is reduce the poem to the bare outlines of the allegorical situation in such a way that it could be easily imagined as a single, simple picture, and then he drew from it, roughly in the last four lines, an explicit moral lesson that could easily be summarized in a *sentence*. This technique of abridgement in such a way as to condense a long literary development into a particularly vivid and easily visualized scene that serves as a preamble for a moral lesson to be associated with it for easy recall was to be used later in the sixteenth century in the para-emblematic series of *Figures de la Bible* or the *Ovide figuré*.[63]

It is equally tempting to imagine these *argumenta* serving as instructions to artists; as such they could be placed at the head of the individual poems, not to introduce the poem, but to provide a larger space together with instructions to an artist for an illustration. At least that is the design of a late fifteenth-century allegorical poem praising women, *La faulcete trayson et les tours / De ceulx qui suivent le train damour*. In one copy on paper (BN Rothschild 2843) each chapter is preceded by a *huitain* set in slightly larger type than the rest of the text within a much larger space than is needed to accommodate it. Another copy at Carpentras is printed on vellum, and these introductory texts and the adjoining blank spaces have been covered by illuminations of the scenes described in them.[64] The following *huitain* from the Rothschild volume is typical and gives us some idea of how they may have functioned as instructions to artists:

> Comment amours vint saluer honneur
> En ung habit dung gentil faulconnier
> Et ressembloit estre parfait chasseur
> Prompt a voler et prendre le gibier
> Honneur le fist sans point en varier
> Son serviteur et mist en sa maison
> Et se voulut en luy du tout fier
> Par quoy depuis fut reprins par rayson. (sig. a6ᵛ)

For the next three pages *Amour* and *Honneur* talk, and at first at least the *huitain* provides a frame within which to situate this loosely dramatic narrative. Toward the end of this chapter *Honneur* takes *Amour* into an orchard, where he falls in love with the lady; this development leaves the *huitain* behind and prepares the next chapter.

Robertet probably composed his *huitains* for the *Triumphs* around 1476, and artists soon began drawing inspiration from the pictorial descriptions of these and similar compositions. Besides their influence on manuscript illumination in the early sixteenth century, the memory of such versions of the *Triumphs* is clearly evident in a stained-glass window in the church at Ervy in the Aube. Italian artists had been looking to the *Triumphs* for inspiration throughout the fifteenth century, but this window, dating from 1502, is one very early and particularly interesting example of the impact of the *Triumphs* on French art. Its six panels represent the triumphant personifications in chariots; each chariot is accompanied by a whole *cortège* of attributes and personifications and, closely integrated into the scene, two biblical verses on banderoles provide the initial commentary, while a cartouche at the bottom of each panel contains a French explanatory *huitain*. For Simone, this window represents the beginning of a new period in which an Italian artistic influence interacts with the French tradition of the *argumenta*.[65]

At the same time, this window foreshadows in very important ways the development of the emblem form in the 1530s. Among the attributes on Fame's robe, we notice many eyes, ears, and mouths, along with a globe, a ship, a compass, and a ruler. Her chariot is crushing the three Fates. The biblical verses are from Genesis (6: 4): 'Sunt potentes seculo viri famosi' and Ruth (1: 95): 'Valor apud cunctos fama percrebuit.' The *huitain* glosses as follows:

Renommée surmonte la Mort
Par ouye, par bouche et par yeux
Car le juste, sans estre mort
Resplendit en terre et ès cieux
(Renommée) pervole en tous lieux
Par justice, droit et promesse;
(Elle establit) jeunes et vieux
En béatitude et lyesse.[66]

The form is very much like that of the emblem, and indeed, certain emblem books, such as the *Mikrokosmos* of 1579, did retain this form with the biblical verse, picture, and verse text, until the end of the sixteenth century. Still, the relationship between the parts is somewhat looser than in an emblem, even though the poet does attempt to justify the presence of the attributes within the general framework of the personification, much as an emblematist would do. Elsewhere, as in the Triumph of Love, the choice of vocabulary ('immunde Lubricité,' 'fole amour') make the *huitain* description itself into a moral commentary.

During the sixteenth century, Petrarch's *Triumphs* continued to provide a fertile theme, a context, and a form for an astonishing variety of works of visual and literary art. As Franco Simone has noted, French interest in the

Triumphs was centred in Rouen during the early part of the century. The first pictorial representations of the *Triumphs* in France appear in the sculpted friezes of the Hôtel de Bourgthehoulde; the first French manuscripts of the *Triumphs* were produced by a Rouen scriptorium at the command of Cardinal Georges d'Amboise; and the first French translation, this one in prose, was done in Rouen by Georges de La Forge.[67] Later, royal *entrées* all over France were constructed around the idea of the triumphal procession, but nowhere were *entrées* more closely modelled on Petrarch's creations than in Rouen, where, in 1550 for example, Henri II's *entrée* was accompanied by magnificent allegorical chariots devoted to Fame and Virtue.[68] As late as 1560, the Petrarchan triumphs were still providing artists in Rouen with themes, as, for example, in the magnificent windows of the Church of St Patrice. But by this time, the model still appealed only in conservative centres like Rouen, for the decadence of the form was becoming noticeable as in Ronsard's not unironic triumphal procession of Bacchus (1555), or in the carnival, ramshackle procession in Bruegel's 'Triumph of Time' (1574).

Another proto-emblematic form using the pretext of the processional also emerged in the fifteenth century; this was the Dance of Death, which remained a vehicle of choice for the expression of the *memento mori* theme throughout the Renaissance. In the early fifteenth century, a charnel-house was erected at the great central cemetery of the Holy Innocents in Paris to receive the disinterred bones displaced as the cemetery proved incapable of meeting the growing needs for consecrated ground in those parishes it was supposed to serve. One of the earliest *Danses macabres* was painted on the south cloister wall of this charnel-house in 1424. It was presented as a continuous, unified processional, in which vaguely skeletal figures led living men toward their natural end. Beneath the painted processional, verse inscriptions explained that these living men each represented a type, a class, or a condition within the social hierarchy of late medieval France.

Although the charnel-house was demolished in the seventeenth century to make way for road construction, the verses and what is presumably a good approximation of the scenes illustrating the dance have been preserved in two manuscripts at the Bibliothèque Nationale, and an incunable *Danse macabre*, first published by Guy Marchand in 1485.[69] In one illustration, we see the Pope and an emperor, and in another, a monk, a usurer, and a poor man, from whom the usurer is extracting his due, all being spirited away in the dance to their death by the vision of that death itself.[70] The first edition contained thirty characters, usually distributed two to a page, although occasionally three characters fit into one illustration. The following year, Marchand reissued the Dance with ten additional actors, and before the end

Biſduo ſūt q̄ cordeten⁹ ſub pectore miſi. Mors mea. iudiciū. barathri nox. lux para

Vado mori ſenior. iam finis tpis
inſtat. Jamq̄ patet mortis
ianua. vado mori.

Vado mori pulcer viſu: diſi
mors ipſa decori: Vel forme
neſcit parcere. vado mori

Le mort
Homme darmes plus ne reſte:
Allez ſans faire reſiſtence.
Cy ne pouez rien conqueſte.
Vous auſſi: homme daſtinence
Chatreux: prenes en pacience.
De plus viure nayez memoire.
Faictez vous valoir a la danſe.
Sur tout homme mort a victoire.

Le chartreux
Je ſuis au monde pieca mort
Par quoy de viure ay moings enuie
Ja ſoit que tout hōme craint mort
Puis que la char eſt aſſouuie:
Plaiſe a dieu que lame rauie
Soit es cielx apres mon treſpas.
Ceſt tout neant de ceſte vie.
Tel eſt huy: qui demain neſt pas.

Le mort
Sergent qui porte celles mace:
Il ſemble que vous rebellez.
Pour neant faictez la grimace:
Se on vous greue ſi appellez.
Vous eſte de mort appellez.
Qui luy rebelle il ſe decoit.
Les plus fort ſont toſt rauallez.
Il neſt fort quauſſi fort ne ſoit.

Le ſergent
Moy qui ſuis royal officier:
Comme moſe la mort frapper
Je faſoye mon office hier.
Et elle me vient huy happer:
Je ne ſcay quelle part eſchapper:
Je ſuis pris deca et dela.
Malgre moy me laiſſe apper.
Enuiz meurt qui appris ne la.

Fig. 12. Carthusian and sergeant. *La Danse macabre de Guyot Marchant* (1486).

of the fifteenth century, he had produced an equally popular dance for female actors. The original Marchand Dance of Death presumably reproduced, with minor concessions to changing fashions in dress and the like, the alternating chain of the living and the dead as it was presented on the wall of the charnel-house. But because of the nature and limitations of book format, a reader can see only part of this chain at any one time (fig. 12).

Above the illustration, a short Latin text presents proverbial wisdom concerning the art of dying, and beneath the truncated processional, Death identifies each of his guests in a French *huitain* and invites him to join the Dance. Here is the way Death addresses the Carthusian monk and the sergeant:

Homme darmes plus ne reste:
Allez sans faire resistence.
Cy ne pouez rien conqueste.
  Vous aussi: homme dastinence
Chatreux: prenes en pacience.
De plus uiure nayez memoire.
Faictez vous valoir a la danse.
Sur tout homme mort a victoire. (sig. a-viii[r])

The somewhat relieved Carthusian claims that he is already used to being dead to this world, and is ready to die. But his companion, the indignant sergeant, reacts with his mace held high, as if to ward off mocking Death:

Moy qui suis royal officier:
Comme mose la mort frapper
Je fasoye mon office hier.
Et elle me vient huy happer:
Je ne scay quelle part eschapper:
Je suis pris deca et dela.
Malgre moy me laisse apper.
Enuiz meurt qui appris ne la. (sig. a–viii[r])

Early bibliographers and bibliophiles classified the different versions of the Dance as emblem books,[71] but Praz was probably right to exclude them from his vast bibliography. Nevertheless, they can be characterized as proto-emblematic in certain ways. First, picture and text are combined in a regularly repeated format. Second, the form of the Dance is loosely tripartite, with the Latin text above and the French *huitain* below the picture, and in the balance struck between illustration and text, the picture complements the text in a way that is not simply illustrative in a narrative or descriptive sense. Finally, like emblems, the situations of the Dance deal with types, and these types have been placed in a theatrical setting as emblems could be, beginning in the late sixteenth or early seventeenth century. The explicit connection with the emblem tradition proper comes with Holbein's late version of the Dance and with the various emblems composed on the theme by Corrozet, Montenay, and others.

In the late fifteenth century, Franciscan preachers never tired of thundering apocalyptic sermons exhorting all men to meditate upon their impending and ineluctable end. Death haunted the consciousness of the French during these times of renewal following the long period of famine and pestilence that accompanied the Hundred Years' War, and the *memento mori* theme was a choice subject for sermons anyway. Can we perhaps even imagine Franciscans preaching on the theme within the charnel-house itself? The setting would have been ideal, for they would have been able to refer their listeners to the visual arguments of the painted dance, as preachers must have done with the biblical scenes that decorated the churches. Mâle (361–2) speculates on the basis of an eighteenth-century summary of a now missing document then in the archives of the church at Caudebec, not far from Rouen, that the dance was actually performed in that church in the late fourteenth century in a way that recalls liturgical drama from the high Middle Ages.

One of the important techniques of the late medieval sermon was the use of ecphrastic, or pictorially vivid and dramatic description, and summaries in rhymed, rhythmic form. Those theologians who prepared compendia of exempla, stock themes, and mythological commonplaces for use in sermons sometimes condensed their exempla or allegorical personifications of the virtues and vices into sententious *argumenta*, often rendered more memorable by the use of rhythm and rhyme. Here, for example, in a passage noted by Beryl Smalley, is the Dominican John Ridevall's fourteenth-century rendering of Fulgentius' description of Saturn:

> Opi mariatus, senio gravatus,
> capite velatu et falce sceptratus,
> vultu desoltus, pudendis orbatus
> et prole cibatus.

Ridevall then goes on to moralize each phrase of his easily remembered ditty.[72] Fulgentius, however, had presented the fable of Saturn in a more narrative form with less distinction between the different parts of the myth.[73] And as Gombrich (139ff.) has noted, these medieval inventions survived in emblem literature; his example is Ripa's personification of

Amicitia, which Erna Mandowsky has shown to be borrowed from Holcot's moral 'pictures,' and Holcot was a follower of Ridevall.[74]

But Ridevall's method of condensation and presentation, which is similar to that of the *argumenta*, is more important for understanding the impact of these preachers' aids on the structure of the emblem as it was to emerge some two centuries later. Sometimes repeated grammatical forms, such as a series of questions and answers, a series of rhetorical questions, or some other form of anaphora – what the French sometimes call a *construction kyrielle* – would be used to develop and reinforce rhythms that were supposed to make the message stick better in the mind of uneducated listeners in a still largely oral culture.[75] In the fifteenth century, similar techniques were used, as we have seen, to condense proverbial wisdom into rhymed verse, where the attributes of personifications or parts of allegories (understood in the original sense as extended metaphors) were commented on individually and seriatim. This trend toward the analytical dissection of allegories was emphasized by illustrations in the proverb collections and the new personifications of the virtues, and it hastened the fragmentation of the traditional allegorical structures, as commentary always tends to do.[76]

The combination of illustration, rhyme, and paginal compartmentalization continued to be used in a variety of ways in the early sixteenth century, as in the case of the first French version of Erasmus' *Praise of Folly* (see below, 100–3). By the middle years of the sixteenth century, this technique for the presentation of texts that involved the fragmentation of the unit into short sections that could be introduced by a vaguely summarizing condensation in rhymed verse and a supporting illustration was being applied to the Bible. There began to appear a new series of illustrated 'Bibles' with the severely abridged text often paraphrased in rhymed quatrains, and with the complete text left implicit. The relation between text and pictures in these Bible anthologies recalls that of the *Bibles moralisées* and other typological works of the fourteenth and fifteenth centuries, one of which was even called the *Biblia figurata*. The different Renaissance versions of the *Figures de la Bible* enjoyed immense popularity in France from the late 1530s through the 1570s, and many of the emblematists, including Corrozet, Gueroult, Paradin, and Simeoni composed the paraphrased texts for these works.[77]

Like the rhymed proverbs and *dictz pour faire tapisserie*, they were apparently intended to provide models for artists and artisans, or possibly to be clipped from books to decorate modest bourgeois households. Such, in any event, is the suggestion implicit in Gilles Corrozet's address 'Aux lecteurs,' which serves as a preface to one edition of his rhymed texts for Holbein's *Historiarum veteris testamenti icones*:

Ces beaux pourtraictz serviront d'exemplaire
Comment il fault au Seigneur Dieu complaire:
Exciteront de luy faire service,
Retireront de tout peché & vice
Quand ilz seront insculpez en l'esprit
Comme ilz sont painctz, & couchez par escript.
Doncques ostez de voz maisons & salles,
Tant de tapiz & de painttures sales,
Ostez Venus & son filz Cupido,
Ostez Helene & Philis & Dido,
Ostez du tout fables & poësies
Et recevez meilleures fantasies.
Mectez au lieu, & soient voz chambres ceinctes
Des dictz sacrez, & des histoires sainctes
Telles que sont celles que voiez cy
En ce livret. Et sy faictes ainsy,
Grandz & petis, les jeunes & les vieulx
Auront plaisir, & au coeur & aux yeulx.[78]

It is interesting to note here the reaction against the subject-matter of humanistic art by a prominent Renaissance *libraire* of impeccable humanistic training, bias, and interests.[79] Such, however, is not our concern here, and it is more important for my argument to note how Corrozet is suggesting, through the use of words like 'insculptez' that suggest simultaneously the arts of memory and interior decoration, that these paraphrases might be used like the *dictz moraulx* or Alciato's emblems; that is, that they might provide edifying motifs for interior decoration in such a way as to turn any bourgeois house into a kind of memory house preaching the sermon of its owner.

Each paraphrase in the series is displayed on a single sheet in the following manner: at the top of the page the biblical verse about to be elaborated is presented in Latin; beneath it an illustration interprets the biblical scene narrated in the Latin verses; finally, at the bottom of the page, a French quatrain expands the verse or verses in a way that situates the scene illustrated in the woodcut within the context of a narrative development. Here is an example from the 1539 edition of the Corrozet-Holbein version (fig. 13). The biblical passage is represented as being from 'IIII. Regum II.' and reads as follows: 'Elias diuidit aquas pallio. Raptus in coelum non inueniuntur. Eliseum irridentes pueri, lacerantur ab ursis.' Actually, this passage appears to be a condensation of four different verses of the second chapter of 2 Kings as it appears in the King James version (8, 11, 23–4). The selection of

ELIAS diuidit aquas pallio. Raptus in cœlum non inuenitur. Eliſeum irridentes pueri, lacerantur ab urſis.

IIII. REGVM II.

Vn chariot de feu ardant rauit
Le bon Elie, & plus on ne le veit.
Enfantz ſont mortz, & des Ours ſuffoquez
Car ilz ſ'eſtoient d'Eliſee mocquez.

Fig. 13. 'Elias diuidit aquas pallio.' *Historiarum veteris testamenti icones* (1543).

elements to be illustrated from this chapter has apparently been governed by the pictorial potential of the different moments in the narrated action.

Each of the elements retained has been fitted into the illustration, even though they occur at successive moments in the narrated time span; in the luxuriously produced *Bibles moralisées*, on the other hand, each moment of the fragmented narration has its own illustration. The three story moments are rendered in French with no real effort to shape them into a narrative:

Un chariot de feu ardant ravit
Le bon Elie, & plus on ne le veit.
Enfantz sont mortz, & des Ours suffoquez
Car ilz s'estoient d'Elisée mocquez.[80]

Even the relationship between the different moments is none too clear, and so the composition affords a point of entry into a doctrinal or moralizing commentary, either oral or, potentially, written. How might this commentary develop? The text might be used as an example of the advantages we may receive from our trials and tribulations. At least, that was the way le Père Berthod used the story of Elias in one of his *Emblesmes sacrez* of 1665. He begins his forty-sixth emblem with a verse from 2 Timothy (2: 5): 'Non coronabitur, nisi qui legitime certaverit ...' The illustration shows two hands emerging from clouds and holding crowns: one crown is halo-like, while the other appears to be made of laurel leaves. A meditation in prose (II, 341–3) is followed by an example, the tribulations of Elias, whom God permits eventually to make miracles and then be transported into heaven in a chariot of fire.[81] The miracles do not appear in Corrozet's quatrain, but they are referred to in the first Latin verse: 'Elias diuidit aquas pallio.' Since the French and the Latin do not entirely coincide, there remains a certain space for commentary that can reconcile the two texts and, not incidentally, generalize the implicit message as Berthod later did.

In short, during the fourteenth and fifteenth centuries there developed in France a whole panoply of techniques and models for the use of illustration or ecphrastic description to support the message being presented in a discursive text. These techniques and models were no doubt related to the arts of memory, to the characteristics of scholastic teaching, and to the general tendency toward a more visual orientation of thought in the late Middle Ages. They were increasingly conditioned by the development of printing and its absolute dependence on the compositional model of the codex page opening. And these were the trends that would culminate in the production of the emblem in the middle third of the sixteenth century.

4

Proto-emblematics in the Early Sixteenth Century

The decade when François Ier came to the throne was a period of intense proto-emblematic activity at court, and much of this activity centred on the queen mother, Louise de Savoye. The French court apparently became interested in 'hieroglyphic' signs in 1509 following Louis XII's return from Venice, where Aldus had just published the *Hypnerotomachia Poliphili* in 1499, and Horapollo's *Hieroglyphics* in 1505. Horapollo's *Hieroglyphics* were partially translated into French for the queen mother shortly after François took the throne, and their translator described them as useful when one wanted to 'escripre les gestes des Roys en marbre et tapisserie.' As an example the translator produced what Anne-Marie Lecoq calls 'l'hiéroglyphe de Marignan,' in which a chained bear representing the Swiss is held captive by a crowned lion.[1] The scene is interesting precisely because it does *not* resemble contemporary Italian humanist renderings of so-called hieroglyphics,[2] but rather recalls the *tableaux vivants* that were so common in French courtly ceremonies in the early sixteenth century. Indeed, we are witnessing here what would seem to be a conscious conflation of a medieval form with newly discovered humanist concerns in the interest of a more stylish and intriguing presentation of political propaganda; this is not an isolated occurrence, as I have tried to show elsewhere.[3] In another example from around the same time, François Demoulins composed for Louise de Savoye a treatise on the virtues in which the personifications use configurations of symbolism borrowed from the *Hypnerotomachia Poliphili*.[4] These personifications attest to the same desire for variation in the mode of presentation of conservative themes and forms in an attempt to make them more fashionable and attractive to their potential audience.

Other proto-emblematic compositions at this court were more closely linked to medieval traditions of allegorical biblical exegesis, while still looking forward, as far as format is concerned, to the emblem books that were to appear a bare decade or two later. These little works of edification and political propaganda were often produced by Godefroy le Batave, the court illuminator; François Demoulins, François d'Angoulême's tutor; and another Franciscan, Jean Thenaud. In them, we often find medallion-shaped illustrations, perhaps with biblical verses that serve as a kind of *inscriptio*, and explanations in French. Since the high Middle Ages, writers and preachers routinely adapted the biblical text to the purposes at hand, sometimes changing it slightly, sometimes incorporating fragments of it in their discourse, like formulas, without much concern about what the text originally meant. For a courtly audience, the Psalms would provide an ideal starting point for building such works, since the Psalms were familiar to everyone, clergy and laity alike. It has been observed that Augustine, like other Christian writers, wrote not only in Latin, but '"in Psalms," so imbued is his language with their phrasing and vocabulary.'[5]

If such compositions, then, look back in subject matter to the vernacular sermon traditions of biblical exegesis, they also look ahead in form to the emblem. Not only are they tripartite compositions, as has often been noted, but they are emblematic, too, in the way they use biblical quotations. To take an example from the *Dominus illuminatio mea* that François Demoulins composed and Godefroy le Batave illuminated on commission for Louise de Savoye to welcome her victorious son back from Marignan in 1516, we find each verse of Psalm 26 illustrated and developed in such a way as to produce a commentary on the event to be celebrated. For example, verse 14, *Expecta dominum, viriliter age, et confortetur cor tuum et sustine dominum*, serves as the caption for a scene in which Louise is handing a cross to her son (fig. 14). The relationship is explained in the *subscriptio*:

> Madame aymant myeulx lame spirituelle du Roy son filz. que le corps materiel. luy presente la Croix Et luy dyt Monseigneur Mon defenseur. Mon repoux. Mon desir. Mon maistre. Mon filz. Et mon amy. Festina lente
>
> Attends Dieu ton liberateur. faictz virilement, fortifie ton cueur. Et soutiens noustre siegneur.[6]

At first glance there is nothing particularly emblematic about this composition apart from its tripartite form. But upon closer inspection we see that the biblical passage is inserted into a new and different context, that of the royal situation, in a way that is bound to surprise, while still retaining its

Fig. 14. 'Expecta dominum.' François Demoulins, *Dominus illuminatio mea*. BN ms fr. 2088, f. 10v.

appearance as a biblical citation. Even if the royal situation is taken to be divinely ordained, this passage is still being presented *consciously*, *flagrantly* out of context, and that surprising fact forms part of its interest. This text exaggerates the rhetorical technique of earlier Christian writers and transfers it into a secular domain; the biblical text becomes a quotation as the distance increases between the original context and the ad hoc context to which it was being applied.

Emblems often involved this kind of 'quotation,' in which the quoted passage, or motif, hovers between two contexts in such a way that the intended message is conveyed with a sense of surprise (that the passage could be thus interpreted), and with the authority that attaches to the text or tradition from which the quote was drawn. We have already seen this technique at work in the stained-glass windows at Ervy (see above, 80). We can assume that it was used widely with biblical texts before Alciato adapted it for use with the pagan motifs that were of interest to the humanists, and were by then much better-known to a broad literate audience through their newfound place in the curriculum of the schools.[7]

Likewise, *tableaux vivants* and other festival décor from the period 'quoted' well-known symbolic motifs to comment in unexpected ways on contemporary events; hence they can be very useful documents for our understanding of the symbolic mentality that underlay the rhetoric of propaganda at the time. Among the many examples discussed by Anne-Marie Lecoq, the Lyons royal entry of 1515, described in a manuscript now at Wolfenbüttel, is perhaps the most revealing in this regard. The first spectacle presented to the young king was an allegorical ship being towed on the Saone by a winged deer, upon which the Connétable de Bourbon was perched (fig. 15). On the one hand, he is recognizable by the flaming sword he is holding, which had been a traditional device in the Bourbon family since the fifteenth century.[8] But on the other, he is identified as a role player in an allegory: he is also labelled as the *Guide Loyal.*

So this is an allegory that functions in a very curious way; each of the *figurants* is a recognizable player at court and, at the same time, a personification of some virtue, quality, or type. It is, at the very least, interesting to speculate that the necessity of the assumed role within the economy of the allegory may have been intended to legitimize or confirm the character's everyday role in the economy of the court.

The other players in this little scene represent the king, Claude de France, and her sister Renée, along with Jean-Jacques Trivulce at the tiller. The allegory simply transforms these characters into abstract forces and provides a syntax to relate them to one another and, through the allegorical

Fig. 15. 1515 Lyons entry of François Ier.

roles they are made to play, to a particular situation. Naturally, this situation is not immediately evident, and must be explained in some kind of text. Hence, the composition functions in exactly the same way as an emblem with the text presenting an allegorical decoding of the message hidden in the ideogrammatic scene. Perhaps it might be enlightening as well to compare the roles played by the various actors to occasional devices that silently present messages about their bearer in a particular situation.[9]

Lecoq shows the same pattern being repeated in other entries and manuscripts prepared for the royal family in the period between 1504 and 1525. It is also clear that the same rhetoric governed the invention of medals and motifs for interior décor in the royal châteaux that were being renovated at the time. There, royalty and members of the court are disguised as personifications and mythological beings, but the disguises and allegorical surrogates for royalty never made them unrecognizable. Indeed, it may have been the desire to distinguish the person beneath the disguise that prompted royal portraitists to a greater degree of individualizing realism;

François, for example, would always be distinct from the allegorical or mythical persona he had adopted for the moment, for if he wished to be associated with the mythological creature or abstract virtue he was pretending to be, he did not wish to be subsumed by it. This tendency to separate the person from the role he is playing must have been a firmly established article of courtly decorum, for early in the second book of *Il Libro del Cortegiano*, Castiglione expressly advises that a costume disguise be designed so that it shows as much of its wearer's nobility as it hides of his identity.[10]

Equally important signs of what I would call a proto-emblematic mentality in France are to be found in the use of allegorical fragments as vehicles for all sorts of propaganda, both personal and political, in courtly festivities and decorative schemes; the taste for allegory fairly pervaded all court life and public pageantry.[11] All these manifestations are closely allied to the emblematic mode, and they go far in explaining the immense and immediate popularity of the emblems when they made their appearance in the 1530s.

Some of the allegorical tableaux staged in Rouen in the early years of the century might even, with little exaggeration, be called living emblems. Josèphe Chartrou has described examples of such presentations on the stages of Rouen in 1508 and 1517. In the first of these tableaux, spectators witnessed a three-headed dragon emerging from a rock labelled Italy. One head represented Milan, another Genoa, and the third, in the form of an eagle, Rome. A porcupine (from the device of Louis XII, where it was combined with the motto *De pres et de loin*) then came out of an allegorical forest called France to combat and defeat the dragon. Nine years later, on Robec bridge, the salamander entered into battle with a bull and bear to symbolize François's battle with the Swiss cantons.[12] The propagandistic nature of these scenes foreshadows the propaganda emblems used later in the century by both Catholics and Protestants in the religious wars. Tableaux of this kind were in fact so much a part of the culture that they provided a vehicle for satire, as in the famous farce of M. Cruche, which is recalled at the beginning of the twenty-fifth *nouvelle* of Marguerite de Navarre's *Heptameron*.[13] There the salamander is once again the hero of a ludic allegorical struggle, in which the king triumphs over another kind of adversary, the aging husband of his mistress.

At Fontainebleau, which François Ier began to renovate in 1527, his emblematic signature, the salamander, provided the basis for many recurrent decorative motifs, and its murals were composed of more complicated allegorical scenes with specific epideictic intentions. These murals were so

Fig. 16. *L'Amour profane.*

closely allied with the emblem tradition that Pierre Dan's seventeenth-century description of them is universally classified as an emblem book. One of the allegorical scenes he describes as an emblem is to be found in the Galerie François Ier, and portrays the monarch as a philosopher king chasing blind Ignorance from the temple of the Muses.[14]

The work at Fontainebleau bears witness to a fashion for allegorical designs in interior decoration, and many of the best-known tapestries of the period contained allegorical projects in which a text was always present, either implicitly or, just as often, explicitly. An example that comes immediately to mind is the famous *Dame à la licorne* series, but perhaps more interesting in this context, there also existed rebus tapestries of which the pair *L'Amour sacré* and *L'Amour profane* at the Musée des Arts Décoratifs are fascinating examples (fig. 16). Here the message is presented in attributes and then spelled out on interpretive banderoles as was common, we may suppose, in tapestries modelled after Henri Baude's *Dictz.*[15]

The close relation between text and illustration in an emblem book appears today in no way extraordinary; conditioned by practices of printed illustration developed over four hundred years, we are quite used to illustrations intended to 'illustrate' or support the message being carried by the text – even if we understand the relation between picture and text quite differently from the emblematists. Indeed, the modern reader finds illustrations unrelated to the text disconcerting. Yet many of the illustrated books produced in France during the first quarter of the sixteenth century lack precisely that close relationship between text and illustration that we take for granted. Part of the reason for this common discrepancy is that, for the editions of secular works, and especially for those published in smaller formats (octavo and even quarto), publishers often simply drew 'illustrations' from stocks of vignettes that they had begun to accumulate during the late fifteenth century. According to Robert Brun, it is very rare to find a woodcut from this period that was executed especially for the work it was 'illustrating.'[16]

Consequently, illustrations in these books bear a tenuous relation at best to the text, and while their role is sometimes that of generic, as opposed to specific, illustration, it is often reduced to little more than pure ornamentation because of the limited choice of woodcuts available. Furthermore, unlike the sumptuous illustrations of the great books of hours published at this time by Simon Vostre, Thielmann Kerver, and others, the woodcuts in these little secular books were usually no more than summary sketches, sometimes clumsy and crude as well. Brun has concluded that they should probably be understood as 'schémas' waiting to be completed by the art of an illuminator or rubricator; for books were still being modeled on manuscripts, and manuscripts provided the standards by which all book production was still judged.[17] Given the schematic nature of some early emblem illustrations, it is possible that the emblem texts were intended, at least in part, to provide guidance to an illuminating artist, or more likely, to the artisan who would develop one or more of these sketches into a tapestry or stained-glass window.

Against this background, the illustrations of Brant's *Narrenschiff* must have appeared as something of an innovation, and emblems, especially as they were printed in the Wechel edition of Alciato in 1534, to be quite revolutionary, the epitome of a new conception of woodblock book illustration. As early as the beginning of the sixteenth century there were experiments with a regularly repeated format where an illustration and text were united on a single page. Baron Heinecken, the early print collector and connoisseur, claimed the honour of originating this formatting technique for the publisher of a mnemotechnic manual printed in 1502 and entitled *Ars memorandi notabilis per figuras Evangelistarum.*[18] Sandra Hindman has described this work as a 'pictorial and written guide to memorizing the Gospels,' and suggested that here, as elsewhere at the time, the pictures served as teaching devices.[19] In the 1502, 1507, and 1510 editions I have consulted,[20] all the chapters of the four Gospels are represented by symbols displayed in a series of fifteen woodblocks. Three, four, or five pictures are used for each of the Evangelists, and in each picture the various signs are displayed on the body of an animal, bird, or human being. The signs are disposed in the form of a cross and numbered for easy and rapid scanning and correlation with the descriptive labels and explanatory verses by Peter de Rosenheim that are printed on the facing verso.

These distichs summarize each chapter, and begin with successive letters of the alphabet for easy recall of the proper sequence. For example, the sixth part of the *Primo imago Ioannis* shows the five loaves, two fishes, and a sign of Christ on the cross disposed in a sort of medallion (fig. 17); it is labelled 'De quinq*ue* panibus & de eucharistica.' Since it is the first of the explanatory texts, the twelve-line explanation is prefaced this way: 'Quae singula subiectis reminiscimur versibus ...' (a-ii^{r}) Lines eleven and twelve correspond to the sixth sign that I have just described, and they read as follows: 'Foena iacent vbi millia quinq*ue* cibat: fieri vult / Rex: mare calcat: amen est caro vita cibus.' So it would appear that the regularly repeated format and close coordination of picture and text may have originated in various mnemotechnic compositions, including works like these or Murner's *Logica memorativa*, but also the *Danse macabre* and other aids for preaching. This is the paginal pattern that Wechel and Janot were to adapt for the earliest emblem books.

Among illustrated works of secular literature from this period where we also find a close coordination of picture and text, one of the most interesting and famous antecedents of Alciato's emblems is Sebastian Brant's *Narrenschiff*, which has occasionally, if erroneously, been classified as an emblem book. Published in Basel in 1494, the *Narrenschiff* must have had an immediate and durable success in France, where one Latin and three

Prima Imago Ioannis

Vna uigena diſtichoq; Ioannis clauditur euangelium hoc eſt Viginti capitibus & uno.
Primum De Trinitate & de uerbo incarnato &c. II. De nupcijs in Chana Gallileę & numularijs extra templum pulſis. III. De Nicodemo. IIII. De muliere Samaritana circa fontem & de Regulo. V De probatica piſcina. VI. De quinq; panibus & de euchariſtia.

Quę ſingula ſubiectis reminiſcimur uerſibus.

Alta docens aquila.uerbum caro fit.ueniuntq;
Vox teſtis.alij tres quoq; Nathanael.
Bis tria uaſa replent noua uina.fugat quoq; fune
Vendentes.templum ſoluite ſignat eis.
Cęlica dogmata dat Nicodemo.tingit uterque
Pręfert Baptiſta.pręedicat atque Ieſure.
Dum laſſus fonte reſidet.ſe Samaritanę
Pandit.curatur Regule filius hic
Extra piſcinam iuſſit tibi languide ſurge.
Nil ſine patre facit.credite uel Moyſi.
Foena iacent ubi millia quinq; cibat.fieri uult
Rex.mare calcat.amen eſt caro uita cibus.

Fig. 17. *Rationarum Evangelistarum* (1507), sig. a-i^{v}-a-ii.

French translations (actually 'adaptations' or 'paraphrases' would more correctly describe these versions) appeared before 1500; it continued to be reissued throughout the first half of the sixteenth century.

Remarkable woodcut illustrations incorporated into Brant's text give relief to a regularly repeated and fairly standard format reminiscent of that of the emblem. Even though some students of Brant's work feel that various chapters may have been composed separately and circulated as *fliegende Blätter*, the book gives the impression of being a unified literary entity in contrast to the earlier anthologies of illustrated proverbs, which lack the central theme and pretext of Brant's work. Here the theme is folly; the pretext is the ark-like ship, that traditional metaphor of society, designed here to ferry across the sea of life a collection of fools, representing all the types in the galaxy of late medieval European society. The tone, as we might suspect, is consistently satirical, with a strong implicit suggestion of paradox underlying many of the developments. Like most earlier illustrated books, Brant's intention was to edify, and the work's usefulness for this purpose is amply demonstrated by the numerous extant sermons based on different chapters from Brant's collection.[21]

Brant's form resembles that of the emblem because the three-line introductory *argumentum*, taken together with the accompanying picture, poses a riddle (at least in certain cases) that will be resolved in a moral lesson by the long poem whose title sets the theme to be developed. But as Holger Homann concluded from his study of Brant's work, the long text seems largely detached from the illustration; illustrations are not often referred to in the text, and Homann cannot see the illustration here as a 'functional component' (*Funktionsglied*) of an integrated whole. The picture merely reproduces the situation or part of the situation for the *Leseunkundigen*; it is merely a supplementary text in the *libri laicorum* tradition.[22] Tiemann interprets this lack of correlation somewhat differently, claiming that in such compositions picture and text are independent illustrations of the same moral theme, the one indicated in the title.[23] Actually, the way this work is illustrated may simply be an example of the process of transition between the often ornamental illustration of late fifteenth-century printed books already discussed and illustration as a *support* of the text as it was increasingly to become in the early years of the sixteenth century. In this transitional stage, then, we may be able to view illustrations as visual *argumenta*.

A close examination of Brant's form will show how different it is from that of the emblem, and that difference is clear in almost any chapter of the *Narrenschiff*. The eighth poem's title, 'Nit volgen gutem ratt,' could conceivably serve as the title of an emblem. In the woodcut we see a man pulling a plough; he is followed by a fowler with a bird on his wrist (in the left-hand half of the illustration). Above the woodcut we read these lines: 'Wer nit kan sprechen ja und neyn / Und pflegen ratt umb gross und kleyn / Der hab den schaden im allein' [Who cannot answer no or yes / And spurns advice as valueless / Must bear his own unhappiness].[24] The problematic relationship between this textual *argumentum* and the following illustration is very nearly emblematic in the tension between the pictured scene, which the reader will assume to be the vehicle for a metaphorically expressed message, and the text, which presumably contains that message. But the message is not immediately evident, for the short introductory text hides the analogies that link the two. This tension is resolved in the long poem, which begins this way:

Der ist ein narr der wys will syn
Und weder glympf / noch moss dut schyn

Und wenn er wysshheit pflegen will
So ist ein gouch syn faderspyl /
Vil sint von worten wyse und klug
Die ziehen doch den narren pflug
Das schafft das sie uff ir wyssheit
Verlossen sich und bschndikeit
Und achten uff kein dromden ratt
Biss jn ungluck zu handen gat

[A fool who with the wise would go
Yet reason, measure cannot show,
And e'en when speaking wisdom's word
A cuckoo is his fowling bird.
Some men are wise in what they say
But hitched to folly's plow they stay;
The reason is that they rely
Upon their shrewdness keen and sly
And heed to no one's counsel pay
Until misfortune comes their way.]

The paradoxical situation presented in the picture is described in the first part of the quoted text. The cuckoo represents folly well, for this bird would be of no use to the fowler's hunt, while the plough, it would seem, figures a kind of slavery not unlike the folly of stubbornness in regard to good advice not heeded. Or perhaps the picture is suggesting that only a fool would try to hunt and plough at the same time. We may suppose the picture is literalizing metaphorical pieces of proverbial wisdom. Whatever pieces of good advice this picture suggests by negative implication, it is in the end nothing more than a pretext that leads into, and is subordinated to, the sermon-like development in the last two-thirds of the text (24 lines) where a series of biblical examples exhorts the reader to take full advantage of good advice freely offered.

Illustrations from early French editions of Brant's work were also used in the first French edition of Erasmus' *Praise of Folly*, in a way that is highly instructive for our understanding of the background against which the emblem took shape. In 1520 Galliot du Pré issued a French version of Erasmus' *Moriae Encomium* under the title *De la declamation des louenges de follie.*[25] In this illustrated *vulgarisation*, the work is partitioned into thirty-five chapters, each of which begins with an illustration of a French quatrain that serves as a vague and imprecise *argumentum* for the section or episode to follow. The same format had been used during the fifteenth

Des ſouenges de follie.

Des nourrices de folie. Chap.iiii.

Par delices inſaciables
De viure trop mignottement
Sont ſes folz nourriz proprement
Trop menger ſont choſes greuables

Fig. 18. 'Des nourrices de folie,' Erasmus, *De la declamation des louenges de follie.* (1520), f. 6[v].

century for the presentation of Latin or French translations of Petrarch's *Triumphs* (see above, 76–81).

Chapter 5 of Du Pré's *Declamation* is entitled 'De la divinité de follie,' and a large woodcut, taken like all the rest from one of the early French editions of Brant's *Narrenschiff*,[26] dominates the page. It shows a fool (as identified by his cap) in a rain of insects and beasts from heaven, where there sit two men on clouds; one is bearded (the sign of a sage) and has horns, while the other is clean-shaven and has the appearance of a young man. The quatrain reads: 'Lauctorite & la puissance / De follie sont estimee / Comme maiestez increes / Transcenda[n]s humaine iactance' (f. 7ᵛ). The illustration does not seem to be particularly well suited to the passage in question, but rather serves here simply as part of the inventory of fools, presenting two types – the young man and the old cuckold, and more vaguely, the discussion of the child and the doting old man a little farther on – clearly enough to make any commentary unnecessary.

Chapters 4 and 7 are both illustrated by a picture of several women carrying lanterns as they arrive at the door of a house and knock (fig. 18). Chapter 4 is entitled 'Des nourrices de folie,' while chapter 7 is captioned 'Medee/Circes/Venus/Aurora/et plusieurs sont refformez en ieunesse par la vertu d'aucuns enchantemens/fontaines/charmes et autres choses.' From the appended texts there is no way for a modern reader to realize that the women are carrying lanterns and knocking on the door to heaven; this we can learn only from Brant's 'De l'obmission de bonnes oeuvres' (f. 101ʳ):

Quiconque a sa lampe remplie
Duylle sa lumiere remplist
Et si apres est desemplie
Et de bien faire nacomplist
Parce que sa vertuz nemplist
La porte des cieulx descouverte
Aux bons ne luy sera ouverte.

Galliot du Pré used this illustration more generically than Marnef had done in his illustration of Brant's text, since it was not made specifically for the work he was editing; and this is clear in the *argumentum* to chapter 7: 'Pour en jeunesse revenir / Nallez point crier ma loquence / Vers la fontaine de jouvence / Car a folie fault venir.' Almost the entire chapter is devoted to youth, why all the gods are young, and how only folly can bring youth back through love and wine. So while the portrayal of young (?) women lifts Du Pré's use of this illustration above the level of pure decoration, it does not 'illustrate' in the modern sense, and its relation to the text remains puzzling at best.

To take another example, chapter 11 is entitled 'De lestat de mariage'; the illustration shows the interior of a comfortable house with a fool holding a backgammon board and lifting a broken vase above his head; at his waist hangs a purse and he is identified by his fool's cap. Standing by, in the left-hand half of the picture, there is a lady and child. The quatrain reads: 'Quant a lestat de mariage / Maintenant se fait par luxure / Nompas pour faire geniture / Est ung cas en la loy saulvaige' (f. xvii^{r} [actually xix^{r}]). While Erasmus does speak of marriage and gamesters, this introductory combination of picture and *argumentum* only vaguely recalls the tenor of Erasmus' text, and it may be said, as Tiemann has done concerning Brant, that these introductions are more like independent, but parallel, developments on a common theme than actual summaries of the text. Still, the title and rhymed *argumentum* do provide the explanatory transition between the picture and the text, just as they would, for example, in many of the expanded-form emblems of Corrozet and Coustau. The illustration provides a commentary, too, on the long text, but that commentary remains implicit until the *argumentum* links the two. And it would appear that Erasmus' work continued to be associated with emblem literature, however independently of his intentions, well into the seventeenth century.[27]

A variety of other works from the same period also seems to foreshadow the emblem form and its internal structure in different ways. First, there is the absolutely essential example of Erasmus' *Adages* (1500), which not only provided emblematists with a rich new source of materials, but also suggested how proverbs could serve as the point of departure for digressive moralizing discussions in a humanistic vein. Many of the trends and developments we have been looking at come together in a manuscript, *Speculum principis*, recently brought to light by Jean Michel Massing.[28] Composed between 1512 and 1515 for the *dauphin* François d'Angoulême by François Demoulins, it contains illustrated adages from Erasmus alongside the complicated allegories familiar to us from other works by Demoulins, and the illustrated *dicts* of Henri Baude. While the work is dominated by versions of Erasmian adages not too dissimilar from emblems, the technique is that of the illustrated proverbs, and we can see the difference by comparing the way Alciato translated adages into emblems with the way adages are presented here. One of the drawings exhibited was a literal, pictorial transcription of *Delphinum cauda ligas* (*Adages*, I, iv, 93), which the text describes in a way that is reassuring for François d'Angoulême, the *dauphin* (fig. 19).

Fig. 19. 'Delphinum cauda ligas.' François Demoulins, *Speculum principis*, f. 17.

As Virginia Callahan has shown, Alciato was a friend of Erasmus, and some of his emblems show interesting similarities with *Adages* in Erasmus' collection.[29] So while it is not surprising to find that many of Alciato's emblems had Erasmian adages as their point of departure, it is interesting to see what Alciato does with these adages. Emblem 16, *Sobrius esto, et memineris non tenerè credere: haec sunt membra mentis*, shows a disembodied hand with an eye in the palm; it is the *Oculatae manus* of *Adages*, I, viii, 31. Alciato conflates this image from Plautus (*Asinaria*), expressing the old saw 'Seeing is believing,' with a saying of Epicharmus and an anecdote concerning Heraclitus calming a mob by displaying a pennyroyal (*pulegium*), while Erasmus confines himself to citations from Plautus and Terence. Unlike Demoulins, Alciato conflates several proverbial sayings or memorable examples, thus setting the adage within the mosaic of a broader context of commonplaces. Here, as in other emblems based on adages, the adage is illustrated, while the text conflates or subverts the message it carries.[30]

Against the background of many examples like this one, even an emblem drawn from the Greek Anthology may remind the reader of one of the adages; hence, *In silentium* (12) recalls *Stultus stulta loquitur* (*Adages*, I, i, 98, although it may ultimately be traced back to an Anthology epigram). The emblem couples motto and epigram with a man in scholar's dress with a finger raised to his lips. But what, we may ask, could have attracted Alciato to this adage and epigram? I would suggest that the reason is to be sought in the popularity of the theme of the finger raised before one's lips in the late Middle Ages. There is a Quentin Massys Allegory of Folly at the Worcester Museum of Art, where Folly has a finger before her lips, and the fourteenth of the *Proverbes en rimes* warns that 'derriere le doigt on ne se peut cacher,' as does the *Vénus domestique* in La Perrière's *Theatre* (18). So we may be in the presence of yet another example of conflation, this a complicated one where a medieval proverb is conflated with an ancient epigram to produce a typically emblematic variation.

Whatever the case, Alciato's followers also must have mined Erasmus' collection of *Adages*; we know, for example, that La Perrière drew heavily on the *Adages* in composing his *Theatre des bons engins*, and on the *Parabolae* for *La Morosophie*.[31] Perhaps Aneau was thinking of *Adages*, I, i, 70 when he composed an emblem on the theme of *Homo homini lupus*, and the examples could be multiplied. The emblems are in many respects the children of the *Adages*.

On other fronts, editions of Petrarch's *Triumphs* still provided artists and engravers with ample experience in translating a text into pictorial terms, and the bestiary tradition remained strong and strongly pictorial with Pierre Gringore's *Menus propos* (see above, 30). Books of hours also did much to set new standards for the combination of picture and text. In the magnificent examples from the first third of the century, printers bound picture and text together with an elaborate, dominating frame that, following the example of manuscript practice, often filled out the entire page. This typographical artifice encouraged, and perhaps even mandated, a close relation between picture and text – such as the one we see in the late medieval books of hours but that had been lost in much early printed book illustration. Perhaps the most pertinent example for understanding the dynamics of emblems is to be found in the presentation of the traditional allegory of the months in these books. In his Hours of 1522, for instance, Kerver's presentation of July shows a mature man surrounded by his household with the following quatrain: 'Saige doibt estre ou ne sera iamais / Lhom*m*e quant il a quarante deux ans / Lors sa beaulte decline desormais / Lom*me* en Juillet toutes fleurs so*nt* passa*ns*.'[32] This tradition was continued in a more secular mode by Gueroult in his *Hymnes du temps et de ses parties* (Lyons, 1560) and by Ronsard in his *Sept aages de l'homme*, engraved by Gillis Hoorbe (Paris, 1595).[33]

Although his own production is only marginally proto-emblematic at best, Geoffroy Tory is a valuable witness to the mental attitudes current in the first third of the century that helped make the rapid acceptance of emblems possible in France. Through studies in Italy, Tory developed an attitude toward the art of printing and book composition that combined Renaissance classical ideals with his own medieval allegorizing bias. In Italy he learned new techniques of printing and design, but as Gustave Cohen has explained: 'Tory ne peut pas considérer une chose, lettre, forme, dessin, sans chercher à en découvrir le sens moral et la valeur symbolique ... Tout mythe antique, tout récit biblique, toute pierre des *Lapidaires*, tout animal des *Bestiaires*, était susceptible, aux yeux de l'exégète ou de l'interprète averti d'une quadruple interprétation, morale ou tropologique, allégorique ou théologique.'[34]

In *Champ Fleury*, the curious treatise on the design of letters that he published in 1529, Tory plumbs the allegorical meaning of letters and translates it into the form and composition of those letters. As a result, Tory was less impatient with rebus signs than Rabelais, for example, since he tended to place them, along with ordinary letters, in the semantically charged category of ideogrammatic writing, as the Renaissance also did for the newly discovered Egyptian hieroglyphics. But we should not mistake this for a purely humanist attitude: the allegory of letters goes back at least to the second half of the thirteenth century, and seemed to enjoy a lively and uninterrupted popularity from that time until the Renaissance of the sixteenth century.[35] One of his explicated letters occasionally used in emblem books is the Pythagorean Y (fig. 20), which recalled for Tory the paths of moral choice open to man: sin leading to hell and virtue leading to heaven, following the motif of Hercules' dilemma at the crossroads.[36]

One of Tory's exercises in experimental printing design also appears today as something of a forerunner of the emblem format. Simon Colines published *AEdiloqium ceu Disticha, partibus Aedium urbanarum & rusticarum suis quaeque locis adscribenda. Item, Epitaphia septem, de Amorum aliquot passionibus Antiquo more, & sermone veteri, vietóque conficta* in 1530–1, and this little typographical masterpiece was probably intended in some measure to publicize Tory's prowess as a designer. The first part contains 154 epigrammatic distichs suitable for decorating the various parts of a house and the implements one might find in it. Although they are not

LE TIERS LIVRE.

Inuidia.
Superbia.
Libido.

IEn porrois dire beaucop daultres belles cho=
ses, mais pour ceste heure ie passeray oul=
tre, venant a deseigner & descrire
nostre derniere lettre Abecedai
re & Attique Zeta. Laquel
le Frere Lucas Paciolus
na pas mise en sa Di
uina proportione,
et la cause pour=
quoy il a omi=
se, ie ne le pu
is entẽdre,
ne ne mẽ
soucye.

Fig. 20. Pythagorean Y. Geoffroy Tory, *Champ Fleury* (1529).

illustrated, these distichs are emblematic in their mnemonic intention and in their relationship to the site of their inscription. The second part is composed of seven 'epitaphs' in Latin prose, extending from one to three pages, and they all end with a salutation coupled with a collage-like composition of two interlocking hearts and various implements or animals (for example, a rope, a kicking horse, or a boar). In spite of the title of the modern partial reprint, *VII Epitaphes d'amour et emblemes*, these compositions are not really emblems in any meaningful sense; they lack the moralizing tone and the allegorical relationship between picture and text that we expect to find in an emblem. Yet, this is another early example of a textual format in which the picture is one with the text and where together they are intended to form a single entity.

One further undertaking by Tory bears witness to an already lively interest among the French of that time in the pseudo-Horatian *ut pictura poesis* idea. In 1529, Tory translated the *Tableau de Cebes de Thebes* into French. With its moralizing descriptions of an ancient work of art, this little treatise recalls the epigrams of the Greek Anthology, but it was even more interesting to early French emblematists because of its more insistently didactic, moralizing tone. In the following years, Denys Janot published another illustrated translation of this work by Gilles Corrozet, one that used illustrations from Corrozet's *Hecatomgraphie* and also included a number of new emblems by Corrozet.[37]

In short, all the elements of illustrated book format used in the composition of emblem books and all the ancient precedents for the ideogrammatic presentation of a message in a picture were well-known and had been thoroughly explored and tested in France by the end of the first third of the century. Most especially, the combination of title, picture, *argumentum*, and exposition had been firmly established as a perfect vehicle for popularizing abstract, complicated, or ironic allegories like Petrarch's *Triumphs* or Erasmus' *Moriae encomium*. Generally, it would seem, these *vulgarisations* had the goal of moral edification, and it was with this intention that Brant used the model in the composition of his tantalizingly proto-emblematic *Narrenschiff*.

Taken as a group, these examples evoke a cultural climate that would have been particularly hospitable to an idea such as the one Alciato was developing during the 1520s. This climate goes far in explaining the flowering of the emblem form in France between 1534 and 1555, a flowering that, it should be repeated, was unique in Europe at that time. Nowhere else did Alciato's book have progeny before the 1550s, and I would argue that the reason is that there was to be found in France at the time a delicate balance between medieval habits of reading and communicating and the Renaissance interest in printing technique and the ideogrammatic precedents of antiquity. There, as in Italy, the most important part of painting was the literary exercise of 'invention.' The literary description of pictorial allegory was already common – in part because that is the way ancient art was usually known, and in part because of the ancient models provided by Anacreon and other classical poets, who used the description of a real or imaginary work of art as the pretext for poems of love or other aspects of life. As a result, French culture of the early sixteenth century was possessed of a habit of thinking about texts in visual terms and pictures in literary terms that could be easily, and as if naturally, exploited in emblems.

PART II

EMBLEMS IN RENAISSANCE FRANCE

5

Alciato and the Humanist Background of the Emblem

In spite of numerous early Renaissance prototypes and late medieval compositions that might even be considered emblems in everything but name, it was Andrea Alciato (1492–1550), an eminent Italian humanist and jurist of international reputation who, in the 1520s and 1530s, shaped the emblem idea around a word pregnant with aesthetic and epistemological implications. Around 1530, he exploited the idea in a collection of about one hundred emblems in a more or less fixed form that included a title, a picture, and a verse text, often epigrammatic in shape and construction.[1] He added a few emblems to subsequent editions published in the 1530s, and then in 1546, Aldus published an edition containing eighty-six new emblems, of which two were unillustrated. By the time Alciato had composed the last of his 212 emblems (published in the first cumulative editions of 210 or 211 emblems by Guillaume Rouille and Macé Bonhomme between 1549 and 1551), the nucleus of a 'genre' had been formed.[2]

For want of solid, specific documentation about the process by which Alciato isolated the emblem idea,[3] it is difficult to do much more than speculate about the ways different models may have inspired him as he developed the form, and it is equally difficult to judge the extent of any single influence, given the multiplicity of possible sources. Traditionally, that is to say since the earliest prefaces and theoretical writings, several sources have been advanced with reasonable justification; these sources fall into two groups, one textual and the other pictorial. The textual model generally adduced is that group of Greek epigrams contained in the so-called Planudean Anthology, and it is the influence of the Anthology that is the most obvious and easiest to document. Among possible visual precedents, Francesco Colonna's *Hypnerotomachia Poliphili* and the *Hieroglyphics* of Horapollo surely provided Alciato with stimulating pictorial and ideogrammatic models, but very few emblems can be traced directly to either work, and they both bear a relationship to the *emblemata* that remains problematic at best.[4]

Janus Lascaris issued the first edition of the Anthology in 1494, and it quickly attracted attention throughout Europe. In his youth, Alciato took a particularly keen interest in these epigrams; nine of his translations appeared in the Soter edition of Greek epigrams in 1528, and many more, 153 in all, in Cornarius' selection from the Planudean Anthology published in 1529. Thirty of these epigrams found their way into the first edition of the emblems published two years later, and the 1531 edition also contains eight translations from the Anthology that had not been published in Cornarius' selection. It would seem at first glance that his interest in the Anthology waned somewhat after 1531, for in subsequent editions only one of the newly composed emblems they contained was a translation from the Anthology, and the tree emblems are only distantly inspired by Greek epigrams.[5] The explanation may lie rather in an evolving conception of the emblem increasingly perceived by its creator, or so it seems, as a more autonomous form, a form perceived less and less to be derivative from the conception of epigrams as inscriptions, following the original rationale of the Anthology and the Italian humanist understanding of the form in the fifteenth century.[6]

In any event, the importance of the epigrams in the Anthology must not be underestimated as models for the development of the emblem, for the relationship between the two may help explain how the first authorized edition of the emblems came to be published by Christian Wechel. Hutton has claimed that 'Miniature selections from the Anthology probably issued with a view to the schools, form a prominent feature of the history of the Greek epigrams in the sixteenth century. The evidence at hand indicates that the idea of these selections originated with Christian Wechel.'[7] It seems likely, then, that Wechel saw in Alciato's emblems yet another kind of *vulgarisation* of Anthology or Anthology-like material appropriate for the public he was already catering to in the schools. This hypothesis receives some support from a remark by Steyner concerning the illustrations in the preface to his edition: 'Utilissimum itaque nobis visum est, si notulis quibusdam obiter, rudioribus, gravissimi authoris intentionem significaremus, quod docti haec per se colligent ...'[8]

Furthermore, it is fairly certain that many of Alciato's early readers must have understood his work within the humanist fashion for epigrams in imitation of those of the Greek Anthology. Lucas Cranach used one by Georg Sabinus as the inscription in his paintings of Cupid and the bees, a subject

Alciato later turned into two emblems (112, 113). Cranach, as Michael Bath has shown, probably encountered this epigram after Theocritus in the milieu of Philip Melancthon, Sabinus' father-in-law.[9] Melancthon himself showed a lively interest in epigrams of this sort, as evidenced by his anthology of epigrams[10] published, at least on occasion, with illustrations by Jost Amman. In the section 'Epigrammate de politiis,' we find moralizing epigrams with titles like *In vitam aulicum* (115) and when they are illustrated, their format recalls the by-then-fashionable emblems. There is even one, albeit unillustrated, emblem epigram by Alciato in this collection (*Quod non capit christus rapit fiscus*, 114–15).

We get some sense of the range of this fashion in a copy of Alciato's *Emblematum libri duo*,[11] where an early hand has noted sources and parallels of the emblems in Ausonius, Erasmus, Aesop, Caspar Velius, Bernardino Dardano, Marullus, and Sleidanus. The texts copied there make it clear that any generic associations Alciato's work may have inspired were certainly with the kind of epigrams fashionable in the circle of neo-Latin humanist poets. For example, emblem 90 (*Ferè simile ex Theocrito*) recalls for this annotator epigrams by Ercole Strozzi and Jo. Stigelius,[12] while 103 (*In dona hostium*) inspires a quote from Erasmus: 'Aiaci datus ensis ab Hectore, baltheus Aiace / Hectori, utrique suum donum erat exitio.'

At Bourges, Alciato had apparently won a reputation as an excellent teacher; in the late seventeenth century, the biographer Isaac Bullart described his method this way: 'Aussi sans s'arrester dans les routes que Bartol, Balde, Castrense, & Accurse avoient suivies; quoy qu'il reverast le nom, & la doctrine de ces grands Interpretes du Droit; il passa plus avant: il tempera l'austerité de leur discipline par les douceurs du bien-dire; & par une invention nouvelle & hardie, il la fit paroistre en ses Ecoles toute parsemée des fleurs de la Rethorique, & ornée des plus riches dépoüilles de l'Histoire.'[13] This is just the way Alciato presented moral wisdom in the emblems, and if Bullart is right in claiming that Alciato used this method of teaching for the first time at Bourges (1531), it would be tempting to see a relationship between the new pedagogical method and the new manner of didactic presentation that Alciato characterized by the technical, juridical term *emblema*. Perhaps Wechel took an interest in the emblems because he saw just such a relationship between the illustrated epigrams and Alciato's successful method of teaching. Fifteen years later, Aneau's *epistre dedicatoire* to his translation of Alciato's emblems makes it clear that he was well aware of the educational potential of emblems,[14] and later in the century Plantin used the same format we have seen in Brant's *Narrenschiff*, in the French version of the *Moriae encomium* and, finally, in emblems, for moralizing *vulgarisations* in the editions of Aesop he was preparing for use in the schools.[15]

Even though Karl Giehlow demonstrated that Alciato knew and used Filippo Fasanini's early Latin translation of the *Hieroglyphics* (1517) in the composition of his emblems,[16] the complex relationship between emblems and this kind of ancient ideogrammatic model remains nonetheless rather obscure. The prestige of hieroglyphic signs, whether authentic or not, was great during the Renaissance, and for the humanists, the principal sources of this symbolism were ancient obelisks and funeral monuments, along with Plutarch, Ammianus Marcellinus, and Horapollo's *Hieroglyphics*. Manuscripts of the *Hieroglyphics* had been circulating among Italian humanists since the Florentine monk, Christoforo Buondelmente, brought the work back with him from Greece in 1419. Its impact was reinforced by the simultaneous rediscovery or reassessment of other ancient texts, often of a Neoplatonic cast, concerning such supposedly ideogrammatic signs.[17]

Aldus published the first edition of the *Hieroglyphics* in 1505 together with Aesop's fables, and this may say something about the way both works were understood at the time; in 1515 Trebatius translated them into Latin and Fasanini published another Latin version in Bologna two years later. The work was soon discovered by the French humanists at the court of François Ier; a partial French translation was done for Louise de Savoye[18] and Trebatius' translation was published in Paris in 1521.[19] In addition, Geoffroy Tory claimed in 1529 to have translated Horapollo into French for a friend,[20] and Kerver published the first vernacular version in 1543, under the title *De la signification des notes hieroglyphiques*.

Alciato specifically compared his emblems to the hieroglyphics only once, and then as if in passing, in his *De verborum significatione* of 1531. While he did borrow a few signs from Horapollo's arcane glossary, hieroglyphics seem to have played a small role in the economy of the entire collection of emblems; it is fair to assume such models were important mainly in providing justification after the fact for the combination of picture and text to present a message by means of a vehicle that was simultaneously discursive and ideogrammatic. In any event, Alciato's followers seized upon this idea as a legitimizing rationale for the mechanics of the emblem: first an image would stimulate the 'intuition' of a moral truth, and then a discursive explanation of the cosmic analogy would show how this compelling revelation had come about. Such was the power of this generally unstated rationale that some editions of Horapollo's *Hieroglyphics* were illustrated as if they were emblems, beginning with the Kerver edition of 1543. Even though Filippo Fasanini did have the idea as early as 1517 of illustrating his

Fig. 21. 'Comment ilz denotoient ung homme imparfaict ou embrion.' Horapollo, *De la signification des notes hiéroglyphiques* (Kerver, 1543).

translation of the *Hieroglyphics* to enhance his reader's comprehension of the signs, he did not in fact have his text illustrated[21] and editions of the work came to resemble emblems only with the French versions beginning in 1543 (fig. 21). So it would appear that emblems actually influenced the perception of hieroglyphics more than hieroglyphics influenced the creation of the emblems.[22]

Incorrectly understood for the most part, Horapollo's corrupt 'glossary' of the ancient Egyptian language was crucial mainly because it was the principal and richest source of these enigmatic signs. As such, Neoplatonic speculation on natural language and on the symbolic structure of the universe sometimes centred on it. The reason hieroglyphs so intrigued humanists of a Neoplatonic inclination was their supposedly close participation in the essence of the things they represented and the quasi-magical power they thereby possessed. They were seen as the 'holy symbols of the cosmic elements,' and in the earliest writings on the hieroglyphics, the term *stoicheia* designated Egyptian writing while continuing to carry its normal meaning of 'elements of nature.'[23]

Relying on a tradition that ultimately goes back to the description of beauty in Plato's *Phaedrus*, Renaissance Neoplatonists exalted the sense of sight above all others; and they listened to Plato's distrust of written language while ignoring his equally distrustful attitude toward visual signs like the highly regarded enigmatic hieroglyphs (*Phaedrus*, 275c–276a). This blindness was possible in large measure because the humanists actually looked less to Plato himself than to the Neoplatonists of late antiquity as their source of inspiration and authority; these were the philosophers who provided the bulk of Renaissance arguments in favour of ideogrammatic languages and justifications for the deductive allegorical interpretation of signs and texts. Plutarch was the first to use the term 'hieroglyphics' this way in his essay on Isis and Osiris, and much Renaissance animal symbolism was informed by his discussion of the use of animals in Egyptian and other ancient systems of symbols.

But among all the Neoplatonists, Plotinus was the prime authority on the symbolic use of the hieroglyphics during the Renaissance, at least for the Neoplatonists. It was Plotinus who suggested similarities between Egyptian hieroglyphics, intelligible forms, and beautiful statues as examples of all art. Plotinus used the word *agalma* for both the statue and the intelligible form the sculptor has in mind as he makes it; he also used the word to refer to Egyptian sacred writing,[24] and in his commentaries on Alciato's emblems, Mignault gave the plural *agalmata* as a synonym for emblems. As late as 1666, the Jesuit emblematist Pierre Le Moyne was still using Plotinus' image of the sculptor who gives form to shapeless matter as he carves a beautiful statue from a block of marble, to explain the elaboration of the emblematic composition.[25] Plotinus' central statement on the hieroglyphics occurs in the eighth book of the *Enneads V*:

> Similarly, as it seems to me, the wise of Egypt – whether in precise knowledge or by native intuition – indicated the truth where, in their effort towards philosophical statement, they left aside the writing-forms that take in the detail of words and sentences – those characters that represent sounds and convey the propositions of reasoning – and drew pictures instead, engraving in the temple-inscriptions a separate image for every separate item: thus they exhibited the absence of discursiveness in the Intellectual Realm.
>
> For each manifestation of knowledge and wisdom is a distinct image, an object in itself, an immediate unity, not an aggregate of discursive reasoning and detailed willing. Later from this wisdom in unity there appears, in another form of being, a copy, already less compact, which announces the original in terms of discourse and unravels the causes by which things are such that the wonder rises how a generated world can be so excellent.

For, one who knows must declare his wonder that this wisdom, while not itself containing the causes by which Being exists and takes such excellence, yet imparts them to the entities produced according to its canons. This excellence, whose necessity is scarcely or not at all manifest to search, exists, if we could but find it out, before all searching and reasoning.[26]

This passage summarizes the Greek misunderstanding of the largely phonetic Egyptian hieroglyphic signs as ideogrammatic figures and insists on the value of the synthetic intuition of wisdom in a way that seems to downgrade the analytic presentation of knowledge in discursive writing. Nevertheless, the passage does go on to acknowledge that the intuition, once grasped, should then be elaborated in a discursive presentation that will 'unravel' the causes of the relationships that made possible that originally wondrous intuition. In other words, the hieroglyph is, in this view, to be presented with a visual sign and a discursive explanation.

Moreover, Plotinus had suggested that such a conception of ideogrammatic hieroglyphs provides an ideal approach to understanding all pictorial art. When this approach is accepted and applied, it almost guarantees an emblematic perception of art objects; and Ficino did as much as anyone to make that approach acceptable throughout the Renaissance. In his commentaries on Plotinus and on Jamblichus' *Book on the Egyptian Mysteries*, Ficino elaborated upon this bias, suggesting among other things that such ideogrammatic languages delight men because of their use of similitude, and further that the intuitive perceptions they foster resemble the ways of God's knowledge: 'For God has the knowledge of things not as a manifold discursive knowledge of things, but as the single and permanent (*firma*) idea of the things.'[27]

As a result, the prestige of these signs was immense; and the Neoplatonic understanding of them probably did much to form an emblematic appreciation of art that was more general than we are often inclined to imagine in the twentieth century. In the seventeenth century, the Abbé Marolles arranged his vast collection of prints and drawings in volumes according to artist or subject-matter. Those volumes from the section devoted to emblems and devices contain materials that suggest quite clearly that his idea of the emblematic was broader than ours. His was still an emblematic vision of the world, conditioned by this conception of the hieroglyphics and summed up in the epigraph to his catalogue: 'In imagine pertransit homo,' from Psalm 38. The further fact that Marolles pasted emblems into albums in a way to minimize blank space suggests that his idea of the 'book' was also different from ours, at least as far as emblems are concerned. The presentation and packaging of this collection may do much to explain why incomplete emblem books are quite normal, especially when it is taken with Warnecke's observation about emblematic *alba amicorum* that 'presque tous ces livres sont non seulement rares, mais ils se trouvent presque toujours dans un état défectueux. Il est, du reste, souvent impossible de constater leur intégrité, en absence de toute table de matières. Tantôt les gravures d'un livre se trouvent dans l'ouvrage d'un autre auteur, tantôt on trouve des copies d'une image imitée par plusieurs graveurs et exécutée de différentes manières.' In any event, we can conclude that much art was considered emblematic in the late Renaissance that does not fit the strict definitions laid down by modern historians of the form.[28] Perhaps that is why Menestrier's definitions of the emblem often seem to be adrift in a sea of vagueness and near contradiction and lack the rigour modern historians require.

But there was a different, and less exalted, conception of the hieroglyphics that we see for the first time in Alberti, and that was elaborated by Beroaldo and Pio, following the lead of Diodorus Siculus and Apuleius around the turn of the sixteenth century. This conception can perhaps be characterized as Aristotelian, in that the signs are understood to be built metaphorically on natural properties of the object in such a way that they may stand for anything else that possesses that property. This, according to Denis Drysdall, must have been the way Alciato understood the hieroglyphs, and it is certainly the conception that was most operative in the actual making of emblems and, especially, devices throughout the rest of the century.[29]

The early French translation of Horapollo done for Louise de Savoye suggests that this more mundane understanding of the hieroglyphics was prevalent in France as well. The dedication proceeds as follows 'Doncques pour mon essay et commencement mest venu entre les mains ung livre en grec lequel a fait ung aucteur nomme Orus apollo en egyptien, qui parle comment et enquelle maniere les prestres degypte escrivoient leurs secretz sans lettres seulement par figures de bestes & aultres choses lequel ma semble plaisant. Car il descript la nature de plusieurs bestes mieulx que aultre livre qui se puisse trouver. Et ceulx qui scauront ce livre pourront escripre par figures les gestes des Roys en marbre & tapisserie.'[30] Here the hieroglyphics are seen simply as convenient signs for the ideogrammatic presentation of political propaganda, perhaps in a decorative way, in sculpture and tapestries. In this passage, one senses no awareness of the supposedly sacred, mysterious quality of this ideogrammatic vocabulary; for this author the signs simply 'describe' the symbolic nature of several animals better than other symbolic systems.

For two reasons, such a reception or understanding of the hieroglyphic signs in France during the early years of the sixteenth century is in no way surprising and should not be unexpected. First, the hieroglyphic signs are related to the *Physiologus* tradition, which was preserved in French bestiary lore through the middle of the sixteenth century.[31] Consequently, as is clear from this dedication, the Egyptian symbols were not considered new or strange in France. Second, as Barbara Tiemann has noticed, there was a progressive secularization of the moral interpretation of all bestiary lore throughout the late Middle Ages. This process of desacralization of certain symbolic systems explains, at least in part, why our translator saw Horapollo's *Hieroglyphics* as no more than convenient rebus-like ideograms.[32] Such was later to be the attitude, at least in practice, of the emblematists toward the hieroglyphics; they simply served as another source of analogies for varying the emblematic presentation of conventional wisdom in order to make it more memorable.

As this position suggests, there was also a practical side to the symbolism of the hieroglyphics to which the emblematists could not remain indifferent. Here the analogies seemed to emerge more from a *jeu combinatoire* of endless surprises than from the rigid necessities of an ancient tradition – as was generally the case with medieval bestiary symbolism. Very often Horapollo proposed indifferently two or more symbols to express the very same concept or, alternately, one symbol that would express a multiplicity of ideas or entities. Eternity, he tells us, can be represented either by the sun or the moon, which are the eternal elements, or by a serpent in gold with its tail concealed by the rest of its body. Conversely, the hawk could represent a bewildering – at least for the twentieth-century reader – variety of things: God, something sublime, something lowly, superiority, victory, Ares, Aphrodite. A freedom from semantic determinism characterizes the symbolism of this system, and it parallels most interestingly the semantic ambiguity of Renaissance vernacular languages.[33] Horapollo seems to have taken such freedom for granted in a way that must have been difficult in the Middle Ages when the hierarchical, unified, cathedral-like ordering of human knowledge tended, in the abstract at least if not in practice, to force the presentation of a given idea in a single, constant, and as if obsessive, image.

In the late Middle Ages, artists had already begun, as in the case of the personification of the virtues,[34] to exercise greater freedom in their presentation, but they were not entirely successful in detaching the old symbols from the ideas with which they had traditionally been associated. The example provided byHorapollo gave impetus to this trend and stimulated the even further loosening of these traditional symbolic bonds, because he confirmed and encouraged medieval practice as far as it was opposed to the medieval theory of symbolic coherence and unity. As such, Horapollo confirmed medieval practice as against medieval theory and probably provided significant support in the formation of a variety of allegory peculiar to the Renaissance.

The emblematist presumably used this new freedom for its shock effect; the surprise resulting from the use of a well-known motif to present an idea other than the one traditionally associated with it had an indisputable mnemotechnic value. Alciato's emblem 144 provides a perfect example. Augustus Caesar's dolphin-and-anchor motif must have seemed immutably linked in the early sixteenth century to the motto *Festina lente*. As such, it was perhaps the most famous of all Renaissance printer's marks, gracing each of the elegant Aldine editions; and composers of devices looked to the combination as one of the most perfect ancient examples of their art. What a surprise then to find the motif here illustrating the theme *Princeps subditorum incolumitatem procurans*, and what a fine memory place the famous motif provides for the exhortation developed in the epigram!

We learn from Mignault that the dolphin foresees storms, while the anchor, which the dolphin secures in times of danger, represents salvation. The *Festina lente* configuration of the dolphin and anchor is absent from Steyner's illustration, as if he did not realize the intended connection between Vespasian's device and the advice to kings from Ammianus Marcellinus and Plutarch.[35] Steyner shows a cheery dolphin apparently tugging at an anchor (fig. 22a), unless it is a reminiscence of Erasmus's adage *Delphinum cauda ligas* (I, iv, 93), and what we may take to be Alciato's intention did not become clear until 1534 (Fig. 22b), when a new illustration represented the pictorial organization he had presumably sanctioned.

One of the first works to demonstrate how the hieroglyphic signs might be explicitly integrated into a literary work on a large scale and in a more or less systematic way is Francesco Colonna's curious *Hypnerotomachia Poliphili* – even though Colonna's symbolic collages bear a rather tenuous relation to Horapollo's work. This book intrigued the Renaissance, but is remembered today mainly because, in its Aldine and Kerver editions, it inspired some of the finest and most elegant woodcuts to be produced during the European Renaissance. Colonna would have his reader believe that he finished this, his only work, on the first of May 1467, having undertaken it several years earlier. One of the main authorities on the question, Giovanni Pozzi, suspects, however, that it was composed much later, probably just before its publication by Aldus in 1499.[36] The mystery surrounding Colonna's attempts to hide the origins of his work in the mists of a per-

Dum dormit, dulci recreat dum corpora somno,
Sub picea & clauam cæteraq; arma tenet.
Alcyden pygmæa manus prosternere letho,
Posse putat, uires non bene docta suas.
Excitus ipse uelut pulices, sic proterit hostem,
Et secum implicitum pelle leonis agit.

PRINCEPS SVBDITORVM IN-
columitatem procurans.

Titanij quoties conturbant æquora fratres
Tum miseros nautas anchora iacta iuuat.
Hanc pius erga homines Delphin complectitur imis
Tutius ut possit figier illa uadis.
Quam decet hæc memores gestare insignia reges,
Anchora quod nautis, se populo esse suo.

MVTVVM AVXILIVM
B 2

EMBLEMATVM LIBELLVS. 25

Princeps subditorum incolumitatem procurans.

Titanij quoties conturbant æquora fratres,
Tum miseros nautas anchora iacta iuuat.
Hanc pius erga homines Delphin complectitur, imis
Tutius ut possit figier illa uadis.
Quam decet hæc memores gestare insignia Reges,
Anchora quòd nautis, se populo esse suo.

Fig. 22(a). 'Princeps subditorum in columitatem procurans.' Andrea Alciato/ *Emblematum liber* (Steyner, 1531), sig. B2; and (b) *Emblematum libellus* (Wechel, 1534), p. 25.

sonal legend was compounded by its publication by Aldus Manutius, who had until then published only serious, philological works. The reason why the learned Aldus published this neoclassical rendering of a dream of love in an illustrated quasi-vernacular edition may lie in the suspicion, current throughout the sixteenth century, that this was an excellent alchemical handbook in which Colonna guides his hero, in the opinion of the poet and alchemist Nicolas Le Digne, into 'la Cabale sainte des Chimiques secrets.'[37]

Although alchemical works did, on many occasions, take an emblematic form, this book is of interest as a proto-emblematic model for other reasons. In many fifteenth-century illustrated printed books, the link between text and illustration is tenuous at best, and sometimes non-existent to the twentieth-century eye. Such is not the case here; Colonna describes and explains the initiatory hieroglyphs as they are presented to the eyes both of Poliphile and the reader in the adjacent illustrations. The combination of description, illustration, and explanation is reminiscent of Plotinus's remarks on the hieroglyphic signs and seems to foreshadow the presentation of symbols in later emblem books.

The fortunes of this work in France were great. Rabelais knew and used it in the elaboration of different parts of his great narrative.[38] It was published in France in 1546 by Kerver in a translation by Jean Martin, and issued twice more before the 1600 edition with an introduction by Béroalde de Verville, who perhaps as much as anyone appreciated its alchemical insights. And the hieroglyphic decorations for Renaissance court pageantry were more often inspired by this work than by Horapollo himself, of which one of the best-known examples is the elephant and pyramid in the 1548 Lyons entry for Henri II and Catherine de Medicis.

The Greek epigrams and Egyptian hieroglyphics, then, were the most immediate ancient influences on Alciato's work, and they provided the impetus and justification for his developing vision of a new genre. The fact that they were all well-known and highly appreciated in France suggests that they were not seen as breaking with certain medieval traditions and explains, in part at least, why the emblems were so quickly and enthusiastically welcomed in France. But unlike epigrams, the emblems moralized the description, and unlike hieroglyphs, the analogical link needed to be explained in an emblem because these signs were always taken out of their specific cultural context without being integrated into the syntagmatic framework of any allegorical narrative. Conservative, then, in its drive to moralize, the emblem was new in its tendency to couch its lessons in new signs as if it were a metaphor for the newly discovered individual point of view with its distinctive perspective on a constant focal point in reality.

6

The Dissemination of the Emblem Idea in France

In the years immediately following Christian Wechel's publication of the *Emblematum libellus* in 1534, the French appear to have been more receptive to Alciato's idea than any other culture in Europe. So they would continue to be throughout the first generation of emblem books. The transition to a second generation clearly took place in the decade of the 1560s. Following the lead of Achille Bocchi's *Symbolicarum Quaestionum*, published in Bologna in 1555, printers began to use copperplate engravings in preference to woodblocks in illustrating emblem books; it was then that France ceased to be the centre for the production of emblem books, while Italy, the Low Countries, and Germany were beginning to produce volumes of emblems in increasing numbers and with increasing regularity. During this period Plantin began publishing emblem books, and German editions of Alciato began to appear with some regularity. As I have suggested elsewhere,[1] inflationary pressures probably made it difficult for French printers to renew their stocks of woodcuts as the old blocks wore out, and it was not until the 1580s that Parisian printers again began issuing more than an occasional new edition of Alciato. Lyons never recovered to the extent of regaining its place as a centre for the publication of emblem books.

Before the 1560s, however, France dominated the field of emblem book production in every way. All but four of the some fifty editions of Alciato published before 1560 were printed in France.[2] Clearly, many of these thousands of copies were produced for export. French editions of Alciato's emblems were, for example, known and appreciated in England soon after the Wechel editions began to appear;[3] yet there were never any editions of Alciato published in England. Although the first extensive manuscript collection of English emblems dates from the 1560s, no English emblem book was published before the 1580s, and even then it was produced in Leyden. The reason is simple: English printers were simply not equipped to produce emblem books of any typographical sophistication until the middle third of the seventeenth century.[4]

So from the standpoint of European printing history, it is well worth noting that French printers and *libraires*, especially in Lyons, were the ones who took the lead in disseminating this popular work. To a certain extent, we can only assume that their initiative reflects a particular interest in emblems, either on their own part or on that of their milieu and local clientele. Still, if emblem books were produced in France in good measure because French printers were prepared to take advantage of the new fashion, there does exist some convincing material evidence to suggest a real interest on the part of the French reading public as well. The first French translation of Alciato was published several years before the emblems were available in any other European vernacular.[5] Le Fevre's translation was frequently reprinted throughout the century, and by the time the first Italian and Spanish translations were available, Barthélemy Aneau had a second French translation ready for what must already have been a sizeable audience. These two were joined by yet another complete French translation, that of Alciato's commentator Claude Mignault, published in Paris by Jean Richer in 1583, and several translations of individual emblems that, however, sometimes remained in manuscript.[6]

It seems plausible to explain this lively interest by a vigorous tradition of pictorial allegory and by the way textual illustration was used in late medieval and early Renaissance France. In exploring this background, we have encountered numerous proto-emblematic compositions in royal entries and in devotional manuscripts prepared for François Ier and members of his family, or in certain bestiaries and *dictz moraulx pour faire tapisserie*. The compositional practices and epistemological habits that contributed to the shaping of such works continued to exercise a very real influence on French emblem books even after the success of Alciato's emblems had provided a clearly delineated model for what was soon to become a new genre. In fact, it is not impossible that these traditions exercised a certain influence on Alciato himself, and in this regard, it is perhaps worth noting that Alciato's stays in France parallel in a most suggestive way the chronology of the composition and publication of his emblems. If, as seems likely, Alciato began to develop the idea of the emblem as early as 1521, it would have been just after his return from Avignon. But those emblems that may have been composed as a Christmas present in 1521 were not published until Alciato returned to France to teach and lecture at Bourges in 1531.

Of course, no really convincing conclusions can be drawn from what are perhaps merely biographical coincidences, but it is at least clear that the early French emblematists understood Alciato's emblems within the context of these traditions. That probably explains why La Perrière called his 'bons engins' emblems when many of them actually resemble Pierre Sala's illustrated proverbs more closely than they do Alciato's emblems.[7] Indeed, early French emblems often resemble Alciato's compositions only to the extent that they express conventional moral wisdom in a hybrid form that combines picture and text in ways that make each part more or less dependent on the other for its effect; but that is the way illustrated proverbs had worked since the second half of the fifteenth century (see above, 58–62). Alciato had, perhaps unwittingly, modernized a traditionally French way of presenting moral wisdom, and, more important, he had given compositions of that sort a name around which a body of generic expectations could easily and quickly develop. That perhaps is why he inspired imitators in France earlier than he did elsewhere. For whatever reason, however, eight collections of emblems and annotated devices were composed and published in France during the period between 1534 and 1560, while none was published elsewhere in Europe before 1555.[8]

Several anecdotes will help gauge the extent to which the growing fashion for emblematic compositions penetrated different cultural milieux in France during the middle years of the sixteenth century. The vogue was such that Pierre Du Val's *Puy du souverain amour* in Rouen proposed that each author compose a *dizain* in the form of an emblem for its 1547 competition. The results of this contest were published in an exceedingly rare illustrated volume in 1547 and, subsequently, in an unillustrated Lyons edition.[9] This *puy*'s interest in emblems must have dated from 1543 or earlier, for in that year the *puy* presented its contest winner, Guillaume Durant, with a copy of Corrozet's *Hecatomgraphie*.[10] It is interesting to note parenthetically this early preoccupation with emblems in Rouen, for that is where the 'new iconography' of the virtues, as Emile Mâle called it, developed in the second half of the fifteenth century, and where Petrarch's *Triumphs* were first illustrated in proto-emblematic ways (see above, 76–81).

A good command of emblematics could serve a poet in other circumstances as well; it was a tool of polemic, first in literary quarrels like the one between Marot and Sagon, and then, as we shall see later (197–206), in partisan propaganda during the religious wars. The title-page (fig. 23) of the brochure *Defense de Sagon contre Clement Marot* (1537) bears a composition resembling a printer's mark. A palm tree is presented as weighted

Deffense de Sagon
Contre
Clement Marot.

On la vend au mont Sainct Hylaire, deuant
le College de Reims.

Fig. 23. Title-page. *Defense de Sagon contre Clement Marot* (1537).

Epiſtre a
MAROT PAR FRAN-
cois de Sagon pour luy monſtrer que
Frippelipes auoit faict ſotte cõparaiſon
des quatre raiſons dudit Sagon a quatre
Oyſons.

VELA DE QVOY.

Fig. 24. Title-page. *Epistre a Marot par Francois Sagon* (1537).

down by a heavy stone; the explanatory legend, 'Pondere pressa, altius extollitur,' could serve as the motto of a device. But here the device does not serve as a printer's mark; rather, it is a satirical emblem, and it may be the first of many in sixteenth- and seventeenth-century France. As will become clear in the text of the brochure, it refers to Sagon, the author, who is claiming to be fortified by Marot's attacks.[11] Here the emblematic composition serves as a visual, symbolic prologue to the text to come, following a model observed in certain biblical manuscripts dating from the early Middle Ages, and recently used in François Demoulins' dialogue for the young *dauphin*, François d'Angoulême.[12] It was also a model that would be used in seventeenth-century emblem books of the kind that proposed metaphorical models and rhetorical strategies for sermons.

In another of the brochures from the same collection, this one entitled *Epistre a Marot par Francois Sagon pour luy monstrer que Frippelipes avoit faict sotte comparaison des quatre raisons dudit Sagon a quatre Oysons* (1537), the title is illustrated with Wechel's illustration for Alciato's *In silentium* (12) with the scholar holding a finger to his lips (fig. 24).[13] To the reader remembering Alciato's warning that one may appear erudite until he opens his mouth, this illustration provides the perfect preface to the scathing attack to come. And this attack, in its first pages at least, is keyed to the theme of knowing when to be silent and when to speak, for although Sagon claims to have plenty to reply, he remains silent because of the improper and undignified nature of the forum. The insolence of Frippelippes has indeed struck him dumb, and so he is going to let Linotte, Marot's washerwoman, reply in his stead. The emblem serves here as the inspiration for Sagon's rhetorical strategy. Clearly emblematics had already found a place in French literary culture, and every time one of these illustrations was used in another context or copied into a different setting it carried the weight of Alciato's text as an implicit commentary.

In order to understand the nature of Alciato's appeal for the French, it may be helpful to begin by isolating those characteristics and interests common to his early French imitators. With the notable exception of Maurice Scève's *Délie*, the emblem form did not have much impact on French poetry during the sixteenth century, at least not on the surface. And no major French poets composed emblem books *per se*. Later in the century, Etienne Jodelle, Rémy Belleau, Jean Passerat, and Amadis Jamyn did compose devices, but their inventions betray a distinct lack of enthusiasm and show an equivalent lack of inspiration, suggesting that they were the product of a courtier's duty rather than a poet's inspiration.[14] Yet, the form did attract very respectable, and respected, humanists like La Perrière, Corrozet, and Aneau.[15] This situation may suggest that the emblem was not considered to be a 'literary' form at all, but rather one of the rhetorical strategies of a mode of communication.

Corrozet was the only Parisian to compose an emblem book during the period, and most emblematists gravitated to the cultural centre of Lyons rather than Paris, at least after 1540. The music publisher, Jacques Moderne, issued the first illustrated Lyons edition of Alciato in 1544, and his example inspired great interest in emblems among other Lyons printers and writers. Some of these writers maintained close and congenial relations with publishers; there is, in fact, some evidence that emblem books were often commissioned by publishers who had a ready stock of woodcuts and wished to take advantage of this popular, and possibly lucrative, new discovery.[16] Balthasar Arnoullet actually did commission the emblematists Barthélemy Aneau and Guillaume Gueroult in 1549–50 to compose a two-part bestiary, in a form that goes far in reminding us of the very close relationship between the medieval bestiary tradition and Renaissance emblem books.[17] From remarks in the preface to Aneau's *Picta poesis*, one is tempted to assume that Macé Bonhomme had also commissioned Aneau to compose this emblem book.[18]

Corrozet was a *libraire* himself, and his training as a humanist was clearly intended mainly to prepare him for his profession. Guillaume Gueroult, on the other hand, perfected his education as a typesetter and corrector, first in his native Rouen, and then in printing shops across France, before settling in Lyons.[19] Presumably, he met Aneau while they were working together as correctors for Gueroult's brother-in-law, Balthasar Arnoullet. Another example of this kind of relationship between emblematists and *libraires* was the friendship, some ten years later, between the Hungarian humanist and emblematist, Johannes Sambucus, and Christopher Plantin. Close ties like these between emblematists and printers point up the emblematist's dependence upon printers and engravers for illustrations and for the composition of paginal formats that would distinguish his creations from simple illustrated epigrams. Some at least of the early emblem books must have been more the project of a printer's *atelier* than the poetic creation of a solitary artist as the Romantics were to conceive this act two or three hundred years later; indeed the creation of emblem books would seem to problematize the whole notion of the author as far as the Renaissance is concerned.[20]

If, as we can now do with some confidence, we take the emblem text to be the central part of the composition, and even see the emblem as a textual phenomenon, and if we give printers and booksellers in France much of the credit for the development of the genre *as* a genre, it is possible and enlightening to look at the emblem from a different perspective. Perhaps it will then be easier to understand the creation of the emblem within the context of the development of early printed book illustration. From that perspective, the emblem will emerge as a conscious attempt to make the best of a less than ideal situation. Much early book illustration, as has been abundantly noted, was not adapted to the work it illustrated. Having been created perhaps for a very different text, it sometimes was no more than pure ornamentation with no, or very tenuous, relations to the surrounding text. In this regard, early printed book illustration would not have stood very favourable comparison to late medieval manuscript illumination, which is much more closely related to the text it illustrates and must have served as a benchmark for printed illustration (given the numerous attempts to make printed books look like luxurious manuscripts).

Why, then, do we find an apparent lack of regard for the relation between text and illustration in early printed books, and what were its consequences? Although it must have been expensive to produce a set of woodblock illustrations adapted to a particular text, it could not have been much more so than to produce some of the most elaborately illuminated fifteenth-century manuscripts. Technique was not so primitive as some commentators would lead us to believe, although it was not so highly developed as that of the most accomplished illuminators. But unlike the illumination, the woodblock could be used more than once; so the temptation to milk the most profit possible from a given set of blocks must have been great among those printers working in that most proto-capitalistic of Renaissance industries.

When Galliot du Pré published the first French translation of the *Moriae encomium* in 1521, he expressed his hopes in a quatrain entitled 'Le marchant a son livre': 'Va et cours selon tes fortunes / Follie/simulant tes faces / Mais quelzques choses que tu faces / Rapporte force de pecunes.' The illustrations for this volume came from the set used to illustrate early French editions of Brant's *Narrenschiff*, such as that of G. Verard in 1497. Naturally, the fit is not perfect, but it is better than the one between pictures and text in certain late fifteenth-century editions of Olivier de La Marche's *le Chevalier delibere*, for example, where everything is spelled out with labelled figures and explanatory banderoles. Blocks, as Marian Rothstein has recently reminded us, could be modified in different ways, and sometimes the banderoles were even morticed so that their text could be easily changed.[21]

The fit between illustration and text would become better in such books illustrated with ready-made blocks, as the stocks of available woodblocks expanded with the increasing wealth and activity of booksellers, who traded blocks or sold them to other printers.[22] But when a *libraire* commissioned a set of blocks for a specific book, would he not be tempted to instruct the artisans not to make them too text-specific, precisely so they could be used more than once? Then the illustrations could be used either specifically or generically. That is, they could represent a specific text such as Brant's 'Du maulvais exemple des plus grans' or serve as a generic representation of a family (husband, wife, and child) in Erasmus' 'De l'estat de mariage' (see above, 100–4).

The value of such approximate illustrations must still have been considerable. The reader would approach the following text wondering how that text would elucidate the illustration, and would quickly realize that the illustrated scene could be 'glossed' in a variety of ways. That realization would prepare him for the experience of reading an emblem, where the same scene, or even the same illustration, could be viewed from different hermeneutic perspectives. In the emblem books by La Perrière and in Corrozet's *Hecatomgraphie*, no illustrations are repeated, but there are repetitions in Aneau's *Picta poesis* and Gueroult's *Le Premier Livre des emblemes*, while cuts from the *Hecatomgraphie* were used to illustrate quite different emblems in the collection appended to Corrozet's 1543 translation of Cebes' *Tablet* (see below, 176–8). There, too, we see the same slippage toward a generic representation that does not have the specificity of relationship evident in the original combination of emblem text and illustration. Still, for a sixteenth-century reader these illustrations, and many others like them, must have seemed to be just so much unshaped raw material awaiting the sculpting chisel of some didactic text that would give them an edifying sense and direction. And conversely, these illustrations would endow the text with a concrete presence that it might not otherwise be perceived to have.

Emblem texts, as we have seen in anthologies of poetry containing epigrams by Alciato and other early emblematists, could easily be detached from their accompanying illustration, but then we notice that they are often no longer identified as emblems. Perhaps it did take an illustration, in the beginning at least, to make an emblem. But paradoxically, if that was the case, it was because the illustration was the least important, the attached, part. However, this hypothesis must be considered with caution because there did exist partially unillustrated editions of Alciato – or in the editions of his complete works in 1548 and 1549, an entirely unillustrated set of emblems. But in cases like this one, the term 'emblema' cannot be understood to be generic; it is, as Bernhard Scholz has argued, simply the *title* of a collection of epigrams (see above, 127).

Whatever their role in the actual production of emblems, the humanist writers credited with authoring the earliest emblem books were usually engaged as well in pedagogical pursuits of one sort or another. These were men who could not help but be interested in the potential usefulness of the emblem form as a pedagogical aid. Aneau was a progressive and successful principal of the important Collège de la Trinité in Lyons. At one point in his career, La Perrière served as *prieur* of the Collège St Mathurin in Toulouse, while Sambucus' first lecture in Paris, at the Collège Royal in 1551, dealt with pedagogy. Later in the century, Alciato's translator, editor, and commentator, Claude Mignault, composed two works devoted to specific pedagogical problems.[23] And as we have seen, Alciato himself had the reputation of being a superb teacher.

Translations of emblem books also provided a vehicle for demonstrating the comparative worth of different vernaculars in the nationalistic debate that raged throughout the sixteenth century. Aneau's translation of Alciato was intended, at least in part, to demonstrate that French was capable of the concision of Latin. Wolfgang Hunger claims much the same thing in the preface to his German translation of Alciato (Wechel, 1542), and in a paper read at the international conference on emblems in Glasgow in 1987, Karel Porteman proposed that the Dutch translation of La Perrière's *Le Theatre des bons engins* can best be understood in the context of the struggle to develop Dutch as a literary language.[24]

Perhaps this involvement with pedagogy and the development of literary vernaculars explains why the emblematists usually were more than casually interested in history. In the sixteenth century, after all, history was valued mainly as a vehicle for moral instruction or political propaganda. As such, it was used to demonstrate the workings of different lines of conduct and the results that could be expected from them. As moralists, then, the emblematists concentrated on the anecdotal aspects of history that could so easily be turned into exempla of the kind one often finds moulded into emblems or devices. But history also fed the drives for national identity that fuelled efforts to develop vernaculars capable of challenging the domination of Greek, Latin, and Italian. And finally, as numismatists and archaeologists, these scholars were attracted by the visible, concrete memorabilia of classical antiquity, especially coins and medallions, and the examples they could provide for the decorative use of emblem motifs.[25]

Such interests go far in explaining the predilection of these humanists and polymaths for a form so perfectly suited to the didactic presentation of moral commonplaces and historical exempla, and they suggest that these bourgeois scholars must have had in mind a bourgeois public intent on self-improvement rather than the courtly audience imagined recently by Jean Mesnard.[26] The vast number of editions of emblem books published in the sixteenth century attests to their popularity, but it is difficult to delimit and describe the composition of their public and gauge the exact nature of the emblem's impact in France following its introduction in the 1530s. In fact, there remains very little concrete evidence of the extent to which the emblem form penetrated bourgeois mentality directly, even though the subjects of many Renaissance emblems suggest that they were certainly composed with this class of society in mind.[27] Albert Labarre's survey of private Amiens libraries inventoried between 1500 and 1573 in connection with inheritances lists only two books of emblems in the several hundred libraries surveyed. A.H. Schutz found hardly any more in his investigation of inventories to determine what kind of vernacular books were contained in Parisian libraries during the same period.[28] Perhaps all these libraries contained other emblem books that were not considered important enough to warrant a separate listing in the inventories; at least such a conjecture may be valid for books in small formats where worn woodcuts were used, but it may need to be disputed for larger or better illustrated volumes such as Corrozet's *Hecatomgraphie* or Georgette de Montenay's *Emblesmes ou devises chrestiennes*.[29]

A partial explanation may lie in one of the traditional uses of illustrated books. In his very first preface, Alciato urged artisans to use his emblems as a source of designs for interior decoration, and his imitators normally repeated this suggestion. So it is likely, as Emile Picot once proposed, that many of these books found their way into the hands of artists and artisans who may well have cut them up to use as models for their work.[30] Humanists and poets also probably kept emblem books, as well as iconographical encyclopaedias, among their *usuels*, where steady use must certainly have shortened their life.[31]

Yet the consumption of emblem books and iconographies by artists, artisans, and poets could not be imagined to account for all that part of the vast production from the middle years of the sixteenth century that has now disappeared.[32] It is perhaps not unreasonable to theorize that, during the period between 1535 and 1570, some emblem books were also being cut up to provide edifying decoration in modest bourgeois households. Such woodcuts would have replaced xylographic illustrations and broadsides used for similar purposes in the previous century, when they served as talismans on walls or inside tombs, inside voyage trunks (*coffrets de voyage*) that could thus be made into portable altars, inside books, or even sewn into clothes.[33] One such crudely printed and coloured xylographic broadsheet showing 'Le Monogramme du Christ et la Madeleine' is preserved on the inside cover of a *coffret de ferronnerie* at the Bibliothèque et Musée Calvet at Avignon.[34] In turn, the emblem woodcuts must have begun to give way to another kind of 'tableaux des pauvres,' the copperplate *estampe* in the 1560s.[35]

Among Anne d'Urfé's manuscript emblems composed in the 1590s, we still find one entitled 'Pance à ta fin,' and it is expressly designated, with its awful pun, as an emblem intended for a dining room.[36] This emblem suggests that, if emblem woodcuts were used to decorate modest houses, their role would have been more to turn the home into a 'memory house' presenting the family's moral program than to provide pleasing decoration. If such were indeed the case, then their size would not have been an impediment to their function.[37] Moreover, such use would not be discouraged by the composition of emblem books since most of the emblem collections compiled during this period have no unifying principle in theme or philosophy that would be violated by breaking them up. We could even say that emblem books were made to be broken up, and in fact, emblem books were commonly broken up in another less literal way when the texts of individual emblems or selections of emblems by Corrozet or La Perrière were reprinted, often without any illustration, in contemporary anthologies of poetry.[38]

At the same time, some sort of decorative use of emblems is actually encouraged by their presentation. Sometimes, as in La Perrière's *Theatre*, where the woodcuts are larger than those Janot usually used to illustrate books of that size, the emblems seem designed for some kind of decorative use. Sometimes they were printed on high-quality paper or vellum, and sometimes, as in the case of Georgette de Montenay's volume of emblems, they are printed on only one side of a folio; this practice continued for the publication of religious emblems in the seventeenth century, especially in Germany, as with the emblem books of Daniel Cramer.

Paginal composition of the most successful emblem books was also consonant with this use; the illustration and epigram are united on a single page or on two facing pages, and the engraving is framed in most cases, either alone, with the motto, or with both motto and epigram. In some editions of La Perrière's *Theatre* and Corrozet's *Hecatomgraphie*, no illustration detached from the book – for example, to be hung in some bourgeois home or pasted into another book or manuscript (see below, 145–6) – would contain another illustration or part of an illustration on the back. But a book like Aneau's *Picta poesis* in which this kind of compositional unity was neglected was not for that reason much less popular than those where more attention was paid to formatting and presentation; indeed, Aneau's book may have seen as many as seven editions in French and Latin between 1552 and 1564, while La Perrière's elegant *La Morosophie* of 1553 was never re-edited. And in fact, the Palmer mansucript recently edited by John Manning shows that illustrations could just as easily be taken from Aneau's book as from any other; when the author needed pictures on a single recto and verso, he would simply have one or the other sketched in by an artist.[39]

We know that Giovio had decorated his study with a collection of devices, and the printer's preface to Claude Paradin's *Quadrins historiques de la Bible* of 1553 contains further indications that emblem illustrations may have been used for this kind of decoration. De Tournes exhorts the reader this way: 'si tu n'as le loisir de lire & jouir de la lettre comme tu desirerois, tu puisses pour le moins tapisser les chambres de ta memoire des figures d'icelle, & plus honnestement, selon nous, que tu ne fais les chambres & salles de ta maison des histoires ethniques [images paiennes].'[40] De Tournes is using the instructions metaphorically to urge the building of a new memory house for those who do not have the leisure to read the Holy Word itself. There is no reason to doubt that, in those times when the cross-over between the literal and the figurative was so easy and natural in either direction, de Tournes' advice was transferred to the decoration of actual houses in such a way as to replicate 'memory houses.' And we know that Paradin's work, with the magnificent illustrations by Bernard Salomon, did in fact provide motifs for many kinds of decorative programs in pottery, embroidery, and the like during the second half of the century.[41]

This work belongs to a genre that Robert Brun has classified as *Figures de la Bible*.[42] Such works enjoyed considerable popularity from about 1520 until quite late in the century, and were often composed by such emblematists as Corrozet, Gueroult, and Simeoni, and the popularity of these works in France may well have rivalled that of emblems in the wake of the Council of Trent.[43] Their illustrations were sometimes prepared by the same artists who had illustrated emblem books, and if de Tournes is maintaining due proportion in his comparison, the 'histoires ethniques' he is referring to are more likely to be mythological emblem illustrations and the elements of interior decoration they might have inspired than the magnificent paintings of the Ecole de Fontainebleau. Gilles Corrozet had said substantially the same thing some twenty-five years earlier in his French introduction to Holbein's *Historiarum veteris testamenti icones* (see above, 85–8), and likewise in the preface to his translation of *Le Tableau de Cebes* of 1543 he situates this *tableau* in an imaginary memory house:

> Or voions nous plusieurs tableaux dorez,
> Dont les palais sont tresbien decorez,
> Pour les couleurs dont ilz sont revestuz:
> Mais cestuy cy tout doré de vertus,
> De sainctz propos, & bon enseignement,
> De nostre estrit [sic] doit estre l'ornement:
> L'aiant tousjours devant nostre presence,
> Pour contempler, & y prendre plaisance:[44]

If the advice of Corrozet and de Tournes was followed, these biblical pictures, even more than emblems, would turn the bourgeois home into a memory house comparable to that used by ancient orators and, later, medieval preachers, until at least the time of Ramus and probably beyond.

If this were the case, that does not mean emblems were completely displaced as elements of interior decoration. That is very clear in a collection of emblems formed by Anne d'Urfé around 1590.[45] The Urfé family residence in the Forez contained among its decorative motifs many emblems and devices, and at least one of d'Urfé's emblems bears a clear indication that it was intended to provide edifying decoration for a dining room. Entitled 'Sur celluy [emblem] de la Mort mis dans une salle,' it has as its motto 'Pance à ta fin,' and the accompanying quatrain urges: 'Vous qui prenez esbat dans se petit sejour, / soit mangeant ou bevant, contemplez cest'image, / memorial certain à checun s'il est sage / de se qu'il deviendra en mourant quelque jour' (92). Possibly all sixty-six of his compositions, composed along the lines of this example, were intended to provide motifs for inspirational pictorial decorations in the home of the poet or the homes of his friends, like Louis Papon – who actually did paint rather crude illustrations for part of the series – and which have been preserved in the manuscript at Caen. If that is the case, d'Urfé would be following, whether wittingly or not, the advice of Du Bartas when he counselled: 'Pour regler ta maison ne li point les escrits / Du fils de Nicomache, honneur des bons esprits: / Ne fueillete celuy que le proverbe antique, / Pour ses discours sucrez, appella Muse Attique: / Puis que la seule araigne instruit chacun de nous, / Et du soin de l'espouse, & du soin de l'espoux.'[46] Some evidence does exist that d'Urfé knew Du Bartas's work,[47] and in any event there must have been a developing fashion at this time for relatively small, and affordable, images specifically designed for the houses of the modest middle classes.

This is clear from the increasing production of larger *estampes* in the later years of the sixteenth century. As the quasi-emblematic genre of the *Figures de la Bible* was increasingly assimilated into the mainstream of emblem literature, and as the emblem became more and more the vehicle for religious expression following the publication of the earliest Protestant and Catholic emblem books around 1570, small collections of single-sheet emblems were produced by engravers like Sadeler and Crispin de Passe in the Low Countries. These large-format prints, where the illustration totally dominated the text (fig. 25), were obviously intended for decorative rather than pedagogical purposes.[48]

More important, if such prefaces were heeded, they would lead to a shift away from emblem books as they were made in the middle years of the six-

Fig. 25. 'Non tibi, sed religioni.' Andrea Alciato, *Emblemata* (1599), Johannes Sadeler.

teenth century, and make them more like later religious emblems and other kinds of edifying literature. Whether prefaces and other admonitions like this one actually played a significant role, such a shift did occur in France after 1560, in the wake of the Council of Trent. At that time, devices became even more popular at court than they had been in the time of François Ier. Several editions of Paradin, Giovio, and Simeoni were issued during the period, and they were beginning to be supplemented, as such collections would continue to be throughout the seventeenth century, by the more personalized anthologies we find in manuscript collections of devices.[49] Emblem books proper, however, seem to have been replaced to a certain extent by other kinds of vaguely emblematic illustrated literature like the *Figures de la Bible* and the *Ovide figuré* that Simeoni composed in 1559 following the typographical and literary models provided by emblem books and *Bibles figurées*.[50] And it would appear that, late in the century, the emblem tended to merge with the class of *Figures de la Bible*, as we see, for example, in Bernard Sellius' *Emblemata sacra* of 1593 (fig. 26).[51]

Fig. 26. 'Elusa mundi potentia.' Bernardus Sellius, *Emblemata sacra* (1613).

Between 1560 and the end of the century, only five new emblem books were published in France. Three were in Latin, and one of these may have been meant mainly for non-French audiences.[52] None of the five was popular enough to require more than an edition or two. Would it, then, be fair to say that the emblem book had passed out of fashion in France? This is a very difficult question to answer. On the surface, after a quick count of editions, that would indeed seem to be the case; but there are many considerations that complicate the question in the extreme, and that cannot be ignored. Febvre and Martin have suggested that inflationary pressures in the third quarter of the sixteenth century began to make it prohibitively expensive for French printers to produce the kind of fine woodcuts for which French emblem books of an earlier period have become justly famous.[53] If one looks, for example, at a Rouille edition of Alciato from the

1560s, it is clear that Rouille's stock of woodcuts for this book – acquired from Macé Bonhomme, who used them first in 1548 – was badly in need of renewal.[54] Renewal is never easy, and when it came, French printers often converted to copperplate illustration, even though it was more expensive, because it was better suited to tastes increasingly formed by the techniques and effects of painting.

Even though the copperplate technique had been well-known in France since the fifteenth century, it was the domain of goldsmiths and remained somewhat neglected by French printers until the flowering of the Ecole de Fontainebleau in the 1540s, when the famous portraitist, Claude Corneille, began to use the technique. Thanks to Mantegna, Dürer, and others, copperplate had, however, always enjoyed more prominence in Italy, Germany, and the Low Countries, where publishing houses were therefore more ready than the French to cater to the changing tastes of the 1560s.[55] At this time, too, emblem books began to enjoy a surge of popularity in the Low Countries and in Germany. So, like French printers thirty years earlier, publishers in these countries may very well have planned their production to satisfy a foreign, and at least partly French, public interested in emblem books, while catering to a growing local clientele as well.

Hints that German and Dutch emblem books did indeed make their way into France come down to us from the end of the sixteenth and beginning of the seventeenth centuries. We know, for instance, that Etienne Tabourot des Accords – who, according to Jean Mesnard, was a nephew of Alciato's translator, Jehan Le Fevre – possessed a copy of the emblematic *stambuch*, *Emblemata saecularia*, which had been produced by J.-T. de Bry in Frankfurt in 1596.[56] In the early seventeenth century, the Parisian, Louis Lhuillier, *fils*, possessed a Latin emblem book published in Holland by Raphelengius; in his copy all the Latin mottoes and texts have been translated into French and neatly transcribed beside or beneath each passage (fig. 26).[57] Printers in the Low Countries also occasionally published emblem books in French. The most important example is Christopher Plantin's publication in the 1560s of the Jacques Grévin translations of the emblems of Hadrianus Junius and Johannes Sambucus,[58] although there were many more polyglot emblem books in which one of the languages was usually French. So it is possible that France became a net importer of emblem books rather than an exporter, as it surely had been during the period from 1534 to 1560.[59]

On the other hand, France may simply have produced enough emblem books during the middle years of the century to satisfy the needs of its reading public for a very long time, and this may have induced the French book trade to de-emphasize the production of emblem books to a certain extent. Perusing volumes of Alciato's emblems published in France during the middle years of the century, one immediately senses that copies of early editions remained in use over considerable periods of time. Sometimes their long useful life is indicated by the names of multiple owners; at others, copies interleaved to be used as *alba amicorum* bear traces of use over long periods of time. One vellum copy of Wechel's 1536 French edition at the Bibliothèque Nationale, for example, contains the signatures of Charles Bredin and of G. Guiflier, the last being dated 1627, and manuscript notations suggest that it served as a *livre de raison* in the early seventeenth century. And, shortly before his death in 1778, Louis-François Jamet, the great eighteenth-century scholar and bibliophile, was still making marginal notes in a 1536 French edition of Alciato he had purchased in 1741![60]

Actually, evidence of Alciato's enduring popularity in France is quite common. In the 1580s, for example, Jean de La Jessée translated several of Alciato's emblems into French, apparently as part of a program of exercises in poetic style; they were published between other translations of epigrams by Muret and Dorat, thus suggesting that Alciato remained one of the important neo-Latin models for the epigram.[61] So the durability of sixteenth-century copies of emblem books and the disruptions caused by the religious wars may go further in explaining the dearth of editions of Alciato's emblems in France before Jean Richer and Marnef began to publish a new series of editions in Paris in the 1580s than any waning of interest on the part of a basically conservative bourgeoisie.

Emblem books played multiple roles in the life of late sixteenth- and early seventeenth-century France. Sometimes they were interleaved in binding to serve as *alba amicorum* for students as they travelled around Europe from university to university. Interleaved copies of Aneau's *Picta poesis* (1552), Sambucus' *Emblemata* (1584), and many other emblem books have been preserved and bear witness to the peripatetic life of their student owners.[62] Beginning in the 1560s, the use of emblem books as *alba amicorum* was quite widespread, both in France and throughout Europe. The friendship books apparently originated in Germany around 1550, and quickly gained popularity among university students, who used them during their scholarly wanderings to collect autographs, obtain proof of contact with famous scholars, or preserve thoughts and memories from student travels.[63] In his *Life of Ramus*, Nancel recounts how Ramus once replied to a request from a German student for his autograph by adding his motto, a half-line taken from Virgil, 'Labor improbus omnia vincit,' to an emblem in the student's *album amicorum* (*Quod ipse sua manu adscripsit emblemati uni de multis, quae Germani quidam ei porexerant*).[64]

One particularly revealing example is the album that Johann Reibolt of Plauen in Saxony used when he was a student in Paris in 1571. Now in the Spencer Collection at the New York Public Library, bound in a 'contemporary Parisian roll-tooled and stamped binding,' according to the catalogue description, this volume contains a 1564 Rouille edition of Alciato in French, a 1566 de Tournes *Metamorphose d'Ovide figuree*, and a 1566 Plantin Sambucus. The first two works were interleaved, although not very systematically, with some interleaving even in the preface and the index; the Sambucus was not, having only a group of blank leaves inserted at the end. Nearly all the painted arms and inscriptions are to be found in the Alciato. Binding the three works together to make the volume we have today obscured parts of several inscriptions, and it would have been next to impossible to paint the elaborate heraldic crests on the pages bound as they now are. Perhaps the original 'album,' then, was simply an unbound copy of the Alciato.

In that copy we find the usual mixture of heraldic arms and short inscriptions. For those friends short of inspiration, often those who had a heraldic crest to brighten their page, there was a stock phrase they would copy with slight variations: 'Virtute ac eruditione egregio (or praestanti) viro (or Domino) Ioanni Reibolt Plauensi in perpetuam amicitiae memoriam ...' (fig. 27). Others offered thoughts more or less inspired by one or another of Alciato's emblems. Facing Alciato's 'Caquet' (*Garrulitas*), for example, we find a 'quatrain' – 'L'ennemy qui appertement se demonstre / Ennemy n'est à craindre: mais celuy / qui combien qu'il soit ennemy, toutesfoys il / feint une amytie, est à craindre & digne de haine' – and the following Latin distich: 'Scilicet ut fuluum spectatur in ignibus aurum / Tempore sic duro est inspicienda fides.' The inscriptions express variations inspired by the commonplace simply stated in Alciato's emblem. Others are more straightforward. Facing page 27 with its version of *Qua dii vocant, eundum*, the author piously adds, 'Et quo fata vocant pietas secura sequitur.' Or facing page 71, *Non illicitum sperandum*, someone else solemnly opines that 'Spes afflictos maxime consolatur.' There are very few inscriptions in the Ovid, and it appears that they all could have been made after the volume was bound.

Jean de Tournes published the first volume intended expressly for this purpose in 1558, and his *Thesaurus amicorum* had three printings before 1560. The outward appearance of this volume is vaguely emblematic: in the first part, empty frames invite inscriptions or emblematic compositions while, in the second half, a number of portraits are accompanied by

D'ALCIAT. INIMITIE. 199

INIMITIE.

Contre les Detracteurs.

Trainebaletz, & sots Maistre d'eschole
Osent sur moy vomir leur chaude chole,
Que feray-ie? rendray-ie la pareille?
Prendre seroit la Cigale par l'æle.
Car que vaut il males mousches chasser?
Ce qu'on ne peut aboli : faut laisser.

Cecy est escrit d'affection indignee à l'occasion de quelque Maistre d'eschole, qui auoit osé detracter de l'Alciat, dont se sentant irrité luy si grand, par si peu & vil (comme il dit) sagement s'abstient de respondre. Car le Iurisperit prise trop peu le Grammarien, ou literateur humain.

Effort fait en vain.

Le chien veut prendre en nuict la lune aux dents,
Car d'autres chiens cuyde estre la dedans.
En vain abaye: & gecte aux vēts voix lourde:
Car son cours fait tousiours Diane sourde.

Comme les chiens en vain iappent, à la lune: laquelle ils ne sauroyent mordre: Ainsi les detracteurs, enuieux comme chiens, en vain mesdisent d'vn grand personnage: auquel il ne sauroient nuyre, mais sans les ouir, poursuit tousiours le cours de ses vertus.

N 4

Fig. 27. Johann Reibolt's *album amicorum* (1571–3). Andrea Alciato, *Emblemes*, Lyons, Rouille, 1564.

mottoes of the people portrayed. Beside Marot's portrait, for example, we read 'A la vertu la mort n'y mord.'[65] Like emblem books, these volumes sometimes had a very long useful life; one copy of the de Tournes *Thesaurus* preserved in Lyons was not used until 1602 when the son of the original owner began to use it to collect autographs from his classmates.[66]

Beginning in 1592 Johann-Theodor de Bry published a series of editions of two emblem books, entitled *Emblemata nobilitati* and *Emblemata saecularia*, specifically designed to serve as *alba amicorum*. First come a group of 'Interpretationes emblématicum,' followed by the pictures with engraved mottoes beneath them or on banderoles within the pictures. These pictures are interspersed with empty frames elaborately decorated and shaped like shields, inviting the inscription of the arms of the autographer. These works were obviously well-known in France. I have already noted that the copy of the *Emblemata saecularia* belonging to Tabourot des Accords is now in the Leber Collection at the Bibliothèque Municipale de Rouen, and an interesting copy of the *Emblemata nobilitati* that once belonged to a Rouennais, Jacques (de) Massieu, contains occasional inscriptions of friendship that document his travels in Germany; we learn from them that he was in Wurzburg in September 1595 and again (still?) on 7 April 1596, but we find him in Frankfurt the next day; the last inscription dates from 1606. Above a *memento mori* (that de Bry used twice), for example, Jo. Paulus Salesius wrote these words: 'Pone me ut signaculum super cor tuum, ut signaculum super bracchium tuam quia fortis est ut mor dilectio. Cant. 8.' in October 1595; elsewhere Horace is quoted.[67]

Beginning in the second half of the sixteenth century illustrated books, including books of emblems, were often dismembered to provide illustrations for manuscripts, or to change the illustrations in other illustrated volumes. As Ruth Mortimer has noted, such replacement illustrations are quite common in books such as the illustrated Kerver editions of Horapollo's *Hieroglyphics*.[68] And the practice continued well into the seventeenth century in books as varied as Jean-Jacques Boissard's *Theatrum vitae humanae* and Erasmus' *Moriae encomium*.[69] One of the earliest collections of English emblems was Thomas Palmer's *Two Hundred Poosees*, a manuscript composed in the 1560s and illustrated mainly with woodcuts taken from Alciato, Aneau, Paradin, and other emblem books.[70] One of the most interesting manuscript volumes illustrated this way in France contains *Imitations et traductions de cent dixhuict emblemes dAlciat, Assavoir cent treize du premier livre et cinq du deuxiesme livre*.[71] This collection, comprising mainly sonnets, was the work of the transplanted Parisian, Simon Bouquet, who passed his unhappy years in Anjou working up his versions of the emblems, and composing other occasional poetry.

Late in the sixteenth century, and at least in part after the submission of the Ligue in 1594, Bouquet assembled this volume in the following manner. At the top of each page, he began by writing the Latin motto of one of Alciato's emblems (fig. 47). Then directly beneath the motto Bouquet pasted the corresponding framed illustration and Latin epigram cut from a copy of the 1583 Marnef edition of the emblems. He did not retain the printed motto because the format in that edition couples the motto to the number of the emblem. But Bouquet's collection of imitations is not organized according to the by then standard arrangement of Alciato's emblems. The mention of two books in the title provides the only clue we need to know that he was following the rather different numbering in a copy of one of the editions published by de Tournes and Gazeau after 1547, or by Plantin after 1565, which must have served as his working text. Although many of Bouquet's poems are fairly straightforward translations of Alciato's Latin, others provide interesting examples of the way the generalized wisdom of Alciato's emblems might be particularized for application to specific situations, much as propaganda emblems were being used at the same time (see below, 195–7).

The Bouquet volume is one of many manuscript collections of emblems and devices composed in France in the second half of the sixteenth century. These collections are quite varied, but for the modern reader their goal and intended readership are usually clearer than those of published emblem books. They included volumes of devices with accompanying verse texts as in the Maréchale de Retz collection,[72] collections of what are probably in some sense personal emblems, such as the ones in the manuscript Théodore Courtaux attributed to Jean-Baptiste Chassignet, or again the little love emblems of Louis Papon and the more serious ones of his friend, Anne d'Urfé.[73]

While each of these manuscript collections of emblems and devices is in some way unique, certain patterns can be seen in the way they were produced, and in the reasons why they were created. First, it is clear that many of these collections were intended to stand as finished products – these were not final working drafts intended to provide textual material and rough designs for printers and engravers. O.C. Reure has remarked, for example, about the manuscript that Loys Papon, a fine calligrapher and moderately accomplished Forezian artist, produced in 1596 containing 29 of Anne d'Urfé's emblems, that it is 'disposé absolument comme un livre imprimé' (8). The same could be said for the other manuscripts produced by Papon.

Other emblem 'manuscripts' were produced with figures engraved on sheets large enough to accommodate a manuscript text. The kind of book that comes immediately to mind is the dedicated *album amicorum*, the kind of partially blank book we have just been studying. But there were other collections of emblematic prints presumably designed to serve as the illustrations for manuscript emblems. The clearest evidence that books were produced this way may be found in the collection of emblematic engravings by Pierre de Loysi (the elder) printed on large paper around 1615. Each engraving is accompanied by a couplet, and in the copy now at the

Bibliothèque Municipale de Besançon, where no further texts have been added, the engravings measure 90 mm × 110 mm and are situated near the top of sheets measuring 285 mm × 190 mm (Courtaux, 5), thus leaving ample space for printed or manuscript texts. In one set of these engravings, manuscript sonnets have turned the compositions into four-part emblems.[74] The Dartmouth College Library possesses a manuscript collection of emblems by René de Bruc with engraved illustrations by Juan Dolivar (fig. 1); this manuscript dates from around 1680, and the engravings were produced from what is perhaps an autograph manuscript now in the collection of the University of Illinois.[75] We may speculate that other emblematic engravings, like those of Heinrik Goltzius, for example, may also have been prepared to accommodate similar personalized textual developments.

Manuscripts like these were obviously intended for small, specifically delimited audiences, and they may sometimes be considered to be personal epitomes, distilling the moral wisdom of their author (or the person for whom they were composed) and commenting obliquely on events that had touched their lives, sometimes in order to draw a general moral lesson. As Loys Papon explains in his 'Discours sur la vie et moeurs de Anne d'Urfé,' d'Urfé's emblems represent 'les diversités dont il a esté traicté, et les resolutions de son dessein pour l'advenir' (32). It would seem, then, that at least some of these manuscript collections of emblems were vastly expanded versions of the owner's device, which was as if refracted into a multitude of emblems that could, in turn, be generalized to provide a summa of personal wisdom, and perhaps a metaphorical moral biography of the subject as well.[76]

Perhaps the best-known French manuscript collection of emblems from the sixteenth century is the *Liber fortunae*, attributed to Jean Cousin and now part of the collection of the Bibliothèque de l'Institut in Paris (ms 1910). Dated as having been completed in 1568, it is one of the earliest collections of emblems to have some thematic unity, composed as it is of a series of variations on the theme of Fortune. Its author was a military man from the Nivernais, Imbert d'Anlezy, and if we take his preface at face value (even if it is not literally true, it probably does represent an ideal), then this collection represents a life's work, done in fragments to serve as a set of ahistorical commentaries on the life and times of this soldier and courtier.[77]

On page 68 we see men representing the three estates working at anvils (fig. 28); the soldier is shaping a sword, the senator seems to be working on a shepherd's crook, while a commoner is making a wheel. The motto reads SUAE QUISQUE FORTUNAE FABER, and the Latin epigram explains: 'Si te dura premat: si fallax decipiat sors, / Non est cur adeo tristia fata

Fig. 28. 'Suae quisque fortunae faber.' Jean Cousin, *Liber fortunae.*

gemas / Has super incudes quid cuditur aspice: sortem / Quisq*ue* suam propria fabricat, ecce manu.' On page 71, we find a development of this epigram in French: 'Nous somes maistres et fabricateurs, de nous mesmes, de notre fortune, delaquelle lung en retire honeur, et biens: l'aultre infamie, honte, et domage, comme il se voit icy en l'ymage, du chevallier, du senateur, et du laboureur. Don de nous mesmes, et non poinct della fortune, nous debvons doloir, et plaindre les trombes et trombettes, et cornettes, mis en la marge, signifife [sic] la renommee laquelle (comme voix humaine) resone par tout le monde.' The reference to trumpets and cornets recalls the device facing the emblem on page 69, where a monumental frame contains a quote in Latin from Homer beneath a device included in the frame at the top. Beneath the frame itself there is a Latin distich, and on pages 70–1, in addition to the French text cited, there are prose explanations in Latin, Italian, and English. Later in the volume, the Italian and English explanations are missing.

All one hundred compositions are developed along these lines, with infinite variations upon the theme and personification of Fortune. The presentation is that of a printed book, but we would hesitate to claim that this is a copy for the printer, even though Kerver's name (misspelled) does appear on the title-page. Perhaps that title-page is simply a bit of whimsy, intended to make a manuscript look like a printed book, as Papon was to do some twenty years later in another French province.

While it is impossible to know how many manuscripts like these may have existed and circulated in late sixteenth- and early seventeenth-century France, it is fair to suppose that the ones I have been discussing are far from unique. As we shall see in the next section, the impact of emblematics on French culture at that time was varied and ubiquitous. We find emblems in sermons, and devices everywhere in political propaganda and courtly festival. This was the time when the French began to write about the theory of the emblematic forms, and the time too when poetic imagery was most clearly emblematic.

Yet the French all but ceased publishing new emblem books after 1570. Jean Mercier's *Emblemata*, published at Bourges in 1592, appears as a clear anomaly, one final humanist echo from a city that had already become a provincial backwater. This collection, by its exceptional nature, serves as a reminder that Paris had become the dominant centre of French publishing by the end of the religious wars. When French publishers again began to issue new editions of Alciato's emblems, it was in Paris that it happened. The Lyons printing industry had become marginalized by inflationary pressures, competition from the Low Countries, and the general effects of the religious wars.

The emblem books by Jean-Jacques Boissard were clearly produced for an international market, even when they were published in French, and their particular humanist cast attaches them to flourishing German traditions exemplified by Reusner and Rollenhagen rather than by any French model.[78] All of these books were, of course, known and used in France.

Perhaps the market had simply been captured by German and Dutch publishers like Feyerabend and Plantin. But the paradox remains that, despite little publishing activity in France, the emblematic mentality had probably become more pervasive than at any time before or since. The composition of emblems in France must by then have been seen as a rhetorical exercise with an instrumental value for expressing specific messages of almost any sort, and hence emblems no longer called out to be published in independent collections but could accomplish their function in manuscripts or scattered throughout otherwise unemblematic works.

7

The Construction of the Early French Emblem

In *The Emblem and Device in France*, I analysed the sixteenth-century theoretical understanding – if one can call it that – of the emblem in France, and the differences perceived to exist between the emblem and related forms like the *devise*, *impresa*, *revers de médaille*, enigma, and hieroglyphics. In practice, the emblem was understood somewhat differently, and much more broadly than it was in any theoretical writings that have come down to modern scholarship. More important, there is wide discrepancy between the actual construction of emblems in sixteenth-century French emblem books and most modern definitions of the form.

No emblem book published in sixteenth-century France exactly reproduces the format of any other, and any attempt to reduce this variety to a rigid generic model is as unproductive when one considers the books themselves as it is when studying the incipient theory of the emblematic forms. Early French emblems range from La Perrière's untitled combinations of a picture with a *dizain* to the four- or even five-part compositions of Corrozet, Gueroult, and Coustau that not only have a title for each emblem – or even two titles in some emblems by Gueroult and Coustau – but also a long development in verse (Corrozet, Gueroult) or prose (Coustau) that amplifies on the quatrain or explains the relation between the other textual components and the illustration. It is not even possible to accommodate all emblems by generalizing the definition to the point of saying only that a sixteenth-century emblem has at least a picture and a text, for many of these emblems were published without pictures, and some were apparently not even intended to be illustrated.[1]

In her study of sixteenth-century French emblem books, Alison Saunders attempts to reduce this dissimilarity to a single generic model.[2] She claims that the early emblem is a three-part invention with a titular inscription, picture, and epigram. She notes that by 1545, in the first of a series of de Tournes editions, La Perrière's *Theatre* was made to conform to this model by the addition of titles, and that the long verse amplifications in Corrozet's *Hecatomgraphie* or the 'narrations philosophiques' in Coustau's *Pegma* are, in fact, nothing more than commentaries, comparable to those that were appended to Alciato's emblems with increasing regularity in the second half of the sixteenth century.[3]

This is a relatively elegant solution to the problem, and one that is, on the surface, quite seductive. The new format of La Perrière's emblems in the Lyons editions does indeed argue powerfully that there existed considerable pressure for generic conformity to the model developed in Wechel's editions of Alciato, but we should not forget that the pressure was not so great that Etienne Groulleau felt obliged to add title/mottoes in the editions of *Le Theatre des bons engins* he issued between 1548 and 1554.[4] Nor did La Perrière himself feel compelled to compose titles for the emblems of his *La Morosophie*, published in 1553, even though his prefaces suggest that he was more conscious of the generic implications of the form than others using it at the time; and when Théodore de Bèze composed a group of forty-four emblems as an appendix to his *Icones* of 1580, he was content to use a two-part form, composed of a picture and a short, more or less epigrammatic text.[5]

When Lanteaume de Romieu translated Coustau's emblems into French, he, too, apparently felt some pressure for generic conformity, for he deleted the *narrations philosophiques* as well as alternative emblem texts proposed by the Latin original. And there is a copy of the complete work at the Arsenal where the long prose texts were carefully excised, and the volume put back together as if they never existed.[6] But we should remember that Romieu felt obliged to put them back in the 1560 edition, thus suggesting that they may not simply have been considered somewhat superfluous commentaries for curious scholars, but rather a necessary adjunct to the rest of the composition, or perhaps even an integral part of it. It is interesting to compare these texts with Junius' commentaries on his emblems; Junius labelled his commentaries as such and grouped them at the end of the volume where they could easily be deleted. They were indeed omitted from the Dutch version, and while they are also lacking in the 1567 French edition, the commentaries may be found in the 1570 edition of that translation.[7]

Moreover, the analogy between the fourth part of Corrozet's emblems and later commentaries on Alciato's emblems quickly becomes less compelling when it is confronted with actual emblems from the *Hecatomgra-*

phie. Commentaries on Alciato's emblems were never done by Alciato himself, whereas Corrozet and Coustau were both ostensibly the authors of the 'fourth part' of their emblems. Usually, the long verse text in Corrozet's emblems bears a relation to the other three parts that is distinctly different from that of commentaries such as those composed on Alciato's emblems by Aneau or Mignault. Indeed, Corrozet's text is sometimes essential to our understanding of the point of the emblem.

In 'La fin nous faict tous egaulx' (D4^{v}–D5^{r}), the long poem is an absolutely integral part of the emblem; it explains and describes the illustration and relates the picture to the two other textual components. The illustration shows a man sweeping the pieces of a chess set from the board into a sack, presumably at the end of a game. The quatrain makes no allusion to this scene as it simply expands on the title: 'La terre est eguale à chascun, / Par tous les pays & provinces, / Aussi tost faict pourrir les princes, / Que les corps du pauvre commun.' The first three parts of this emblem do not, then, explicitly link *signifiant* and *signifié*; that is not really necessary as long as one recognizes the activity pictured in the woodcut, for the comparison was a commonplace that probably did not require much comment for certain audiences. The long text simply spells out what the *cognoscenti* would know anyway; for those readers it is a dispensable commentary, and a congratulory affirmation of what these readers had already realized. But for the uninitiated reader who was most likely more typical of Corrozet's intended audience, this long explanation is a necessary component of the composition, identifying as it does the pictured scene, explaining the game, and making the proverbial comparison in the most explicit terms possible. That text will dispel any doubts Corrozet's reader may have had about the board representing the *jeu de dames*, or an accounting table (*eschiquier* = exchequer).

Whether or not one of these long texts was a commentary must, then, have been a function of the audience reading it. And the more conservative the audience, the more the distinction between work and commentary becomes blurred. The late Middle Ages, as A.J. Minnis explains, distinguished between the *scriptor*, the *compilator*, the *commentator*, and the *auctor*. Following St Bonaventure, Minnis describes the activity of the last two as follows: 'The *commentator* strives to explain the views of others, adding something of his own by way of explanation ... the *auctor* writes *de suo* but draws on the statements of other men to support his own views.'[8] Statements by Corrozet himself, as well as his practice in many of the emblems, make him look more like a compiler or a commentator than an author, but in that case it is impossible to separate the commentary from the emblem pure and simple; as Michel Foucault has reminded us, there can be no commentary without a sovereign, primitive text whose meaning the commentary works to uncover.[9]

Even in one of Saunders' examples, 'De tromperie pauvreté' (D5^{v}–D6^{r}), where the long text begins as if it were a commentary, with the statement 'Cest embleme nous faict scavoir ...' the situation is far from simple, for this poem continues with a passage addressing the figured player directly: 'Car toy pipeur qui veulx avoir ...' (l. 3), as in 'L'ymage de Fortune' (see 165 below). Accounting for ten lines in a total of twenty-four, this highly personal and dramatic harangue is very different from an ordinary, impersonal 'commentary' of the kind Mignault wrote on Alciato's emblems some thirty years later. Then, the text does revert once more for the last twelve lines to a generalizing mode suitable for commentary, where the poet introduces a new comparison, that of the 'loup afamé,' and draws more sententious conclusions,[10] but the contrast with the preceding harangue makes it even clearer why one cannot consider this text to be a 'commentary.'

In 'Insuffisance' (B2^{v}), to take an even better example, the quatrain tells us only that 'Moy pauvre chien de ma nature, / Sy hastif suys à devorer, / Qu'en recepvant ma nourriture / Je ne l'ose pas savourer.' The relation between the title and the pictured dog, which is devouring its food without tasting it, remains obscure and puzzling without the explanation given in the long text, where we learn that the dog's devouring his food as quickly as he can is comparable to the miser's insatiable appetite for wealth he does not even enjoy. The analogy, at least to modern eyes, is so tenuous and seemingly marginal that the long text could not be taken away without rendering the composition meaningless – unless, of course, the comparison was proverbial in ways that are certainly not evident from the text itself.

In Gueroult's emblems, the quatrain often resembles an *argumentum* of the sort we found prefacing Petrarch's *Triumphs* or sections of the first French translation of Erasmus' *Eloge de la folie* early in the century (see above, 100–3). For example, his sixth emblem, 'La femme prudente,' is prefaced by the following ditty: 'Femme qui est sage / Ne court ça, ne la, / La folle & volage: / N'ayme que cela.'[11] Hardly an epigram as we generally understand it, this text seems to stand as a précis of the main text, more closely allied to the title than to the text that follows. Seen this way, the main text cannot in any meaningful sense be considered to form a 'commentary' on the quatrain.

In Coustau's *Pegma* of 1555 the situation is somewhat more complicated, for some of his emblems are not illustrated, while others have more than one verse text coupled with a single prose *narration philosophique*. Some of these prose texts could be considered simple commentaries, but others do not function as commentaries in the way we understand the term today. The emblem 'Sur le tombeau de Chiron' pictures a dead centaur (as is clear from its position atop a tomb with its four legs extended rigidly in the air; fig. 29). Following the quatrain more or less abandoned in the French version, a second text on the next page entitled 'Aliud' serves as a second *subscriptio* in the Latin version and simply asks, over the space of twenty lines, the questions: Why is he dead? Why did he forsake the gift of immortality that the gods had bestowed upon him? The prose narration explains that it is because his human nature pushes him to die.[12] An even clearer example, this one from the French version, is labelled as being 'Sur le chameau & beuf de Plutarque,' and the titular inscription 'L'homme envers l'homme, Dieu,' can be found in Erasmus' *Adagia* (I, i, 69). The *dizain* recounts the fable of the camel that refused to help the tired ox with its load; the ox then died, and in the end 'l'ingrat chameau fut forcé justement / Porter le beuf & son fardeau ensemble: / Refuser donc ne faut ingratement, / Faire un plaisir, qui les autres assemble' (398–9). The relation between fable and adage becomes clear only in the prose narration, where Coustau warns: 'ceux qui auront moyen, devront aviser, qu'ilz ne dedeignent l'adversité d'un autre ...' (400), suggesting that man *should* be like a god to his fellow man. The link is unexpected because, as Erasmus tells us, the expression 'Man is a god to man' is 'usually said about one who has conferred sudden and unlooked-for salvation, or who has brought help by some great benefaction.'[13] An emblem like this one, then, goes far in explaining why Lanteaume de Romieu felt obliged to translate the *narrations philosophiques* for the 1560 French edition.

Examples such as the ones we have been considering show that the long texts in the emblem books by Corrozet, Gueroult, and Coustau are, in general, no more similar to commentaries than they are to the shorter epigrammatic text. Of course, it depends on how one defines 'commentary.' Is the fourth part *essential* to the understanding of the composition by the *intended* reader? If so, and if it is the work of the author of the composition, it is not, it seems to me, meaningful to call it a 'commentary.' Perhaps the *entire* text of an emblem is a commentary upon a picture; if so, the emblem would assume a particular stance in relation to pictorial art, and even other poetic texts.[14] There is, I believe, some reason to do so, but that would vitiate the argument that some parts of the emblem are commentaries upon other parts of the text.[15] Or at least it would render that argument meaningless.

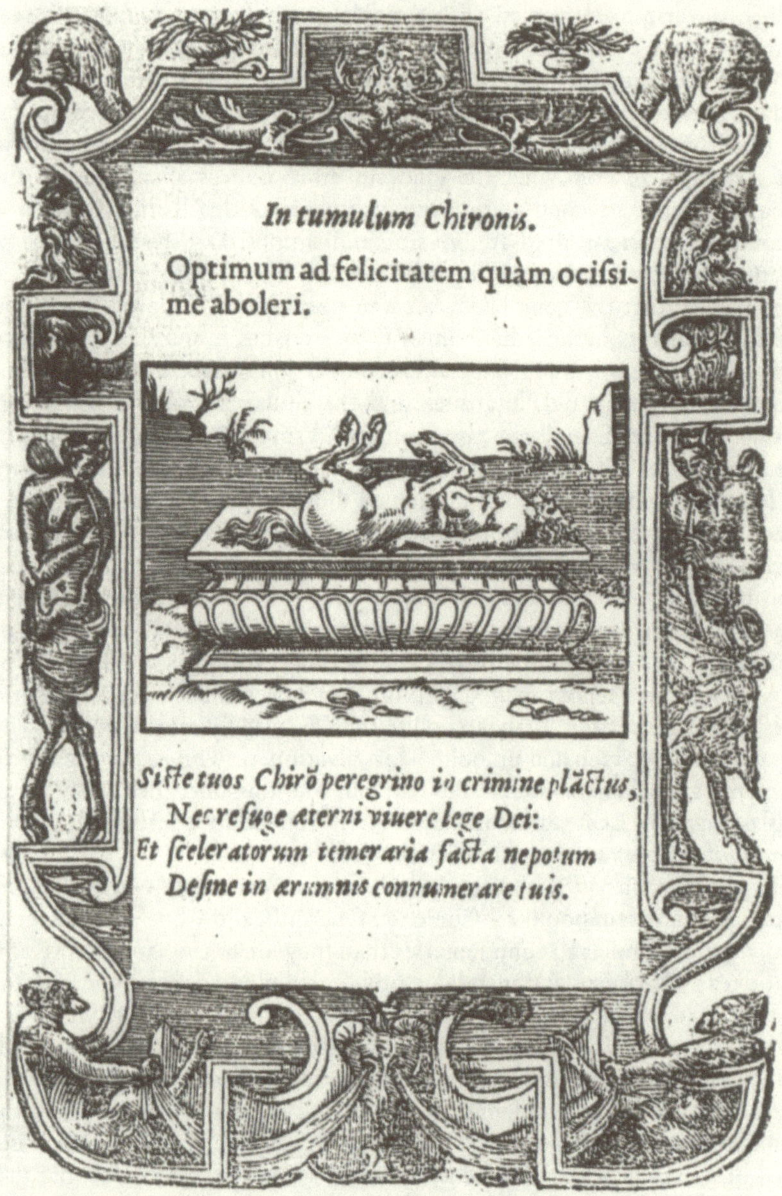

In tumulum Chironis.

Optimum ad felicitatem quàm ociſsimè aboleri.

Siſte tuos Chirō peregrino in crimine plāctus,
Nec reſuge æterni viuere lege Dei:
Et ſceleratorum temeraria facta nepotum
Deſine in ærumnis connumerare tuis.

Fig. 29. 'In tumulum Chironis,' Pierre Coustau, *Petri Costalii Pegma* (1555), p. 15.

If one accepts my line of reasoning, one is forced to conclude that the emblem as a genre was a highly unstable entity that could take a variety of forms, although there was some pressure throughout the middle years of the century for it to conform to the model devised by Alciato and his early French printers. Perhaps the best solution to the problem of classifying emblems by their parts is to adapt Peter Daly's happy compromise that proposes a system distinguishing between 'emblem books in the strict sense, i.e., the tight three-part form as introduced by Andrea Alciato' – and 'expanded forms' such as Henry Hawkins' 'complex nine-part structure.'[16]

Naming the parts of the emblem is as difficult as agreeing on the number of parts an emblem can have. Henkel and Schöne settled on the terms 'inscriptio,' 'pictura,' and 'subscriptio,' but this system is far from uniformly satisfactory.[17] First, the use of terms implying spatial relationships above and below the picture forces the assumption that the emblem is necessarily a three-part invention, with those parts distributed in a particular way. Second, the prefixes in- and sub- tend to subordinate the different texts to the picture, when in fact the picture was generally a secondary and subordinate element in the conception and execution of French Renaissance emblems, at least during the middle third of the century. Finally, the prefixes suggest a certain positioning of the parts of an emblem in which the two textual components would, respectively, precede and follow the picture.

Bernhard F. Scholz has become convinced that such positioning was indeed an integral part of the emblem form,[18] but in at least two of Gueroult's emblems (5: 'Amour par labeur est dompté' and 12: 'Ne s'accointer de plus grands que soy'), the quatrain accompanies the titular inscription above the picture, or the picture falls between lines two and three of the quatrain, as in emblem 2 (fig. 30), thus suggesting that the positioning implied by Henkel and Schöne's terms was not an absolute requirement of the genre as it was beginning to be understood, but was rather more often a question of the compositional limitations involved in producing a given book.[19] Confirmation of the irrelevance of the positioning of the parts of an emblem comes in the *Jardin d'honneur,*[20] where Corrozet's emblems have no title and the quatrain has been moved to the title's position above the illustration in all twenty-five of the emblems from *Hecatomgraphie* reproduced there.

William S. Heckscher and Karl-A. Wirth had earlier named the parts of the emblem the 'lemma,' epigram, and icon.[21] This system poses nearly as many problems as that of Henkel and Schöne, but it is ultimately more

Ainſi eſt deceu le trompeur
D'vn plus caut & fallacieux.

Fable du Coq & du regnard.

LE regnard, par bois errant,
Va querant,
Pour ſa dent tendre paſture,
Et ſi loing en la fin va,
Qu'il trouua:
Le Coq par meſauenture.
Le Coq (de grand peur quil ha)
Sen volla,
Sur vne ente haute & belle:
Diſant, que maiſtre regnard,
N'ha pas l'art:
De monter deſſus icelle:
Le regnard, qui l'entendit,
Luy à dit:

Fig. 30. Guillaume Gueroult, *Le Premier Livre des emblemes* (1550), emblem 2, p. 8.

stimulating to debate and useful for helping us understand what an emblem is. First, very few emblem books were composed in such a way that the text was actually, or only, an epigram. Second, the picture was an 'icon' in only the most general of senses; and in some regards, it may even be misleading to speak of the emblem picture as an icon. Indeed, the *Oxford English Dic-*

tionary cites as obsolete all the meanings of the word that seem pertinent to its use in characterizing the emblem picture (and hence not likely to come to the mind of non-specialist readers), except for its use in the Eastern Church to refer to the representation of a sacred person that is itself regarded as sacred and therefore venerated. This is just the problem that the medieval Latin church in the West wished to avoid,[22] and while the distinction between representation and symbolization did, on occasion, become blurred in western Europe during the Renaissance,[23] it was a trend constantly fought in scientific thought as it was also in the Church, at least until the Council of Trent, when a rewriting of dogma encouraged the trend toward baroque incarnation in art, and exacerbated the dispute with the Anglicans over the question of transubstantiation.

Using the word 'lemma' to describe the titular inscription is likewise fraught with difficulties. As an English word, Webster's defines 'lemma' as 'a preliminary or auxiliary supposition accepted as true and used in a demonstration of some other proposition.' But if one goes back to its Latin and Greek roots, it can mean argument, title, or assumption. If the introductory statement of an emblem were a 'lemma' in any of these senses except that of 'title,' it would take the form of a proverb, as the motto of a device sometimes did,[24] or maxim, and correspond to the motto of a device, or the first term of a syllogism. Such is sometimes, but not always, the case in the emblems composed by Alciato, or in those by writers who imitated him in French. But 'lemma' could also mean heading, classification, commonplace, or title. In this sense, it is an appropriate, if perhaps unsatisfyingly general, term for describing the first part of most emblems. But if the term is carefully circumscribed to mean *only* 'the heading or theme of a scholium, annotation, or gloss' (*OED*), it is not only an appropriate, but even an enlighteningly descriptive term.[25]

In the more general English sense, the word could be applied with complete accuracy to many introductory statements in Corrozet's emblems, but by no means to all. Corrozet was the first in France to use the third part of the emblem, and his titles are every bit as varied in form as those of Alciato; alongside maxim-like 'lemmas' such as 'Doulce parolle rompt ire,' we find more topical titles, as in 'Liesse et tristesse' or 'Amytié entre les freres,' or even descriptive labels, such as 'L'ymage de témérité.'

Although La Perrière apparently did not compose his emblems with any kind of titular inscription, the reception and publishing history of his *Theatre des bons engins* provide many interesting insights into the function and place of this 'third part' of the emblem in its economy. What may be the first edition of the *Theatre* by anyone other than Janot was issued by

Denys de Harsy in Lyons. There, the illustrations have been replaced by titles, but these maxim-like statements are not descriptive substitutes for illustrations. Rather they point to a different conception of the emblem, one in which the emblem text can be seen as a development upon some commonplace elaborated in the title. As such they provide a good example of the reasons Heckscher and Wirth's term 'lemma' is more appropriate than Henkel and Schöne's *inscriptio* for characterizing this part of an emblem.

Then, in 1545, Jean de Tournes initiated a series of editions in which La Perrière's *dizains* had titles (fig. 31), but in the main quite different ones from those in de Harsy's edition, and they were accompanied by new pictures that occasionally brought the illustration into closer conformity with the text; de Tournes printed each three-part composition, as it was now constituted, on the same page. This model would seem to have been the most successful one, as the de Tournes version may have seen as many as seven editions by de Tournes and his heirs through the early 1580s.

What are we to make of the titular inscriptions that attached to the emblems of La Perrière's *Theatre* after the first Janot editions? These emblematically attached new texts could, as we shall see, take a variety of forms, and perhaps serve a variety of purposes. When we consider those versions where the emblems were published alone – that is, when they were not published as part of an anthology – titular inscriptions are found only in Lyons editions. The Parisian editions of Janot and of his successor, Etienne Groulleau, do not have such inscriptions, and hence La Perrière's authorship of either group is at the very least to be viewed with sceptical caution. Indeed, given the differences between the texts published by Janot in the 1540s and those of the de Tournes edition of 1583, we may even suspect that La Perrière's control over his own emblem texts was limited.[26] The second characteristic of these titles is that they differ depending on the publisher of the emblems, thus suggesting that the publisher rather than the author may have have been responsible for their addition.

In fact, there are quite striking differences between some of the texts added by Denys de Harsy and those used by Jean de Tournes. Yet, interestingly, while many of these texts are different, even in meaning, others are similar or, in a few instances, identical, as in the case of the first motto, 'Pour vivre en paix et tranquilité.' Among those that bear little or no resemblance to their counterpart, we see, for example, that de Harsy captions the fourteenth emblem 'De vraye amitié,' while de Tournes simply takes the first line of La Perrière's *dizain*: 'Pour peu de cas trebuche foy

EMBLEME XVIII.

Ce qu'eſt requis en la femme prudente.

EN tel eſtat que voyez,noz anceſtres,
Dame Venus iadis voulurent paindre,
Bien cõgnoiſt on,que les ſouuerains maiſtres
En la faiſant,ne ſe voulurent faindre,
Et pour l'effect du ſens miſticque attaindre,
Par la tortue,entendre eſt de beſoing,
Que femme hõneſte ne doibt pas aller loing,
Le doigt leué,qu'à parler ne s'aduance,
La clef en main,denote qu'auoir ſoing
Doibt ſur les biens du mary,par prudence.

Fig. 31. Guillaume de La Perrière, *Le Theatre des bons engins* (Lyons: Jean de Tournes, 1546), no. 18.

legere.' As in this case, the difference is substantial in well over half the captions for the emblems.

While it is difficult, given our rather imperfect understanding of the structure of paroemic locutions,[27] to distinguish between proverbs and the more learned form of the maxim, it would appear that de Tournes's captions are closer to proverbial diction than de Harsy's more formally structured inscriptions with their heavy reliance on imperative infinitives, or straightforward affirmative sentences, and less reliance on metaphor. For instance, the *inscriptiones* attached to *dizain* 77 are similar in subject-matter but very different in expression; de Harsy proclaims that 'tous biens se consument en fol Amour,' while de Tournes suggests rather that 'Qui suit Amour, enfin aura disette.' The more colurful presentation of de Tournes is common throughout the collection, and would tend to argue for a less humanist source and orientation for these texts than for those of de Harsy. But there is little other evidence to support this very tentative hypothesis.

Occasionally, a substantive difference in the two titular inscriptions suggests a different interpretation of the text. De Harsy labels *dizain* 63, on Occasio, 'Labourer doibt lhomme quand il est temps,' while de Tournes advises, 'Ne refusons Fortune, quand à nous se presente.' How might we explain the curious mixture of similarity, or occasionally identity, with great differences of expression and sometimes of meaning? We could speculate on the possiblity of influence coupled with attempts at improvement, but it may be more rewarding to regard these titular inscriptions as more or less proverbial summaries of different, but often similar, interpretations or readings of the *dizains*. If that were so, it would give us unique insights into the dynamics of reading at the time. And this hypothesis receives some confirmation in the activity of anthologizers like Corrozet, in such collections of excerpts as his *Parnasse des poetes françois modernes contenant leurs plus riches & graves sentences, discours* ... of 1570. That is, they summarized readings of short poems or excerpts from longer ones in sententious titular inscriptions not so different, either in their diversity or in their often proverbial cast, from the ones we have encountered in the editions of the *Theatre* by these two Lyons publishers. One of Corrozet's selections comes from Ronsard's 'Voyage de Tours': 'Bien fol est qui se fie en sa belle jeunesse, / Qui si tost se desrobe, & si tost nous delaisse, / La rose à la parfin devient gratecu, / Et toute avec le temps par le temps est vaincu' (f. 10^{v}). He captioned this fragment with the title 'Beaulté n'est qu'une fleur.' With or without the picture of a thorny *rosier*, this passage, thus titled, might well remind the reader of emblem 30 in La Perrière's *Theatre*, which begins with the observation 'Qui veult la rose au verd buysson saisir, / Esmerveiller ne se doit s'il se poingt' (ll. 1–2) that leads to the following conclusion: 'Par quoy penser doit tout homme scavant, / Que volupté n'est jamais sans douleur.' (ll. 9–10)

It has long been recognized that La Perrière often built his emblems around adages by Erasmus.[28] The captions for the de Harsy and de Tournes editions do not take account of that influence, but it must have been well-known, for a copy of Janot's second edition at the Folger Shakespeare Library in Washington, DC, has captions in Latin, German, and Spanish added by a late sixteenth- or early seventeenth-century German reader. And this writer, it would appear, referred back to Erasmus wherever possible in establishing parallels. The fifth emblem is captioned *Spes pretio non emenda*, in a very slight variation on Erasmus' *Spem precior emere* (*Adages* II, iv, 5), a *rapprochement* obviously inspired by lines 5 and 6: 'C'est grand abuz de laisser son bon heur / Pour ung espoir de promesse incertaine,' and one that situates the emblem within a network of commonplaces evoked when not actually stated in the adage in question. For emblem 7 our German reader cited Erasmus' *Irritare crabones* (I, i, 60), while in emblem 43 the Latin *Alia vita alios mores postulat* clearly recalls Erasmus' *Alia vita, alia diaeta*, without quoting it verbatim (I, ix, 6). Sometimes this copy contains more than one inscription per emblem, and often in a different hand. And they may serve as diverse commentaries on the text. For example, emblem 77 (fig. 32) is captioned here *In amores meretricios*, and then, perhaps as an afterthought or perhaps to another reader, the *dizain* recalls an adage of Erasmus, *Sero sapiunt Phryges* (I, i, 28) ['the Phrygians learn wisdom late']. This is a real commentary; it gives us a glimpse of an early reader's reaction to the text while also suggesting that such readers tended to see the emblems within a context of commonplace wisdom best summed up in the *Adages*.

These various examples of possible 'inscriptiones' for La Perrière's emblems make it clear, I believe, that there was no real consensus on the *kind* of title appropriate for any given combination of picture and text, and the only term that is really enlightening about the form of the titular inscription is 'lemma,' used in the restricted way I have suggested above. But it is not necessarily ideal, and this problem of terminology provides further confirmation that the Renaissance emblem cannot be defined in a neatly monolithic way, at least not through the first stage in its development. Rather, it suggests that so many things were happening simultaneously in an emblem that the form of individual emblems must be analysed in some detail, but also that we will probably need to forgo, at

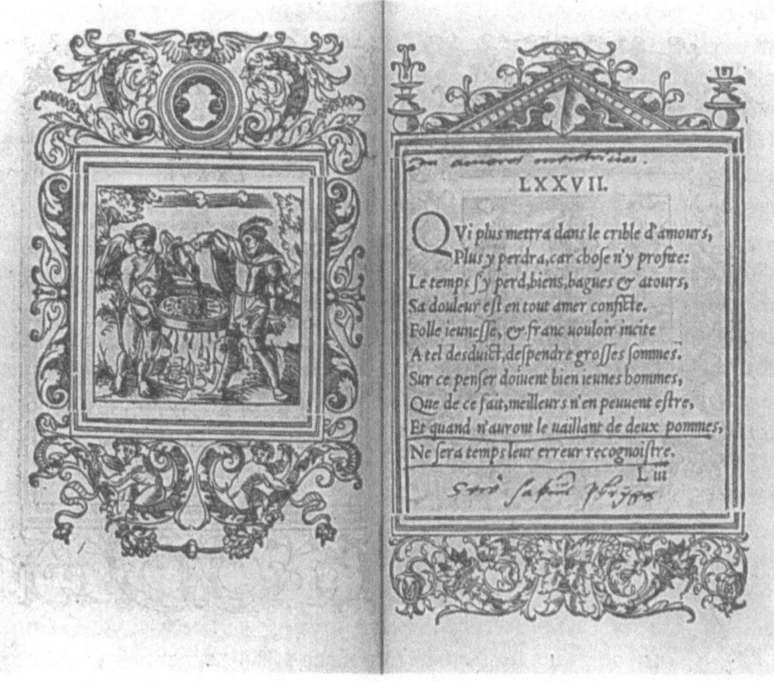

LXXVII.

QVi plus mettra dans le crible d'amours,
Plus y perdra, car choſe n'y profite:
Le temps ſ'y perd, biens, bagues & atours,
Sa douleur eſt en tout amer confitte.
Folle ieuneſſe, & franc uouloir incite
A tel desduict, deſpendre groſſes ſommes.
Sur ce penſer doiuent bien ieunes hommes,
Que de ce ſait, meilleurs n'en peuuent eſtre,
Et quand n'auront le uaillant de deux pommes,
Ne ſera temps leur erreur recognoiſtre.

L iii

Fig. 32. *Le Theatre des bons engins* (1540), no. 77.

least in large measure, any attempt to arrive at a synthetic model that will satisfactorily describe all emblems.

It is possible to look at the emblem as a way of commentary on traditional themes and motifs; but it is equally possible to see it as an implicit (or explicit) dialogue between author and reader, in which the reader plays a newly dynamic questioning role. In this regard, the emblem reminds one of the first mythological encyclopaedias of the Renaissance, Georg Pictor's *Theologia mythologia* (Freiburg iB, 1532), where, in dialogue form, Theophrastus teaches his disciple, Evander, about the appearance and allegorical meaning of the Gods. Evander asks questions about the pictures and Theophrastus answers. Giovio used the dialogue form in his pioneering treatise on devices, and other theorists, including Tasso, used it too in writing on the *impresa*, as if to enact the process of reception they were imagining in their conception of the emblematic forms.[29]

In his translation of Alciato's emblems, Aneau still considered the 'emblems' to be the texts, and he classified many of them as either a *probleme*, a *dialogue*, an *apostrophe*, an *apodixe* or *evidence*, or a *prosopopee* (fig. 33). With the exception of apodixe, these terms are fairly familiar. Apodixe, or *apodioxis*, involves the rejection of an argument as absurd. Such labels seem to 'frame' the picture, and turn it into a motivated composition. Herbert Read has claimed that 'composition is born out of containment, out of imposed discipline.'[30] Indeed such labels, like any emblem text, provide our perception with the discipline that turns a scene into a *motivated* composition. The text is the frame that imposes unity on the scene, which would otherwise remain ambiguous or infinitely polyvalent in boundless, unfocused space.

Most emblems adhere to one of these models, or some combination of them. Perhaps the most interesting for our understanding of the dynamics of composition and intentionality in the making of emblems use the question-and-answer format, following a technique common in the Greek epigrams. In such emblems, it is either a figure in the illustration, an animal, or perhaps a personification, that speaks as in a prosopopoeia,[31] or the imagined viewer will discuss the picture with the imagined narrator in a dialogue. The long verse text of Corrozet's emblem 'L'ymage de fortune' begins this way:

> Dy moy (fortune) à quelle fin tu tiens
> Ce mast rompu duquel tu te soustiens?
> Et pourquoy c'est aussi que tu es paincte
> Dessus la mer, de ce long voille sceincte?
> Dy moy aussy pourquoy n'a quelle fin
> Soubz tes piedz sont la boulle & le daulphin?
> C'est pour monstrer mon instabilité
> Et qu'en moy n'est aulcune seureté. (sig. F7)

Here we have a combination of prosopopoeia and dialogue. In such cases, the interlocutor is the fictive viewer of the work of art being interrogated, and the work of art responds. As such, emblems like this one are allegories of the process of reading an emblem, for as the reader's questions describe the picture, they also trace the path of his inquiring gaze and sort out those objects that would have been considered at the time to be charged with symbolic significance. Following the model proposed by such a re-enactment, the reader begins by posing questions about the illustration or the relation between the illustration and the title that will be answered by the author through the text.

This approach to the pictured artefact is necessary because the world of the emblem is a world of allegorical fragments; it is a landscape cluttered

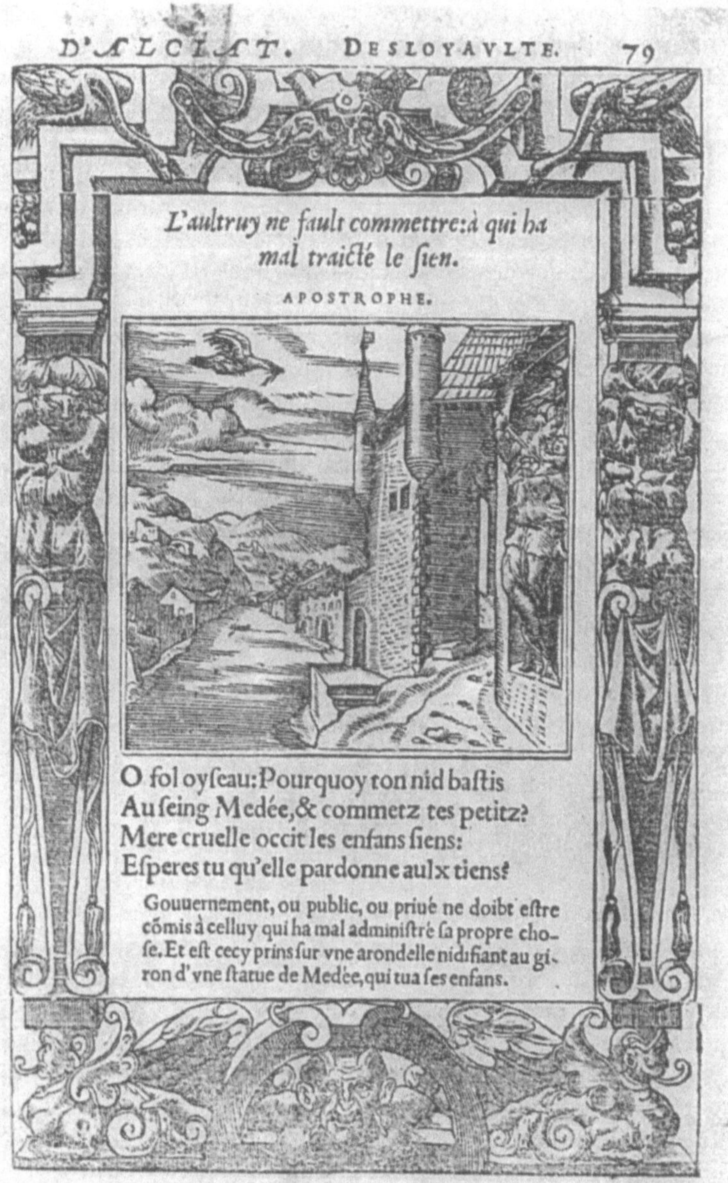

D'ALCIAT. DESLOYAVLTE. 79

L'aultruy ne fault commettre: à qui ha mal traicté le ſien.

APOSTROPHE.

O fol oyſeau: Pourquoy ton nid baſtis
Au ſeing Medée, & commetz tes petitz?
Mere cruelle occit les enfans ſiens:
Eſperes tu qu'elle pardonne aulx tiens?

Gouuernement, ou public, ou priué ne doibt eſtre cõmis à celluy qui ha mal adminiſtré ſa propre choſe. Et eſt cecy prins ſur vne arondelle nidifiant au giron d'vne ſtatue de Medée, qui tua ſes enfans.

Fig. 33. 'L'aultruy ne fault commettre: à qui ha mal traicté le sien.' André Alciat, *Emblemes* (1549), p. 79.

with the debris of a collision of sign systems. Lacking the narrative framework of a complete allegory, the structure of the early emblem picture provides no context to guide the viewer's understanding of the signs before him. The sense of the sign is then initially polysemous because of its tacitly acknowledged place in more than one sign system. So its intended meaning remains undecidable without some interpretive text, and the picture, or even the surrounding emblems in the collection, generally provide nothing to indicate within which sign system it should be considered. Later, first in the *Morosophie* as in the fig-tree emblem discussed in note 23, and then much more clearly in Rollenhagen's emblems, double images often solve the problem, and obviate the need for a text, at least for the knowledgeable reader. But this development came later, and never completely supplanted the model I have been describing.

To the extent that the reader hesitates over the meaning of the motifs, or sees multiple possibilities for interpretation, he is becoming conscious of himself as a reader, and hence begins to prepare himself for a more active, and eventually freer and more creative role, as a reader. For any reader of emblems is, as I have argued elsewhere, potentially a maker of emblems since the deciphering of an emblem entails the realization that the emblem motif could have been used differently.[32] In this sense, the emblem, perhaps more clearly than any other literary form, shows how the reading process was beginning to evolve toward the highly active role it assigns to the reader in today's interaction with a text.

Corrozet and La Perrière both seem conscious of the importance of an increasingly dynamic reading process in making an emblem work; *Theatre*, 63, is a straightforward, and as if literal, re-enactment of the way any emblem is supposed to work, for the questions are a reader's or viewer's questions, and it is clearly the author who is answering the questions, acting as the reader's companion and guide.

Quel est le nom de la presente ymaige?
Occasion, se nomme pour certain.
Qui fut l'autheur? Lysipus feit l'ouvraige:
Et que tient elle? ung rasoir en sa main.
Pourquoy? pourtant que tout tranche soubdain.
Elle a cheveulx devant, & non derriere?
C'est pour monstrer qu'elle tourne en arriere,
S'on fault le coup, quand on la doit tenir:
Aux talons a des aesles? car barriere
(Qu'elle que soit) ne la peult retenir.

This is an individual and human voice answering the questions of another individual; although the authorial voice is better informed than its interlocutor, it is not the impersonal voice of omniscient authority, nor is it the voice of some figure within the illustration reciting as in a prosopopoeia, as Fortune was doing in the emblem by Corrozet just quoted. This, of course, is clear from the use of third-person verbs.

But if at first, and in the absence of a text, a babel of voices seemed to emanate from the emblem picture, or indeed perhaps from any picture, the emblematist worked nonetheless with constellations of traditional imagery that might come from the body of ancient maxims and proverbs supplied by the discoveries of the humanists, as, for example, the Pythagorean dicta used by La Perrière in several emblems of his *Theatre* (7, 8, 9, etc.), late medieval proverb and bestiary lore, and ancient mythology. For an emblem to have its full effect, it needed to be clear that it was working some unexpected, even if minor, variation on a traditional or familiar motif, and so the emblematist needed to be aware of his sources even when he did not cite them, and might even willfully subvert them. It is therefore interesting to note in this regard that, in the revisions of his emblems for the third edition of the *Theatre*, for example,[33] La Perrière compressed the description of the picture in the first four lines of emblem 69 to make room for the comment 'Maint bon autheur, grec et latin declaire,' as if to assert that the reader should be familiar with his subject, even if he were not.

To understand the dynamics of the emblem illustration, scholars have generally done little more than invoke, as indeed the emblematists themselves were wont to do, the vague idea of hieroglyphics and ideogrammatic writing. But this strategy on the part of sixteenth-century writers may simply have been a ploy to give a still very conservative art form a patina of humanistic respectability.[34] In fact, emblem illustrations were seldom like hieroglyphics. They may have been done by artists or craftsmen little attuned to what was going on in the text, or they may be generic illustrations that were used to illustrate more than one text.[35] Such a cavalier attitude toward the illustration of emblem books in the early years of the form may result from the understanding that the illustrations were actually little more than sketches for an illuminator, as Robert Brun has suggested for earlier book illustration in general;[36] taken metaphorically, this understanding of the illustration would lead us to see the text as embroidering upon, or 'illuminating' the sketchy woodcut scene.

But some illustrations seem to have been made for the emblems they illustrate; then, the idea of the mirror, of the *speculum*, understood both in a highly metaphorical way and also in a more literal way than we are accustomed to doing, may help us understand better the mechanism of some of the more disconcerting emblem designs. On the verso of Michelangelo's 'Punishment of Tityus,' he traced an improvisation of the resurrected Christ by holding the drawing to the light. A letter from his friend, Sebastiano del Piombo suggested that he do the same thing with his (now lost) drawing of Ganymede, the companion piece to this one, and add a halo to produce for the cupola of the Medici chapel a St John of the Apocalypse ascending to heaven on the wings of Christ the eagle.[37] In *Studies in Iconology*, Panofsky suggested a link here to the *Ovide moralisé*, where Ganymede is made to represent St John,[38] but what is more important to my argument is that the form of one figure suggests another figure. One figure or shape can 'masquerade as another as we shall see in mythological portraits from the time (206–11 below). Formal *rapprochement* can, I would suggest, provide the impetus for a search for other analogies between the two formally similar figures.

The improvised figure is, of course, a mirror image of the original (unless it is the other way around), and as such it draws one into the Renaissance topos of the mirror and reversal.[39] The mirror was a metaphor of imitation as emulation from the Middle Ages to the seventeenth century, as in the innumerable *Specula* that carried the moral instruction soon to be provided by emblem books. One of the principal topoi associated with the mirror metaphor was the *memento mori*, as we see in Lucas Furtenagel's portrait of Hans Burgkmair and his wife (c. 1529) with a mirrored reflection showing (their) skulls.[40] That emblem books consciously continued this tradition of serving as a metaphorical mirror to show one's true self is clear from the mirrors that were decorated with devices either as in Rémy Belleau's *Bergerie* or in paintings like the *Madeleine* by Artemisia Gentileschi.[41] The theorist Henry Estienne confirmed this function of such inscriptions when he advised gentle ladies to place their devices on their mirrors so that they might contemplate their moral ideals while inspecting their physical beauty.[42] This advice echoes Italian theorists, especially Capaccio, who situated the device in the realm of the portrait.[43] But it also echoes the Neoplatonic idea that desire is the mirror of the heart, or as Maurice Scève puts it: 'Si le desir image de la chose que plus on aime / Est du coeur le miroir' (diz. 46).[44] But perhaps La Perrière sums up the emblematic view of mirrors best when he declares:

> Lors que la dame au miroir se regarde,
> Et qu'elle void la beaulté de sa face,
> Fault que de vice en tant se contregarde,

> Que deshonneur à sa beaulté ne face:
> Si belle n'est pour lors, fault qu'elle efface
> Par ses vertus, le deffault de nature:
> Beaulté de corps tourne à desconfiture,
> S'elle se plonge en plaisirs reprouvez.
> Icy noter peult toute creature,
> Que les miroirs à ces fins sont trouvez. (emblem 37)

We see a distinct nuancing of the Neoplatonist position on beauty here, but the big difference is that the skull begins to be replaced by a more positive ideal, and a more individualized one. Even though the *memento mori* was to take on renewed life in baroque still lifes, a medieval attitude is beginning to be supplanted here by a more optimistic Renaissance view of man's condition.

Michelangelo's drawing provides the clue necessary to link this metaphor to the kind of artistic imitation that came to manifest itself in printed and engraved copies of paintings or drawings, for they were almost always mirror images of the originals, and consequently bear an indelible reminder that imitation always involves change. To the extent that imitation implies variation rather than identification, the emblem is a particularly innovative vehicle of Renaissance imitation, and may be seen as linked to illustrated proverbs by the fact that imitation was simply another manifestation of formulaic expression. The formulaic always carries the presumption of possible variation; formulaic repetition may intend to reproduce the model exactly, but in an oral culture that can never be guaranteed. By the Renaissance, the use of some formula, as a quotation, was never tautological, that is, never identical in its effect or meaning. That is so if only because an incipient awareness of the implications of point of view made every context different and thus inflected the formulaic utterance to fit a particular situation, as in Demoulins' use of the Psalms to praise a king other than David (see above, 90–2). Point of view changed the oral formula into a quotation.

Viewed from the perspective of production, printing was the privileged domain of the emblematic; that is, the explicitly text-oriented, relatively small-scale, a-narrative, and fragmentary illustration that does much to distinguish print culture from manuscript culture is particularly conducive to the emblematic positioning of texts in relation to such pictures. To the extent that the emblem is conditioned in its very nature by the requirements and implications of printing, it is a visually oriented phenomenon, even when it is most textual. For as we have seen, the text, from Fournival

Fig. 34. Karl Audran. Political Allegory.

to Tory, was to some extent always considered to be a pictorial representation of oral language.[45] This view of the text requires a metaphorical understanding of the written word, and metaphor based on analogies between the literal and the figurative, between the interior and the exterior is the very stuff of emblematic thought. Liberated by the examples of the hieroglyphics and the extremely forced analogical practices of the *ars memorandi*, the emblematists looked relentlessly for new and striking analogies of their own. Why not, then, analogies of form? In an age obsessed with form, formal similarities surely provided one of the important conduits for syncretic *rapprochements*. But in that case, the similarities that grounded the analogy would be found not in nature, but in art, for nature does not make radically different entities truly similar in shape. Or if it does, then they do not function in the same way.

Many analogies of the emblematists and those who worked in their orbit seem ridiculous to modern eyes. An example is Karl Audran's allegory on the conquests of Louis XIII in the Alps (fig. 34). In it we see fluvial divinities around a magnetic stone marked with the arms of France, and that stone is attracting laurel-wreath crowns.[46] It was certainly well-known that

Fig. 35. 'Non tuis viribus.' Georgette de Montenay, *Emblemes ou devises chrestiennes* (1571), no. 5.

magnets did not attract any kind of object indiscriminately, but only those composed of iron. What kind, then, of cultural *vraisemblance* might this curious event have been thought to possess in the early years of the seventeenth century? As it turns out, this composition was modelled on one made for the Italian Accademia della Parthenia, where the magnet is attracting the links of a chain. Against what must have been a fairly well-known background such as this, Audran's composition must have seemed incredibly witty and perfectly acceptable within a particular context of symbolic compositions.[47] But the magnet had already been assimilated to the attractive power of God's love through another kind of formal resemblance, that of the homonym, as in this case *aimant-aymant*, from Georgette de Montenay's emblem 5, *Non tuis viribus* (fig. 35).

Analogies of form could develop too from the kind of iconographical abstraction that is common in the artist's or draughtsman's presentation of objects. These abstractions turn into conventions, and as Michael Camille has noted,[48] the use of iconographical conventions has a generalizing effect. Only an obsessed nominalist with the eye and imitative talents of the most refined mannerist could capture all the formal peculiarities of an individual peach, but who, before the great botanical illustrators of the post-Linnaeus period, should want to do such a thing anyway? Normally, the artist will abstract a general shape and translate it into a two-dimensional iconographical pattern. And for the convenience of reference these patterns are sometimes characterized analogically by the names of other objects that have more or less the same shape; hence waves are presented as mountains, and the peach, perhaps, as a human heart. These comparisons carry little obvious meaning, but they can provide the impetus for emblematic comparisons that make them meaningful. Alciato used the formal analogy between the peach and man in his emblem *Albutij ad D. Alciatum, suadentis, vt de tumultibus Italicis se subducat, & in Gallia profiteatur* (143), where the comparison turns first on the resemblance between the shape of the peach tree's leaf and that of a human tongue, and then on that of the peach and a human heart, in order to found an exemplum imagined by Albutius to help persuade Alciato to move to France. The peach tree, we learn, is foreign to our shores, but its fruit has improved by being transplanted, and the tree is like Alciato because its leaves are shaped like human tongues, thus suggesting Alciato's eloquence, while its heart-shaped fruit evokes the wisdom of Alciato's heart.[49] This iconographical formula for a peach probably emerged from the lore of herbiaries and ancient natural history. And while it may have become conventional in the workshops of some illustrators, the form is rarely evident in any illustration of Alciato's emblem (fig. 36). The emblematist nevertheless applied it to a very specific situation through the medium of analogy in order to produce an emblem.

Early emblem illustrations were constructed with a relatively limited number of formal models. Naturalistic scenes can be divided into three groups: 1) the presentation of examples from natural history in the bestiary tradition as expanded with the wealth of examples provided by such ancient natural historians as Pliny; 2) a single, but significant moment from the story of a fable or an exemplary episode from ancient history; and 3) scenes from everyday life that demonstrate some proverb. Other models are situated more clearly within what Walter Ong once characterized as allegorical space.[50] These include mythological scenes and personifications, symbolic collages, and the literalization of proverbial metaphors. Somewhere in between we find variations, often of a paradoxical nature, on such standard structural motifs as the scales or the ship on the sea of life.

An example of what I call a 'symbolic collage' is Corrozet's emblem 'L'heure de la mort incerteine,' where symbolically charged objects are combined in an obviously ideogrammatic combination (see above, 40). While such constructions appear to be ingeniously original, they are some-

Albucij ad. D. Alciatum ſuadens,
ut de tumultibus Italicis ſe
ſubducat, & in Gallia
profiteatur.

Quæ dedit hos fructus arbor, cœlo aduena noſtro,
Venit ab Eoo perſidis axe prius:
Translatu facta eſt melior, quæ noxia quondam
In patria, hic nobis dulcia poma gerit:
Fert folium linguæ, fert poma ſimillima cordi,
Alciate hinc uitam degere diſce tuam.
Tu procul à patria in pretio es maiore futurus,
Multum corde ſapis, nec minus ore uales.

Fig. 36. 'Albutij ad D. Alciatum.' Andrea Alciato, *Emblematum libellus* (1534).

times shaped along archetypal models that may go back to prehistoric times. An example is La Perrière's 'Lievres & chiens couronnes soutiennent' (*Theatre*, 92; fig. 37). The prince, metonymically abstracted into a sceptre and crown, comes between the animals confronting each other, while at the same time supporting the crown and sceptre. This formal model may be found in heraldic arms, but, despite Praz's claim[51] that La Perrière took it from Machiavelli's *The Prince*, it actually goes back to neolithic times where it represented a taming of the savage forces of nature through the submissive posture of the animals, and human creative power through the symmetry of their positions.[52]

The repertoire of usable motifs was actually quite limited, and left little room for what we think of as original composition, for the intended audience needed to recognize the emblem motif and be somehow surprised by the way it was being used in a given emblem. Hence, motifs were often

XCII.

PRince qui veult que ſa vertu fleuró
ne,
Et que ſõ bruict ſoit en tous lieux famé:
Pour aſſeurer ſon ſceptrꝫ & ſa courõne,
Fault que des ſiens il ſoit crainct & amé.
Par ce moyen ſera bien reclamé,
Et des ſubiectz honnoré nuict & iour.
Le liepure crainct le chiẽ à grãd amour.
Deux ennemys ferme paix entretiẽnẽt
Craictꝫ & amour tiẽnẽt Roys en ſeiour.
Liepures & chiẽs les courõnes ſouſtiẽnẽt

N ii

Fig. 37. Guillaume de La Perrière, *Theatre des bons engins* (1540ns), emblem 92.

subjected to curious mannerist variations. Sometimes a motif was functional; that is, it played a role in the economy of the personification or allegory. But occasionally it served simply as an identifying attribute or a relatively general background *support*, or foil, for some symbolic action. In La Perrière's emblems the eagle can either enter into the economy of the symbolic action, as in emblem 52, where Aesop's 'L'aigle se plainct comme mal fortunée, / Quand d'une flesche on l'a frappée à mort,' because the feathers came from an eagle; or the eagle can serve simply to identify Jupiter, as in emblem 57. Fortune's sail is simply an identifying marker in *Theatre*, 20, as is Cupid's blindfold in *Theatre*, 81 (fig. 38), where it actually impedes Cupid's gardening. Or sometimes the motif falls between the two functions as in Corrozet's emblem 'Vertu meilleure que richesse' (sig. O1^{v}), where the palm branch weighs more heavily in the scale than worldly riches. The palm is a traditional sign for virtue because of its qualities of resistance. But it also functions in the economy of the design of this emblem by being lighter than gold; as a result, it can usefully indicate the paradox to be explained in the long text.

When the picture was not executed for the emblem it was being used to illustrate – or sometimes even when it was – it was common too for ele-

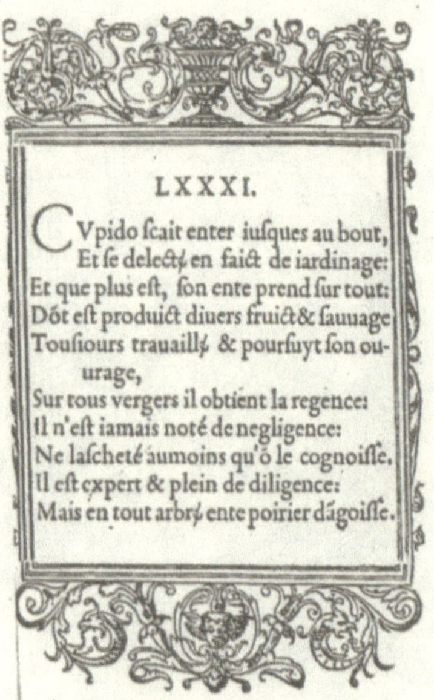

LXXXI.

Cvpido ſcait enter iuſques au bout,
Et ſe delecte en faict de iardinage:
Et que plus eſt, ſon ente prend ſur tout:
Dōt eſt produict diuers fruict & ſauuage
Touſiours trauaille & pourſuyt ſon ouurage,
Sur tous vergers il obtient la regence:
Il n'eſt iamais noté de negligence:
Ne laſcheté aumoins qu'ō le cognoiſſe.
Il eſt expert & plein de diligence:
Mais en tout arbre ente poirier dãgoiſſe.

Fig. 38. Guillaume de La Perrière, *Theatre des bons engins* (1540ns), emblem 81.

ments of the emblem picture to go unattended in the emblematic interpretation of it. In one of the *Emblemes* that accompanied his translation of the *Tableau de Cebes* (1543), 'N'entreprendre trop d'affaires à une fois,' (f. 50), Corrozet used an illustration from his 1542 translation of Aesop[53] that can be taken to be a generic hunting scene, but the fox pictured there is not even mentioned in the emblem text, and the same is true of the deer in Gueroult's emblem 21, 'Irriter ne faut d'avantage l'homme courroucé,' where the poet concentrates exclusively on the horse and rider.

When elements of the illustration are used in a symbolic development, they may be used syntagmatically or paradigmatically. An example is the fire that Corrozet uses in his rendering of 'Accroissement d'yre est à eschever' (*Hecatomgraphie*, G1v). In the woodcut a man appears to be striking a fire with a sword. The quatrain explains: 'Ne frappes le feu d'une espée / Quand il est en sa grand' challeur, / Se l'ire n'est bien attrempée, / Ne soys trop importun parleur.' In the long text, the fire becomes the 'feu d'ire' (G2r) and the sword is the 'glaive de la bouche' (G2r). Thus, the two elements mesh and begin to take shape as the syntagm of some as yet unarticulated allegory. Moreover, when La Perrière presents the 'dict pitagoricque' upon which this emblem is based ('Le feu de glaive attiser ne convient'), he explains that it will be reduced 'en sens alegoricque' (*Theatre*, 7, ll. 1, 4).

Emblemes. LIIII.

De leſcripture ſaincte.

Il n'appartient indifferentement
A tout chaſcun uoir la ſaincte eſcripture,
Sinon aux bons, parfaictz d'entendemēt,
Suyuantz l'egliſe & ſa doctrine pure:
Car il en uient ſcandaleuſe aduanture
De la bailler à gens trop curieux.
Couſteau trenchāt faict treſgriefue bleſ-
ſeure
Entre les mains de l'homme furieux.

Fig. 39. 'De l'escripture saincte.' Gilles Corrozet, *Emblemes* (1543), f. 54.

Corrozet also used this *Hecatomgraphie* illustration for another emblem in the sequence appended to his translation of the *Tableau de Cebes*. Entitled 'De l'escripture saincte' (f. 54), this emblem (fig. 39) warns that the Bible is a dangerous weapon in the hands of those who are not prepared to receive and understand the Holy Word. The sword represents the Bible, but the fire has no specific *signifié*. That is, it has no equivalent term in the hypothetical four-term homology introduced by the equivalence between the sword and the Bible; the whole scene simply evokes the damage that can be done by wielding weapons imprudently or improperly. Here an example of a dangerous or imprudent act is connected to another (the misuse of the Bible) through a metaphor (the sword representing the Bible); and the reader will know this is imprudent against the background of other emblems and perhaps proverbial lore.

Saunders[54] finds the illustration to be 'used less satisfactorily' in this emblem than the one in the *Hecatomgraphie* with the same woodcut, but

XXI.

QVi porte espée estant oingte de miel,
Monstre qu'il est du rang des hipocrites,
Qui soubz doulceur, tiennent caché leur fiel,
En euidence ung iour seront reduictes
Leurs faulcetez, & cautelles mauldictes:
Car tel uerra, qui oncques n'a eu ueue,
Leur espée est bien trenchante & ague.
Qu'ilz ont uoulu en ce point de miel oingdre,
Ce nonobstant, une mouche menue,
Ne lerra pas à les asprement poindre.

D iii

Fig. 40. Guillaume de La Perrière, *Theatre des bons engins* (1540ns), emblem 21.

this one may be more enlightening about the formation of emblems, since the cut was apparently not made for this emblem, but for the earlier Corrozet emblem. Stephen Rawles tells us that it was used only in these two places (unlike some of the cuts in the *Hecatomgraphie*, which were used in the illustration of as many as eleven different works).[55] Obviously, the action portrayed would have limited its possible applications, and the fact that it was not used indiscriminately suggests that Janot did care about the appropriateness of a given illustration to the text it was illustrating. And despite Saunders' disdain, the illustration is perfectly appropriate for an emblem discussing the Scriptures. Charles, cardinal de Bourbon, had chosen for his device a flaming sword, and it was to recall his guiding maxim that proposed the Scriptures as the true sword of prelates;[56] so Corrozet was working here within a clearly accepted emblematic context. The difference is simply that this emblem turns on a metaphor built paradigmatically by comparing two situations from the storehouse of commonplaces about dangerous actions. The *Hecatomgraphie* emblem, on the other hand, is a fragment of an allegorical syntagm.

Corrozet's illustration for this Pythagorean dictum is formally quite different from that of La Perrière (*Theatre*, 7), but La Perrière does have another emblem whose illustration could well have served as a formal model for that of Corrozet or, more likely, could have been made following the same prototype. In *Theatre*, 21, we see a man brandishing a sword surrounded by flies, and he is positioned much like the man in Corrozet's emblem (fig. 40). The revised text of this emblem in the third edition provides a particularly clear clue to the meaning that cannot be gleaned from inspection of the picture: the sword is 'greased with honey': 'Qui porte espée estant oingte de miel, / Monstre qu'il est du rang des hipocrites' (ll. 1–2). Such people are hypocrites because 'soubz doulceur, tiennent caché leur fiel,' (l. 3). But this will do them no good because it is clear that their sword is sharp ('bien trenchante & ague'), and even if they do anoint their sword with honey, bees will still sting them. There has been a transfer of qualities here: now it is the sword that represents anger, or bad blood (*fiel*).[57]

The paradigmatic use of signs is most conspicuous in the reading of plants and animals. The cypress and the fig tree were particularly intriguing to emblematists. In *Le Theatre* La Perrière moralizes on the fact that 'Le Cypres est arbre fort delectable, / Droict, bel, & hault, & plaisant en verdure: / Mais quant au fruict, il est peu proffitable' (emblem 65), while in *La Morosophie* (emblem 81), he more optimistically reflects that 'le Cyprés ha semence fort menue, / Mais son ramage est beau, & tient grand place: / Raison de soy (avant que soit cogneûe) / Est fort petite, et puys fait grosse trace.'

Such emblems are interesting in part because they demonstrate how the symbolic vocabulary of early French emblems can be used in many ways, and indeed must be used in many ways because it is in fact quite limited. The ground rules for this quasi-ideogrammatic language were set in large measure by La Perrière and Corrozet, who each composed two collections of emblems. La Perrière, at least, was aware of the role he was playing in creating a genre; this is clear in the introductory remarks to his *Morosophie*, where he claims credit as the first to compress his emblems into quatrains in both Latin and French.[58] If he is aware of being first, this means others were perceived as doing something different in the past, but within a common generic context, and it also means that La Perrière expects to serve as a model for those who will follow him. And by indicating that the quatrain will be his choice of epigrammatic form, La Perrière underlines the importance of uniformity in shaping a generic pattern. Although we often see hints in Corrozet's emblems of what he may have thought an emblem to be, we find in no writer from the period as acute a sense of participating in the formation of a genre as we do in La Perrière.

Occasionally, there is in these early emblems an interesting discrepancy

Fig. 41. 'La statue de Caia Cecilia.' Gilles Corrozet, *Hecatomgraphie* (1540), N8^{v}.

between the illustration and the text that reminds us no single, unified creative impulse guided the elaboration of most emblems. Greta Dexter and Jerome Schwartz have already noticed a sort of subversive tension between illustration and text in certain of these emblems.[59] Their examples, taken from La Perrière, can be supplemented by others showing the same kind of tension in the work of Corrozet. In 'La statue de Caia Cecilia' (fig. 41), the woodcut shows the statue of a naked woman (she is clearly on a pedestal). The statue is positioned in an open landscape and there are some objects on the ground around her. The quatrain reads: 'Toute femme pudicque / Doibt estre domesticque, / Non pas aller dehors / Pour mielx monstrer son corps' (sig. N8^{v}). This naked woman makes no more than a gesture to 'pudicité' and she is clearly 'dehors.' The long text points out the 'queloigne' (= *quenouille*?), *fuseau*, and *pantoufle*, which are the attributes of domesticity; but in the illustration that, Stephen Rawles tell us,[60] was made for the *Hecatomgraphie* emblem, they seem to be scattered far from the statue, and as if carelessly abandoned, rather than 'pres' as the long text suggests they should be. In short, the illustration seems, if not to contradict the text, at least to establish a certain distance or tension between the two that could not go unnoticed by competent readers who were used to reading significance into the oppositions near/far, dressed/naked, inside/outside. And since there was still a strong Church tradition that one did not read a picture independently of the text that was supposed to inform it with meaning, the competent reader might well have looked on an illustration such as this one as willfully subversive.

In other illustrations made for these emblems, we notice other types of discrepancies. Corrozet's emblem on 'Calumnie' (L6^{v} – L7^{r}) is interesting on many accounts (fig. 42). First, it enacts that part of the emblematic process involved in the description and interpretation of works of art, for the long text is devoted entirely to a moralizing or allegorizing description of Apelles' version of Calumny. But this 'description' may, following a long tradition, actually have been a 'prescription' for the artist who designed the woodcut, and that woodcut is not a perfect reflection of the description. The long text tells us that Calumny holds a torch in her right hand (l. 15), but the woodcut has put it in her left hand; the text tells us that Envy is in front of Calumny (l. 22), but this is not entirely clear in the illustration.

Such problems have to do both with the imprecision of the woodcut illustration as compared to late medieval illumination and with the requirements of disposition within a restricted space. One might object that these discrepancies between text and illustration simply indicate some jamming of the channels of communication between the author and an artist who may not have understood the text very well. If that were to be perceived as a normal occurrence, such discrepancies would not be considered meaningful, and indeed, if personifications were perceived in a purely allegorical space, then they might not even be perceived as discrepancies at all; that is why Cupid, in one of Van Veen's love emblems, can use his bow to row the raft made from his quiver furiously in one direction while the sail made from his blindfold billows out behind, suggesting that the wind is pushing him in the other direction.[61]

Calumnie.

A tort & par faictz indecentz
Deuant les iuges d'ignorance
Calumnie porte nuyſance
Contre les iuſtes innocentz.

Fig. 42. 'Calumnie.' Gilles Corrozet, *Hecatomgraphie* (1540), L6v.

But such was not, I believe, the case in any absolute way. First, the emblem, as I would argue, came into existence in part to provide an allegorical framework for moralizing meditations upon objects, birds, and beasts that must increasingly have been perceived within the single, and increasingly dominant, context of empirical reality. And such discrepancies would therefore have been noticed. Perhaps the best evidence for this can be found in one of the illustrations for La Perrière's *Theatre* in the series of editions Jean de Tournes began to publish in 1545. Jerome Schwartz has noted the discrepancy between text and illustration in the emblem of the

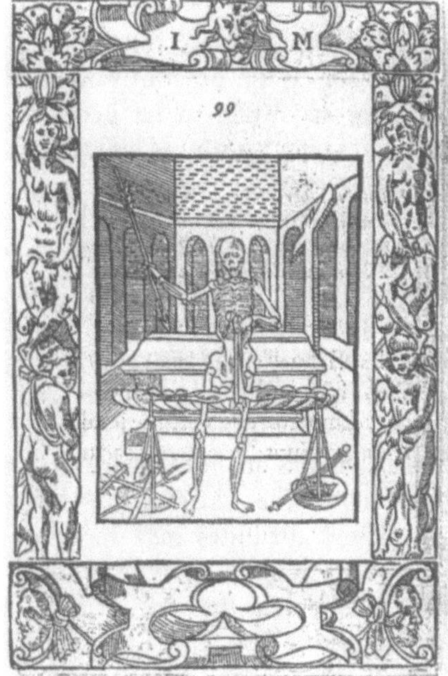

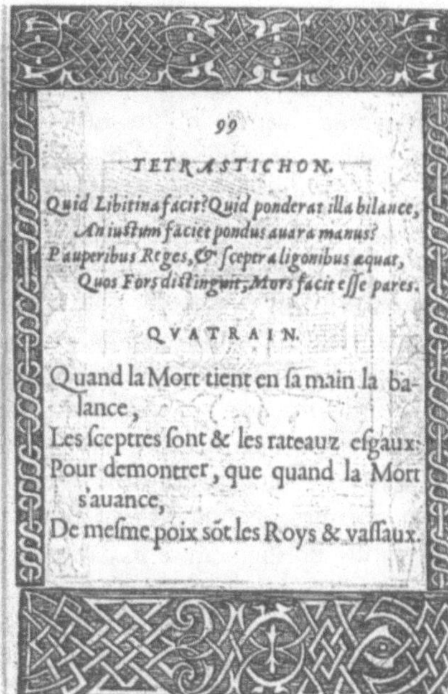

99

TETRASTICHON.

Quid Libitina facit? Quid ponderat illa bilance,
An iustum faciet pondus auara manus?
Pauperibus Reges, & sceptra ligonibus æquat,
Quos Fors distinguit, Mors facit esse pares.

QVATRAIN.

Quand la Mort tient en sa main la balance,
Les sceptres sont & les rateaux esgaux:
Pour demontrer, que quand la Mort s'auance,
De mesme poix sōt les Roys & vassaux.

Fig. 43. Guillaume de La Perrière, *La Morosophie* (1553), emblem 99.

domestic Venus in the Janot editions of the *Theatre*,[62] where the illustration shows her outside and naked in clear contradiction to the text. De Tournes corrects this inconsistency with a clothed Venus who is clearly situated in the inside portion of a scene equally distributed between an inside and an outside (fig. 31).

Usually, however, the scene collaborated with the text to deliver an unambiguous message. The imagined scene could carry its edifying message in a number of ways. It might function as a parable, in which a moral is drawn from an occurrence of everyday life by pointing out its paradigmatic exemplarity. An example would be Corrozet's emblem 'Amytié entre les freres' (E8^v–F1), portraying a father showing his sons the value of unity by demonstrating how difficult it is to break a bundle of sticks that has been tied together. But if emblems like this one are comfortably situated in the realm of everyday reality, others present paradoxical situations that are impossible among the constraints of physical reality and make sense only in an allegorical space. Such is the case when La Perrière uses the image of the scales in the *Theatre* to show that 'Pour peu de cas trebuche foy legere, / Et pour ung rien soudain amont se lance: / Une plumette, ung grain de cheneviere, / Plus poisera, contre elle à la balance' (emblem 14). At the end of *La Morosophie*, we find Death in the form of a skeleton, holding a set of scales where the tools in one pan balance the obviously lighter crown and sceptre in the other (fig. 43), for according to La Perrière: 'Quand la Mort tient en sa main la balance, / Les sceptres sont & les rateaux esgaux: / Pour demontrer, que quand la mort s'avance, / De mesme poix sont les Roys et vassaux' (emblem 99). These emblems depend nevertheless on physical nature to the extent that they deny it to create the paradoxes necessary to show that, despite appearances, 'foy legere' is really much less substantial than it may appear and that all men are indeed equal in death.[63]

As we have seen (72–6), the late medieval revolution in the presentation of personifications in art was based on a system of definition by epithet, and hence personifications and the gods of ancient mythology were perceived in the early Renaissance as composite characters, whose qualities are manifest in an assemblage of attributes that reinforce one another like strings of synonymous epithets in a Renaissance text. These attributes may function through metonymy, as with the *fuseau*, *quenouille*, and *pantoufle* in Corrozet's 'La statue de Caia Cecilia,' which are the implements of domesticity, while Fortune's attributes – the wheel, the sail, and so on – are metaphorical.

Other late medieval techniques of pictorial coding could also be used in constructing emblem pictures, even when the source of the scene was fashionably humanist. La Perrière provides an interesting case in the second emblem of his *Theatre*. There we see Bacchus and Venus ensnaring Minerva: '... ce que nous fait entendre, / Que vin & femme, attrapent le plus saige.' The homely, proverbial cast of this last line alerts us that the context is not classical but late medieval and proverbial. The three characters are no more than convenient ciphers for love, drink, and the wise man. And although the net may recall the snare of Hephaistos (*Odyssey*, VIII, 266ff.), it is actually the snare of love that was so common in medieval art, either in the form of intricately knotted ropes (as in the Oxford manuscript of the *Roman de la Rose)* or as a net covering a man (as in a marginal illustration of the Smithfield Antiphonary). Classical references do no more here than provide a pleasant patina of fashionable humanist lore to update age-old wisdom that is far from cutting its ties to its medieval sources. Indeed, the net provides a kind of visual emphasis that makes the scene even more effective by using commonplace visual cues in an unexpected context.

Many of the early emblems were built around pictures that showed isolated plants or animals, following the models of the bestiaries and herbiaries, or they presented mythological figures and personifications as they had been elaborated, often with literary models, in one or more of the traditions of painting. Such is the case, for example, with the Calumny of Apelles that, following Botticelli, Coustau used as the basis for an emblem in his *Pegma.*[64] Such models were not abandoned, and indeed they were institutionalized in the language of emblems by the iconographical manuals, most notably that of Valeriano. But besides these kinds of figures, there developed a growing taste for the kind of symbolic collage one sees, but rarely, in the emblems of Corrozet and La Perrière.

Such composites are not unrelated to the northern allegorical still-life paintings of the late sixteenth and early seventeenth centuries, still lifes used more often than not as a *memento mori.* In France we see a trend toward an increasing use of this kind of composition in the emblems of Georgette de Montenay, where the Germanic influence of the Lorraine artist Pierre Woeiriot helped change the course of French emblematics. It is here that the commonest rhetorical figures, containing dead, or dying, metaphors, are brought vividly to life by their translation into nightmarishly concrete literalizations that break all bonds with banal everyday reality in a way that the earlier literalizations of the *proverbes figurés* almost never did.

There was very little religious imagery in most of the early books, and since she was a Protestant writing as a Protestant, we might expect to find much more than we do in Georgette de Montenay's *Emblemes et devises chrestiennes.* The Protestant attitude toward imagery was so iconoclastic that we might on the other hand, be surprised Montenay even composed emblems at all. As Simone Perrier has noted, she may have used statues of Christ, and the like, in order to put additional distance between symbol and reality.[65] In any event, since it was unacceptable to work variations on traditional Christian symbolism, the effect here was achieved mainly through vivid and often fascinating literalization of metaphors that had faded through constant use.

The emblems of Jean-Jacques Boissard and Jean Mercier seem to have been somewhat isolated exceptions as far as the French tradition is concerned. They are both in a humanist tradition much more alive in the late sixteenth century in Germany than in France. Indeed, as I have already suggested (149), Boissard worked under the influence of German humanists and artists, such as Theodore de Bry. Probably we can get a better idea of the late Renaissance French emblem and its place in the culture of the time from the manuscript emblems of Loys Papon and Anne d'Urfé than from the few volumes that were published after 1570.

The construction of Loys Papon's love emblems is particularly revealing of the formal motivation of such compositions. This group of thirty-six

Fig. 44. 'La fermesse d'amour.' Loys Papon, *Enblemes et devises d'amour*. c. 1580.

emblems, presumably composed in 1581, follows a nearly 1200-line 'Discours a Mademoyselle Pamfile' in a manuscript that was prepared to look like a printed book.[66] The section of the manuscript of interest to us here is entitled 'Enblemes [sic] et Devises d'Amour.' In the prose *envoi* addressed to Mlle Pamfile, presumably his *destinataire unique*, Papon describes the collection as 'quelques stances mises au pied des Emblemes amoureux' (9). May we then understand the pictures to be the 'emblemes' and the texts to be the 'devises d'amour' (here in the more common Renaissance sense of the word as 'discours' or 'propos')?

If the 'emblems' here are pictures, they are not ordinary pictures representing narrative, naturalistic, or mythological scenes. Rather, all but six of these pictures represent symbolic collages explained by texts that, for their part, are not really to be understood as part of the so-called 'emblem.' We must then assume that Papon labelled these compositions as emblems because each is so composed that its parts must be read as symbols and decoded in relation to one another in such a way as to yield some message, in the form, presumably, of a syntagm. So the 'picture'-emblem turns out to be a 'text' anyway, and the other text becomes an elucidating commentary, but one that is often essential in the decoding process – it is a 'commentary' only in principle.

Some of these constructions are built, at least partially, with rebus signs. Thus, 'la fermesse d'amour' is an S formed of the two parts of a broken bow, with the arcs closed (*fermés*) by an arrow. This variation on a *devise* of Valentine Visconti, which Papon could have found in Paradin's *Devises heroiques*, still represents fidelity, but in a novel twist, Papon introduces

Fig. 45. 'Loeilhade amoureuse.' Loys Papon, *Enblemes et devises d'amour*. c. 1580.

the idea of love metonymically through the use of Cupid's bow, broken in two, together with an arrow to create the sign in a virtuoso display of mannerist emblematic bricolage (fig. 44)! Elsewhere, Papon turns to the common pun on feathers (*pennes = peines*), but generally he avoided such pure rebus signs in favour of visual pastiches of common emblematic signs like the caduceus, formed in the same way from Cupid's implements, together with the flames, tears, and other attributes of Petrarchan love. Nevertheless, the presence of some rebus signs suggests how the pictures are to be 'read.' I say 'read' because these pictures are meaningless viewed in their totality, as unified single scenes; they must be deciphered syntagmatically with each sign being decoded and then understood in relation to the other parts of the composition and its position within the whole composition.

'Loeilhade amoureuse' is a good example of Papon's technique (fig. 45). In the picture, we see a winged eye, reminiscent of Alberti's famous device, shot through by two arrows; at the sides and above, we see flames, while below tears are falling. The text explains: 'Loeil qui volage assault un autre oeil plus aigu, / Et qui sans se deffendre, y demeure vaincu, / Transverssé de ses tretz jette flammes & larmes.' The metaphors from the old Petrarchan tradition used to underpin the rhetoric of this text were by that time dead or dying, and had recently borne the brunt of a world-weary Ronsard's irony in his sonnets for Hélène. But the picture gives them a semblance of life that was perhaps to pique the interest, or at least curiosity, of Mlle Pamfile.

Papon's process is even clearer in 'L'Esquif d'amour' (87); the picture is well described in the first three lines of the *sixain*: 'Cest arc mis en esquif ou la trousse est en bas, / Sur la corde tendue, aux sagettes d'un mas, / Double-ayle sur la hunne air-souflé de ce voyle.' And the image established in the subject of this sentence is explained in the predicate: 'Montre en combien de ventz aux vagues de plesir, / Soubz les rames d'Amour, vogue nostre desir / Mais tousjours un escueil fait perir la nacelle.' The pessimistic last line is not shown in the picture, but it does remind us that the meaning of these images can only unfold in time. These images make sense only as texts.

In this sense, these 'emblems' hark back to hieroglyphics as they were understood at the beginning of the sixteenth century. That is, they are combinations of signs that can hypothetically stand alone as an ideogrammatic text, but will in reality need to be explained by a text because they lack the syntagmatic articulations of discursive language that would permit the reader to understand exactly how the different parts of the collage are related to one another to form the message they obviously contain. The hieroglyphic inscriptions in Colonna's *Hypnerotomachia Poliphili* functioned the same way in that work, and that is perhaps why the hieroglyphics were taken as a model for the early emblem, even when so few hieroglyphic signs were actually used in the creation of emblems.[67] Papon talks about hieroglyphics in his introduction to Anne d'Urfé's emblems, and in the illustrations for some of those emblems, he drew heavily on Valeriano's *Hieroglyphica*.[68]

Papon was an artist, of sorts, and it is to artists that we should look to understand some of what was happening in the creation of emblems in the late sixteenth century. For several reasons I have alluded to in passing, French printers came rather late to the use of copperplate engraving, especially in emblem books for which mid-century woodblocks were recut and reused until the end of the century and beyond. Artists preferred the copperplate technique, for they could control their production much more closely than with the woodblock prints, which require the intermediary of technicians. At the same time, printers lost some of their control over the production of emblem books, since the more costly copperplate engravings needed to be printed on special presses, often in another shop, and increasingly the artist became the originator or 'author' of emblems. This is the case with Theodore de Bry, and later Jacques Callot and Albert Flamen. And since these plates were often used in more than one suite of emblems, the pictures increasingly became the starting-point of the emblem, and so a myth of emblem production was born, not to be dispelled until very recently, as research has begun to show that the early emblem was really a textually based production.[69]

PART THREE

EMBLEMATICS AND THE STRUCTURING OF A CULTURE

8

Emblematics and Court Culture

'Applied emblematics' are typically the last subject treated in a study of emblems, but paradoxically, it is only to the extent that parallels and analogues may be found between emblems and other cultural phenomena of the *ancien régime* that emblems in themselves are relevant to the broader study of cultural history. As I have suggested elsewhere, it is historically most interesting to understand the emblem as a particularly revealing symptom of an epistemological condition that colours thought and, especially, its expression from the late fifteenth through the early eighteenth centuries. As a result, it is sometimes heuristically fruitful to characterize similarities between emblematic structures and the artistic composition or rhetorical organization of other cultural artefacts as examples of 'applied emblematics.'

In the account that follows, I shall understand the expression, translated from the German *angewandte Emblematik*, to refer very broadly to the application of the principles of emblematic construction, as they have been described in the earlier parts of this study, to literary composition and the making of other vehicles of cultural communication, whether for courtly ceremony, interior décor, or political propaganda. But I shall also take it to refer to the ways an audience, whether contemporary or modern, 'applies' these same principles to the understanding of pictorial compositions or literary works and, more generally, to the reading of early modern French culture.

The notion of 'applied emblematics,' then, encompasses both the use of symbolic motifs in ways that can be characterized as emblematic in settings other than emblem books, and the reception of discourse and art objects in ways that are conditioned by a familiarity with the structure of emblems or other emblematic forms such as the *impresa*. Emblematic portraiture, mod-

Fig. 46. 'Ardorem extincta testantur vivere flamma.'

elled on medallic portraits and their symbolic reverses, is particularly interesting, because it provides examples both of motifs used emblematically in painting and of complete emblematic compositions fully integrated into the portrait design.[1] The symbolic composition may be found on a reverse or a portrait cover, or it may be integrated into the portrait itself. In the first case, a portrait and a full *impresa* may be juxtaposed in some suggestive way, as in the device of palm and laurel branches with the motto *Virtutem forma decorat* on the reverse of the portrait of Ginevra de' Benci (1474) by Leonardo da Vinci at the National Gallery in Washington. Later, the full *impresa* was often displayed in the portrait itself, more or less discreetly relegated to some marginal space, as in the case of Clouet's engraved portrait of Catherine de Medicis, where her device of tears falling on quicklime with the motto *Ardorem extincta testantur vivere flamma* is positioned beneath her likeness in the lower margin (fig. 46).

On the other hand, a motif with no text may appear so obviously foreign to the naturalistic setting in which it is embedded as to be meaningful only in an emblematic way in relation to the other components of its setting. Such is the case in the Rogier Van der Weyden portrait of Francesco d'Este at the Metropolitan Museum of Art in New York; the sitter is holding a hammer and ring that are generally taken to be part of some as yet unidentified device, because they are clearly not purely ornamental and yet have no naturalistic relation either to each other or to the rest of the setting. Another example of the same kind of ostensibly unnatural juxtaposition may be found in Dürer's 1519 portrait of Maximilian holding a pomegranate (Kunsthistorisches Museum, Vienna). Here we can be almost certain it was intended as a device because the *Tot Zopiro* and pomegranate device of his relative Philip, as it was anthologized around 1600 by Typotius, suggests that this was a family device passed from a member of one generation to a descendant in the next (as occurred with François Ier's salamander device, which he inherited from Charles d'Orléans). In all such portraits, the elements we take to form the device do not have any other role assigned to them by the decorum of portraits. And so the emblematic model permits the viewer to 'read' an element that would otherwise be unreadable, as he contextualizes it as the motif of a device belonging to the sitter.[2]

Portraits can be emblematic in other ways as well. A case in point is Holbein's portrait of Erasmus at Longford Castle. There we see Erasmus standing at a parapet with his hands resting on a handsome book. On the fore-edge, where we would not necessarily expect to see a title, one can read the Greek inscription ΗΡΑΚΛΕΙΟΙ ΠΟΝΟΙ [The Labours of Hercules]. Perhaps the fore-edge inscription is a metaphoric summation of Erasmus' work, but certainly not in any boastful way. In the adage with the same expression, Erasmus tells us that the meaning is rather that such labours procure for their author a modicum of fame and a maximum of envy. Letters from Erasmus to Alciato in 1528 and again in 1531 make it clear that the expression remained very close to his mind and way of thinking, and might even be suitable as the motto for an Erasmian device, with any one of a number of possible scenes.[3]

When such a fragmentary motif or allusion in painting or discourse can be interpreted or integrated only in an allegorical way, it becomes, as I have contended,[4] an emblematic image. The emblematic image lies between the naturalistic and the allegorical because, on the one hand, its presentation is often highly realistic while, on the other hand, its lack of naturalistic links to the surrounding setting makes it understandable only through some kind of allegorical interpolation. Such is the case with almost any *impresa*, and it is true too in such emblematic portraits as the Ermine or Sieve portraits of Queen Elizabeth. These are 'emblematic images' simply because they may be understood to find a place in the economy of the whole only through an emblematic reading of them.

Following this criterion, it is evident that emblematic imagery was common in the decorative arts and festival décor throughout the period under consideration. Although by the later seventeenth and eighteenth centuries, complete emblems were commonly used in programs of interior decoration, especially in Germany and Austria,[5] such an explicit use of emblematics was rare in the sixteenth and early seventeenth centuries; the remarkable ceiling at Dampierre-sur-Boutonne or Lady Drury's Oratory at Hawstead Hall, both lavishly decorated with complete emblems and dating from the late sixteenth or early seventeenth centuries, are nearly unique.[6] The reason is, I think, that early in the period no need was felt to signal the emblematic, whereas by the eighteenth century, with its increasingly naturalistic view of the world, the emblematic needed more than ever to be bracketed, framed, and set apart from the surrounding world. And that is why we find more emblems *per se* in decorative schemes as we move toward the end of the *aetas emblematica*.

Applied emblematics may, however, be understood to comprise more than decorative schemes for attire, households and their contents, court and religious festivals, printers' marks, frontispieces and bookbinding design, reverses of medals, and the like. Throughout the seventeenth century, Jesuit schools, it would appear, taught the composition of emblems in the *classes de rhétorique*.[7] The rationale for including the art of making emblems in the pedagogical program of confessional schools must have been largely practical; the strategies of emblem composition provided useful compositional techniques for sermons, political propaganda, and instructional manuals.[8]

If the rhetorical structure of much upper-class and official communication followed the lines of emblematic models, then it would appear equally reasonable to expect texts and pictures to be read against a background of expectations bred from the same sources. And reading did function this way from the very early years of the *aetas emblematica*. That is, like emblems, certain types of pictures were interpreted in idiosyncratic and partial ways that made them serve as convenient vehicles for moral or doctrinal messages that would be unexpected in relation to the traditional ways of interpreting such imagery. No longer was a picture expected to express, icon-like, a single and immutable reality, in which the *signifiant* was coterminous with its *signifié*, and actually participated in it to some extent. This trend mirrors the abandonment of a conception of language in which there was believed to exist some intrinsic and essential relation between word and thing, and its replacement by a conception of language as a system of arbitrary signs.[9] Syncretism and the breakup of the monolithic view of the universe from the medieval Catholic perspective fostered these trends as they encouraged a multiplicity of interpretations, depending on an increasingly individualized point of view. Already, in the Middle Ages, images could be interpreted *in bono* or *in malo*, and sometimes in a variety of ways. This possibility was expanded during the Renaissance, and the Pandora's box thus opened formed the basis for the development of the emblematic mode of thought.

The relation between the emblem form and a mode of thought, manifest in various ways in art and discourse, is particularly evident in direct and conscious adaptations of canonical emblems for particular and individualized situations. One striking example is Simon Bouquet's *Imitations et traductions de cent dixhuict emblesmes dAlciat* (see above, 145–6). Although many of Bouquet's poems are fairly straightforward translations of Alciato's Latin, others provide interesting examples of the way the generalized wisdom of Alciato's emblems might be used to structure solutions to the particularized dilemmas that arise in everyday life, or to describe particular political situations. When, for example, a neighbour – 'un certain hobereau d'anjou,' the subtitle tells us – urges Bouquet to sell the rest of his inheritance in Paris and buy a property near him in Anjou, Bouquet lets Alciato's famous emblem *Aliquid mali propter vicinum malum* (165; f. 10^{r}), with its title from Plautus combined with Aesop's fable of the two pots, shape his decision to steer clear of what could be a dangerous friendship with a powerful neighbour (fig. 47).

As in this case, Bouquet's application of Alciato's general moral lessons to particular circumstances or situations is often mediated by a subtitle that can work powerfully in orienting our reading of Bouquet's version. Such is the case with Alciato's emblem 193, *Amor filiorum / Amour envers ses enfants*, which Bouquet has subtitled 'Contre les putains qui les estouffent' (f. 22^{v}). Even though the poem itself remains very close to Alciato's epigram, the subtitle recalls sordid rumours that circulated about the court of Henri III, and thus turns Alciato's moralizing emblem into a satirical one for the readers of Bouquet's French.[10] When Bouquet takes up Alciato's emblem *In eos qui supra vires quicquam audent* (58, f. 10^{v}), the resulting satire is even more explicitly developed as Bouquet turns from Alciato's subject-line, expressed in the quatrains, to a strong, clear attack on the Ligue in the tercets. The reader does not come upon this attack unexpectedly, for the subtitle addresses the emblem 'Aux ligueurs veincuz par le Roy.' The quatrains present Alciato's rendering, somewhat expanded, of

In eos qui supra vires quidquid audent.

Dvm dormit, dulci recreat dum corpora ſomno
Sub picea, & clauam cæteraque arma tenet,
Alciden pygmæa manus proſternere letho
Poſſe putat, vires non bene docta ſuas.
Excitus ipſe, velut pulices, ſic proterit hoſtem,
Et ſæui implicitum pelle leonis agit.

Contre ceux qui entreprennent plus quilz ne peuuent
Aux ligueurs vaincuz par le Roy.

Hercule soubz vn pin voulut prendre repos,
Ayant soubz luy la peau du lyon estendue,
tenant entre ses bras sa pezante massue
Le doux sommeil en fin se coulla dans ses os:
Le peuple pigmean de loccir tint propos.
Mais leur peu de valeur leur estoit mconnue,
Car sesueillant hercul comme poux il les tue
Bref au lieu de combatre ilz luy tournent le doz
Presomptueux ligueur cela te doit apprendre
Contre la magesté de ne plus entreprendre
Si ne veux esprouuer vn triste repentir
A la sedition retire donc la bride
Ou tu esprouueras henry second Alcide
Qui leffort de son bras ta desia faict sentir.

Fig. 47. *In eos qui supra vires quicquam audent.* Simon Bouquet, *Imitations et traductions de cent dixhuict emblesmes dAlciat*, f. 10v.

the story of the Pygmies who try to kill the sleeping Hercules. Then the tercets develop the following comparison:

Presomptueux Ligueur cela te doit apprendre
  Contre la mageste de ne plus entreprendre
  Si ne veux esprouver un triste repentir
A la sedition retire donc la bride
  Ou tu esprouveras henry second Alcide
  Qui leffort de son bras ta desia faict sentir.

Bouquet's choice of this emblem as a vehicle for attacking the Ligue must have been prompted not only by Alciato's motto, but also by the motif of Hercules, which makes this emblem fit perfectly with one of the traditional mythological characterizations of the French king in the sixteenth century as the *Hercule gaulois*.[11]

Although Bouquet names few names in his variations on Alciato, one senses that many of his satirical pieces are directed against very specific *bêtes noires*. His version of Alciato's emblem *Quod non capit Christus rapit fiscus* (147, f. 31ᵛ), for example, is directed 'Contre un certain tresorier de lespargne.' The rebirth of such *ad hominem* satire in the sixteenth century must have had its origins in the development of Renaissance individualism and, stimulated by the religious wars, became increasingly common in the second half of the century.[12] Emblematic images in various settings often served as vehicles for political satire and government propaganda. Satirical devices, or criticism of personal devices with a satirical intent, were used to focus attacks on Henri III and the cardinal de Lorraine; and Henri IV used the devices created for the *jetons* he distributed as *étrennes* to publicize and advance specific political goals.[13]

For more complicated attacks, emblem-like compositions were developed. A number of examples have been preserved in Pierre de L'Estoile's precious album, *Les Belles Figures et drolleries de la Ligue*.[14] One piece is entitled *Fides vitrea*; within an oval frame containing the legend *Sic Judam fregerat aurum*, a woman's hand throws pieces of money into a cup, which breaks, thus spilling most of the money (fig. 48). Beneath the picture, one reads the following verse from Psalm 108: *Fiant filii ejus orphani et uxor ejus vidua*, and the accompanying sonnet is pure invective against the traitor Vitry; it ends with following four sardonic lines: 'Croirons-nous donc, Vitry, ces choses bien nouvelles, / Qu'un Vitry, c'est a dire un traistre et un trompeur, / Un infidelle Arabe, ayt vendu son honneur, / En trahissant Meaux au Roy des Infidelles?'[15] It is interesting to note the use of one of

Fig. 48. 'Fides vitrea.' *Les Belles Figures et drolleries de la Ligue*, f. 29.

the Psalms here, for the Psalms, as we have seen, had been integrated into political propaganda in France throughout the Renaissance, although not usually for satirical ends.[16]

Compositions like this one often date from the period following the death of Henri III when Henri de Navarre was trying to consolidate his hold on royal power. Some are satirical and directed, as in the previous example, against the party of the king presumptive. Others are political propaganda designed to advance Henri's cause; in both cases the emblematic form works equally well. In 1594 Jean Le Clerc published one such composition as a broadside entitled 'La Delivrance de la France par le Persee François' (fig. 49). L'Estoile's editors describe the engraving this way: 'Andromède (la France), entièrement nue, est enchaînée sur un rocher, au milieu des flots. A gauche, le monstre à tête de bélier et à corps de dragon se retourne, à l'approche du Persée françois (le Roi de Navarre), monté sur un

La deliurance de la France par le Perſée François.

FRANCE, comme Andromede à la mort fut offerte,
Mal voulue des ſiens, & d'vn peuple eſtranger,
Son pays fut ſon mal, ſa guerre, & ſon danger,
Où ſon bien deuoit eſtre, y demeuroit ſa perte:
Le ciel faſché de veoir vne iniuſtice aperte,
Vn Perſée enuoya à fin de la venger,
Vn Perſée François qui la vint deſgaiger
Des vagues de la mort, qui l'auoient ja couuerte:
Le monſtre qui gardoit entre ſes dens ſa mort,
Sentit combien le bras de Perſée eſtoit fort:
Comme feit l'Eſpagnol de HENRY quatrieſme.
FRANCE, ſois luy fidelle, & ne te laiſſe plus
Attacher de doublons, & ne croy aux abus
De ceux qui ont rongné l'or de ton Diadéme.

A Paris, par Iean le Clerc, rue S. Iean de Latran, à la Salemandre. Auec Priuilege du Roy. 1594.

Fig. 49. 'La Delivrance de la France par le Persee François.' *Les Belles Figures et drolleries de la Ligue*, f. 31.

cheval ailé et prêt à le frapper d'un coup d'épée. A droite le Grand Prêtre et la Synagogue regardent du rivage, avec stupeur, l'évenement qui se prépare.' The following sonnet serves as a gloss for the picture in such a way as to form a complete emblem:

France, comme Andromède à la mort fut offerte,
Mal voulue des siens, et d'un peuple estranger,
Son pays fut son mal, sa guerre, et son danger:
Où son bien devoit estre, y demeuroit sa perte.
Le Ciel, fasché de veoir une injustice aperte,
Un Persée envoya afin de la venger,
Un Persée François qui la vint desgaiger
Des vagues de la mort, qui l'avoient jà couverte:
Le monstre qui gardoit entre ses dens sa mort,
Sentit combien le bras de Persée estoit fort:
Comme feit l'Espagnol de HENRY quatriesme.
FRANCE, sois-luy fidelle, et ne te laisse plus
Attacher de doublons, & ne croy aux abus
De ceux qui ont rongné l'or de ton Diadème.[17]

Although the comparison is explicit from the very beginning, with an apostrophe to France in the first line, and a clear periphrastic reference to Henry IV in the second quatrain, the quatrains are mainly devoted to expressing the mythological situation, which will then receive its specific political application in the tercets. There, as was often the case in propaganda emblems, the moral precept that usually falls at the end of an emblem is replaced by an exhortation, in this case urging the French to unite behind their new king.[18]

Françoise Bardon has shown that the illustration of the motif comes directly from Reusner's *Emblemata* of 1581 (254) where the Perseus and Andromeda episode is used as an example of 'Principis boni imago.' For Reusner the motif is used to represent something more general, but with Andromeda representing Ecclesia, we see that even his emblem is not entirely detached from current events. Nevertheless, the placard is wedded to an event, or political situation, in a way that makes it inapplicable, unlike Reusner's emblem, to any other situation. Reusner provides the open form, the empty vessel; the placard provides the use or application of the image. The French chose this vessel, at this time and in these circumstances, in part at least because of the similarity in form between this myth and the legend of St George, to whom the French were particularly attached, and because

Reusner had already associated the myth of Perseus with the image of the good king.[19]

Another example is the emblematic use of the story of Milo of Crotona in the placard entitled 'Le prix d'Outrecuidance, et Los d'Alliance' (fig. 50). Coustau had used this motif to build an emblem 'Contre gens rempliz de leurs sens,' a criticism of pride, and this model was followed in the Netherlandish *Mikrokosmos* of the 1570s. Toward the end of the century, Boissard's emblem on Milo is entitled 'Eventus stultorum magister.' This is the emblematic context that prepared the placard emblem SIC FRANCIA DIVISA COALESCIT, with the tree representing France, and Milo, her proud enemies.[20] As usual, the choice of motif appears to be motivated by a familiarity with the image that must have been prepared, at least in good part, by the emblem books. Like emblems, too, this composition engages the viewer's interest by the lack of evident relationship between the title and the composition itself; that will become apparent in the dense prose that captions the different parts of the picture.[21]

The reference to the Spanish in the Perseus and Andromeda placard sonnet provides an important clue to the motivation behind the other major group of satirical French emblems dating from this period. The tensions resulting from Henri IV's wars with Spain produced or rejuvenated the unflattering national typing of the Spanish nobility that provides the subject matter for the *Emblesmes sus les actions et perfections et meurs du Segnor Espagnol. Traduit du Castillien.*[22] 'Hardly an emblem book proper,' according to Praz,[23] this collection of sixteen satirical engravings does, nevertheless, illustrate the very loose understanding of the word 'emblème' around the turn of the seventeenth century,[24] and it also highlights the trend toward more politically engaged and propagandistic uses of the emblem forms after 1570. Quite simply, the author of this little collection has taken a series of proverbial expressions, based mainly on animal proverbs, to sketch out a caricature of the *miles gloriosus* the French imagined the Spanish nobleman to be in the closing years of the sixteenth century.[25]

In the first engraving we see our hero, under the caption 'Un ange en l'Eglise,' (3) kneeling in prayer before an altar. Then we see him as 'Un diable en la maison' (5). Next, the Spaniard is portrayed at table with a wolf seated on the floor nearby as a silent reproach that he is 'un loup en table' (7). In the fourth engraving, we see the Segnor seated on a chamber pot accompanied by a pig ('un pourceau en sa chambre,' 9), and so on.[26] In most cases, the animal and the cavalier share an allegorical space in a vivid visual translation of the proverbial equivalence. Such is the case to show that he is 'un Lyon en garnison' (15), but more realistically, the author shows him fleeing *like* a

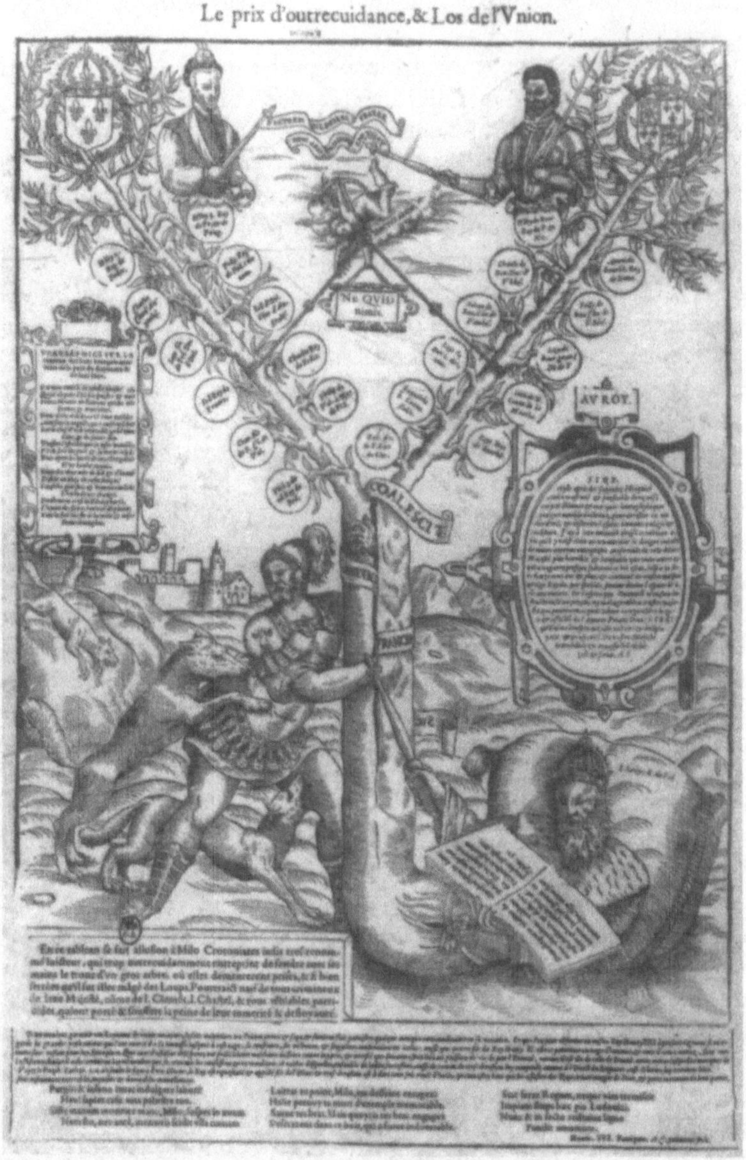

Le prix d'outrecuidance,& Los de l'Vnion.

Fig. 50. 'Le prix d'Outrecuidance, et Los d'Alliance.' *Les Belles Figures et drolleries de la Ligue*, f. 31ᵛ.

rabbit (and followed by a hare) to demonstrate that he is 'un Lievre estant assiegé' (17–18). In each case, the proverbial subject is amply expanded into a relatively long piece of doggerel that nearly fills the verso of each folio and faces its illustration on the following recto, at least in some of the early editions; in one of the 1608 editions, however, the text begins beneath the illustration and continues onto the *following* verso.[27] This case provides yet more confirmation that the emblem was not conceived as having any particular spatial disposition (see above, 157–8).

Among the most interesting editions of this work are French and Dutch-German versions published as broadside 'comic strips' in the early seventeenth century (fig. 51).[28] Other examples of political satire and propaganda were published this way through the early years of the seventeenth century. In the *Tableau et Emblemes de la detestable vie et malheureuse fin du maistre Coyon*,[29] the satire is clearly directed against a particular individual, and the butt of this allegorical animal satire is Concino Concini, who had risen rapidly after the death of Henri IV to become governor of Péronne, Roye, Montdidier, and Amiens as well as Maréchal de France, and then as quickly fell beneath accusations of the usurpation of power and rumours that he had had a hand in the death of Henri IV. The six scenes (fig. 52) present an elaborate allegory detailing the governor's career and serve as a warning that attempts to gain absolute power do nothing but turn the world upside-down.[30] This elaborate quasi-narrative development marks a departure from earlier practice, and it recalls a tendency evident in certain seventeenth-century collections of devices such as Chaumelz's life of Anne of Austria, where a more or less chronological series of devices represents stages and scenes from the queen's life in such a way as to suggest a biography.[31]

Most of the examples collected by L'Estoile for his album, however, are single, generally a-narrative, scenes with textual exegesis or labels. While they are seldom called emblems, they often do contain emblematic elements, and are structured along the lines of other sixteenth-century emblems. One engraved broadsheet, entitled 'Le soufflement et conseil diabolique d'Esperon a Henry de Valois pour saccager les Catholiques,' shows a meeting between Henri III and several notables of the Church including the cardinal de Bourbon and the archbishop of Lyons. One of the identified participants is distinguished, as was often the case in court festivities such as marriages and tournaments, only by the device on his back: ULTIME CL ... MANE ...[32]

It must have been around this time, too, that broadside emblems began to be published as memorials to deceased persons of high rank or

Fig. 51. *Emblemes sus les Actions & meurs du seignor Espagnol.* 1609.

TABLEAU ET EMBLEMES DE LA DETESTABLE VIE ET MALHEVREVSE FIN DV MAISTRE COYON

MYTOLOGIE DES EMBLEMES DV COYON.

1.

Fortvne ſabaiſſe & ſe hauſſe
Comme ce Coyon nous faict voir,
Mais lorſqu'il croyoit tout pouuoir,
Luy-meſme eſt tombé dans la foſſe.

2.

Mãgot leur Suſçon & Babin
Sont tout au plus haut de la roüe:
Et au bas, quand le Coyon joüe,
Vielle-foy, Du Vray & Nanin.

3.

Du Vray, Vielle-foy, & Nanin,
Sont maintenant au haut eſtage,
Le Coyon n'eſt plus dans la cage,
Abas Mãgot, Suſçon, Babin.

4.

Le Coyon fit caſſer le verre
Où trempoient les trois fleurs de Lys:
Mais paſſant ſur le pont-leuis
Vn Vitry-êt l'a mis par terre.

5.

A ceſte fois la beſte eſt priſe,
Sortez Coyon; Car par les lois,
Ceux qui attentent à nos Roys,
N'ont point d'Aſyle dans l'Egliſe.

6.

Coyon, vous en ſerez pendu;
Ce n'eſt pas ainſi qu'il faut plaire;
Trancher du Roy, faire & deffaire,
Cela n'eſt-il pas defendu?

7.

Au moins, que ma queüe on ne rongne,
Ny mes oreilles ny mon nez,
Et par les ruës ne traiſnez
Mon corps, ainſi qu'vne charongne.

8.

Vous ſerez pour voſtre arrogance,
Traiſné, deſchiré, mis au feu,
Et cela ſemble encore peu,
Pour vanger le peuple de France.

En ce Tableau que nous voyons,
La Conchine peut recognoiſtre,
Que les François ont vn grand Maiſtre,
Et qu'ils ne ſont-pas, Tous Coyons.

Ce qu'il eſt depeint à l'enuers,
N'eſt pas arriué ſans myſtere,
Le Coyon qui vouloit tout faire,
Renuerſoit ainſi l'Vniuers.

Qui Le onore?
François ou Italien.

A Paris, Chez les 24. & 25. Auril.
1617.

Fig. 52. *Tableau et Emblemes de la detestable vie et malheureuse fin du maistre Coyon.*

outstanding accomplishment. Ruth Mortimer tells us, for example, that Jean Mercier's fiftieth emblem was originally published in a slightly different form as a broadside memorial to the great Cujas, Mercier's former mentor in his legal studies; and 'devises en veuvage' as Brantôme called them were commonly published as broadsheets or short plaquettes in the seventeenth century.[33] Actually, there is less difference between such a broadside memorial and the satirical comic strip attacking Concini than would at first appear. As with medieval portraits, emblematic characterizations of people were never neutral; they always carried a charge of praise or blame, but whichever they carried, they functioned the same way.[34]

Much the same could be said for propaganda devices, but it was more common to use *jetons* for their distribution than broadsides. In his *Mémoires*, Sully explained how he had regularly composed devices for the *jetons* he offered annually to Henri IV as his *étrennes*.[35] These devices generally carried a political message and were intended to be used for propaganda purposes. Here is an example of the way such a device might work. During the uneasy period of Henri de Navarre's consolidation of power following his accession to the French throne, the duc de Savoie saw what he took to be a propitious opportunity to enlarge his duchy. He met with initial success, and boasted of it on commemorative *jetons*: 'ce Duc qui croyoit avoir bien pris l'occasion d'attacquer Henry IV durant les troubles de la France en s'emparant du Marquisat de Salustes, fit battre des jettons ou de la monnoye, où il y avoit un Centaure qui fouloit aux pieds une couronne Royalle avec ce mot. OPORTUNE, *à propos*;'[36] but Henri's counter-offensive proved decisive and 'apres cette glorieuse victoire pour contre pointer la devise du Duc, mon oncle [Robert (III) Estienne] inventa celle-cy pour les jettons du Roy de l'année 1601, sur lesqueles on voyoit un Hercule domptant un Centaure, avec ce mot OPORTUNIUS ...'[37] Such an exchange recalls the *tableaux vivants* of the beginning of the century, where the actors played out allegorical battles between the figures of the devices of monarchs and principalities (see above, 93–4). The only difference is that these devices are beginning to follow the rules made fashionable by the Italian theoreticians, who were only just beginning to be read at the courts of Henri III and Henri IV.[38]

Devices of this sort tended increasingly to be used for particular occasions, whereas more general public relations often took other emblematic forms. Allegorical or mythological portraiture was often constructed emblematically; early and dramatic confirmation of the relation between portraiture and emblematics may be found in a portrait of François Ier painted as a composite deity by Niccolò Bellin da Modena around 1545 or a little later (fig. 53).[39] A *trompe-l'oeil* frame incorporates a *huitain* into the portrait in a way that gives it the form of a complete emblem, in which the *huitain* helps the viewer decode the iconography of this strange portrait:

Francoys en guerre est yn Mars furieux
En paix Minerve & Diane a la chasse.
A bien parler Mercure copieux
A bien aymer vray Amour: plein de grace
O france heureuse honore donc la face
De ton grand Roy qui surpasse Nature.
Car lhonorant tu sers en mesme place:
Minerve, Mars, Diane, Amour, Mercure.

As in an emblem, the text relates all the disparate, rebus-like components of François's costume and indicates the artist's intention in forcing these attributes into an uneasy and 'unnatural' union around the recognizable person of the king. As in any emblem, it is difficult, if not impossible, to separate the text from the illustration. The conceit-like ending in the last two lines loses much of its meaning and all of its force without the painting, and conversely, the painting is all but incomprehensible without the text. Edgar Wind's insufficient attention to the text leads him to characterize the painting as 'androgynous,' which condition he then allegorizes to signify the universal man. But that sense was almost certainly not intended, since it leaves the painting open to nuances of bisexuality totally inappropriate in this context.[40] The poem does not draw a moral lesson from the portrait here, nor does it make insinuations about the king's sexuality, but instead develops an extravagant *éloge* of the king, as was increasingly common in noble devices.

Although it is not common to find Renaissance paintings where the emblematic design has been elaborated as explicitly as it has been here, much of the artwork used to embellish the new Renaissance châteaux was nonetheless conceived with a clearly emblematic intention. While tapestries and woodcuts may have been turning bourgeois homes into 'memory houses' full of moral platitudes, the more luxurious châteaux were often decorated with device-like motifs that tended to nourish a narcissistic cult of the owner's personality. Examples that come immediately to mind are Fontainebleau and Chambord, where the mark of the salamander gives everything the personalized imprint of the king who helped change the entire architectural conception of the noble residence in Renaissance France. And the emblematic decoration of a château such as Fontainebleau,

Fig. 53. Niccolò Bellin, Portrait of François Ier as a composite deity.

which François began to renovate in 1527, is by no means limited to a single, if almost obsessively, repeated motif. The emblematic inspiration here is so pervasive that the seventeenth-century description of Fontainebleau by the Jesuit Pierre Dan is actually classified as an emblem book by Praz and others (see above, 94–5). Murals were composed of complicated allegorical scenes with actors so clearly recognizable that each scene seemed to carry a specific, if implicit, message not unlike the text of an emblem, and much more precisely particularized than the message of an allegory.[41]

As in the case of the allegorical portrait discussed above, this art was aimed in some measure at transforming the king into a demigod following the model of deification of the ancient Roman emperors. The advantages of this public-relations charade must have been great and quite obvious. It would detach the king from the realm of mortals and their foibles and make him larger than life for the awe-struck spectators of this masquerade; the king would seem to be leading the life of a glorious hero among the abstractions of the ancient *psychomachia*, and shoulder to shoulder with the famous citizens of the city-state of ancient mythology, all made familiar and fashionable by an increasingly humanistic program of education. It would be perfectly acceptable, too, to the monarch's subjects who were prepared for a *dédoublement* of royal roles by the principle of the king's two bodies that emerged in medieval political theology.[42]

The minor decorative arts contain other examples of the same kind of statement designed to invest the monarch or some other august personage with a god-like aura and heroic proportions. In 1555, Anne de Montmorency commissioned an enamel plate from Léonard Limousin that reproduced Raphael's famous *Banquet of the Gods*. Upon close inspection, it is clear that Jupiter resembles Henri II, while Catherine de Medicis and other members of the court have been portrayed in the stately guise of Raphael's Olympian banqueteers. Edouard Bourciez even speculated that the blond nude is Diane de Poitiers![43] So there must have been a whole program tending to assimilate royalty to the world of ancient mythology as it was conceived by Renaissance humanism. And the process of assimilation always functions the way an *impresa* did; that is, it worked to elevate the subject to the level of a noble type and lift him out of the everyday realm of individuality. It was, therefore, serious business, and that is why Henri II took the trouble to have his official device composed by Giovio almost immediately upon his accession to the throne.[44] Another enamel by Limousin, this one now in the Frick Collection in New York, shows that the nobility used allegory in the same way. This enamel presents portraits of members of the Guise family within the allegorical framework of a Triumph of Faith, and we are able to identify Charles de Guise, cardinal of Lorraine, by his ivy and pyramid device, which, however, is no longer surmounted by the crescent, as it had been, for example, in Paradin's collection, for Henri II was now dead.[45]

Even on the grander scale of emblematic programming for the interior decoration of noble residences, Fontainebleau was far from being an isolated example of such public relations manoeuvres. In fact, the use of applied emblematics to turn a noble residence into an extension of the mythological masquerade designed to create a public persona is perhaps better exemplified by the case of Diane de Poitiers and her residence at Anet. There, all decoration seems to be consciously subordinated to the central allegorical design, surely intended to support the transfiguring identification with Diane's mythological namesake. Her goal would have been to put distance between herself and more ordinary ladies of the court and develop a kind of cult that would assure her of the king's worshipful favour. Or as Françoise Bardon has explained it:

> Diane voulait être assimilée à la déesse austère et chaste dont elle portait le nom, elle désirait cette assimilation par fierté intime, pour ne pas être confondue dans la race subalterne des maîtresses royales, et elle réussit à faire douter du caractère véritable de ses rapports avec le roi; ... Il y avait une troisième raison: les séductions de l'allégorie étaient nécessaires pour conserver à l'amour du roi, non seulement sa fidélité, mais sa poésie. Cet homme, qui n'était pas très intelligent, était sensible au romanesque et à l'aventure; il subit d'autant plus facilement le pouvoir de cette femme extraordinaire qu'elle lui fût présentée comme le reflet de quelque divinité. L'étonnante beauté de Diane bénéficiait des perfections de nudités sans défaut en marbre, en peinture, en émail, soumises aux yeux du roi.[46]

Better yet, the myth could provide a narrative frame that would channel activity inexorably toward a desired end,[47] and devices were among the most common and effective instruments for recalling this narrative frame. In this case, Diane's elegant little hunting lodge near Rouen, 'le Paradis d'Anet' as Du Bellay called it, was the principal vehicle for the expression of the metamorphosis of Diane and her lover; it was designed to be the temple for her cult. So the decorative motifs were to serve a complex psychological function, and for this reason they had to be composed of something more than simple hunting scenes or paintings that recalled the myth of Diana the huntress in general terms. Devices and other emblematic compositions were used to make the deifying transfiguration explicit and bind the king to the cult of his mistress in the kind of apotheosis we have been discussing, and because the assumption of a device entailed a personal engagement not unlike a promise to fulfil the ideal expressed by the device.

Poets played an important role in developing the highly allusive and carefully coordinated decorative scheme to be executed by Italian mannerists at Anet. Pontus de Tyard, for example, contributed the designs for a series of paintings on the theme of fountain and river myths, which probably once adorned what is now the Galerie des Glaces. In the text of his instructions to the artists, Pontus began each *projet* by recounting the fable he was going to use; instructions for the painting followed along with the explanatory epigram (in reality, a sonnet) that was to be placed beneath the painting.

Here, for example, is the way he presented the myth of Narcissus. The title is to be 'Huitiesme Fable de la Fontaine de Narcisse.' After recounting Pausanias' version of the legend, he proposes the following 'Description pour la Peinture': 'Faudroit peindre une jeune fille morte, toute resemblante a Narcisse: et faudroit qu'en un paisage solitaire et escarté, Narcisse fust couché aupres d'une fontaine, en laquelle son image se representeroit, comme dans un miroir: il seroit peint d'un visage mourant. Ainsi sa seur, son image, et luy seroient tous semblables.' The painting, whose composition would re-enact the myth, would be explained by the 'Epigramme de la fontaine de Narcisse' in the following way:

Narcisse ayme sa seur, sa chère seur jumelle,
Sa seur aussi pour lui brusle d'ardeur extreme:
L'un en l'autre se sent estre un second soymesme:
Ce qu'elle veut pour luy, il veut aussi pour elle.
De semblable beauté est ceste couple belle,
Et semblable est le feu qui fait que l'un l'autre ayme,
Mais la seur est premiere à qui la Parque blesme
Ferme les jeunes yeux d'une nuit éternelle.
Narcisse en l'eau se void, y pensant voir sa seur:
Ce penser le repaist d'une vaine douceur,
Qui coulee en son coeur, luy amoindrit sa peine.
De luy son nom retint l'amoureuse fonteine,
Dans laquelle reçoit, quiconque aymant s'y mire,
Quelque douce allegeance à l'amoureux martire.[48]

While this composition does lack the moralizing dimension usually associated with emblems, it is emblematic in every other sense. The final tercet takes the particular mythological situation and provides it with an interpretation that has general significance for all those who truly love. In this sense, it recalls many of Maurice Scève's *dizains*, and in a more general way, it combines the synthetic simultaneity of visual perception with the analytic presentation of the discursive narration of a story in time. The poet achieves this effect in part by his use of the present tense consistently until line 12, where the *passé simple* sets a distance between the scene described and the general commentary.

Closer perhaps to the central emblematic tradition, much of the decoration at Anet is developed around amorous courtly devices. Many of them were composed during a visit to the château in the late 1550s by Gabriello Simeoni, who was largely responsible for the publication of Giovio's *Dialogo* in France and who collected and published many devices of his own: 'Et par ce que je apperceu leans une fontaine qui ne parloit point, comme tout le demeurant faisoit, & que en la basse gallerie du grand jardin estoit quelques places vuides, j'entreprins en passant mon temps de faire la fontaine parler, & remplir la gallerie de semblables devises.'[49] This passage is interesting in many respects. First, it shows that signs no longer automatically carried a message, as the proliferation of possible meanings and the rise of a scientific naturalism caused readers or viewers to restrain their interpretive instincts, inherited from the Middle Ages, unless they had some guidance and encouragement from a text. Second, 'deviser' meant 'to talk,' so perhaps we are in the presence of a use of the word 'devise' that indicates it meant, among other things, texts that make signs speak in certain ways. If that is the case, then the *devise*, like the emblem, would be a primarily textual form, as it is still understood in modern French.

Here is the way devices were used in the decorative schemes at Anet. The ceiling of the Salle de Gardes was divided into several panels; on two of these panels were painted the arms of Diane and Henri. On the other panels, there alternated two devices: one was composed of an arrow and two laurel branches intertwined with a banderole bearing the motto *Sola vivit in illo*, while the other was Henri's famous device composed of a crescent and the motto *Donec totum impleat orbem*. The beams separating the panels bore other devices such as the one composed of a javelin and the motto *Consequitur quodcumque petit*.[50]

Even when they were not explicitly organized around a particular theme as at Anet, devices were often used in the decoration of the hall and gallery ceilings in Renaissance châteaux. A celebrated example is the château of Dampierre-sur-Boutonne in the Charente. François de Clermont built this intimate little château on an island in the Boutonne in 1475. Jeanne de

Vivonne, the wife of his grandson, Claude de Clermont, and the mother of Catherine de Clermont, the future maréchale de Retz, commissioned the famous ceiling of the 'Haute Galerie' after the death of her husband in 1545. In the opinion of Maria Antonietta de Angelis, however, the ceiling was executed much later in the century, or even in the early years of the seventeenth century.[51] This lacunar ceiling contains sixty-one emblems and devices in stucco, each framed within a caisson or coffer.[52] Some of these compositions reproduce devices included in the sixteenth-century collections printed in France and Italy, and while six seem to have a biblical inspiration, many of the rest resemble emblems by Alciato, Corrozet, La Perrière, Camerarius, Aneau, Covarrubias, de Boria, and Bruck. Indeed, twenty of the ceiling emblems are exact reproductions of printed emblems.[53]

This château was not an isolated exception. Devices and emblems adorned the ancestral home of the d'Urfé family in the Forez. The chapel is particularly interesting; Claude d'Urfé began work on it in the 1540s, following the model of an Italian *camera depicta*. Various intarsia panels contain his device, and such emblematic motifs as the chameleon, a bird with a worm in its mouth, and Androcles and the lion.[54] At the Château du Perron at Pierre-Bénite, near Lyons, Enzo Giudici found several devices decorating the *soffitto*, and they bear such a 'soprendente corrispondenza' with certain of the *emblesmes* of Scève's *Délie*, that Giudici concluded that 'Délie' belonged to the Gondi family![55] Perhaps the inscriptions on the beams in Montaigne's *librairie* were also intended to function as devices, and it is even more likely that the shipwreck scene painted over the doorway to this *librairie* was part of a quasi-emblematic composition like those of Pontus de Tyard at Anet.[56]

We know that emblems and devices were used in the decorative schemes of libraries, following a tradition that goes back to the late Middle Ages. When the library of San Giovanni of Parma was decorated by two Bolognese artists in 1574–5, they followed the directions of the abbot, who had reserved for himself the right to choose the *materiam picturae*, and designed their frescos around emblems by Alciato.[57] Devices were frequently used during the seventeenth century in French Jesuit libraries, such as the one at Dijon.[58] This tradition would seem to go back to the late Middle Ages when, for example, the old cathedral library at Puy en Velay was decorated with personifications of different parts of the quadrivium: grammar, logic, rhetoric, and music, each explained by a Latin inscription in the form of a prosopopoeia on a banderole. Grammar, for example, exclaims that 'Quicquid agant artes, ego semper praedico partes.'[59]

Devices and emblems could also be used in other settings for the decoration of a Renaissance residence. While Alciato gave artisans general encouragement to use emblems for this purpose, Aneau specifically recommends that his 'Figure de Mariage' be used to decorate a 'ciel de lit,'[60] and the variety of settings in which one could find emblems and devices is truly remarkable. Perhaps better than any history could ever do, the Grand Palais exhibition devoted to the Ecole de Fontainebleau in late 1972 began to demonstrate the extent and variety of uses of the emblematic forms during the middle years of the sixteenth century,[61] and now much of that material may be viewed on a permanent basis at the Musée Nationale de la Renaissance at Ecouen. A stained-glass window from Ecouen, for example, had as its central motif the complete device of Catherine de Medicis with its rainbow and Greek motto APLANOS. The door to the chapel at Anet was designed around Henri II's device and his famous H/D monogram, and apparently the Bastie d'Urfé in the Forez contained a door with a palm device.

In one of his enamel *rétables* dating from 1553, Léonard Limousin incorporated the devices of both Henri II and François Ier. Generally, when complete devices were presented in works of art, the close relationship between motto and figure was underlined by the spatial proximity of the two parts, but here the two parts of each device have been separated, as was often the case in presentation copies of manuscripts earlier in the century. The motto is prominently centred at the bottom of the composition, while the figure has been discreetly relegated to a recurring motif in the décor framing the pictured Resurrection.[62] Limousin's less illustrious contemporary, Pierre Reymond, also organized the motifs for his enamelware in an emblematic way. He chose the motif of the triumphal chariot to present the signs of the zodiac allegorically in one set of dishes, and he is best known for his emblematic presentations of the months in the grisaille décors of another set of enamel-on-copper plates.[63] Devices and other kinds of emblematic compositions continued to be used by artists and artisans of the second Ecole de Fontainebleau in enamel and majolica ware through the end of the sixteenth century.

Beginning with the *entrées* of François Ier in 1515 (see above, 92–4), or so it would seem, these royal pageants were ever more heavily dependent in their design upon emblematic motifs and constructions. This is evident in the *entrée* of Elisabeth d'Autriche in 1533,[64] but with the *entrées* prepared to welcome the new king, Henri II, around 1550, a pattern developed whereby devices became an essential part of the epideictic presentation associated with such welcoming ceremonies. This pattern was to obtain at least through the first quarter of the seventeenth century.[65]

Maurice Scève and Barthélemy Aneau collaborated with other artists in the preparation of the spectacular Lyons *entrée* of September 1548. The procession was numerous and the costumes were rich and colourful, but for the interests of this study, the various points throughout the city where the procession was to pause are more important. At different locations in the city, obelisks, triumphal portals, and allegorical tableaux had been set up to express the city's sentiments toward the new king. Each obelisk bore a device that would make it clear that its symbolic message was addressed specifically to Henri. The allegorical tableaux, following earlier models, could be either painted or dramatized by living actors. In one of the *tableaux vivants*, Diane de Poitiers, or a *figurant*, elegantly disguised as her namesake goddess, presented a captive lion to the king as he passed.[66] The painted tableaux on the different portals became more emblematic through their combination of pictorial allegory with an epigrammatic application. The Porte de Pierre-en-Cise had been decorated in such a way as to resemble an ancient triumphal arch or portal

> Au front duquel estoit peinct un parc de France semé de Lys, environné d'une cloison des chiffres et devises Royalles entrelassées d'une subtile grace ... ayant une entrée ouverte, et gardée par un Lion. Et au mylieu dudict parc deux Dames estoient assises en atour de Deesses, celle de la part droicte embrassant l'autre du bras gauche, et luy asseurant la foy de la main droicte, avec un petit chien se jouant à elle, et laquelle signifioit Fidelité. L'aultre luy presentoit un baiser, et de la dextre luy confirmoit aussi la foy, s'appuyant du bras gauche sur un joug de boeuf tout droict pour monstrer qu'elle estoit Obeissance. Dedans le frontispice au dessus d'elles estoit escript en un compartiment de massonerie
> SEDES VBI FATA QVIETAS (534)

Following its use in Leo X's *Suave* device, the yoke had become a sign in the emblematic code to represent a willingly accepted domination, and it is but the most obvious sign that this *entrée* must be understood as nothing more than a coded message, albeit pleasantly so.

Around the composition other inscriptions were placed as well, and this allegory of France is made to speak principally to the king through the emblematic inscriptions. The allegory must have been clear enough in a general sense to any culturally competent viewer, but the inscriptions gave it a more precisely motivated meaning within the context of the *entrée*. Here, as was so often the case in political emblematics, the construction works the way a device does in particularizing a general allegorical statement and directing it to a specific person or, as here, event.

The same technique could be applied just as well to episodes from ancient mythology or from fables. On another of the city's *portes* spectators encountered a painting or *hystoire* of Androcles taking a thorn from the paw of a lion with the following motto: GENEROSE PIO GENEROSA PIETAS (535), which integrates the mythological story into the general allegorical program of the *entrée*. The choice of this episode was determined in large measure, of course, by the presence of the eponymous animal, which makes the specific intended message as clear as if it had been stated in so many words.

Sometimes the entries seem to make explicit reference to specific emblems. Such would appear to be the case in Henri II's Paris entry of June 1549. Atop the arch erected at the Porte St Denis, a scene portrayed the Gallic Hercules in such a way that he resembled the late François Ier, according to the *livret* (fig. 54). Chains proceed from his mouth to the ears of the four representatives of society: the Church, nobility, *conseil*, and *labeur*. The motto, from Cicero's *De Officiis*, explains that *Trahimus, sequimurque volentes*, we are drawn and we follow willingly. The designers could use this emblematic adaptation of a traditional motif with confidence that Alciato's emblem 181 had given the necessary background for reading it just right.[67]

This way of constructing an *entrée* was not in any way exceptional, and the ceremonies accompanying the Rouen *entrée* on 1 October 1550 are equally interesting as an example of this use of emblematics. Aside from the *entrée* proper, there was also a parade of allegorical triumphs – principally Fama, Victoria, and Fortuna – past the royal tribune. Preceded by numerous horsemen, one of whom was carrying a banner covered with eyes, Fama's chariot, as it is preserved for us in a manuscript at Rouen, was drawn by two elephants; she had her foot posed on a skeleton and, like several members of her retinue, was holding a trumpet. On the side of her chariot, we read Henri's motto, *Donec totum impleat orbem*. The motto is all the viewer needs to understand that the composition is talking not about Fame in general, but about the fame of a particular, and as if named, individual.

Two white horses draw Victory's chariot; crowned with laurel and surrounded by trumpeters and trophies, Victory herself proudly holds aloft a palm branch. As in each triumph, there is a two-line inscription. This one reads: 'Victorem comitatur. adest Victoria. palmam / Illa refert, Captos & spolia ampla trahit.' Two white unicorns draw Fortune's chariot; adorned with a sail-like scarf and seated on a wheel, she is crowning Henri.[68] Such *tableaux vivants* remind the viewer of a myriad of Renaissance representations of Fortune, and it would appear that festivities of this kind often

Fig. 54. 'Hercule gaulois.' Henry II's Paris entry, 1549.

relied in their design on the iconography of emblems and related forms. The personifications in the cathedral library at Puy en Velay, for example, provided the inspiration for a series of such tableaux during François Ier's visit to that city in 1533.[69]

Similar constructions became commonplace in *entrées* and other kinds of festive ceremonies throughout the century. Devices tended increasingly to dominate in the emblematic structuring of motifs in such ceremonies, and during Charles IX's visit to Bayonne in 1566, they were used in a new way that was to become typical. In this pageant, five virtues were followed by the nine muses, who had come to offer 'les presens des Chevaliers aux Dames.' These presents were pendant-shaped medallions bearing the devices of the Chevaliers; each device is developed around a personification of one of the muses and has a Greek motto. Later in the ceremonies nine 'amours' present another group of similar medallions to another group of ladies; this time the devices have Latin mottoes.[70] The use of devices in choreographing ceremonies like this one in such a way as to provide them with a kind of coded motivation was common well into the seventeenth century.[71]

The use of devices for such courtly coding went far beyond the rather formal and official domain of *entrées*, weddings, and other royal or noble ceremonies, where their use was often reduced to identifying participants and focusing attention on particular points of a political program. Kurt Weinberg has shown how a complex network of symbolic motifs, derived in large measure from courtly devices, provides an interesting counterpoint to the surface action in Madame de Lafayette's *Princesse de Clèves*.[72] It would appear that devices had provided a conduit for occult communication at court since the very early years of the French Renaissance. Marot often hints at that function in his epigrams,[73] and Brantôme provides us with some very instructive anecdotes concerning the role of devices in courtly society of the time.[74]

According to Brantôme, Marguerite de Navarre had a considerable reputation for composing devices, and it was presumably she who composed the devices that François presented to his mistresses. The vehicle for the presentation of such devices was often ladies' jewellery, and we get a glimpse of what such jewels must have looked like in Jean Passerat's designs for jewellery for Catherine de Medicis.[75] But men also displayed devices, either in rings, as did Erasmus,[76] or in cap brooches,[77] which were especially popular in early sixteenth-century Italy. In his *Autobiography*, Cellini notes the mode in passing and complains that, although he had made many of them, they always involved very hard work.[78] Among others, he crafted a medal of 'indescribably fine effect' for Federigo Ginori; chiselled on a plate of gold, 'Atlas had the heaven upon his back, made out of a crystal ball, engraved with the zodiac upon a field of lapis-lazuli.' Beneath this design was inscribed the motto *Summa tulisse juvat* (101). As Cellini tells it, Federigo brought his friend Luigi Alamanni to meet Cellini, with whom he was duly impressed, and after Federigo's death, the Atlas medal came into Alamanni's possession. Alamanni presented it, together with some of his writings, to François Ier, who liked it so much that he wanted to meet Cellini, and thus began their long and complex relationship (107).

Later, when the duke of Ferrara came to terms with Pope Paul II, he commanded a medal from Cellini to commemorate the reconciliation. The reverse 'showed Peace, represented by a woman with a torch in her hand, sitting alight a pile of weapons ...' (315–16). The inscription reads 'Pretiosa in conspectu Domini,' meaning that peace had cost a mint! Although it does not follow all the rules for an excellent device, this is a perfect example of the occasional device. It is a sardonic propaganda piece, and one that is situation specific, it gives a secular meaning to a religious formula, and it is hermetic for those not informed of the situation that generated it, but not obviously so.

If only because of the cost involved in their manufacture, jewellery and other personal effects decorated with devices and other emblematic compositions were generally restricted in the first half of the sixteenth century to the court and its circle. With the coming of the religious wars, many powerful and wealthy nobles defected to the camp of the Protestants. They brought the fashion with them, and used devices to reflect their positions in much the same way as the propaganda emblems we have already encountered (see above, 195–206). One particularly interesting example is a pilgrim flask made by Antoine Sigalon in southern France around 1581 (Metropolitan Museum of Art, New York). It bears the arms of John Casimir of Bavaria, surrounded by grotesques holding rosaries. Beneath the arms we see a device; the motto on a banderdole appears to read *Constantia et sincere*, while the body consists of laurel and palm branches crossed within a ring. The ring reinforces the theme of fidelity, since it contains a diamond, and the back of the ring takes the form of clasped hands, thus producing yet another sign of fidelity.

The use of multiple signifiers in order to make the precise intended *signifié* clear was, of course, common among poets and painters in the first century of the *aetas emblematica*.[79] Less common, but extremely interesting, is the impact of the frame surrounding the device on the application of its meaning to a particular situation, that, for example, of a Protestant nobleman. The device, as it is described above, could characterize a Catholic or a Calvinist equally well. But the grotesques holding rosaries on either side of the device make clear the confessional character of the profession of faith expressed here.[80] As with occasional devices, the contextual setting of a personal device was important in understanding its precise meaning.

In the case of the medallion Alamanni gave to François, we can assume that the emblematic design delighted the king's vanity as much as its workmanship pleased his discriminating taste, for, judging from the following anecdote about the king and his ladies, good devices were very highly esteemed at the French court in the middle years of the century. When François left Mme de Chasteaubriand for Mme d'Estampes, his new mistress made him promise to take back all the jewels he had given to her predecessor, 'non pour le prix et la valeur, car pour lors les perles et pierreries n'avoyent la vogue qu'elles ont eu depuis, mais pour l'amour des belles devises qui estoyent mises, engravées et empreintes, lesquelles la reine de Navarre sa soeur avoit faites et composées; car elle en estoit très bonne maistresse.' So François sent a gentleman to pick them up. When he arrived, Mme de Chasteaubriand pretended to be ill and asked him to come back three days later. By the time he returned she had had an opportunity to melt all the jewellery down into 'ingots' so that she could give back everything but the devices! The king found her gesture so admirably spirited that he returned the gold to Mme de Chasteaubriand for her to keep as well![81]

These examples make it clear that the device was an increasingly popular vehicle for communication at court, and while we would have no reason to expect members of the court to be reading emblems, much imagery of courtly ceremony and pageant is clearly emblematic, through its fragmentary nature and its particularized and often idiosyncratic meaning. The emblematic was the ideal form for such decoration because it was *not* narrative like allegory. The emblem made its point at the moment it was perceived, before the pageant had passed on, or before the spectator had moved away to other business.

9

Emblematic Structures in Renaissance Literature

One elegant manuscript of Marguerite de Navarre's *Heptameron*, dated 8 August 1553, is bound in red and green morocco with a cartouche on the cover bearing the device of a vine twined around a tree trunk, with the motto *Sin' et doppo la morte*, together with the monogram of Adrien de Thou.[1] This binding goes far in reminding us that Marguerite spent her life in an intellectual and artistic milieu heavily influenced by emblematics. Although her own sunflower device, with the motto *Non inferiora secutus*, was criticized on technical grounds in the seventeenth century,[2] it was clearly quite famous a century earlier, when the gender of words was a bit less rigidly fixed. In fact, Marguerite was so deeply involved in the traditions and movements that produced the earliest French emblems that her device probably gives as good an idea as any of the state of the art in the middle of the sixteenth century. We have already seen how much of the proto-emblematic activity in early sixteenth-century France centred on her mother and her brother's court (see above, 89–94). And her interest in such forms must have been taken for granted, for on the occasion of her visit to Toulouse in 1533, the *capitouls* of that city commissioned La Perrière to compose a group of emblems, the first to be composed in France and the core of his *Theatre des bons engins*, published by Janot some six or seven years later.[3]

Robert Cottrell has shown how the relation between text and illustration in the 1547 edition of *La Coche* is reminiscent of certain, if not all, aspects of the emblematic.[4] And several of the *nouvelles* of her *Heptameron* contain emblematic images that often play crucial roles in the structuring of the story. The sixteenth *nouvelle*, for example, and the ensuing discussion, provide a superb example of the way late medieval allegory evolved into, on the one hand, a dust of fragments that could be used emblematically to ornament a text and, on the other, a loose rhetorical frame for the presentation of a message or, as here, of a dialogue/debate. In this story a Milanese widow swore never to remarry, nor to love again. However, a Frenchman pursued her with such tenacity over a period of three years that she gave in to his entreaties, and they swore 'perpetuelle amytié' to each other. The metaphor of the hunt surfaces from time to time in the telling of this tale, with verbs and similes like 'pourchassa' and 'elle le fuyoit comme le loup fait le levrier.' As the lady describes how in the end she finally gave in to her lover's entreaties, she explains that 'comme la bische navrée à mort cuyde, en changeant de lieu, changer le mal qu'elle porte avecq soy, ainsi m'en allois-je d'eglise en eglise, cuydant fuyr celluy que je portois en mon cueur, duquel a esté la preuve de la parfaicte amityé qui a faict accorder l'honneur avecq l'amour.'[5] The image of the deer that aggravates its wound by fleeing the hunter had been common in the rhetoric of love since Petrarch borrowed it from Virgil; and following its use in a mourning device by René d'Anjou in the fifteenth century, it was turned into emblems by Corrozet and Scève before Du Bellay and other Pléiade poets worked their own variations on it.[6]

The image as it is used here could be characterized as emblematic in several ways. First, it is ornamental; that is, it has no structural role in the rhetorical exposition. Rather it is as if attached to, or embedded in, the text for illustrative reasons very much in the original sense of the Latin *emblema*.[7] Second, the image is reproduced as it might be found in a number of places, and very much as the commonplace it was understood to be. But the use of the image is anything but commonplace. The lady's flight does not aggravate the wound of love in the sense of producing stress and conflict, as in most uses of this image, but rather brings her to an understanding of the reality of her suitor's love, and of her own love for him. And it seems to conflate with another variation on the image of the deer that we find, for example, in *Délie*, diz. 46, where we discover that 'Plus fuit le Cerf, & plus on le poursuyt': the lover's pursuit is the continuing proof of his love. So in reality, the image is emblematic in three ways; the exterior form of the image is commonplace, the sense is novel and unexpected, and finally it is not necessary to the construction of sense in the passage where it is inserted.

The metaphor of the hunt continues to inform the discussion that follows this *nouvelle*, but the rhetorical context is different; it derives from a traditional allegorical frame that serves as a rhetorical matrix, a rhetorical vehicle that is quite different from the highly elaborated and self-conscious emblematic image in the story itself. Hence the 'chasseur' and 'chassées' as well as the simile of the 'cerf' surface from time to time, but as if from some stereotypical rhetorical code not unlike the Petrarchan vocabulary that became, as Leonard Forster describes it, the code for speaking of love in the sixteenth and seventeenth centuries.[8] The background of this code may be seen, for example, in various late medieval works such as the series of early sixteenth-century tapestries for Guy de Baudreuil on the theme of 'The Hunt of the Frail Stag' (Metropolitan Museum, New York).[9]

In the discussion following *nouvelle* 19, Dagoucin ventures that there are some who love so perfectly that they would rather die than even feel a desire, let alone commit an act, that would impugn the honour and chastity of their lady. Saffredent replies, with what must be considerable disdain, that such lovers 'sont de la nature de la camalercite [chameleon], qui vit de l'aer.' This image originated in Plutarch, and was taken up by Alciato in emblem 53 to describe flatterers. D'Aubigné uses it in *Princes* (ll. 235–6) in a way that is emblematic in the same sense as the deer image discussed above, but here the image is used in a very different way. We could call what Saffredent is doing emblematic typing, an activity that is related to the craft and cult of the device; that is, he is using a well-known emblematic image as an epithet to characterize a person or group.

In other *nouvelles*, emblematic images become important structuring devices. Either the emblematic image is used to replace causal links that relate different parts of a single story, or it can provide a canvas, a framework, upon, or within, which the story can be deployed. We find an example of the first use of such imagery in the thirtieth *nouvelle*, the story of an unnamed widow and her incestuous relation with her son. As is often the case when Marguerite presents a type-cast character such as this one, 'la jeune dame vefve' is never named or otherwise described. The word 'jeune,' however, betrays the flaw in this type that contains the seeds of its own destruction. For the widow denies her youth and puts all her energies into being the perfect mother, the mother-type. As her son grows, Nature teaches him other lessons, Marguerite tells us, and the mother learns that he lusts after one of her maids. The mother unwisely substitutes herself for the maid at the appointed meeting in order to teach her son a lesson. But Nature takes the upper hand, and her precipitous fall into incest is succinctly explained by a pivotal emblematic image: '... tout ainsy que l'eaue par force retenue court avecq plus d'impetuosité quant on la laisse aller, que celle qui court ordinairement, ainsy ceste pauvre dame tourna sa gloire à la contraincte qu'elle donnoit à son corps' (230). This clearly emblematic image, with no other comment, provides the transitional explanation for her fall, in which she forgets 'le nom de mere,' that is, in which she abandons the 'mother' type in which she had invested all her energies. The pivotal image replaces causal explanation in the structuring of the story.[10]

Sometimes, the story is structured in such a way as to conjure an all-encompassing image that organizes the reader's perception of the action and directs his moralization of the story. We find such a case in the twenty-sixth *nouvelle*, where a young man finds himself torn between his attraction to a wise lady and a foolish one. The young seigneur d'Avannes, dissatisfied with his father, who is 'rude et avaritieux,' lives with his uncle; at a wedding dance one day, he meets an old gentleman and his lovely young wife, and so ingratiates himself that the fifteen-year-old is invited to come and live with them as if he were an adopted son. A total lack of what we would today call psychological realism in the 'adoption' of a handsome young nobleman by a wealthy old commoner and his young and beautiful wife removes the story from the very start from the space of everyday pragmatics, and into that of the fairy tale, which is an allegorical space,[11] the space of parable. In any event, the trio live an idyllic life until the young *seigneur* becomes interested, as he approaches his seventeenth year, in women, and turns his attention to a lady from Pampelona. The reader is alerted to the allegorical dimension of the tableau that emerges by the way the two ladies are set in parallel over the question of their qualities as housekeeper, the first being implicitly compared to the *Venus domestique* of the emblem tradition, while the other is presented as a bad *mesnagiere* and hypocritical imitator of the ideal. Later the young nobleman is compared, quite in passing, to Hercules. That reference sets the story, for the knowledgeable reader, against the background of Hercules at the crossroads, trying to choose between vice and virtue,[12] and points the direction to what I take to be the intended moralization.

These *nouvelles* are not isolated examples. Other French prose writers of the sixteenth century also showed themselves to be keenly interested in emblems and emblematic structures. Rabelais was passionately curious about Egyptian hieroglyphics and, whether unwittingly or not, structured more than one episode in his narrative in emblematic ways, or against an emblematic background. The passage that comes immediately to mind is Panurge's deciphering of the *impresa*-ring sent to Pantagruel by the Parisian lady, a ring that contained one of the atrocious rebus devices that Rabelais professed to detest: 'Di amant faux pourquoi m'as tu laissée?'[13] As my colleague Jerome Schwartz has shown, emblematic structuring may also be found in Jacques Hyver's collection of *nouvelles*, the *Printemps*, and emblematic images were used in the discourses delivered at the Palace Academy of Henri III.[14]

By the turn of the seventeenth century, French preachers were consciously turning to emblematic imagery to express the ineffable, especially as concerns such things as the Virgin's graces. Jean Bertaut, for example, did not believe these graces could be 'represented' 'à l'egal de leur verité,' and this, in his opinion, explained why the Church described them rather 'en termes qui sentent l'hieroglyfic, & l'Embleme, qu'en paroles expresses et nuës.'[15] References to emblems were particularly common in the writings of Jesuits such as Seguiran, who seems to expect of his audience some familiarity with Alciato, and a little later the Jesuit Etienne Binet published his manual, *Essay des merveilles de nature*, which encouraged an emblematic deployment of imagery in sermons throughout the seventeenth century.[16]

In short, the emblematic was used, and consciously so as often as not, to structure all kinds of Renaissance prose, and although poetry, too, was often structured in ways that recall the organization of the emblem, the influence is not so clear, nor so self-conscious. Elsewhere I have tried to show how emblematic images might usefully be defined and how they might be used in the structuring of poetry.[17] Probably some of the best examples of emblematic images in poetry may be found in the religious verse of the late sixteenth century, and some examples from this corpus will show very clearly what one might call the emblematic structuring of imagery in literature that would not otherwise be classified as emblematic.

In one of his *Lettres touchant quelques poincts de diverses sciences*, d'Aubigné reports that Henri de Navarre preferred poetry from the court of Navarre to that of the fashionable imitators of Desportes, because 'ils sont si coulants que le goust en est aussy tost escoulé: les autres,' continued the king, 'me laissent la teste pleine de pensees excellentes, d'images et d'amblemes, desquels ont prevalu les anciens.'[18] Many poets and readers of serious verse must have agreed with the king in the last quarter of the sixteenth and the first quarter of the seventeenth centuries. Close attention to the religious poetry of Sponde, Chassignet, Du Bartas, and to a certain extent d'Aubigné himself, shows that these poets as well as less prominent writers, both Catholic and Protestant, such as Florent Chrestien, La Roche Chandieu, and Gabrielle de Coignard, were all marked by the same mentality that spawned the immense popularity of emblems. This is not to say that all of their imagery was emblematic, but on occasion, especially when they wished to draw specific new moral lessons from traditional images, all of these poets would organize their presentations in ways that appear to be modelled closely on the composition of emblems.

The use of emblematic models in such cases may well have helped prepare techniques for the construction of the highly incarnate imagery that characterizes baroque poetry during the first half of the seventeenth century. We find one highly explicit example among the *Octonaires de l'inconstance et vanité du monde*, composed by Antoine de La Roche Chandieu around 1580. Following the long poetic tradition of instructions to artists, he orders:

Orfevre, taille-moy une boule bien ronde,
Creuse et pleine de vent, l'image de ce Monde;
Et qu'une grand'beauté la vienne revestir,
Autant que ton burin peut tromper et mentir,
En y representant des fruicts de toute guise,
Et puis tout à l'entour escri ceste devise:
Ainsi roule tousjours ce Monde decevant
Qui n'a fruicts qu'en peinture et fondez sur le vent.[19]

And it was a goldsmith-engraver, Etienne Delaune, who took up the poet's call and actually did illustrate many of these epigrams; the imagery was indeed so pictorially incarnate that it was able to call forth engravings, just as Georgette de Montenay's emblem texts did for Pierre Woeiriot. I say 'pictorially' because the image Chandieu presents is not taken from nature, but from art, and is built from art's iconographical conventions.

Before turning to other examples from this body of poetry, it will be useful to look at a love sonnet by Etienne Jodelle that provides a classic and more easily analysable example of emblematic structuring than almost any other poem I know, or at least any poem that does not explicitly draw attention to its emblematic character the way La Roche Chandieu's *huitain* does. Jodelle gave his sonnet a title: 'Sur la devise de la Cygalle,' and it proceeds this way:

Quand le chien d'Erigone ou l'avant-Chien encore,
Au plus fort de l'Esté d'une ardente cuisson
Seiche toute herbe aux champs, avançant la moisson
Que le soleil doré de son or mesme dore:
Du plain jour l'aspreté, qui tout humeur devore,
Vient tous gosiers d'oiseaux fermer à leur chanson,
La Cygalle sans plus renforçant son haut son,
Sans fin de voix et dueil, l'oeil du grand monde honore.
Or tu es la Cygalle, et ta Dame un Soleil,

Mais au chaud de l'Esté ton chaud n'est pas pareil,
Ny ton beau chant au chant de la rauque Cygalle:
  Car ta Dame peut faire ainsi qu'aucun flambeau
N'egalle à ton avis son lustre en tout si beau,
Qu'aucun chaud, qu'aucun chant, ton chaud, ton chant n'egalle.[20]

The quatrains clearly suggest the picture of a cicada, the summer sun, and a field of ripening grain, suspended in time like any pictured scene by the use of the present tense throughout. But what does the picture suggest? As in a typical emblem text, the first tercet equates the cicada and sun with a lover and his mistress, before making the emblematic point in the last five lines that the solar heat of her beauty makes the poet/lover sing with unparalleled beauty. By telling us that this sonnet is a development on a cicada device, the poet reveals that he is thinking in emblematic ways as he is writing these verses, and thus betrays the motivation for the structure he has chosen.

It would appear that the composition of emblems in France between the late sixteenth and early seventeenth centuries was an exercise that did not generally have as its goal publication; indeed, as we have seen (146–50 and 185–8 above), several unpublished collections of emblems from this period have been preserved in more or less carefully prepared, and sometimes even elegant, manuscripts that seem to have been intended as their final form. It would appear then that in France the composition of emblems was coming to be seen as a personal and private exercise, for one's own benefit, that of his family, or the enjoyment of his friends, rather than for the broader, more anonymous, readership that publication would assume. The imagery of such poetry was often intended to become literally incarnate, as is clear in Chandieu's *octonaire*. The pictures thus produced could be used in the kind of interior decoration that might serve as a meditational program.

The personal meditative practices implied by such programs of small-scale moralizing poems and pictures as have been preserved were encouraged by the Church and explained in manuals modelled on Loyola's *Exercices spirituels* in the wake of the Council of Trent. Occasionally, we catch a glimpse of the role emblematic models might have played in shaping a personal meditation, as in a sonnet composed toward the end of the sixteenth century by Gabrielle de Coignard.[21] In the quatrains, the poet tells of her pleasure slumbering beneath a leafy elm, beside a gently flowing stream, on a hot summer day; when she awakes, she exults at the beauty of the sky and '[son] esprit va prendre une haute carriere / Voulant de l'intellect fendre le ciel vouté.' A sudden shower cuts short her proud reverie, and '[son] esprit mouillé fut contrainct s'abbaisser.' Wryly the poet superimposes an emblematic picture on her experience, and that picture serves as a mediator, permitting her to draw from this little spiritual adventure a lesson in humility: 'Ha! vaine dis-je alors: voicy le vol d'Icare, / Il ne t'appartient pas de veoir chose si rare, / Ne monte point plus haut qu'on ne te veut hausser.' The knowledgeable reader will appreciate the unexpected variation here on emblems by Alciato (104, *In Astrologos*) and others, and he will note that, in fine emblematic fashion, the last line presents a moral exhortation of paroemic dimensions.

The influence of emblems on late Renaissance religious poetry has been quite widely acknowledged, but the exact nature of that influence and its significance have never, to my knowledge, been carefully analysed. The reason lies in the difficulty in determining what constitutes an emblematic image and in isolating it from other kinds of poetic imagery. Henri de Navarre claimed to like poetry from the court of Navarre because it left his mind full of 'images and emblems.' What might he have meant by 'emblem,' since he clearly was not talking here about illustrated emblem books in the strictest sense of the term? This question can be answered only by distinguishing between an emblematic image and a metaphor or simile that uses traditionally emblematic materials.

Jean de Sponde's eighth *Sonnet de la Mort* presents, in my view, a perfect model of the unillustrated emblematic image as it appears in late Renaissance religious poetry. The first quatrain presents the emblematic picture:

> Voulez-vous voir ce trait qui si roide s'eslance
> Dedans l'air qu'il poursuit au partir de la main?
> Il monte, il monte, il perd: mais helas! tout soudain
> Il retombe, il retombe, et perd sa violence.

Instead of the metaphorical articulation that is so common in Ronsard and that would yield something like 'Comme ce trait qui si roide s'eslance,' the reader is presented with a picture that the poet will comment on, and eventually moralize, for him. The phrasing 'Voulez-vous voir' does not automatically have to introduce a picture, but while a clever engraver could make all the details of the next three lines visible simultaneously to a viewer, this action, given its speed, is largely invisible to the naked eye. Yet the immobilized arrow in flight was common in emblems and *imprese*; there is an example in the emblems of Georgette de Montenay (embl. 14; fig. 55); two in Scipione Bargagli's *Dell'imprese* (191, 203), and one in Rollenhagen (I, 24). Furthermore, the action is fragmented here ('Il monte, il monte, il perd') in a way it might be presented in a picture or series of

EMBLE'ME CHRESTIEN 14

A ceſt archer inſenſé ſembloit bien
Qu'à chef viendroit de la choſe entreprinſe:
Mais ſur l'enclume il ne proufite rien,
Pleignant trop tard la peine qu'il a prinſe.
Les ennemis de Chriſt & ſon Egliſe
Lairront ainſi arc, fleſches & eſcu:
Car trop vaine eſt toute leur entreprinſe.
Le fils de Dieu ne peut eſtre vaincu.

Com

Fig. 55. 'Operam perdere.' Georgette de Montenay, *Emblemes ou devises chrestiennes* (1571), no. 14.

pictures. Finally, the expression 'Voulez-vous voir' tends to separate the image from the course of daily life by implicitly inviting the reader to turn his attention to the image (and away from something else) and isolate it in an allegorical space where it has only moral meaning.[22] Ronsard draws a comparison from an image without excerpting it from its setting in nature: 'Comme on voit sur la branche au mois de mai la rose.' Such spatial and temporal coordinates as 'sur la branche' and 'au mois de mai' are generally lacking in what I characterize as an emblematic image. In the end, the expression 'Voulez-vous voir' has a framing effect that makes the image pictorial by bracketing it from everyday experience.

The textual presentation of such an image often enacts this originary process of isolation by setting the image into the text without making it truly part of the discursive development of that text. Here we might take as an example an image from Montaigne's 'Apologie' that I have already discussed elsewhere:

> Je croy qu'il [l'homme] me confessera, s'il parle en conscience, que tout l'acquest qu'il a retiré d'une si longue poursuite, c'est d'avoir appris à reconnoistre sa foiblesse. L'ignorance qui estoit naturellement en nous, nous l'avons par longue estude, confirmée et averée. Il est advenu aux gens véritablement sçavans ce qui advient aux espics de bled: ils vont s'eslevant et se haussant, la teste droite et fiere, tant qu'ils sont vuides; mais, quand ils sont pleins et grossis de grain en leur maturité, ils commencent à s'humilier et à baisser les cornes. Pareillement les hommes ayant tout essayé et tout sondé, n'ayant trouvé en cet amas de science et provision de tant de choses diverses rien de massif et ferme, et rien que vanité, ils ont renoncé à leur presomption et reconneu leur condition naturelle.[23]

While this passage was published in its entirety in the 1580 edition of the *Essais*, one is tempted to speculate that the image of the heads of wheat was an addition to a more primitive state of the text,[24] for the entire sentence containing the image and the word 'Pareillement' that begins the next sentence could be deleted without any damage to the underlying argument. This image is a quintessential addition as Montaigne defines it in 'De la vanité' (III, 9; 941b), where he characterizes this kind of addition as 'quelque embleme supernumeraire.' We find the same kind of images, embedded in the text in precisely the same way, in the early seventeenth-century sermons of Bertaut, Seguiran, and Camus (see above, 225).

While this characterization would apply equally well to some images we have examined in Marguerite de Navarre's *Heptameron*, especially in the thirtieth *nouvelle*, the situation in poetry is somewhat different. There the text is a fragment, as if for some kind of mosaic. The detail of description in a sonnet by Sponde, unlike that in Ronsard's metaphorical descriptions, reminds one of the ever-increasing accumulation of detail in the ever more laborious emblem illustrations of the time. Detail in an emblem never functions to link the image with the surrounding world, but is entirely inward-directed, and subordinated to the didactic goal of the emblem, and in Sponde's sonnet serves as a foundation for a point-by-point comparison between the flight of an arrow and the life of man. This comparison, in turn, prepares the reader for the typically emblematic exhortation with which the sonnet closes: 'hé! commence d'apprendre / Que ta vie est de Plume, et le monde de Vent.'

The emblematic image does not need the grammatical articulation of a simile because it is predicated on the assumption of a strict microcosmic parallel between man and the world.[25] When Du Bartas says that 'Le monde est un grand livre,' he means that it is a book of emblems. This view of the world descends from the monolithic medieval world-view that was generated by the Roman Catholic power structure and was reflected, for example, in the bestiaries, but it is a view of the world that is no longer monolithic and, at least hypothetically, monovalent. The implications of nominalism had made this grand design seem increasingly implausible, and the refraction of a generalized point of view into an infinity of autonomous points of view that developed as a corollary of Renaissance individualism made it possible to juxtapose the microcosm with elements of the macrocosm in a vast variety of what must have seemed equally legitimate ways. It is this possibility that accounts for the emblem's capacity for endless variation and its potential for surprise. The bestiary was limited by the belief in a single, correct parallel, even when there was disagreement over what the right one was.

Resemblance was an increasingly important criterion of analogy, and since resemblance is a variable element of cultural *vraisemblance*, that which was *ressemblant* in the Renaissance was more dependent on questions of shape, or natural function, than it had been during the Middle Ages. Hence tears could be transformed into pearls, and as Françoise Bardon has shown, players at court could take the shape of the ancient gods. Once the primary analogical link had been made through some kind of resemblance, then the emblematist could forge all kinds of parallels in order to find striking new vessels for old wine.[26]

On a technical level, then, the composition of an emblematic image is a matter of craft, rather than creativity as we have understood it since the Romantics. In his *Sepmaine*, Du Bartas sketches various pictures of man producing works of art. During the first day, for example, he contrasts God's way of creation with the strategies or techniques of an architect who constructs an edifice through the imitation and combination of ideas taken from other, existing buildings:

> ... il prend le frontispice
> De ce palais ici, d'un autre les piliers,
> D'un autre la façon des riches escaliers:
> Et choisissant par tout les choses les plus belles,
> Fait un seul bastiment dessus trente modeles: (I, 188–92)

This is obviously an artisan's way of working, and it closely resembles the technique of composing emblems. The emblematist takes 'les choses les plus belles' from perhaps several ancient and medieval traditions and recombines them in new ways to make 'un seul bastiment,' an emblem book, 'dessus trente modeles.' It is significant that both Corrozet and Du Bartas should use the same image, with its implications of 'bricolage' in the sense of Lévi-Strauss' famous definition.[27] Du Bartas used emblematic imagery of the kind I have been defining mainly in the seventh day when he was discussing man and the standards for his conduct within the world that God had made, although others are scattered throughout the fifth and sixth days. The textual model Du Bartas used for this imagery can, I think, be traced back to La Perrière's *Morosophie* of 1553. With some variations, that model may be described as based on a quatrain structure in which the first couplet provides a description followed by two lines of sententious moralization. By the eighteenth century such a structure was seen as an ideal form for the epigram. In his essay 'Zerstreute Anmerkungen über das Epigram,' G.E. Lessing observed that the classic inscription epigrams were simply informative descriptions, whereas a higher form of epigram would, in his opinion, not be attached to any actual physical object, but rather would elaborate a verbal symbol in the first part in such a way as to excite a reader's curiosity that would be satisfied by some explanation in the last part of the epigram.[28]

A typical example of Du Bartas' application of this model might be his use of the traditional image of the heads of wheat that become more deeply bowed, the heavier they are with grain:

> Que le noble, le fort, l'opulent, & le docte,
> Soit comme roturier, debile, pauvre, indocte:
> Et voyant par les champs blondoyer la moisson
> Des espics barbotez aprene sa leçon,
> Qui plus sont pleins de grain, plus leurs testes abaissent:
> Plus sont vuides de grain, plus haut leurs testes dressent. (VII, 495–500)

We have already seen how Montaigne used this iconographical theme, which goes back to Seneca among others, and which had been, or was to be, taken up for devices and emblems in a number of different ways by Paradin, Taurellus, Schoonhovius, and others.[29] Lines three and four of this passage describe the wheat field, while lines five and six draw a precise, if implicit, lesson, but leave it general enough that it can be applied to the arrogance of nobility, of knowledge, or of wealth. In other words, like any emblem, this passage sketches a truly universal moral lesson.

This image is not an isolated instance of such construction, and indeed the seventh day, given over to rest and meditation, contains a whole series of such lessons drawn from the consideration of the marvellous work that God had wrought. The series of lessons thus drawn from nature focuses on the faithful palm tree, the magnet, the mores of bees, the touching fidelity of the widowed turtle-dove, the spider web, and the whole litany of emblematic motifs that was by then so familiar from the emblem books of La Perrière and others, and that poets like Chassignet were to take up time and time again throughout this period.

While emblematic motifs of this kind do occur elsewhere in the work of Du Bartas, they are seldom linked to generalizing moral commentaries. Rather, when a given animal is brought into the world, it is often accompanied, especially in the fifth day, by an emblematic epithet. That is, when Du Bartas refers to the halcyon (V, 719–30), he recalls its ability to calm the sea while building its nest; it is characterized in such a way as to fit it into a particular kind of world, not to prepare it for a certain kind of action. The editors of the American edition of Du Bartas' works take pains to tell us that this is a belted kingfisher,[30] but such fussy ornithological distinctions would be quite lost on Du Bartas' early pre-Linnaean readers, who would more likely have thought of something more like Alciato's *Ex pace ubertas* emblem (179). If they did do so, then this description would serve a didactic purpose without any explicit moralization. In this way, a great number of descriptions are emblematic in that they silently refer the reader to emblems he already knows.

Elsewhere in the *Sepmaine*, one senses the influence of the iconographical traditions of the emblem, even when any moralizing intention is either absent or secondary to the poet's concern. During the second day, for example, Du Bartas presents the spontaneous generation of a frog: 'Le limon escumeux se transforme souvent / En vert grenouillon ... ' following a tradition emblematically expressed in Horapollo's *Hieroglyphics*. Sometimes Du Bartas recalls the emblematic context with a simple epithet, as Marguerite de Navarre did in the *Heptameron* (see above, 223). In day six (VI, 81) we find a passing reference to the 'chameau troube-rive,' evoking an image that recalls La Perrière's well-known *Theatre* emblem 69, and that Pierre de Loisy copied early in the seventeenth century for one of the so-called *Sonnets franc-comtois*, sometimes attributed to Chassignet (fig. 56a–b). There is no moralization in either case here, explicit or implicit, but it almost seems in such cases that Du Bartas is consciously fashioning a world that will be ready for the emblematist man will become on the last day of this first week.

Fig. 56. (a) Guillaume de La Perrière, *Le Theatre des bons engins* (1540), Emblem 69.

Fig. 56. (b) Pierre de Loisy, 'chameau trouble-rive' (c. 1615).

At other times, Du Bartas combines the emblematic tradition with the taste for enigmas that was so common during the sixteenth century. Numerous volumes of enigmas were published, and one manuscript set of enigmas at the Bibliothèque Nationale is entitled 'Emblemes tres curieux des plusieurs choses fort communes et triviales' and dates from the late sixteenth century.[31] When Du Bartas fashions an emblematic enigma, he describes an animal or object, situates it in a moral context, but does not name it, or names it only at the end of a long descriptive *amplificatio*. One example from the sixth day is his portrayal of the porcupine (VI, 293–308), in a long periphrastic *éloge* of that model of defense preparedness that leaves the beast unnamed, but not unrecognized by the aficionados of the courtly *impresa*, who would remember here Louis XII's famous 'De pres et de loin' device. For those who still might not recognize the porcupine, he uses the verb 'hérisser,' which, of course, gives the secret away completely. Such exercises in mannerist periphrasis had been common in French poetry since the early days of the Pléiade, and it was probably from Ronsard that Du Bartas borrowed the technique.

Not only does Du Bartas borrow frequently from the store of emblematic iconography, but when he does so, he sometimes explicitly characterizes the resulting descriptions as pictures. He often uses the word 'tableaux' in talking about them, and occasionally he is even more explicit as in this metaphor from the fifth day: 'Mon livre ... ne rougi de porter les mouches, ... & cent mil autres vers, / Peints sur ton blanc papier du crayon de mes vers.'[32] With the pun of *vers*/verses 'painting' *vers*/worms, it is clear how self-conscious Du Bartas was about his involvement with the *ut pictura poesis* aesthetic. And that involvement was full of implications for his art. His descriptions are pictorial, too, in that they do not fit into any narrative scheme. And like emblems, these 'tableaux' are usually intended to serve a precise and fairly explicit didactic purpose. In a passage already cited (138 above) it is clear that for the needs of domestic economy, Du Bartas seems to be claiming that an emblematic interpretation of nature is superior to the lessons of the ancients.

As a result, then, Du Bartas appears quite modern in his preference for nature over the authority of the ancients, but at the same time, he is conservative in his use of nature to provide moral guidance for his fellow men. Du Bartas, like his contemporaries in the Low Countries, was turning an ever more attentive eye to the observation of nature in order to construct better tableaux for the instruction and edification of his readers. As he did so, the description came, increasingly, to dominate the moralizing application. Modern readers of Chassignet, who remember his sumptuously sensual and incarnate imagery but have forgotten his sombre moralities, will realize how much he and other religious poets of the time learned from Du Bartas. But this somewhat myopic attention to naturalistic detail, which certainly grew out of a mannerist preoccupation with the perfect execution of detail for its own sake, would eventually spell the end of the emblematic, an end foreshadowed in the amoral baroque descriptions of Saint-Amant and his *confrères* fifty years later, descriptions in which the incarnate, perhaps for the first time, had lost all touch with the transcendent.

Modern readers unaware of the complex and self-reinforcing context of emblems and emblematics lose much of the flavour that appealed so strongly to readers in late sixteenth- and early seventeenth-century Europe from Louis Papon and Anne d'Urfé to John Milton. But can we be sure that contemporary readers saw the links to the emblematic in the poetry they read or the sermons they listened to? In fact, we have much evidence of how emblematics affected the reading process. Some of the ways in which the emblematic habits of processing and organizing information conditioned the reception of French Renaissance writers are evident in emblem books published in the Low Countries. Most often what we find in the works of Jacob Cats and Zacharias Heyns are passages gleaned from literary works and grouped around the commonplace topics provided by emblems. Heyns was partial to Du Bartas, while Cats often cited Montaigne, especially in his 'Sur des vers de Virgile' (III, 5). Ronsard, excerpted and translated, is often recalled in Johan de Brune's *Emblemata of zinnewerck* (Amsterdam, 1624).[33] Some emblem collections then became commonplace books that organized the gleanings of late Renaissance readers. And these texts go far in explaining the tendency toward sententiousness in Renaissance drama and other kinds of writing. All the great Renaissance writers could be read from an emblematic perspective, and, since an author is always attentive to some audience, that perspective must also have conditioned the practice of writing during the Renaissance.

Conclusion

> Malgré son appartenance à l'univers du symbole en général, l'emblème est bien une création spécifique de l'Humanisme: le Moyen-Age avait connu les figures du blason, la Renaissance qui exalte l'individu forge la devise aristocratique; le 'Temps des Cathédrales' avait fréquenté l'allégorie d'institution divine, stable et fondée sur une intrinsèque Vérité, l'emblème, qui est aussi le brusque dévoilement d'un sens second dissimulé derrière le sens littéral, redressement 'anamorphotique' d'une première illusion, ne repose que sur l'invention d'un instant, l'intuition érudite, le caprice humain presque, et ne s'adresse qu'à un besoin d'approfondissement du monde moral, elle travaille sur la virtualité d'une réserve intelligente du signe qui peut aussi passer à un autre référent.
>
> François Epée[1]

The emblematic process was an act of contextualization. As Michael Camille, among others, has noted, late medieval art needed *tituli*, and other textual explanations, in order to limit and delimit the meaning of visual signs.[2] Despite what may have been a nostalgia for an ideogrammatic system that reflected a monolithic view of the world and the cosmos in a complex, but ultimately monovalent, constellation of signs, the Christian Middle Ages in the West, at least in its later years, saw a multiplication of the meaning of visual signs. Earlier the multiple senses of a sign were fused in a way that did not separate the signifier from what it signified. But as art became more naturalistic at a time when nominalism was beginning to focus attention on things in themselves, the signifier tended to become increasingly separate and independent from the message it carried, from its signified, and the whole symbol became, as a consequence, a candidate for analysis. At the same time, biblical exegesis was becoming ever more analytical, and the multiple possibilities for meaning in the sign, of the lion, for example, became individually clear and distinct.

No longer could an illusion of univalent meaning be preserved, as the proliferation of manuscripts following the introduction of paper in the West made it increasingly possible to consult and compare different traditions and interpretations. In biblical exegesis, efforts to make sense of hermeneutic variety and a multiplicity of interpretive possibilities took the form of typological interpretation along the lines of the famous four levels of meaning, which organized different interpretations into various theological categories, much as other kinds of knowledge were being organized around commonplaces. This exegetical development is probably the proximate origin of the kind of contextualization that was to become typical of the Renaissance emblem. But typology was exercised in a sporadic way at best in biblical exegesis, and it could not be applied very well at all to the profane culture that, increasingly, was becoming commingled with a theological culture striving to remain separate, distinct, and pure.

Camille's most striking example is the use of some kind of label to help the viewer decide whether a female figure was a Virgin to be revered or a Venus to be abominated.[3] That medieval artists, writers, and scholars were even aware of such a need to distinguish personae in visual art by means of labels suggests that their schematized forms were viewed as no more than paradigmatic iconographical matrices that became operational in a particular situation only by the addition of some attribute or text. Paradoxically, however, the need to distinguish by means of labels suggests the dangerous possibility of a pairing of personages through some analogy of form; recalling other figures that could be represented by the very same shape, such paradigms could lead to unauthorized *rapprochements* between Christian and pagan, sacred and profane registers, between the Virgin, for example, and Venus. Taxonomies of different sorts were moderately successful in containing such potential imaginative forays, and corresponding to the typological taxonomies at a profane level, proverbs and bestiary lore were increasingly presented in specialized anthologies where they were all interpreted in a single sense – amorous, legal, and the like.

Emerging from these late medieval traditions, the emblem presupposed two things. First, like an empty iconographical form of the kind I have been discussing, the emblematic image is one that can, almost by definition, be interpreted in more than one way, but like medieval images, it can also, by the limitations of its bi-medial structure, carry only one meaning at a time. Second, the emblematic image represents, at least very often, something that exists independently of any symbolic meaning it may carry; it tended to become a radically detachable image, one that could stand alone, independent of any emblematic meaning it might be meant to contain.

The emblematic image was, and increasingly so, especially in Dutch emblems, a naturalistically presented image that could be used in other, non-emblematic contexts, such as the scientific illustration of natural histories. Or it could be taken simply in itself as part of 'nature,' with no thought of any metaphorical or other application or use.

Metaphor, with the neat distinction it makes between signifier and signified, between vehicle and tenor, signals the coming marginalization of the cultural system upon which it depends for its analogies by some other system. This marginalization was a very slow process, and while scientific naturalism was slowly displacing medieval cosmology and its interpretation of the world, the residue of that cosmology continued to provide some of the stuff of emblematic analogies.[4]

So in this transitional world of the late Renaissance, it is not surprising to find that natural history illustration influenced emblem illustration and vice versa. Often, as William Ashworth has shown, it would be impossible to know from the woodcut or engraving alone whether a chameleon is supporting an emblematic analogy in Alciato or Camerarius, or illustrating one of the natural histories such as Pierre Belon's *De aquatibus*, Conrad Gesner's *Thierbuch*, or later the work of Aldrovandi (fig. 57).[5] The signifier had truly become detached from any particular abstract or transcendent meaning outside itself. The signifier was taken, increasingly, to signify only itself, unless of course some contextual signal directed its viewer or reader to do otherwise. Providing such a signal was the function of the emblematic: it fitted an image into a setting that would transform it from a simple part of nature into a metaphorical ornament of some idea.

Hence, some context was necessary during this period for an image to carry any metaphorical meaning at all; we can find what I would consider to be a self-conscious enactment of the need for a context to understand what message the emblematic sign is supposed to be carrying in Jacob Cats' first emblem book, the *Silenus Alcibiades* of 1618. There Cats used the same set of illustrations three times with different titles and texts to gloss them according to three different registers of meaning: the amorous, the moral, and the religious. The same thing happened in a slightly different way when George Wither used the Rollenhagen plates to make new and, in his opinion, better emblems. Wither's attitude somewhat obscures the situation Cats is enacting, but it is revealing in that it underlines the lingering belief that signs possessed an ideal, and as if natural, meaning. Although this belief was increasingly less compelling in the post-Reformation world of competing creeds and the competition they all were waging with the newly emergent scientific view of the world, it nevertheless survived, on

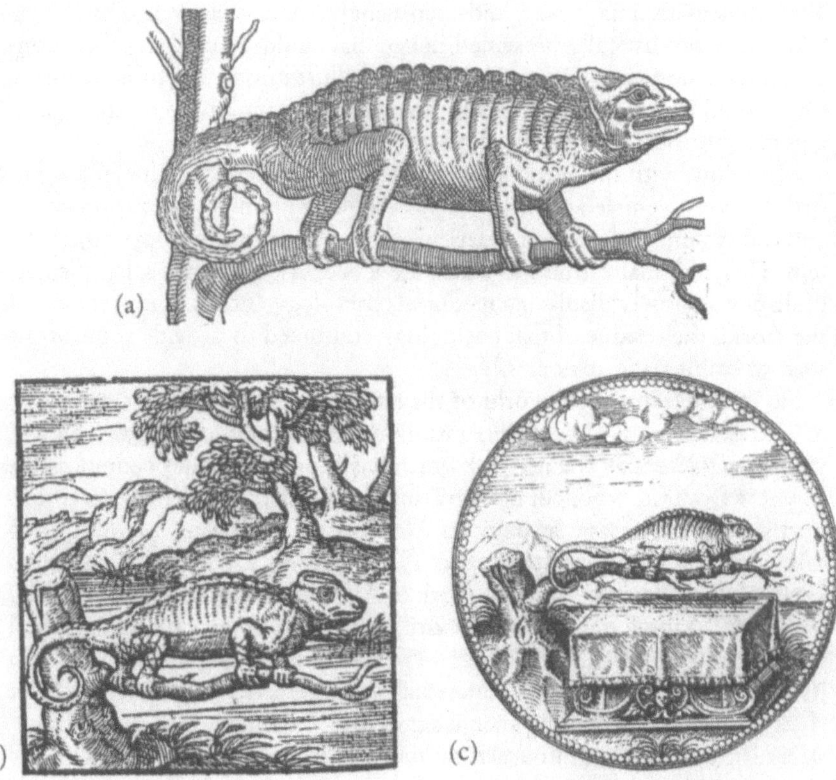

Fig. 57. Chameleon
(a) Pierre Belon, *De aquatibus* (1553). (b) Andrea Alciato, *Emblemata* (Leiden, 1591). (c) J. Camerarius, *Symbolorum et emblematum ex animalibus quadrupedibus* (1605).

the wings of positivism, well into the twentieth century, even though the principle of relativity was explicitly articulated as early as the Renaissance, and even though the source of such truth was seen as shifting from the Christian religion to science.

The interpretation of signs in different ways by Cats and Wither reminds us of the ways bestiary lore and proverbs were made to comment on these different domains in different ways in the late Middle Ages.[6] But what of the emblematic image as it occurs outside the domain of the emblem book *per se*? The emblematic image as I have defined it often appears to be somewhat detached from its surrounding context. It is a framed and bracketed image that can be removed from its setting without diminishing or fragmenting that context in any essential way, even though the image does lose its own role and meaning in the context when this happens. The emblematic image is an ornamental, highlighting device used to draw attention to a message that might otherwise appear trite or dry or abstruse. As in the poem by Jean-Antoine de Baïf cited and discussed in my introduction, the emblematic image tended simply to infuse new life into dead metaphors.

In the passage cited in the epigraph to this conclusion, François Epée used the term 'anamorphotique' in a passing reference to the emblematic process of uncovering the real sense behind the illusion of the literal. That term may be richer in implications for understanding the emblematic than Epée realized. Anamorphosis is a particularly revealing enactment of the perspectival possibilities of the individualized point of view. But rather than empowering the individual, the anamorphic controls the individual perspective by framing or constructing the composition in certain ways that call for specific perspectives on the tableau. The emblem does the same thing. Most emblem pictures, viewed with no frame, or no framing text, appear much different from the way they come into focus once the text has made the reader/viewer understand what he is looking at.[7] This emblematic perspective is an added perspective that emerges, by surprise, from the way the entire composition is put together. It is emblematic because it is 'added.' But is the added perspective the true perspective, a view of the true essence of the scene? Or is it merely 'ornamental'?

The terms 'emblem' and 'emblematic' remain so apt, so right for characterizing the imagery from the period under consideration, because such imagery became increasingly ornamental in this way during the *aetas emblematica*. This etymological sense of the word 'emblem' and its cognates lay heavy on the consciousness of a society whose culture was profusely and profoundly Latin. And the consciousness of this etymological guarantee of meaning must have made the whole notion of the emblem seem particularly appropriate for understanding metaphor in France at a time of its progressive trivialization and eclipse.[8] As a detachable, unessential ornament, the emblematic image could be accommodated to all kinds of situations, since it was no longer *necessarily* attached to a single theme or idea. It is this characteristic of the emblematic image that makes it so well fitted to the mechanisms of festival disguise, where appearance and reality lose contact, as the distrustful baroque consciousness was all too ready to believe to be typical in the presentation of self in the transactions of everyday life. Ornament overwhelmed reality in the baroque age. As one of my students, Didier Course, observed one day, baroque ornamentation tended to obscure and even hide the host on baroque altars. That effect is just the opposite of the effect of ornamental trappings in the Middle Ages, when ornament added to the prestige of religion by inspiring awe, a sense of the marvelous, and a sense of power through its ostentatious assertion of fabulous wealth.

The emblematic embodies a conception of the ornament as something unessential, and thus participates in the trivialization of ornament as it does in the desacralization of language. During the Middle Ages there remained at least the nostalgia of an original language in which the signifier still participated to some degree in the signified. But the western Church resisted the iconicity implied by such a conception of language, and insisted that visual images could be no more than arbitrary and unessential *libri laicorum*. But metaphoricity can be triumphant only when there exists some necessary bond between signifier and signified. And yet the iconoclasm of the Reformation broke language and metaphoricity every time it broke a head from the statue of a saint.

The emblem appears, then, as a transitional form between the reign of the natural sign, and the coming dominance of the arbitrariness of language. From Michel Foucault's perspective on the evolution of intellectual history at the time, we may deduce that the emblematic was subsumed by a conception of language that understood why a hieroglyphic and ideogrammatic conception of language will not work, and will prevent progress. The new conception of language understood normal language to combine the spatial and the temporal in an ideal analytic tool and memory system at the same time. Such a conception of language made the emblem superfluous.[9]

The metaphor was, as a consequence, exiled to the wilderness, especially in France, in the seventeenth and eighteenth centuries. When the Romantics took up the problem – that broken vessel of metaphoricity – they made it whole again by creating a personal and subjective bond between the signifier and its signified. And since that time, the only necessity in symbolism is a personal and subjective one. Real poetry requires some necessary relation between the signifier and its signified, but so does Freudian analysis. And thanks to the Romantic metaphor, both have flourished in the past century and more. Before that time, but after the end of the Middle Ages, European culture lived an interregnum of the sign, the *aetas emblematica*, which prepared the Romantic metaphor to come, out of the ruins a sign system that had carried the wisdom of the West for more than a thousand years.

Abbreviations

AB	*Art Bulletin*
BHR/HR	*Bibliothèque d'Humanisme et Renaissance / Humanisme et Renaissance*
BL	British Library, London
BN	Bibliothèque Nationale, Paris
CWE	*Complete Works of Erasmus*
DVLG	*Deutsche Vierteljahrschrift für Literatur und Geistesgeschichte*
JWI/JWCI	*Journal of the Warburg Institute / Journal of the Warburg and Courtauld Institutes*
PL	*Patrologia Latina*
RenQ	*Renaissance Quarterly*
RSS	*Revue du Seizième Siècle*
SATF	Société des Anciens Textes Français
STFM	Société des Textes Français Modernes
THR	Travaux d'Humanisme et Renaissance
TLF	Textes Littéraires Français

Notes

Introduction

1 The symbolic potential of such an image is expanded even further and becomes even more diffuse in the metamorphosis of the cedar tree into a mythological character in *La Chute d'un ange*, which Lamartine published in 1838.
2 For a discussion of this *précieux* poet and his emblems, see Russell, 'M. de Montplaisir and His Emblems,' 503–16. The following example is cited from a manuscript in the Dartmouth College Library.
3 *Evvres en rime*, ed. C. Marty-Laveaux, IV, 209.
4 For the distinction between the emblem and the device, or *impresa*, see Russell, *The Emblem and Device in France*, chap. 3.
5 These images may be usefully compared to one of the *Devises pour les tapisseries du roy* (BN ms fr. 7819), ed. Marc Fumaroli and Marianne Grivel: 'Pour la Magnanimité, dans la piece de l'element de la terre. Un Sapin, & ce mot RECTA SE TOLLIT IN ALTVM. Sa Majesté qui se plaist dans les choses grandes & elevées va droit à la gloire, ainsi que le Sapin qui se plaist sur les montagnes les plus hautes, & qui s'éleve droit en haut sans jamais se gauchir.' This theme is developed in a six-line madrigal by Charles Perrault (59).
6 'Emblematic Structures in Renaissance French Poetry,' 54–100.
7 'Qu'est-ce qu'une description?' 465–85.
8 For details of these developments, see Russell, 'Directions in French Emblem Studies.'
9 *François Ier imaginaire. Symbolique et politique à l'aube de la Renaissance française.*
10 *Emblèmes et pensée symbolique en Lorraine (1525–1633). 'Comme un jardin au coeur de la chrétienté.'*
11 *Diane de Poitiers et le mythe de Diane* and *Le Portrait mythologique à la cour de France sous Henri IV et Louis XIII.*

12 *Dictionnaire de poétique et de rhétorique*, 3rd ed. 65–84 (for allegory) and 670–742 (for metaphor).

13 See, for example, Kerver's French edition of Horapollo's *Hieroglyphics*, where the hieroglyphics are illustrated for the first time and presented as if they were emblems, or Corrozet's verse translation of Aesop, or even Blaise de Vigenere's translation of Philostratus' *Imagines* (Paris, 1615); cf. Russell, *The Emblem and Device in France*, 96 and passim.

14 *L'Art des emblemes* (1684), 124 and passim. The *Triumphs* are presented this way in BN ms fr. 24461, and Paris, Arsenal ms 5066; for a quasi-emblematic treatment of alchemical materials, see, for example, *Trois traitez de la philosophie naturelle non encore imprimez ... traduit par P. Arnauld* (Paris: Guillaume Marette, 1612); Rouen, Bibliothèque Municipale Leber 1243.

15 See, for example, the late 15th-century presentation of the four cardinal virtues (c. 1470) in BN ms fr. 9186, f. 304, discussed by Rosemond Tuve in *Allegorical Imagery*, 73–5.

16 E.g., 'Emblematic Structures in Sixteenth-Century French Poetry'; 'Montaigne's Emblems'; and 'La Description et l'emblématique dans la poésie française de Du Bellay,' 237–47.

17 *Labyrinthe de l'art fantastique*, 18, citing Emanuele Tesauro.

18 'La Théorie de l'expression figurée dans les traités italiens sur les *imprese*, 1555–1612.'

19 *The Emblem and Device in France*, chap. 4.

1: Book Illustration in Medieval France and the Relation between Picture and Text in the Later Middle Ages

1 Here, and in much of what follows concerning the early history of illuminated manuscripts, I am following Hélène Toubert, 'Formes et fonctions de l'enluminure.' See, too, John Harthan, *The History of the Illustrated Book*, 12–39.

2 *The Book of Memory: A Study of Memory in Medieval Culture*, 248–50.

3 Cf. Carruthers, 226–28, 244.

4 For another example, see René d'Anjou's device with the green orange branch sprouting from a dead tree trunk; see Christian de Mérindol, *Le Roi René et la seconde maison d'Anjou. Emblématique, Art, Histoire*, 130–1, 219, and 315, plate VIII.

5 See Félix Gaffiot, *Dictionnaire illustré latin-français*, s.v. *illustratio*. See, as well, Brian Stock, *The Implications of Literacy: Written Language and Models of Interpretation in the Eleventh and Twelfth Centuries*, 81, on the difference between northern and classicizing art.

6 But we must also not forget the technical side of this art, which is expressed in

the verb *alluminare*, introduced in the eleventh century and used by Dante to characterize the art of painting with the product of a reaction between vegetable extracts and alum crystals; see Giulia Bologna, *Illuminated Manuscripts: The Book before Gutenberg*, 31.

7 *Allegory: The Theory of a Symbolic Mode*, 108–9, where Fletcher, following Aristotle, describes allegory in terms of ornamental diction (*kosmos*), where the ornamental signifies a universe and serves as a symbol indicating rank in a hierarchy.

8 We do, however, find the same subordination, for example, in the Carolingian Stuttgart and Utrecht Psalters. See Harthan, and Robert G. Calkins, *Illuminated Books of the Middle Ages*, 209ff.

9 See E.H. Gombrich, *Symbolic Images: Studies in the Art of the Renaissance*, 151–2. But as Michael Camille's excellent study, *The Gothic Idol: Ideology and Image-making in Medieval Art*, shows, the Church was only moderately successful in this regard.

10 For an example of the use of this theme, see Gregory the Great's characterization of church sculpture as a Bible for the illiterate in his epistles to the Bishop Serenus of Marseilles (*PL*, 77, cols. 1027–8 and 1128–30). For an account of variations on this theme, see W. Tatarkiewicz, *Medieval Aesthetics* II, 104ff.; and L. Gougaud, 'Muta praedicatio,' reproduces several of the *loci classici* of this tradition. On the legitimation of visual art through titular inscriptions, see Michael Camille, 'Seeing and Reading: Some Visual Implications of Medieval Literacy and Illiteracy, 33.

But Avril Henry, in her edition of the *Biblia pauperum*, 17–18, cautions that pictures were used as reminders, and not as ideogrammatic texts in their own right.

11 David Bland, *A History of Book Illustration*, 2nd ed., 57.

12 Quoted by Meyer Schapiro in *Words and Pictures*, 17–18.

13 Cited in what is presumably his own translation, or paraphrase, from Cheltenham, ms 11059, by Léopold Delisle, 'Livres d'images destinés à l'instruction religieuse et aux exercices de piété des laïques,' in *Histoire littéraire de la France ... commencé par des Religieux Bénédictins*, 214. This manuscript contains the expression 'picturae tanquam libri laicorum' after Albert the Great's 'Picturae quae sunt libri laicorum.' See *Journal des Savants*, 1884, 703.

14 As early as the 17th century, Menestrier (*L'Art des emblemes* [1684], 11–12) had noticed the important influence of these epigrams on the early development of emblem literature. On the epigrams themselves, see James F. Hutton, *The Greek Anthology in Italy to the Year 1800*. For their impact on Alciato, see above, 113–16.

15 *The Gothic Idol*, 220–1.

16 'Emblem, Emblembuch,' in *Reallexikon zur deutschen Kunstgeschichte*, V, col. 121.

We find a similar situation in the early 16th-century manuscript containing 20 proto-emblematic compositions built around the verses of Psalm 26, *Dominus illuminatio mea*, to celebrate François Ier's victory over the Swiss in 1516 (BN ms fr. 2088), and beginning in the last third of the 16th century, in some emblem books, like the *Mikrokosmos*. See above, 80–1.

17 *L'Abeille dans l'ambre. Célébration de l'épigramme*, 464–9.

18 Examples of this kind of illustration may be found in 12th-century Bible iconography where the scene derives from a summarizing or interpretive prologue rather than from the text concerned, as in the Bury Bible.

On the increasing specialization and compartmentalization of biblical interpretation, see Marshall McLuhan, *The Gutenberg Galaxy*, 112. On the fourfold system of Biblical exegesis, see Henri de Lubac, *Exégèse médiévale. Les Quatre sens de l'Ecriture*.

It is interesting to note in this regard that, during the passage from the 12th to the 13th centuries, manuscript production was also marked by a parallel specialization, as scribes and illustrators executed separate and distinct parts of a given manuscript. See Michael Camille, 'The Book of Signs: Writing and Visual Difference in Gothic Manuscript Illumination,' especially 138.

19 Such a comparative study might shed interesting light on the relationship between text and picture in the *vitraux*.

20 See *La Bible moralisée de la Bibliothèque Nationale d'Autriche Codex Vindobonensis 2554*, ed. Reiner Haussherr, 5 and passim.

21 As noted by Schapiro, 15.

22 Toubert, 103.

23 Cf. Henry, passim.

24 *L'Art des emblemes* (1684), 61–2. At the beginning of the 17th century, the Jesuit Louis Richeome, whose ideas on the picture and pictorial description closely parallel those of the emblematists, remarked that, unlike the Jews, Christians admire the 'supreme sagesse' by which the old law and testament anticipate the new and which 'a si divinement couché les vives & dernieres couleurs de la loy de grace, sur les ombres & lineamens qu'il avoit tracez en l'ancienne loy.' (15) Second, they admire the 'sagesse du rapport' between the two Testaments. These two causes for *admiration* 'illustrent nostre foy'; they 'affermissent nostre esperance'; and 'Finalement elles enflamment nostre amour envers Dieu; parce que ceste contemplation des figures lointaines, rapportees à la verité presente, nous fait voir l'éternelle charité de la quelle Dieu nous a aymez; ...' (*Tableaux sacrez*, 14–18). As is evident from Richeome's remarks, Biblical typology still played an important role in 17th-century Catholicism; he advises its use in the

composition of sermons, and beginning in the late 16th century, typology was also used in the composition of emblems in France and Flanders.

25 E.g., Galatians 4: 24–31 or Hebrews 8 and 9, but especially 8: 5; for Augustine, see *PL*, 34, col. 625 and 41, col. 505.

26 *Abbot Suger on the Abbey Church of Saint Denis and Its Art Treasures*, 74–5.

27 *Biblia pauperum*, ed. Avril Henry, 32.

28 Henry, 17. There existed, at least in England, a compendium of possible typological parallels that recalls the great Renaissance iconographies and their relation to the making of emblems (*Pictor in carmine*; see Henry, 15).

29 *Etude sur le Speculum humanae salvationis*, 136.

30 Cf. Carruthers, 241–2.

31 Cf. Sandra Hindman, 'Authors, Artists, and Audiences,' in *Pen to Press: Illustrated Manuscripts and Printed Books in the First Century of Printing*, 160: 'Both rubrics and pictures functioned partly as verbal and visual indices to major textual units, ... providing an internal reference system before medieval books received separate indices. Pictures not only functioned as alternate rubrics, but also as visual glosses on a text, providing yet another level of meaning to text and commentary as occurs in Christine de Pizan's *Epistre Othea* (BL Harley 4431 and BN fr. 606).'

32 See, e.g., Emile Mâle, *L'Art religieux de la fin du moyen âge en France*, 3rd ed., 229–46. But if these works provided later artists with iconographical materials, they did not for the most part, as Heckscher and Wirth have noted ('Emblem, Emblembuch,' col. 131), provide the 15th century with formal models. Avril Henry has many excellent examples of such use of the *Biblia pauperum*, 35ff.

33 Adrian Wilson and Joyce Lancaster Wilson, *A Medieval Mirror: Speculum Humanae Salvationis*, 27–8: 'The precise mathematical format of the *Speculum* is reflected in the linear scheme. The text of the first forty-two chapters has twenty-five lines to a column, two columns to a page; the bottom line of the first is rhymed with the top line of the second column. There are four columns or 100 lines to each chapter, filling a page-opening.' And this, of course, would permit the division of the work among many scribes and illuminators.

34 See L. Febvre and H.-J. Martin, *L'Apparition du livre*, 51–5.

35 The first dated illustrated book printed in France was a vernacular version of the *Speculum*: *Miroir de la redemption*, which, like all versions of this book, was printed in movable type.

36 For a particularly clear and concise description of the physical composition of such books, see Pierrette Jean-Richard's catalogue of the Louvre exhibit *Les Incunables de la Collection Edmond de Rothschild. La gravure en relief sur bois et sur métal*, 32.

37 Cf. Henry, 33–4.

38 Although Bland (58) suggests that lay participation in illuminated book production resulted from the decision by the Cistercian order to ban polychrome decoration of manuscripts by monastic scribes, Walter Cahn has shown that while the Cistercian *Instituta* did encourage a relatively sober style of decoration based on drawing, they did not forbid painting in manuscripts ('The Rule and the Book: Cistercian Book Illumination in Burgundy and Champagne').

39 Philippe de Thaon, *Le Bestiaire*, ed. E. Walberg, xxiv–xxvii.

40 See, e.g., Erik Iversen, *The Myth of Egypt and Its Hieroglyphics in the European Tradition*, 47–9.

41 For a different view held by other humanists, see 120–1, and Denis Drysdall, 'The Hieroglyphs at Bologna.'

42 See Florence McCulloch, *Medieval Latin and French Bestiaries*, 34ff. Cf. *Grundriss der romanischen Literaturen des Mittelalters*, Bd. VI, 2.

43 Walberg, i–x.

44 See Xenia Muratova, 'Workshop Methods in English Late Twelfth-Century Illumination and the Production of Luxury Bestiaries,' 53–68.

45 *Dialogue des devises d'armes et d'amours*, trans. Vasquin Philieul, 147; Philippe de Thaon, ll. 1135–76.

The emblematist Barthélemy Aneau composed an emblematic bestiary, *Decades de la description, forme, et vertu naturelle des animaulx, tant raisonnables, que Brutz* as did Guillaume Gueroult, *Second Livre de la description des animaux, contenant le blason des oyseaux.*

46 For the numbering of Alciato's emblems, I am following the standard numbering in the 1621 Padua edition. Cf. *Physiologus*, trans. Michael J. Curley, xxii–xxiii, as well as my discussions of these compositions in 'Emblematic Structures in Sixteenth-Century French Poetry, 87–8, and 'The Needs of the Literary Historian' in *An Index of Emblem Art*, ed. Peter M. Daly, 107–19, together with that of Konrad Hoffmann, 'Alciato and the Historical Situation of Emblematics,' 11–13.

47 *Li Bestiaires d'amours di maistre Richart de Fornival*, ed. Cesare Segre, 3–7. This pseudo-Ciceronian commonplace was understood in the late Middle Ages to come from the *Rhetorica ad Herennium.*

48 Lionel J. Friedman, ed. *Text and Iconography for Joinville's Credo*, 29.

49 Cf. Dürer's marginalia for Maxmilian's prayer-book, where he provides humorous and imaginative explanations of the hymns and prayers contained in it, also presumably to keep the emperor's eye and mind on the spiritual matters being addressed; see Fedja Anzelewsky, *Dürer, His Art and Life*, 170–1.

50 Fournival, *Li Bestiaires*, 3–7.

51 That the written text was translated into an oral message by the act of reading

continued to be literally true until the end of the sixteenth century. This is amply demonstrated by the inventory described and recorded by Robert Barroux, 'Catalogue d'une bibliothèque à la fin du XVIe siècle,' where the transcription shows that each word was pronounced as it was read and then transliterated in the copy as it was pronounced. This idea of the text can be traced to Isidore of Seville (see Carruthers, 169–70).

52 Fournival, *Li Bestiaires*, 3–7.

53 'The Book of Signs,' 135.

54 John V. Fleming, 'Obscure Images by Illustrious Hands,' in *Text and Image*, 1–26.

55 This is clear from Fournival's discussion quoted on 27 above. Cf. Walter J. Ong, *The Presence of the Word*, 111–14.

56 *Pagan Mysteries in the Renaissance*, 2nd ed., 208: 'Thus contrary to the divine intelligence which the reading of hieroglyphs is supposed to foreshadow, the intuitive grasp of them depends on discursive knowledge. Unless one knows what a hieroglyph means, one cannot *see* what it says. But once one has acquired the relevant knowledge, "unfolded" by more or less exoteric instruction, one can take pleasure in finding it "infolded" in an esoteric image or sign.' Cf. A. Henry, 17–18, who takes this fact to invalidate the persistent understanding of medieval art as *libri laicorum*.

57 Cf. Walter Ong, *Orality and Literacy: The Technologizing of the Word*, 39–41, and also Gilbert Durand, who defines allegory as a 'redondance perfectionnante' (*L'Imagination symbolique*, 2nd ed., 10) as well as E.H. Gombrich, *Symbolic Images*, 151–2.

58 *Li Bestiaires*, 11–12: 'Et puis ke je sui primerains veus, selonc la nature del leu j'en doi bien perdre le vois' (12).

59 See H.R. Jauss, 'Entstehung und Strukturwandel der allegorischen Dichtung,' especially 172–4.

60 *Li Bestiaires*, xxii–xxiii.

61 Sig. g-vii^{v}. Cf. Florence McCulloch, 'Pierre Gringore's *Menus propos des amoureux* and Richard de Fournival's *Bestiaire d'amour*,' where she shows the direct influence of Fournival on Gringore.

62 Following the terminology of Gérard Genette, *Palimpsestes*.

63 *Li Bestiaires*, ix.

64 *Bestiaires du moyen âge*, 63–4.

65 Cf. Barbara Tiemann, *Fabel und Emblem: Gilles Corrozet und die französische Renaissance-Fabel*, 30–4.

66 Ed. Lucy Toulmin Smith and Paul Meyer.

67 Tiemann, *Fabel und Emblem*, 101–5. E.g., La Perrière, *Le Theatre des bons engins*, 33: 'N'entreprendre contre plus fort' and Corrozet, *Hecatomgraphie*:

'Entreprendre pardessus sa force'; both are connected this way to the fable tradition, as is clear from the title Corrozet gives to his version of one of Aesop's fables (*Fables*, 1542, 69: 'N'entreprendre oultre ses forces').

68 There exists no modern edition of this work in French although Gianni Mombello promised in *La Tradizione manoscritta dell' 'Epistre Othea' di Christine de Pisan* that an edition would be forthcoming. There exist various English versions of the work. I have consulted *The Epistle of Othea to Hector (Harleian manuscript 838)*, ed. James D. Gordon, and for the French, I have used Lille, Biblio. Munic. ms 175, *Les cent hystoires de Troye, l'epistre de Othea deesse de prudence envoyee a lesprit chevalereux Hector*, BN ms fr. 606, and Philippe Le Noir's edition (Paris, 1522; BN Rés. Ye. 214). The most recent study of this work is Sandra Hindman's *Christine de Pizan's 'Epistre Othéa': Painting and Politics at the Court of Charles VI*.

69 BN ms fr. 606, f. 2^{r-v}. This manuscript provides the source for all further quotes from the *Epistre*.

70 In his *Etudes sur le poème allégorique en France au moyen âge*, 12, M.-R. Jung notes that, in Old French, the word 'allegorie' almost always meant 'sens chrétien' or 'explication chrétienne' and gives Christine's *Epistre* as a particularly clear example of this usage. Cf. Rosemond Tuve's distinction between allegory and moral allegory in *Allegorical Imagery*, 8–20.

71 Le Noir edition, sig. d-i^r–d-i^v. Cf. the Gordon edition, 73–4, the Lille ms, ff. 44^v–45^r (actually 43^v–44^r), and Barthélemy Aneau, *L'Imagination poetique*, 122–3.

72 See Hindman, 61–8.

73 See Henry, 32, and the early editions of the *Danse macabre*.

74 Quoted by J. van den Gheyn in his edition of the miniatures in ms 9392, 5–6.

75 On this development see Russell, *The Emblem and Device in France*, 87.

76 See, e.g., Lille ms 175, ff. 20^v–21^r (actually 19^v–20^r). We see the same apparent inattention to the positioning of illustration in relation to text in other manuscript copies of the *Epistre* (e.g., BN ms fr. 606 or BL Harley ms 4431).

77 On the role of the printers in establishing the format of the early emblem, see Russell, 'Alciati's Emblems in Renaissance France'; Barbara Tiemann, 'Sebastian Brant und das frühe Emblem in Frankreich'; and Claudie Balavoine, 'Les *Emblemes* d'Alciat: Sens et contresens.'

Perhaps this attention to the formation of a visual unit was meant to counter a less close inherent relation between text and illustration than in manuscripts (see Hindman and Farquhar, *From Pen to Press*, 179).

78 On the idea of allegorical space, see Walter J. Ong, 'From Allegory to the Diagram in the Renaissance.'

79 Cf. Hindman and Farquhar, *From Pen to Press*, 3: 'printing gradually omitted organizational features which for centuries had ordered the thought of readers.'

And as Sandra Hindman says in her essay 'Authors, Artists, and Audiences' later in the same volume, '... miniatures tended to preserve a closer relation to their texts than did woodcuts' (179).

80 *Le Livre français illustré de la Renaissance*, 2nd ed., 5–6. See above, 168.

2: The Allegorical Antecedents

1 See Russell, *The Emblem and Device in France*, 155–7.

2 See *Princeton Encyclopedia of Poetry and Poetics*, s.v. allegory.

3 See, e.g., Henri Morier's discussion of allegory in his *Dictionnaire de poétique et de rhétorique*, 65–84.

4 Babette Deutsch, *Poetry Handbook*, 76–7.

5 *Princeton Encyclopedia of Poetry and Poetics*, 12. Cf. Marc-René Jung, *Etudes sur le poème allégorique en France au moyen âge*, 62, where, in a discussion of the *De mundi universitate* of Bernard Sylvestris, Jung observes: 'Mais, dès que l'on essaie de voir clair, de distinguer, par exemple, Natura de Physis on remarque que les personnages allégoriques ne sont pas suffisamment définis par leur nom. Seule l'action, la *fabula*, permet de cerner ces figures de plus près. Nous dirons: l'allégorie réside justement dans cette *fabula*.'

6 Morier, 71–2, following Quintilian's distinction.

7 Cf. Paul Zumthor, *Le Masque et la lumière*, 84–5.

8 'The Painter and the Poet: Visual Design in *The Duchess of Malfi*.'

9 Russell, *The Emblem and Device in France*, 100–1.

10 I am not taking the idea of intentionality here in the narrow modern sense of what an individual author consciously intended, but of what is thinkable within a given society at a given moment in history, and the author's translation of that situation into a function for his work. Emerging from the Middle Ages, art was still mainly didactic, or as I prefer, functional.

11 *Hecatomgraphie* (1540), sig. N3^v–N4. Cf. Gisèle Mathieu-Castellani, *Emblèmes de la mort*, 63–5.

12 On this question, see Michael Bath, 'Honey and Gall or: Cupid and the Bees. A Case of Iconographic Slippage.'

13 *La Théologie au douzième siècle*, 188–9.

14 Gilbert Murray, as quoted by John MacQueen, *Allegory*, 13.

15 Cf. Zumthor, *Le Masque et la lumière*, 78–82.

16 In the discussion that follows, I shall be following Johan Chydenius, 'La Théorie du symbolisme médiéval'; and Armand Strudel, '"Allegoria in factis" et "allegoria in verbis."'

17 Tzvetan Todorov, *Symbolisme et interprétation*, 38–43.

18 MacQueen, 46.

19 Todorov, 92–3.
20 Ibid, 42–3, 99–100.
21 Ibid, 104.
22 Cf. A.J. Minnis, *Medieval Theory of Authorship*, 34.
23 MacQueen, 49–50; for the recent tendency to use this system in literary analysis, and cogent warnings about applying it indiscriminately to literary works, see Morton Bloomfield, 'Symbolism in Medieval Literature,' Cf. Minnis, *Medieval Theory of Authorship*, 34–5.
24 See Chenu, 167–8, where he defines analogy as a 'mot grec qui va prendre au [sic] sens technique ... selon un transfert de l'esprit prenant pied dans les formes sensibles pour percevoir les réalitiés spirituelles ...'
25 In this regard, it is interesting to note that the word 'analogy' presumably did not enter the French language until the 15th century, after having appeared in an early 13th century translation (1213) from the Latin; it would appear that it did not enter the English language until the 16th century.
26 Chenu, 176–7.
27 Ibid, 188.
28 Julia Kristeva, *Semeiotike. Recherches pour une sémanalyse (extraits)*, 55–7.
29 *The Emblem and Device in France*, 164–6. While Bloomfield wisely cautioned, in 'Symbolism in Medieval Literature,' against the wholesale application of the techniques and philosophy of allegorical exegesis as it was practiced in medieval theology to the interpretation of secular literature, there was undeniably some perceived relation between the two as late as the early Renaissance; this is clear in the following passage from Erasmus' *Enchiridion*: 'Jerome reproaches the impudence of those who dare to expatiate on the sacred Scriptures after just completing their secular studies, but how much more impudent are those who attempt the same thing without even having had a taste of the preparatory study. But just as the divine Scriptures themselves do not bear much fruit if you persist in adhering to the letter, so the poetry of Homer and Virgil is of no little profit if you remember that it is entirely allegorical' (*CWE*, 66, 33).
30 Cf. 48–9, and Latini's *argument voirsemblable*.
31 Both testimonials are cited by Sandra Hindman in *Christine de Pizan's 'Epistre Othéa': Painting and Politics at the Court of Charles VI*, 33.
32 As Morton Bloomfield notes in 'A Grammatical Approach to Personification Allegory,' 161–71. See as well Chenu, 190.
33 'Récit et anti-récit: le "Roman de la Rose."'
34 Jung, *Etudes*, 93–8.
35 Carruthers, *The Book of Memory*, chap. 1.
36 Yates, 104.

37 See Rosamond Tuve, chap. 4, especially 296–303.
38 For a discussion of ecphrasis, especially as it applies to this situation, see Jean Hagstrum, *The Sister Arts*, 29. Cf. Carruthers, 229–31.
39 *Symbolic Images*, 135, 138.
40 Beryl Smalley, *English Friars and Antiquity in the Early Fourteenth Century*, 179, 182; for a discussion of one late medieval attempt to illustrate such sermons literally, see F. Saxl, 'A Spiritual Encyclopedia of the Later Middle Ages.' Cf. Carruthers, 229–42.
41 Gombrich, 138; see above, 74–6, for the need for explanations in the new personifications of the virtues.
42 *François Ier imaginaire*, 59.
43 Cf. Carruthers, 226, where, following Carl Nordenfalk, she discusses illustrations as 'pictorial rubrics' and reading aids in other ways.
44 For an account of this revival, see Walter J. Ong, *Ramus, Method, and the Decay of Dialogue*, chaps. 4–6.
45 *Li Livres dou tresor*, ed. Francis J. Carmody, 367. The *argument voirsemblable* resembles the *allegoria in verbis* as defined by Todorov (see above, 42). The argument by contraries is similar to the enthymena as Quintilian defines it (VIII, v, 9ff.).
46 Cf. Morton Bloomfield, 'A Grammatical Approach to Personification Allegory' and M.T. Clanchy, *From Memory to Written Record. England, 1066–1307*, 18ff.
47 On this distinction, see Jung, *Etudes*, 20; and for a different perspective on the same question, Jon Whitman, *Allegory: The Dynamics of an Ancient and Medieval Technique*, 4–10.
48 *Logica memorativa. Chartiludium logice*. This work appears to be modelled on the *Ars memorandi*, used for memorizing the gospels, but it is used for learning logic. There is less regularity in its formatting, and the text is more dominant than in its model.
49 *Pagan Mysteries in the Renaissance*, 2nd ed., 26–7 and note.
50 Jauss, 171.
51 *The Gothic Idol*, 204–5. See as well Chenu, 175.
52 Robert Scholes, *Structuralism in Literature: An Introduction*, 84.
53 Horapollo, *The Hieroglyphics*, 19.
54 *Second livre de la description des animaux, contenant le blason des oyseaux*, sig. A2^{v}: 'Or en la posterité d'icelluy [man] (par sa prevarication premiere) tousjours sont demeurees quelques reliques de sa fragilité, & rebellion: lesquelles reverdissants croissent en telle grandeur, que quelquefoys elles suffoquent la bonne semence que Dieu tout bon espand sur noz coeurs & esprits: & par ce moyen demeure tout le genre des hommes subjet à peché, variable, & degenerant de sa premiere vertu. Parquoy pour le revoquer à la consideration de son devoir,

maintesfoys les animaux irraisonnables luy sont proposez pour mirouers: affin de l'animer à faire bien, & le persuader à prendre exemple aux maux qui adviennent par imprudence, pour ne cheoir en semblables.'

See, too, Pierre Le Moyne, *De l'art des devises*, 136.

55 See, for examples, Dominique Bouhours, *Les Entretiens d'Ariste et d'Eugène*, 296, and especially Henri Estienne, *De l'art de faire les devises*, 100–1.

56 *The Gutenberg Galaxy*, 112.

57 *The Waning of the Middle Ages*, chaps. 15 and 16. For an interesting parallel, see Liselotte Dieckmann, *Hieroglyphics: The History of a Literary Symbol*, 126, where she notes that the rise of enigmatic hieroglyphs in later antiquity coincides with a loss of impetus in ancient philosophy.

58 *The Waning of the Middle Ages*, 216.

59 Huizinga, 205.

60 See above, 41–5, for a discussion of euhemerism. Cf. Liselotte Dieckmann, *Hieroglyphics*, 7: 'Plato's creation of myths to illustrate philosophic ideas is the reverse of the philosophic reading of myth, generally known as the allegorical interpretation. It existed in Greece before Plato's time. Its original purpose was to re-interpret the old legends and myths in terms of a more modern, philosophic mode of thought. It appears as a device to preserve the dignity of old legends at a time when their poetic appeal was no longer sufficient to justify their existence.'

61 *Allegorical Imagery*, 302. In the preface to his *Imagination poetique* (*Picta poesis*), Aneau portrays the composition of his emblems as an exercise in imposed allegory: 'je ne me suis point tant soucié, que pourroit avoir imaginé celluy quiconque en feit le desseing imparfaict, & sans parolle: que d'y approprier de mon invention: ce que me a semblé le plus convenable, & Mythologic a la figure, en partie de moy inventé: en partie prins es tresbons Auteurs, Grecz ou Latins' (7).

62 Jean Seznec, *The Survival of the Pagan Gods*, 85. Cf. Dieckmann, 38: 'It is consistent on Ficino's part that he interprets Plato's myths in the same allegorical fashion. Thus it is of interest that in the *Phaidros* he not only explains in philosophical terms the myth of the charioteer with his two horses, but even adds a sentence of his own on the rotation of the wheels of the chariot – wheels which symbolize, in Ficino's visual imagination, the circle which all things describe in their rotation around the center, God ... This allegorical method is the logical consequence of the Neoplatonic view of the world. From God down to His most material manifestations the same meaning exists on various levels and to various degrees. And the whole world contains and manifests one and the same "wisdom" of which we achieve the highest form humanly attainable if we concentrate on the contemplation of the divine, be it in nature or in art.'

63 E.g., *Metamorphoseos libri moralizati* and *La Bible des poetes de Ovide Metamorphose.*

For a study of these versions, see Ann Moss, *Poetry and Fable: Studies in Mythological Narrative in Sixteenth-Century France*, chaps. 1–3, and Ghislaine Amielle, *Les Traductions françaises des Métamorphoses d'Ovide.*

64 In *From Pen to Press*, 193, where Hindman is paraphrasing from Mansion's second prologue to his edition of the *Metamorphoses* 43:

'Et combien que nostre acteur ovide ait procede par maniere de paraboles de fables et de similitudes qui de prime face semblent de nul prouffit comme dit est: toutesfois qui le clef en scet trouver: et d'icelle en ouvrir lhuis de l'entendement contemplatif: il y trouvera saveur melodieuse glorieuse, confortative et fructueuse chacun a son propos.

Exemple

Nagaires me trouvay en anvers ou pourpris de labaye de saint michiel ou je vey un chesne nouvellement abatu, plain de branches et de fueilles. Pluiseurs gens de divers estas le vindrent veoir pour sa grandeur. Entre lesquelz vint un marechal fevre qui demandoit le tronq dembas pour dessus icellui mettre son englume en sa forge. Il y vint ung bourgois qui demandoit le gros de larbre, pour dicelui faire un sommier en une sale quil faisoit ediffier. Un charpentier y vint qui voulentiers eust eu la flesche dicelui pour en faire des posteaux pour servir a son euvre Le tailleur dimages l'eut volentiers eu, pour en faire un crucifix ou .i. saint xpostle ...

Et moy qui veoye chascun faire son prouffit dicelui chesne: ne mis en oubly mon cas ains recueillay les pommelettes qui croissoient dessus les fueilles afin que de la moisteur dicelles jen attrempasse mon encre pour escripre cestui livre.'

65 See Adrian Wilson and Joyce Lancaster Wilson, *A Medieval Mirror*, 61, discussing BN ms fr. 6275: 'On folio 1 verso and 2 recto there are two miniatures, one showing a group of men felling a tree (Christianity) from which each takes the part that fulfills his need: the swineherd takes the acorns, the carpenter the straight trunk, the fisher the curved branches for boat building, the writer gathers galls to make ink, etc. The other illustration shows five men with three documents with red seals appended. The Prologue states that Holy Scripture is like soft wax which takes the impress of any device, be it lion or eagle, and so one occurrence in one connection, may prefigure Christ, and in another, the Devil.'

66 *Confessions*, book 12, chap. 23–5.

67 Marot added his 'Exposition moralle' to editions of his prose rendering of the *Rose* in 1529, 1531, and 1537. Molinet's was illustrated with woodcuts when Guillaume Balsarin published it in Lyons in 1503.

68 BN Rés. Ye. 22, f. 11^{v}.

3: Proto-emblematics in the Fifteenth Century

1 On the enigmatic quality of medieval allegorical periphrasis, see Jung, *Etudes*, 38 and passim. On the question of presence, see Ong, *The Presence of the Word*, 111–14; Clanchy, *From Memory to Written Record*, 18ff; and Bloomfield, 'A Grammatical Approach to Personification Allegory.'

2 'Proverbe et paradoxe du XVe au XVIe siècle,' 100.

3 E.g., 'Plus par doulceur que par force,' *Hécatomgraphie*, sig. E–ii^{v}–E–iii.

4 Proverbs, then, resemble medieval figures of rhetoric as Marshall McLuhan defined them; that is, they are structures that have no particular content, just like emblem pictures (*The Gutenberg Galaxy*, 46–7).

5 Walters Art Gallery ms 313 (514), published as *Proverbes en rime*. The editors claim (21) that the manuscript dates from the period between 1483 and 1498.

6 Sixteen of these compositions may be found in a manuscript at the Archives départementales de Gap (Hautes-Alpes), ms 153. The text of that manuscript was transcribed by Gustave Cohen, 'Emblèmes moraux inédits du XVe siècle,' in *Mélanges ... offerts à Paul Laumonnier*, 89–96; this fragmentary manuscript can probably be dated to the period between 1510 and 1515. Nearly all of these proverbs are also contained in a manuscript at the British Library that once belonged to Firmin Didot (Add. ms 37527), and some others in BN ms fr. 24461. The British Library manuscript, containing 302 illustrated stanzas, probably dates from around 1500.

Jean-Michel Massing has identified two more pages of such 'proverbs' in the collection of medieval and Renaissance miniatures recently donated by Daniel Wildenstein to the Musée Marmottan in Paris. Massing believes these pages were originally part of the Baltimore manuscript ('Proverbial Wisdom and Social Criticism: Two New Pages from the Walters Art Gallery's *Proverbes en rime*.'

7 See *L'Imagination poétique*, 6–7.

8 Throughout the late Middle Ages and early Renaissance, artists often worked from written instructions or descriptions of lost ancient works. On this question of literary prescriptions and instructions to artists, see, for example, Kenneth Clark, 'Leon Battista Alberti on Painting,' *Proceedings of the British Academy*, 30 (1944), 283–302. The manuscript history of Philippe de Thaon's bestiary (ed. Walberg, v) and Joinville's *Credo* (ed. Friedman, 3–8) make it clear that, even though these texts were intended to be illustrated, the text always preceded, if it did not always govern, the execution of the illustrations.

9 *Proverbes en rime*, 60.

10 *Le Masque et la lumière*, 152.

11 Cf. Morier, 443, where, concerning some examples he has just given, he con-

cludes that 'ces épiphonèmes méritent leur nom dans la mesure où ils sont un luxe du style, efflorescences solaires, feux d'artifices.' How well this sentence could describe rhetorical 'emblems' in Cicero's sense!

12 Cf. Michel Pastoureau, 'Couleurs, décors, emblèmes,' 51–7.

13 Cf. B. Taegio, *Il Liceo*, f. 6v, where he claims that *imprese* 'di parole sole' 'meritano più tosto nome di proverbi, ricordi morali, & enigmi, che d'Imprese ...' For the early history of the *devise* in France, see Russell, *The Emblem and Device in France*, passim, especially 154 and 163. For an account from the perspective of heraldry, cf. Michel Pastoureau, '"Arma senescunt, insignia florescunt." Notes sur les origines de l'emblème.'

14 On Pierre Sala, see Pierre Fabia, *Pierre Sala, sa vie et son oeuvre*. His proto-emblematic works have been most recently discussed by Elizabeth Burin, 'Pierre Sala's Pre-Emblematic Manuscripts.'

15 On the Scève house in Ecully, see V.-L. Saulnier, *Maurice Scève*, 32; some of these compositions are reproduced in E. Giudici's *Maurice Scève poeta della Délie*, vol. 1.

Sala's *Tristan* was edited by L. Muir in the TLF series. For an early study and an imperfect transcription of the first of the proto-emblematic texts, see G.A. Parry, '"Les Enigmes de l'amour" de Pierre Sala.'

16 BL Stowe ms 955, f. 4–4v (as transcribed by Parry). The manuscript has recently been exhibited at the Pierpont Morgan Library in *Renaissance Painting in Manuscripts: Treasures from the British Library*, ed. Thomas Kren.

17 Transcribed in ibid, 170. See as well Burin, 'Pierre Sala's Pre-Emblematic Manuscripts.'

18 F. 9v; Parry, 218.

19 New York, Pierpont Morgan Library ms 422, and BL Add. ms 59677. Allusions in the text of the British Library manuscript permit us to date it from the time of François Ier's Spanish captivity in 1525–6 (see *Renaissance Painting*, 174, n. 17), and a colophon implies that Sala himself was the scribe. See also A. Forni Marmocchi and Gianni Mombello, *Le Raccolte francese di favole esopiane*, 105–7.

Both manuscripts have been studied in some detail and edited by Aurelia Forni Marmocchi, 'Un' opera inedita di Pierre Sala: "Fables et emblèmes en vers"'; and 'Un nuovo manoscritto delle "Fables" di Pierre Sala (con sette favole inedite).'

20 *Proverbes en rime*, 41.

21 Pierpont Morgan ms 422, ff. 3v–4r. Luther used the same fable in an emblematic image in 'The Freedom of a Christian' (1520); see Martin Luther, *Selections from his Writings*, ed. John Dillenberger, 65. Montaigne also used it in 'De l'experience' (III, 13).

22 Pierpont Morgan ms 422, ff. 13v–14.

23 Cf. E. Langlois, *Recueil d'arts de seconde rhétorique*, 218, 272, and passim.

24 Clément Marot, *Oeuvres diverses*, ed. C.A. Mayer, 183–4. This *chant royal* dates from before 1531, and the refrain recalls a famous line from Petrarch's *Rime* (XC, l. 14). Marot's source was probably closer to the French court. Upon the death of his beloved wife, Isabelle de Lorraine, René d'Anjou took up Petrarch's words, along with a Turkish bow whose string had been broken, as a device to express his grief. According to Leroux de Lincey, *Le Livre des proverbes français*, II, 9, this device became proverbial in 16th-century France. See my study of this text in 'Emblematic Structures in Sixteenth-Century French Poetry.' For Corrozet's version, see *Hecatomgraphie*, sig. E–vii^{v}–E–viii.

25 The poems of Molinet and Robertet may be found, together with those of Baude, at Chantilly, Musée Condé ms 509, and in other manuscripts. The most recent complete edition of Baude's *Dictz moraulx pour faire tapisserie* was prepared by Annette Scoumanne; it is based on BN ms fr. 1716. There also exists a 19th-century edition by Jules Quicherat in *Les Vers de Maître Henri Baude*.

26 These meagre biographical details are all brought together in the introduction to the Scoumanne edition, 9–16.

27 This may have been a commonplace title for collections of this sort. The Musée Condé manuscript cited above is entitled *Dicts pour mettre en tapisserie*. In any event, 'dits,' according to Jauss, traditionally dealt with allegory; it was in the *dits*, in his view, that allegory entered vernacular literature ('Entstehung und Structurwandel der allegorischen Dichtungen,' 165).

28 E.g., BN ms fr. 24461 and a copy of it, Arsenal ms 5066, or Chantilly, Musée Condé ms 509. A number of compositions from the Musée Condé manuscript have been reproduced in *Dictz moraulx pour faire tapisserie*, catalogue rédigé par Jean-Loup Lemaître.

29 Ed. Scoumanne, 126. Cf. BN ms fr. 24461, f. 40.

30 Ed. Scoumanne, 128.

31 BN ms fr. 24461, f. 47.

32 On the question of proportion in emblem pictures, see Gisèle Mathieu-Castellani, *Emblèmes de la mort. Le dialogue de l'image et du texte*, 61–5. Cf. Corrozet's use of the butterfly-and-candle motif in 'La guerre doulce aux inexperimentez' (*Hecatomgraphie*, sig. L–ii^{v}–L–iii).

33 *The Emblem and Device in France*, chap. 4.

34 *Second Livre de la description des animaux, contenant le blason des oyseaux*, 20.

35 Cf. Scoumanne, introduction, 19–20.

36 See B. de Fournoux, 'Henri Baude et les fresques du château de Busset,' and A. Bohat, 'Les Peintures murales de la Renaissanceau Château de Busset (Allier),'

Jean Michel Massing (Cambridge) told me recently that he has located a tapestry possibly modelled on one of Baude's compositions.

37 *Le Roi René et la seconde maison d'Anjou*, 217.

38 Princeton ms 92; description by David B. Lawall in 'Notes on a Newly Acquired Manuscript Device Book.'

39 E.g., the volume of René de Bruc's emblems at Illinois or the one at Dartmouth. See Russell, 'M. de Montplaisir and His Emblems.'

40 *L'Art religieux de la fin du moyen âge en France*, 311–17. Mâle gave two examples of this kind of personification from the late 14th century, but he was unable to find any examples in the first half of the 15th century, when virtues were personified without attributes. Rosemond Tuve has suggested, however, in *Allegorical Imagery*, 71–3, that this 'new iconography' of the virtues probably began to take shape around 1450. The example she gives is found in a French abridgement of John of Wales's *Breviloquium de virtutibus*, which accompanies Christine de Pisan's *Epistre Othea* in Bodl. ms Laud Misc. 570.

41 BN ms fr. 9186, f. 304.

42 As Rosemond Tuve points out in *Allegorical Imagery*, 73–4, the relationship between the miniature, including its verses, and the following prose text is problematical, if not completely absent. The manuscript itself dates from c. 1470, while the translation was done in 1403.

This presentation of the virtues must have followed a fairly common model; we find it used, for example, in a presentation of the virtues on the *contreplats* of BN ms fr. 12247, from the early 16th century.

43 '"Arma senescunt, insignia florescunt." Notes sur les origines de l'emblème,' 126.

44 *Symbolic Images*, 138.

45 Mâle's transcription (313) is rather approximate, and it would appear that he has misread line 6 where he transcribes 'voit' instead of 'voir.' Temperance doesn't have the glasses before her eyes, and I think our poet means that glasses help only in seeing at a distance and not close up. It would be excessive to put them on for close work.

Cf. the Temperance in Miélot's *Epistre Othea* (c. 1460), f. 5^v, where she has a clock on her head, a wine pitcher in her right hand, a little *mallette* in the left. She is tightly belted at the waist.

46 On the mechanism of accommodation, see Tzvetan Todorov, *Symbolisme et interprétation*, 25–6.

47 But it is a very special type of rebus that I have analyzed in 'Emblems and Hieroglyphics: Some Observations on the Beginnings and Nature of Emblematic Forms.' For a more general study of the relation between the rebus forms

and proto-emblematics, see Jean Céard and Jean-Claude Margolin, *Rebus de la Renaissance. Des Images qui parlent*, I, 15–28, 53–91, and 137–62.

48 *Le Theatre des bons engins*, (1540ns), 46–7. The turtle as an attribute of Venus comes from Servius, *In Vergil. Aen.*, I, 505, while the key and raised finger are traditional.

49 One particularly striking example is Andreas Friedrich's *Emblemes nouveaux*.

50 Cf. Georges Ritter, *Les Vitraux de la Cathédrale de Rouen*, 81–3, and plates 87–91, and Mâle, 309–18. Cf. BN ms fr. 1863, f. 2^{v}, one of François Demoulins' allegories for the dauphin, François d'Angoulême, where we see Justice, Force, and Temperance together on the viewer's left of the Prince, while Prudence is enthroned to the immediate left behind the prince-amor, and Charity, Faith and Love are grouped to the right. This manuscript is discussed in chapter 4.

51 See Russell, *The Emblem and Device in France*, chap. 4.

52 BN ms fr. 24461 and Arsenal ms 5066; also in BN ms fr. 1717.

53 C.-F. Menestrier, *L'Art des emblèmes* (1662), 14. For further information on Petrarch's influence on emblem literature, see Praz, *Studies in Seventeenth-Century Imagery*, 13–14 and passim.

54 *Le Theatre des bons engins*, 210–11; in the emblem 'Chasteté vainc Cupidon' Gilles Corrozet follows one of the *Triumphs* and explicitly credits Petrarch (*Hécatomgraphie*, sig. C–v^{v}–C–vi).

55 Prince d'Essling and E. Müntz, *Pétrarque, ses études d'arts, son influence sur les artistes*, 106–7.

56 *Etudes sur le poème allégorique en France*, 20.

57 *Pétrarque*, 120–1.

58 See Franco Simone, *The French Renaissance*, 212, 243.

59 Quoted in Jean Robertet, *Oeuvres*, ed. Margaret Zsuppăn, 183.

60 Simone, 217–18.

61 Ibid, 218–23.

62 Robertet, 182.

63 For bibliographical details, see Robert Brun, *Le Livre français illustré de la Renaissance*.

64 See Jean Porcher, 'Un Poème allégorique à la louange des femmes.'

65 For an example of an actual triumphal entry that combines Ovid (Jupiter and the giants) with a biblical verse from Isaiah, see Lecoq, 269.

66 Essling and Müntz, 205. In one 16th-century manuscript now at the Walters Art Gallery in Baltimore (ms W. 476), passages from Petrarch's *Triumphi Cupidinis* and *Rerum vulg. fragm.*, from Ovid's *Metamorphoses*, and from Psalms are expanded into fully developed emblems (see Dennis Dutschke, *Census of Petrarch Manuscripts in the United States*, 45–9).

67 Simone, 229–43.

68 An illustrated record is contained in the *Relation de l'entrée de Henri II, roi de*

France, a Rouen, le 1er octobre 1550, Rouen, Bibliothèque Municipale ms 1268 (Y. 28). Cf. *L'Entrée de Henri II. Rouen, 1550*, ed. Margaret McGowan.

69 *La Danse macabre de Guyot Marchant*. See Mâle, 361–80.

70 Mâle, 365, argues convincingly that we are not looking at thirty replications of Death, but rather at each character's image of himself after death, following the medieval belief that, if one wrote a certain formula in his own blood on parchment, he could see himself in a mirror as he would appear after his death. There is evidence to support this reading both in the texts and in Guyot Marchand's title, *Le Miroir salutaire*.

71 See Praz, *Studies in Seventeenth-Century Imagery*, 371.

72 *English Friars and Antiquity in the Early Fourteenth Century*, 112.

73 Cf. *Fulgentius the Mythographer*, trans. L.G. Whitbread, 49–50, for the full version.

74 'Ricerche intorno all'Iconologia di Cesare Ripa.'

75 Cf. J.W. Blench, *Preaching in England in the Late Fifteenth and Sixteenth Centuries*, 117.

76 See Bernard Weinberg, *A History of Literary Criticism in the Italian Renaissance*, I, 47.

77 E.g., Claude Paradin, *Quadrins historiques de la Bible*; Guillaume Gueroult, *Figures de la Bible illustrée de huictains françoys*; and G. Simeoni, *Figure de la biblia, illustrate de stanze tuscane*. For a complete listing, see Robert Brun, *Le Livre français illustré de la Renaissance*.

78 Hans Holbein, *Historiarum veteris testamenti icones*, sig. A–iii–A–iii^{v}.

79 For the standard biographical account, see S.M. Bouchereaux, 'Recherches bibliographiques sur G. Corrozet.' (In subsequent issues Bouchereaux provided an alphabetical bibliography of Corrozet's works.) See, as well, Barbara Tiemann, *Fabel und Emblem*, 11–20.

80 Holbein, *Historiarum*, sig. G–iv^{v}.

81 F. Berthod, *Emblesmes sacrez tirez de l'Escriture* ... II, 340–8 (emblem 46).

4: Proto-emblematics in the Early Sixteenth Century

1 Chantilly, Musée Condé ms 682. Anne-Marie Lecoq, *François Ier imaginaire*, 255–7, dates this translation from the period 1515–21, or after François's accession to the throne, but before the first Latin translation of the *Hieroglyphics* published in France.

Cf. Lecoq, 209, 279, where we see a case of the biblical story of David combatting a bear to protect his flock compared to François Ier defeating the Swiss bear.

2 For examples of 'hieroglyphs' created in Italy at the same time, see Ludwig Volkmann, *Bilderschriften der Renaissance*, 4–40.

3 In 'Emblems and Hieroglyphics: Some Observations on the Beginnings and Nature of Emblematic Forms.'

4 The treatise on the virtues is to be found in BN ms fr. 12247; on this treatise, see Léon Dorez, 'Etudes aldines, II: Les origines et la diffusion du 'Songe de Poliphile'; Russell, 'Emblems and Hieroglyphics'; and Lecoq, 85–90 and passim.

5 Carruthers, *The Book of Memory*, 88; see also 91.

6 BN ms fr. 2088, f. 10v. On this manuscript, see Myra Dickman Orth, 'Godefroy le Batave, Illuminator to the French Royal Family, 1516–1526,' in *Manuscripts in the Fifty Years after the Invention of Printing*, and Lecoq, 315–22.

7 Another example is the little tract in University of Glasgow ms SMM6 that Jean Michel Massing has recently identified as the work of François Demoulins. See 'A New Work by François Du Moulin and the Problem of Pre-Emblematic Traditions.'

8 See Claude Paradin, *Devises heroiques*, 55.

9 On occasional devices, see Russell, *The Emblem and Device in France*, 32–3, 67.

10 *The Book of the Courtier*, 103.

11 See, e.g., Colette Beaune, 'Costume et pouvoir en France à la fin du Moyen Age: Les devises royales vers 1400.'

12 *Les Entrées solennelles et triomphales à la Renaissance (1484–1551)*, 31–2.

13 See Russell, 'Conception of Self, Conception of Space, and Generic Convention: An Example from the *Heptaméron*,' 159–83, and Lecoq, 177.

14 *Le Tresor des merveilles de la maison royale de Fontainebleau*, 88; cf. 89: 'Au second Tableau est encore representé le mesme Roy armé, & tout de bout au milieu d'une salle, tenant une grenade en main que luy presente un enfant à genoux à ses pieds; & est ce Prince accompagné de quantité de personnes, les uns vieillards, & comme des senateurs, les autres representans des capitaines & soldats. Ce qui est pareillement un Embleme en suite du precedent, par lequel l'on peut entendre que si tost que ce Roy fut élevé à la Couronne & eut pris le maniement des affaires de cét Estat, son dessein ne fut pas seulement de chasser l'aveuglement de l'ignorance de son Royaume, mais encore y establit un bon ordre & police, soit aux choses civiles, ou soit au gouvernement de la guerre: voulant signifier de plus par cette grenade, que tandis que tous ses sujets demeureroient bien unis ensemble, & avec sa majesté, comme les grains de ce fruit, tout ce Royaume iroit fleurissant.'

15 J. Porcher described these two tapestries in 'Deux tapisseries à rébus.' In the early 18th century Roger de Gaignières assembled a collection of sketches of tapestries and stained glass from around France. Much of the Renaissance art thus recorded shows heavy use of *imprese* in the design of such work (BN Dépt. des Est. Pc. 18 Rés.).

16 *Le Livre français illustré de la Renaissance*, 24; and see above, 131–3. Cf. Marian Rothstein, 'Disjunctive Images in Renaissance Books.'

17 Brun, 5–6. See also J.B. Trapp, ed. *Manuscripts in the Fifty Years after the Introduction of Printing*, passim. For an example, see the richly illuminated copy of Aristotle's *Metaphysics* (Venice: Nicholas Jenson, 1483) at the Pierpont Morgan Library (E. 2.78 B). Christopher De Hamel, *A History of Illuminated Manuscripts*, 239, reproduces the frontispiece of the second volume of this work.

18 Commenting on his copy of the 1510 edition of this work, entitled *Rationarium Evangelistarum omnia in se evangelica prosa, versu, imaginibusque quam mirifice complectens*, Leber reports that 'C'est une réimpression du livre fameux intitulé: *Ars memorandi* ... que le Baron Heinecken signale comme le premier ouvrage gravé qui ait paru avec un discours ajouté à chaque image, occupant seul une page (*Idée générale d'une collection d'estampes*, page 395 et suiv.).' (*Catalogue des livres*, I, 7).

19 'Authors, Artists, and Audiences,' in *Pen to Press*, 164–5. This hypothesis would seem to be confirmed by the major recourse to illustration, by Godefroy le Batave and Jean Clouet, in the manuscript version of Caesar's *Commentaires de la guerre gallique*, prepared in 1515 by Albert Pigghe under the supervision of François Demoulins. There Caesar's wisdom is presented in the form of answers to the questions posed by the young king: the intention is purely pedagogical, and the text is pointedly reinforced by the illustrations. On this question, see Lecoq, 229–44.

20 *Rationarum Evangelistarum* ([Pforzheim]: Thomas Anshelm, 1507); Library of Congress, Rosenwald 606 and (Phorcae, 1510); Bibl. Munic. de Rouen, Leber 38. The Bibliothèque Nationale copy (Rés. A. 17929) has no title-page; the catalogue title, *Memorabiles evangelistorum figuras* is taken from a poem by Sebastian Brant on the first page of text.

21 Sebastian Brant, *The Ship of Fools*, trans. Edwin Zeydel, preface, passim. For a more detailed account of the book's fortunes in France, see Dorothy O'Connor, 'Sébastien Brant en France au XVIe siècle'; and Barbara Tiemann, 'Sebastian Brant und das frühe Emblem in Frankreich.'

22 *Studien zur Emblematik des 16. Jahrhunderts*, 22–3.

23 Tiemann, 'Sebastian Brant.' She feels Homann and others may have been led astray by a misconception of the medieval concept of the *illiteratus*, who was not someone unable to read, but rather someone who did not read theology, or sometimes more generally, someone who did not read Latin, as the late Charles Schmitt noted, quoting the introduction to John Wilkinson's translation of Aristotle's *Nicomachean Ethics*, in a lecture at the University of Pittsburgh in October 1978.

24 *Das Narrenschiff*, ed. Manfred Lemmer, 23–4; for the English I have used the Zeydel translation, 78–9.

25 BN Rés. Y[2] 949. Cf. John G. Rechtien, 'A 1520 French Translation of the Moriae Encomium.'

26 *Le Nef des folz du monde.*

27 Holbein's somewhat emblematic marginal illustrations are famous, but there also exists an edition of the *Stultitiae laus*, which was prepared by Charles Patin, the expert on medals, inscriptions, and devices. He gave it an emblematic appearance through the insertion of allegorical illustrations after Holbein. It is clear, however, that these illustrations were not made for this edition, for some are inserted sideways for lack of space. Some subsequent reader of the BN copy judged Patin's illustrations not to be particularly apt, and (as must have been common in emblem books) pasted cut-out engravings of his own choice over some of them.

28 See the exhibition catalogue, *Woodner Collection. Master Drawings. The Metropolitan Museum of Art 1990*, 236ff. These drawings, along with much of the rest of the Woodner Collection, have recently entered the National Gallery in Washington, DC.

29 Virginia Woods Callahan, 'The Erasmus-Alciati Friendship,' especially 135–6. There she quotes Renaudet's characterization of Alciato's emblems as 'an ingenious complement' to the *Adages* of Erasmus. See also, V. W. Callahan, 'Andrea Alciati's View of Erasmus.'

30 For other examples, see Russell, 'Emblème et mentalité symbolique.'

31 See 163–4, and Irene Bergal, 'Word and Picture: Erasmus' *Parabolae* in La Perrière's *Morosophie.*'

32 Reproduced by Brun in *Le Livre français illustré.*

33 One example reproduced by Brun.

34 *Champ Fleury ou l'art et science de la proportion des lettres*, ed. Gustave Cohen, ix–x.

35 Cf. R. Dragonnetti, *La Vie de la lettre au Moyen Age*, 63ff., and H.R. Jauss, 'Entstehung und Strukturwandel der allegorischen Dichtungen,' 162.

36 This was a very common motif in the early years of the century in France. For another example, see the prologue to Jean Thenaud's *Trespassement du glorieux sainct Jhéromme* (1509–15), which was dedicated to Louise de Savoye.

37 Janot published this edition in 1543. Both translations have been reprinted by Sandra Sider in *Cebes' Tablet*. The standard study of the *Tablet* in the Renaissance is Reinhart Schleier, *Tabula Cebetis: Studien zur Rezeption einer antiken Bildbeschreibung im 16. und 17. Jahrhundert.*

On the emblems, see 176–8.

5: Alciato and the Humanist Background of the Emblem

1 Albeit imperfect, due in part to a poor response from libraries in France where the political atmosphere around 1870 was distracting and disruptive, Henry Green's bibliography of editions of Alciato's emblems in *Andrea Alciati and His Books of Emblems* remains basic. It may be supplemented by Georges Duplessis, *Les Emblèmes d'Alciat*. In 1926 P.E. Viard undertook a new bibliography of editions of the emblems; it remains in manuscript (Paris, Biblio. de l'Institut ms 4644: *Catalogue des oeuvres d'André Alciat contenues dans les principales bibliothèques d'Europe*). Mason Tung is preparing a new bibliography with extensive citation of locations; the first fruits of this project may be consulted in 'Towards a New Census of Alciati's Editions.'

Green's work also provides the basic biographical details. Viard's biography, *André Alciat*, is of more interest to legal historians than to students of the emblem. There have been numerous reprints of different editions of the emblems; these have been listed in Andreas Alciatus, *The Latin Emblems*, ed. Peter M. Daly, Virginia W. Callahan, and Simon Cuttler, which provides a facsimile, of the emblems only, from the 1621 Padua edition, and an English translation; volume 2, entitled *Emblems in Translation*, provides 16th-century French, German, Italian, and Spanish versions, together with many more facsimiles. None of the commentaries has ever been edited.

2 The offensive emblem no. 80 *Adversus naturam peccantes*, first published in 1546, was often deleted and was not definitively restored to the collection until the massive 1621 Padua edition.

3 Over the past twenty-five years, the rare references Alciato made to the emblems in his correspondence and other writings have been closely examined, and the debate over their meaning and significance continues. See for example, Hessel Miedema, 'The Term *Emblema* in Alciati'; Holger Homann, *Studien zur Emblematik des 16. Jahrhunderts*, 25–40; Claudie Balavoine, 'Les *Emblèmes* d'Alciat: Sens et contresens'; and Bernhard F. Scholz, '"Libellum composui epigrammaton, cui titulum feci Emblemata.' See, too, Denis L. Drysdall, 'Préhistoire de l'emblème: commentaires et emplois du terme avant Alciat.' Alciato's pertinent correspondence has been published in *Lettere*, ed. G.L. Barni. Most recently, Pierre Laurens and Florence Vuillemier have persuasively introduced Alciato's early *Antiquitates mediolenses* (1508) as another likely source of the emblem idea in 'De l'archéologie à l'emblème: La genèse du *Liber Alciat.*'

4 See Robert Aulotte, 'D'Égypte en France par l'Italie: Horapollon au XVIe siècle'; Giovanni Pozzi, 'Les Hiéroglyphes de l'*Hypnerotomachia Poliphili*';

Claude-Françoise Brunon, 'Signe, figure, langage: Les *Hieroglyphica* d'Horapollon'; and Russell, 'Emblems and Hieroglyphics: Some Observations on the Beginnings and Nature of Emblematic Forms.'

5 See James Hutton, *The Greek Anthology in Italy to the Year 1800*, 196–8; and especially Alison Saunders, 'Alciati and the Greek Anthology.'

6 But, as Saunders remarks (9, n. 22), Alciato often quoted the Anthology in his other works, and presumably throughout his career.

7 *The Greek Anthology in France*, 92.

8 Andreas Alciat, *Emblematum liber*, sig. A–1[v].

9 Michael Bath, 'Honey and Gall, or: Cupid and the Bees,' in *Andrea Alciato and the Emblem Tradition*, especially 68–70.

10 *Epigrammata Philippi Melancthonis Selectiora.*

11 BN Rés. Z. 2518.

12 One of the authors who contributed epigrams to Melancthon's anthology.

13 *Academie des sciences et des arts*, I, 217.

14 *Emblemes*, 4.

15 E.g., *Fabellae aliquot aesopicae in usum puerorum selectae* (BN Z. 17412). This volume, from the library of Pierre-Daniel Huet, also contains Alciato's emblems, those of Sambucus, and the devices of Paradin, all in editions by Plantin or Raphelengius.

16 *Die Hieroglyphenkunde des Humanismus in der Allegorie der Renaissance*, 146ff.

17 E.g., Poggio's discovery of Ammianus Marcellinus, whose writings contain one of the *loci classici* for the Renaissance understanding of the Egyptian hieroglyphics.

18 Chantilly, Musée Condé ms 682 (1529). See 89.

19 On the Latin translations of the *Hieroglyphics*, see Sandra Sider, 'Horapollo' in *Catalogus Translationum et Commentariorum: Medieval and Renaissance Latin Translations and Commentaries*, vol. 6, and Robert Aulotte, 'D'Egypte en France par l'Italie: Horapollon aux XVIe siècle.'

20 *Champ Fleury* (Paris, 1529), f. lxxii[r]. This translation has apparently been lost; the first few words, which Tory quotes, do not correspond to any known French version.

21 See Denis L. Drysdall, 'The Hieroglyphs at Bologna,' especially 233.

22 Cf. Claudie Balavoine, 'Le Modèle hiéroglyphique à la Renaissance,' especially 220.

23 Dieckmann, 21.

24 Ibid., 17–18.

25 *De l'art des devises*, 41.

26 Trans. S. MacKenna, 4th ed., 427. Cf. Emile Bréhier's French translation of this

passage: 'C'est ce qu'ont saisi, me semble-t-il, les sages de l'Egypte, que ce soit par une science exacte ou spontanément: pour désigner les choses avec sagesse, ils n'usent pas de lettres dessinées, qui se développent en discours et en propositions et que représentent des sons et des paroles; ils dessinent des images dont chacune est celle d'une chose distincte; ils les gravent dans les temples pour désigner tous les détails de cette chose; chaque signe gravé est donc une science, une sagesse, une chose réelle, saisie d'un seul coup, et non [une suite de pensées comme] un raisonnement ou une déliberation. C'est ensuite que de cette sagesse où tout est ensemble vient une image qui est en autre chose, toute déroulée, qui se formule en une suite de pensées, qui découvre les causes pour lesquelles les choses sont ce qu'elles sont, qui fait admirer la beauté d'une pareille disposition. Quiconque connaît ces questions, dira certainement son admiration pour une sagesse qui, sans posséder les causes par lesquelles les êtres sont ce qu'elles sont, fait pourtant découvrir ces causes à ceux qui se conforment à elle. Si donc l'on découvre une beauté pareille, qui nous est apparue ce qu'elle doit être, presque sans recherche réfléchie ou même sans recherche du tout, il faut aussi que cette beauté existe avant toute recherche et avant toute réflexion.' *Les Ennéades* V, 142.

27 Dieckmann, 36–7. This passage was first noted by Giehlow, and may be found on p. 1768 of the 1576 Basel edition of Ficino's works.

28 M. de Marolles, *Catalogue de livres d'estampes*. See, too, J.-T. de Bry, *Emblemata saecularia. Moeurs et coutumes au XVIe siècle*, ed. F. Warnecke, 5.

29 'The Hieroglyphs at Bologna'; see, too, Claudie Balavoine, 'Le Modèle hiéroglyphique,' 218–19. On the Aristotelian nature of the *impresa*, see Robert Klein, 'La Théorie de l'expression figurée dans les traités italiens sur les *imprese*, 1555–1612,'

30 See n. 18 above, and Lecoq, 255–7.

31 E.g., Pierre Gringore, *Les Menus propos*, which is based on Fournival's *Li Bestiaires d'amour*, and Barthélemy Aneau, *Decades de la description, forme, et vertu naturelle des animaulx, tant raisonnables, que Brutz*. Cf. Russell, 'Emblems and Hieroglyphics,' 237.

32 Barbara Tiemann, *Fabel und Emblem*. 44–7.

33 Cf. Gisèle Mathieu-Castellani, *Emblèmes de la mort*, 96–7; and for a Neoplatonic explanation of the multiplicity of the signified, see Gombrich, *Symbolic Images*, 159–60: it would appear that the analysis of the symbolic intuition yields this multiplicity.

34 See 72–6.

35 For Mignault's commentary, see, e.g., *Emblemata, cum Claudii Minois ad eadem commentariis*, 524–6.

36 *Francesco Colonna et Alde Manuce*.

37 Quoted by Albert-Marie Schmidt in the introduction to his facsimile edition of *Le Songe de Poliphile*, xv–xvi. A copy of the 1561 edition of this French version at the Folger was bound very early with translations of other Italian and Spanish romances, thus suggesting that the work must also have been read and understood in the Renaissance simply as a romance.

38 Especially the *Cinquiesme Livre*; on this question, see Lazare Sainéan, 'Le songe de Poliphile.'

François Ier possessed a copy of the 1499 edition; see Ernest Quentin-Bauchat, *La Bibliothèque de Fontainebleau et les livres des derniers Valois*, 69.

6: The Dissemination of the Emblem Idea in France

1 'Alciati's Emblems in Renaissance France.'

2 For the most up-to-date survey of editions, see Mason Tung, 'Towards a New Census of Alciati's Editions.'

3 In 'Two Early English-owned Alciato Editions in Glasgow University Library,' Michael Bath has drawn our attention to a copy of the 1534 Wechel edition that belonged to the English jurist Christopher Nevison. Nevison died in 1551, and can be shown to have acquired the volume some time after 1538.

4 See, e.g., Alan Young, 'Wenceslaus Hollar, the London Book Trade, and Two Unidentified English Emblem Books.'

5 Wechel published the Le Fevre translation in 1536. He also published the first German translation in 1542; it was done by Wolfgang Hunger, who had been inspired by Le Fevre's version. The supposed 1540 edition of the Daza Spanish translation was long ago exposed as a ghost (Pedro Campa, *Emblemata Hispanica*, 194), and it seems certain that no Spanish edition was in fact available until the one Rouille issued in 1549, when he also published the first Italian translation by Marquale.

Despite the picture I am painting, the impact and importance of emblem books in French culture of the 1540s and 1550s should not be exaggerated. When the humanist bookseller (*marchand libraire du palais*) Galliot Du Pré died in 1561, his inventory showed 69 copies of the *Hecatomgraphie*, 120 Alciatos, and 10 copies of the 1556 edition of Aneau's *Picta poesis*, as compared to his 860 volumes of various works by Erasmus. But when Guillaume Godard's wife died in 1545, there were 147,000 *livres d'heures* in her inventory! See Annie Parent, *Les Métiers du livre à Paris au XVIe siècle (1535–1560)*, 209–51.

6 Raymond Lebègue noted several French translations of Alciato's emblems among the unpublished poetry of the 16th-century Dieppois poet, Jean Ive, and an 'Imitation d'Alciat' by Loys Thiboust was published in the anthology *Traductions de latin en françoys*. Jean Mesnard reported a 17th-century example in

'Les Traductions françaises d'Alciat.' And there were, of course, the large group of Bouquet translations (see 145–6, 195–7).

See my presentation of some of these translations in 'More French Translations of Alciato's Emblems.'

7 On Pierre Sala, see 63–6.

8 These books are La Perrière's *Le Theatre des bons engins* and *La Morosophie*; Corrozet's *Hecatomgraphie* and *Emblemes* (appended to his translation of the *Tabula Cebetis*); Gueroult's *Le Premier Livre des emblemes*; Aneau's *Picta poesis*; Pierre Coustau's *Pegma*; and Claude Paradin's *Devises heroiques*. In addition, G. Rouille published the first illustrated editions of Giovio's and Simeoni's collections of *imprese* in 1559. All except two of these books appeared in multiple editions/printings, and individual emblems from these collections sometimes turned up in the popular anthologies of poetry from the period.

In 'Chronological List of Emblem Books' appended to Praz's *Studies in Seventeenth-Century Imagery, Part II*, Hilary M.J. Sayles lists dozens of 'emblem books' published outside France before 1555, but the criteria used there have been expanded so much that any sense of generic specificity is completely lost. In this list we find Thomas Murner's *Chartiludium logice*, Paracelsus' *Prognosticatio*, Nicolas Bourbon's *Icones Historiarum Veteris Testamenti* (but none of the other examples of 'Figures de la Bible'), various examples of festival literature, and a bestiary by Guillaume Gueroult. While most of these works are 'emblematic' in some very real sense, they were almost certainly not inspired by Alciato, and cannot be claimed as 'emblem books' in any meaningfully generic sense.

After Bocchi's *Symbolicarum Quaestionum* of 1555, the next pure emblem book was that of Sambucus, published by Plantin in 1564.

9 *Le Printemps de Madame poesie chanté par les vrays amantz au Theatre de magnificence*. Presumably, there are copies of the first edition (Rouen, 1547), with illustrations, at Versailles and the Bodleian. I have consulted it in Jacques Berion's 1551 Lyons edition (BN Rés. Ye. 1694). Emile Picot described the first edition this way: 'Le reste du volume est disposé de façon à ce qu'il y ait au verso de chaque folio un petit bois suivi de quatre dizains qui se développent sur le recto du folio suivant ... Les bois qui ornent le *Printemps de madame Poésie* n'ont pas été spécifiquement gravés pour le livre; ils ont été employés par les frères Du Gord dans diverses publications antérieures ...' and Picot suggests further that some of them may have been purchased from Denys Janot (*Le Théâtre mystique de Pierre Du Val*, 106–8).

10 Picot, 51.

11 This brochure may be found in the volume entitled *Recueil de pièces sur la querelle de Marot et de Sagon* in the Rothschild collection at the Bibliothèque

Nationale (Rothschild 2594); it has been described by E. Picot, *Catalogue des livres composant la Bibliothèque de feu M. le Baron James de Rothschild*, III, 407.

Cf. Alciato, 36 (*Obdurandum adversus urgentia*), which may have served as the model for this composition with its use of the words 'pondus' and 'premo,' but also Alciato, 136 (*Strenuorum immortale nomen*) for its association of the palm with the honour of heroes. It should, however, be pointed out that Alciato's emblems shared much vocabulary and many themes with the neo-Latin epigram literature. Hence Sagon could, for example, also have been thinking of Laurentius Lippius' epigram 'Pondere non premitur, sed sursum palma resurgit, / Hinc ibi victores signa superba petunt.' (in J. Froben's anthology, *Pictorii sacra et satyrica epigrammata*, 64).

12 BN ms fr. 1863; see A.-M. Lecoq's discussion, 80–5.

13 Picot, III, 414.

14 See, e.g., Rémy Belleau's devices for Mlle d'Atri in Arsenal ms 3184, ff. 81–95, and published in the Van Bever edition of Belleau's *Les Amours et nouveaux eschanges*. Some of Passerat's devices are contained in BN ms fr. 894.

15 For biographical details and monographic studies, see John L. Gerig, 'Barthélemy Aneau: A Study in Humanism'; Greta Dexter, 'L'Imagination poétique (à propos de B. Aneau)' and 'Guillaume de La Perrière'; Dexter's preface to her edition of *Le Theatre des bons engins*; S.M. Bouchereaux, 'Recherches bibliographiques sur G. Corrozet'; and H. Oulmont's preface to his edition of the *Hecatomgraphie*.

16 In addition to the recycling of emblematic woodblocks by Janot and his successor, Etienne Groulleau, one can cite Jacques Moderne's 1544 edition of Alciato. His edition of the emblems follows the Wechel 1540 edition except that 12 illustrations are different: the new set of blocks was not finished in time, and Moderne used ones from his *Cy commence la vie de noz premiers parens. Cestassavoir Adam & Eve historie* (c. 1539); the series was complete for Moderne's 1545 edition of the emblems. See Samuel Pogue, *Jacques Moderne*, 42–3.

17 B. Aneau, *Decades de la description, forme, et vertu naturelle des animaulx*, and G. Gueroult, *Second Livre de la description des animaux*. See 70–1, on the emblematic nature of Gueroult's composition.

18 *Imagination poetique*, 6–8.

19 A biographical notice on Gueroult precedes De Vaux de Lancey's edition of *Le Premier Livre des emblemes* (Rouen: Lainé, 1937).

20 See Russell, 'The Emblem and Authority.'

21 'Disjunctive Images.'

22 For examples of such trading, see Emile Picot, *Catalogue des livres composant la Bibliothèque de feu M. le Baron James de Rothschild*, IV.

23 *Oratio de re literaria* and *De liberali adolescentum institutione*.

24 See Denis Drysdall's translation of Hunger's important preface in 'Defence and Illustration of the German Language: Wolfgang Hunger's Preface to Alciati's *Emblems* (Text and Translation),' and Karel Porteman, 'The Earliest Reception of the Ars Emblematica in Dutch.'

25 See Alfred Bonnardot, *Gilles Corrozet et Germain Brice*, on Corrozet's work with the archaeology of Paris. Boissard and Sambucus were *antiquaires* and numismatists. Some examples of the historical writings of the emblematists are Giovio's *Historiarum sui temporis libri*, Paradin's *Alliances généalogiques des rois et princes de Gaule*, and La Perrière's translation of the *Gesta tolosorum*.

26 In 'Les Traductions françaises d'Alciat.'

Sandra Hindman has noted that even the lowest-paid employees in Plantin's shop in the 1560s could probably afford an illustrated emblem book. Her example is a copy of Sambucus that cost only 6 *stuivers* at the time, or about the equivalent of a collator's wage for two days (*From Pen to Press*, 199).

27 Cf. Ken Fowler, 'Social Content in Mathias Holtzwart's *Emblematum Tyrocinia*.'

28 A. Labarre, *Le Livre dans la vie amiénoise du seizième siècle* and A.H. Schutz, *Vernacular Books in Parisian Private Libraries of the Sixteenth Century*.

29 Albert Labarre suggested to me many years ago that emblem books were not considered important (in the economic terms that dictated the rationale of such inventories) because they were not large volumes (i.e., folios or large quartos).

The only mid-16th-century library in which I have been able with certainty to locate more than one emblem book is the collection of Marcus Fuggerus, who possessed a 1548 de Tournes Alciato (now in the Rothschild collection at the Bibliothèque Nationale) and 1548 Groulleau editions of La Perrière's *Theatre* and Corrozet's *Hecatomgraphie* (now bound together as a single volume in the Lessing J. Rosenwald Collection at the Library of Congress). Both volumes contain Fuggerus' signature. It is tempting to speculate that these books were purchased together, perhaps at the Frankfurt book fair of that year.

30 *Catalogue des livres composant la Bibliothèque de feu M. le Baron James de Rothschild*, I, 453.

31 Following Rémy Belleau's death in 1577, the inventory of his library lists copies of Colonna's *Hypnerotomachia Poliphili* and Valeriano's *Hieroglyphica*; see M. Connat, 'Mort et Testament de Rémy Belleau.' See, as well, Paul Laumonnier, 'Sur la bibliothèque de Ronsard.'

32 There were, for example, during this period about fifty editions of Alciato, seven of Corrozet's *Hécatomgraphie*, and at least a dozen of La Perrière's *Theatre des bons engins*. In the sixteenth century it was perfectly normal to issue editions of a thousand or more copies for books like these. We know, for exam-

ple, that Christopher Plantin published Jacques Grévin's French translations of the emblems of Hadrianus Junius and Johannes Sambucus in 1000-copy editions in 1567 (see Lucien Pinvert, *Jacques Grévin*, 268). And Leon Voet, *The Plantin Press, (1555–1589)*,-tells us that Plantin's first edition of Alciato had a press run of 1250 copies.

33 See *Les Incunables de la Collection Edmond de Rothschild*. Xe Exposition de la Collection Edmond de Rothschild, exposition et catalogue par Pierrette Jean-Richard (Paris, 1974), 7.

34 Described in a note by P.-A. Lemoisne in *Les Trésors des Bibliothèques de France*, 157–9.

35 On the use and diffusion of xylographic reproductions of pictures, see L. Febvre and H.-J. Martin, *L'Apparition du livre*, 1971 ed., 62–6. For some visual evidence of such use of manuscript or printed leaves see Petrus Christus' portrait of a female donor at the National Gallery in Washington. Cf. A. Henry for a copy of the *Biblia pauperum* at the British Library that was perhaps printed for use this way rather than to be bound as a book – given the narrow margins. For a good introduction to the printed image in 16th-century France, see Sara F. Matthews Grieco, *Ange ou diablesse. La représentation de la femme au XVIe siècle*, 19–66.

36 *Oeuvres morales et spirituelles inédites*, 92.

37 A Brussels bookseller once told me that, as recently as thirty or forty years ago, devout old Flemish and German ladies still bought emblem books from his father's shop to use this way, detaching emblems for use as *Andachtsbilder*.

38 E.g., *Le Jardin d'Honneur. Contenant en soy plusieurs Apologies, Proverbes et Dictz moraulx: avec les hystoires et figures*, which contains 29 emblems from Corrozet's *Hecatomgraphie* and 32 from La Perrière's *Theatre des bons engins*, according to Frédéric Lachèvre's count (*Bibliographie des recueils collectifs de poésies du XVIe siècle*, 77).

39 *The Emblems of Thomas Palmer: Two Hundred Poosees*, viii–ix.

40 I am quoting from the 1558 edition.

41 See Alison Saunders, *The Sixteenth-Century French Emblem Book*, 271–4.

42 *Le Livre français illustré de la Renaissance*, 130–4.

43 E.g., Guillaume Gueroult, *Figures de la Bible illustrée de huictains francoys* and Gabriello Simeoni, *Figure de la biblia, illustrate de stanze tuscane*. This entire series was illustrated by Bernard Salomon, who also executed the illustrations for the de Tournes/Rouille/Bonhomme editions of Alciato.

44 Sig. A4–A4^{v}. Edited by Sandra Sider in *Cebes' Tablet*.

45 Published by Yves Le Hir in his edition of the *Oeuvres morales et spirituelles inédites*, 67–92. See, as well, O.C. Reure, *Notice sur les emblèmes de Anne d'Urfé avec des stances de Loys Papon*, which reproduces a selection of d'Urfé's emblems in facsimile as they are contained in Caen, Bibl. Munic. ms 211.

46 Du Bartas, *La Sepmaine ou creation du monde*, I, 183 (Bk. 7, 617–22); this passage also recalls the advice of Corrozet forty years earlier (see 85–6).

47 See my study of Papon and d'Urfé, 'Emblematics in the French Provinces: The Case of Loys Papon and Anne d'Urfé.'

48 Johannes Sadeler, *Emblemata evangelica ad XII signa coelestia sive totidem anni menses accommodata*, 1585; BN Dépt. des Est. Ec. 71b, ff. 108–11. Five of Sadeler's large-format versions of emblems by Alciato may be found on ff. 130, 134, 138, and 150 of the same volume; a group of ten such emblems was assembled by Sir William Stirling Maxwell, and may be found today in the Princeton University Library ([Ex]N7710.A35.1874f). William S. Heckscher and Agnes B. Sherman date the group as c. 1599, and note that they correspond to the 1600 Lyons edition of Alciato (*Emblem Books in the Princeton University Library*, 3); but the exact model is not yet clear, for the 1600 Lyons edition uses recut blocks by Bernard Salomon that had served in a number of editions dating back to 1547.

Georgette de Montenay claimed with some reason to have composed the first religious emblems, since she was probably working on them in the 1560s, even though they were not published until 1571. Still, we should not forget that Arias Montanus also published a religious emblem book in 1571, this one with a Catholic orientation: *Humanae salutis monumenta* (Antwerp: Plantin).

49 See, e.g., Paris, Arsenal ms 3184, where a group of Rémy Belleau's devices for Mlle d'Atri (Pt. 2, f. 81–95) are accompanied by some 200 others in an early 17th-century collection that belonged to Hector Le Breton; or BN ms fr. 15257, 'Devises royalles, & heroiques, 1626,' containing approximately 180 devices, taken mainly from Paradin, but often with interesting additional commentaries, and *rapprochements*, some with emblems by Alciato. On Belleau's devices, see 169.

50 For examples with sample illustrations, see *Harvard College Library. Department of Printing and Graphic Arts Catalogue. French Sixteenth-Century Books*, I, 85–128.

51 For bibliographical details, see Russell, *The Emblem and Device in France*, 203, n. 75. The 1593 edition, which I have never seen, was pointed out by Antonio Possevino in *Tractatio de poësi & pictura*, 2nd ed., 313, in a chapter added to this edition where he discusses the nature of the emblem and device, following Mignault, and gives a list of authors. Praz, 324, does not count the 1654 Amsterdam edition of this work as an emblem book.

52 For bibliographical details, see *The Emblem and Device in France*, 84–8, and n. 61.

53 *L'Apparition du livre*, 150ff.

54 I compared a copy of Rouille's 1566 edition at the Folger Shakespeare Library with a copy of the 1548 Macé Bonhomme edition, where the illustrations by

Bernard Salomon and frames by P.V. were used for the first time. Wear is particularly noticeable, for example, in emblems like 'Maturandum' (1548, B4; 1566, B5ᵛ) or 'Prudentes vino abstinet' (1548, B6; 1566, B7ᵛ). But Rouille or his heirs had the blocks recut, and kept using them to 1600 and beyond.

55 *L'Apparition du livre*, 150, and Brun, *Le Livre français illustré*, 95–102.

56 Rouen, Biblio. Munic., Leber 1394.

57 BN Dépt. des Estampes, Te. 39a. *Emblemata sacra e praecipius utriusque Testamenti historiis concinnata a Bernardo Sellio Noviomago & a Petro vander Burgio Figurae aeneis elegantissimis illustrat.* Amstelodami. Ex officina Michaelis Colinii, Anno 1613 (but some of the engravings seem to date from 1592). See n. 51 above.

58 For bibliographical details on the various editions of these translations, see Lucien Pinvert, *Jacques Grévin* and Leon Voet, *The Plantin Press (1555–1589)*.

59 Cf. John Landwehr's statistics on the production of emblem books by country and century in *Dutch Emblem Books*.

60 BN Vélins 2951 and BN Rés. Z. 2522.

61 In the fifth book of his *Meslanges* in *Les Premieres Oeuvres*, 603–4. See my transcription of these translations in 'More French Translations of Alciato's Emblems.'

Cf. the following appreciation of Alciato by J.-C. Scaliger: 'Alciati, praeter Emblemata, nihil mihi videre contigit. ea vero talia sunt, Vt cum quouis ingenio certare possint. Dulcia sunt, pura sunt, elegantia sunt: sed non sine neruis. sententiae vero tales, ut etiam ad usum civilis vitae conferant' in *Poetices libri septem*, 307.

62 Harvard possesses a copy of the *Picta poesis* bound with interleaving for Otto Zeystius in 1576. In the Vatican library there is a copy of the French translation, *Imagination poetique*, which was interleaved in 1568 for Christopher, prince of the Palatinate; this volume contains an autograph inscription by Théodore de Bèze. The Sylvain S. Brunschwig gift to the Princeton University Library contains interleaved copies of Sambucus, *Emblemata* (Antwerp, 1584) and Junius, *Emblemata* (Antwerp, 1565); on these last two volumes, see Howard C. Rice, Jr, 'More Emblem Books.'

63 Cf. Max Rosenheim, 'The *Album Amicorum*,' and J.-J. Rousseau, *Emile*, chap. 5.

64 Nancel, *Petri Rami vita*, 250–1.

65 BN Rés. G. 2640, pt. II, f. 76.

66 For details, see M. Audin, *Le Thesaurus Amicorum de Jean de Tournes*, 7ff.

67 BN Rés. Z. 3734. The volume is bound as an oblong octavo in a contemporary blind-stamped vellum binding, bearing what appears to be a symbolic scene. For the sake of convenience during travels, it may well have been cut down from the

larger format reproduced by Warnecke in his late 19th-century reprint of the 1611 Oppenheim edition of the *Emblemata saecularia*. In fact, I possess one of the emblems reproduced by Warnecke in the same large format. It is interesting to note that these small illustrations were printed on large sheets, ostensibly to provide ample space for inscriptions; that probably explains too why the emblem texts are printed elswewhere in the collection.

We find the same separation of emblem texts, the 'Interpretationes emblematum,' from the pictures and mottoes in Gabriel Rollenhagen's nearly contemporaneous *Nucleus emblematum* (1611–13).

68 *Harvard College Library ... French Sixteenth-Century Books*, s.v. Horapollo.

69 *Theatrum vitae humanae*; Arsenal 4° B. L. 4974 and *Stultitiae laus* (Basel: Typis Genathianis, 1676); BN Y^2 12450bis.

70 This manuscript has recently been studied and edited by John Manning. See his 'Continental Emblem Books in Sixteenth-Century England: The Evidence of Sloane ms 3794,' and *The Emblems of Thomas Palmer: Two Hundred Poosees.*

71 BN ms fr. 19143. For a more detailed study of this manuscript, see Russell, 'Reading Alciato in Sixteenth-Century France,' and the edition of this manuscript that I am currently preparing with Catharine Randall.

72 Cf. Jacques Lavaud, 'Note sur un recueil manuscrit d'emblèmes composé pour la Maréchale de Retz,' See also Enzo Giudici, *Maurice Scève, poeta della Délie*, I, figs. 4–26.

73 Chassignet, *Sonnets franc-comtois inédits*; Loys Papon, *Oeuvres* and *Supplément aux oeuvres*; O.C. Reure, *Notice sur les emblèmes de Anne d'Urfé avec des stances de Loys Papon*; Anne d'Urfé, *Les Oeuvres morales et spirituelles inédites.*

For further discussion of Papon's emblems, see 185–8.

74 These are the sonnets Théodore Courtaux published (see n. 73).

75 See my study of this work in 'M. de Montplaisir and His Emblems.' There are other emblematic engravings by Juan Dolivar in the Département des Estampes at the Bibliothèque Nationale, but they were obviously trimmed and are in old albums; so it is impossible to determine whether or not they, too, were printed on large sheets providing room for additional manuscript texts (cf. BN Dépt. des Est. Da. 43. fol., 6–7; Ed. 65. fol., 154, and Ed. 73. fol., 138, 144).

76 This line of reasoning is inspired to some extent by the collection of devices that was intended to provide a biography of Anne d'Autriche (M. de Chaumelz, *Devises panegyriques pour Anne d'Autriche*). The model dates back at least to the Jesuit Etienne Binet's *Meditations affectueuses sur la vie de la tressainte Vierge Mere de Dieu* of 1632.

77 Published by Ludovic Lalanne as Jean Cousin, *Le Livre de fortune*.

78 Cf. P. Choné, *Emblèmes et pensée symbolique en Lorraine*, 664: 'Par ses relations avec le grand graveur-éditeur protestant Théodore de Bry, l'antiquaire

touche à un moderne réseau de communication d'images et d'idées qui oriente résolument Metz vers l'Allemagne protestante, paradoxe pour une ville depuis longtemps acquise à l'influence politique de la France.'

7: The Construction of the Early French Emblem

1 Indeed, in the first greatly expanded editions of Alciato, those by de Tournes and Gazeau in 1547 and Rouille in 1548, 70 or 80 of the some 200 emblems are unillustrated; cf. Mason Tung, 'Towards a New Census of Alciati's Editions.'

Denys de Harsy published unillustrated editions of La Perrière, Corrozet, and Alciato around 1540, and emblems from *Le Theatre des bons engins* and the *Hecatomgraphie*, as well as many by Alciato, were published without illustrations in various anthologies during the middle years of the century. On this question, see Frédéric Lachèvre, *Bibliographie des recueils collectifs de poésies du XVIe siècle*. Only one in three of the emblems Corrozet appended to his translation of the *Tabula Cebetis* in 1543 was illustrated.

In his 'A Bibliographical Approach to the Illustrations in Sixteenth-Century Editions of Alciato's *Emblemata*,' 146, John Manning suggests that 'the "naked" unillustrated text of the *Emblemata*, as we find it in the authorized *Opera omnia*, probably expresses the author's own ideal intentions for his work,' and it was not uncommon by the turn of the 17th century to find Latin emblems published with no figures (e.g., Andrew Willett, *Sacrorum emblematum centuria una*; Antoine de La Faye, *Emblemata et epigrammata miscellanea*; Gentil Cordier, *Anona prima, in tres partes divisa: emblematum, epigrammatum, variorum*; BN Yc. 8313).

2 *The Sixteenth-Century French Emblem Book*, 143–4, 154, 173, and passim.

3 De Tournes published editions of this seemingly popular version in 1545, 1546 (Marcus Fugger's copy is now in the Rosenwald Collection at the Library of Congress), 1547, 1549, 1553, and 1583.

Denis Drysdall seems to adopt this theory unquestioningly in the introduction to his translation of Hunger's Latin preface to his German translation of Alciato, published by Wechel in Paris in 1542 ('Defence and Illustration of the German Language,' 137–60.) To my knowledge, Hester Black was the first to call these texts 'commentaries' in her preface to the Scolar Press reprint of Hadrianus Junius' *Emblemata* of 1565, but she did so without comment. Barbara Tiemann, too (*Fabel und Emblem*, 105), claims they are commentaries following the model of moralized fables going back to the Middle Ages. Cf. Claudie Balavoine, 'La Mise en mot dans la *Délie* de Scève.'

Aneau initiated the practice of publishing actual commentaries of Alciato's emblems in the Rouille and Bonhomme editions in 1548.

4 He also published emblems from this book in *Le Jardin d'honneur* (1548 and 1550) where he never added titles either. (See Lachèvre for bibliographical details and descriptions.)
5 *Icones, id est verae imagines virorum doctrina simul et pietate illustrium*. When J. Stoer reprinted the emblems in de Bèze's *Poemata varia* of 1597–98, however, they were fitted out with mottoes, often of a descriptive nature. But Stoer apparently had access to only 40 of the original 44 cuts; so four of de Bèze's texts appear beneath empty frames at the end of the collection.
6 Paris, Bibliothèque de l'Arsenal 8° B. L. 32982.
7 See Karel Porteman, 'The Earliest Reception of the "Ars Emblematica" in Dutch,' concerning the Dutch edition; for the 1567 French edition, I am referring to the copy in the Stirling Maxwell Collection (SM659).
8 *Medieval Theory of Authorship*, 94–5.
9 *Les Mots et les choses*, 55–6.
10 We should not imagine, however, that the introduction of a new comparison would necessarily have been seen to make this text into a commentary, because it was not uncommon to do so in ordinary emblem texts, such as this one by Loys Papon (1581):

> Penssers en papilhons, de ces pennes aylés
> Or, argent, & le pourpre, a vos feilhes meslés,
> Pour caduque parade: ou la gloire mortelle
> Nous ternit des ennuys, comm' vn froid, vos verdeurs
> Et vos branches sans fruict, & vos fleurs sans odeur
> Comm' eux nos cueurs en vain, brulent a la chandelle. (*Oeuvres*, 61)

Here the comparison to the butterfly and flame is reinforced by one where cold has the same effect on fruits and flowers.
11 *Le Premier Livre des emblèmes*, 20.
12 Pierre Coustau, *Le Pegme*, 33ff. For the Latin, see *Petri Costalii Pegma*, 15ff.
13 *CWE*, XXXI, 112.
14 See Russell, *The Emblem and Device in France*, chap. 4.
15 Saunders seems to fall into a trap in this regard as she tries to reconcile Aneau's occasionally long-winded didacticism with her contention that brevity is the ideal. She explains that 'Unlike Corrozet and Guéroult he does not separate the explanation from the emblem proper, but incorporates everything into one single verse passage' (*The Sixteenth-Century French Emblem Book*, 173)! François Cornilliat takes a more promising approach to this question when he ventures that longer French texts offer commentaries on the shorter Latin originals ('Physiologie du mariage et de l'emblème: Aneau et Alciat').

16 See, e.g., 'The Union Catalogue of Emblem Books and the *Corpus Librorum Emblematum*,' 131.
17 Preface to *Emblemata. Handbuch zur Sinnbildkunst des XVI. and XVII. Jahrhunderts.*
18 As he explained in the paper 'From Illustrated Epigram to Emblem: The Canonization of a Typographical Arrangement.'
19 We would do well to remember here that, although it does also occur in the subtitle of La Perrière's *Theatre*, Gueroult was the first in France to use the word 'emblème' in his title: *Le Premier Livre des emblemes*, thus indicating a high degree of consciousness that he was working within the confines of a genre.
20 See chap. 6, n. 38.
21 'Emblem, Emblembuch,' cols. 92–5.
22 See E.H. Gombrich, *Symbolic Images*, 151–2.
23 It is evident, for example, in La Perrière's emblem of the fig tree in *La Morosophie*, where its property of bearing fruit without flowers (33) is emblematic of proper friendship where 'les amys par effect / Faut secourir, sans user de promesse.' The scene is a realistic one, with one man giving money to another beneath a tree (fig); representation of the deed cannot be detached from its exemplarity here because of its re-contextualization by the presence of the tree. Actually, a mutual re-contextualization occurs once one realizes the tree is a fig and can link the two scenes through analogy in a way that makes them allegorically redundant in relation to each other. This trend would become magnified in 17th-century Dutch emblem books and genre painting, but it was encouraged as early as the prefaces to Sambucus' emblem book in the 1560s (see Karel Porteman, 'The Earliest Reception of the "Ars Emblematica" in Dutch').
24 See, e.g., Bartolomeo Taegio, *Il Liceo ... Libro secondo*, f. 6v.
25 While the term 'lemma' could also refer to a motto appended to a picture, this sense seems tautological at best and deceptive at worst, to the extent that it could lead to confusion with the motto of a device.
26 See Praz, *Studies in Seventeenth-Century Imagery*, 40–1
27 But see what I take to be the pioneering study by Claudie Balavoine, 'Bouquets de fleurs et colliers de perles: Sur les recueils de formes brèves au XVIe siècle.'
28 In her introduction to the Scolar facsimile of the first edition of *Theatre*, Alison Saunders reports that Henkel and Schöne have judged eleven of the emblems to be so inspired. See as well Irene Bergal, 'Word and Picture: Erasmus' *Parabolae* in La Perrière's *Morosophie*.'
29 Paolo Giovio, *Dialogo dell'imprese militari et amorose*; Torquato Tasso, *Dialogo dell'Imprese*.

30 *Icon and Idea. The Function of Art in the Development of Human Consciousness*, 49–50.

31 Alison Saunders points out that the technique is much more common in Latin emblems than in French translations of them (*The Sixteenth-Century French Emblem Book*, 188–91).

32 *The Emblem and Device in France*, chap. 4. See as well the preface to the Dutch translation of Sambucus' emblems as discussed by Karel Porteman in 'The Earliest Reception of the "Ars Emblematica" in Dutch.'

Mary Carruthers (212–13) has made a case for the medieval reader being freer than previously thought. I would counter that her argument applies only to certain readers, and that those readers, as she describes them, are really 'authors.'

33 On the order of the editions of the *Theatre*, see Stephen Rawles, 'The Earliest Editions of Guillaume de La Perrière's *Theatre des bons engins*.'

34 See Russell, 'Emblems and Hieroglyphics.'

35 On such problems in the illustration of Alciato's emblems, see John Manning, 'A Bibliographical Approach to the Illustrations in Sixteenth-Century Editions of Alciato's *Emblemata*,' and on the use of previously used woodcuts in Corrozet's *Hecatomgraphie*, see Stephen Rawles, 'Corrozet's *Hecatomgraphie*: Where Did the Woodcuts Come from and Where Did They Go?'

36 *Le Livre français illustré de la Renaissance*, 5–6 and passim.

37 See Michael Hirst, *Michelangelo Draftsman*, 103–6. Hirst seems to take this as something peculiar to Michelangelo, but another example would be Rosso's Empedocles/St Roch; see Eugene A. Carroll, *Rosso Fiorentino*, 349. And at the beginning of the Book of the Dead in a Book of Hours from Tours (c. 1530–3; Pierpont Morgan Library M. 452) we see Job on a dung heap visited by his wife and friends; the figure of Job here is purportedly taken from the river god in Marcantonio Raimondi's engraving of the *Judgement of Paris*.

38 Panofsky, 212–13.

39 See, e.g., Jean Frappier, 'Variations sur le thème du miroir,' 134–59.

40 See Lorne Campbell, *Renaissance Portraits*, 195. Cf. Emile Mâle, *L'Art religieux de la fin du moyen âge en France*, 365, on the medieval belief that if one were to write a certain formula on parchment with his own blood, and then look into a mirror, he would see himself as he would appear after death.

41 Artemisia Gentileschi's *Madeleine* at the Palazzo Piti, Florence, shows her looking away from a mirror that appears to reflect her hair and an earring; on the mirror's upper border we read the biblical motto OPTIMAM PARTEM ELEGIT, and behind the mirror we see a skull. For Rémy Belleau, see *La Bergerie*, ed. D. Delacourcelle, 91–5, and A. Eckhardt, *Rémy Belleau, sa vie et sa 'Bergerie'*, 92–3.

42 See *De l'art de faire les devises*, 217–18.

43 Cf. Robert Klein, *La Forme et l'intelligible*, 148.

44 See Russell, 'L'Emblématique et la description dans la poésie française de Du Bellay.'

45 Cf. Carruthers, 221–4.

46 BN Dépt. des Est. Ed. 26 fol., 53.

47 Jennifer Montagu made this *rapprochement* in a talk at the Glasgow International Emblem Conference, 13–17 August 1990, entitled 'Emblems of Academies in Italian Thesis Prints.' See as well her *Index of Emblems of the Italian Academies Based on Michele Maylender's 'Storie delle accademie d'Italia.'*

48 'The Book of Signs,' 135.

49 See the discussion of this image in Russsell, 'L'Emblématique et la description dans la poésie française de Du Bellay.'

50 'From Allegory to Diagram in the Renaissance Mind.'

51 *Studies*, 41.

52 See Herbert Read, *Icon and Idea*, 46–7.

53 'Du regnard & du buisson,' *Ne demander ayde à celluy qui nuyt naturellement, Les Fables du tresancien Esope phrygien premierement escriptes en grec, & depuis mises en Rithme Françoise*, sig. K8^{v}–L1.

54 *The Sixteenth-Century French Emblem Book*, 156.

55 See Stephen Rawles, 'Corrozet's *Hecatomgraphie.*' The *Emblemes* may also be found in *L'Enfer Marot*, 1544 (BN Rothschild 2858) and in Jean Corrozet's *Emblemes ou preceptes moraux.*

56 Claude Paradin, *Devises heroiques*, 55, and Russell, *The Emblem and Device in France*, 64.

57 Cf. Erasmus, *Adagia*, I, viii, 57: *Melle litus gladius.*

58 See Greta Dexter, '*La Morosophie* de la Perrière,' especially 68–9.

59 Ibid, and Jerome Schwartz, 'Some Emblematic Marriage Topoi in the French Renaissance.'

60 In 'Corrozet's *Hecatomgraphie.*'

61 *Les Emblemes de l'Amour humain*, 92–3.

62 In 'Some Emblematic Marriage Topoi.'

63 Cf. Corrozet's 'Vertu meilleure que richesse' (*Hecatomgraphie*, sig. o1^{v}) and Coustau's 'Vertu surmonte tout' (*Pegme*, 121). These are, of course, all variations on a traditional motif; hence, in Steyner's edition of Cicero's *De officiis*, one of the illustrations shows a warrior weighing less in the balance than his captive (f. xix).

64 *Pegme*, 401–6.

65 'Le Corps de la sentence: Les "Emblemes Chrestiens" de Georgette de Montenay,' especially 60.

66 The now lost manuscript of this work was published in Papon's *Oeuvres*. For a

fuller discussion of these emblems, see Russell, 'Emblematics in the French Provinces: The Case of Loys Papon and Anne d'Urfé in the Forez.'

67 See Russell, 'Emblems and Hieroglyphics: Some Observations on the Beginnings and the Nature of Emblematic Forms.'

68 See Claude Longeon, *Une Province française à la Renaissance. La Vie intellectuelle en Forez au 16e siècle*, 540–2.

69 On this evolution, see Michel Pastoureau, 'L'Illustration du livre: comprendre ou rêver?' and Sara F. Matthews Grieco, *Ange ou diablesse*.

8: Emblematics and Court Culture

1 The classic study of emblematic portraiture may be found in John Pope-Hennessy's *The Portrait in the Renaissance*, chap. 5: 'Image and Emblem,' 205–56.

2 The pomegranate is a particularly interesting and often used image in such portraits. In a painting of the Virgin and child at Nantes, Jacopo del Sellaio (1442–93) placed an open pomegranate beside the Virgin, while in L. Lippi's (1606–65) painting of a Lady with a mask, or allegory of dissimulation, at Nantes, the sitter is holding a mask in her right hand, and an open pomegranate before her in her left hand. See, as well, Guy de Tervarent, *Attributs et symboles dans l'art profane (1450–1600)*, s.v. *grenade*. Cf. chap. 4, n. 15, above.

3 See Virginia Woods Callahan, 'Erasmus: An Emblematic Portrait by Andrea Alciati,' especially 73; and William S. Heckscher, 'Reflections on Seeing Holbein's Portrait of Erasmus at Longford Castle.'

4 In Russell, *The Emblem and Device in France*, chap. 4.

5 For one particularly interesting example, see Johannes Köhler's *Angewandte Emblematik im Fliesensaal von Wrisbergholzen bei Hildesheim*, which describes the copious emblematic decorations of this castle; the decorative plan was executed in the early 18th century after emblems by Van Veen, Saavedra Fajardo, and Camerarius.

6 See Maria Antonietta de Angelis, 'Emblems and Devices on a Ceiling in the Château of Dampierre-sur-Boutonne' and Norman K. Farmer, Jr, 'Lady Drury's Oratory: The Painted Closet from Hawstead Hall.'

7 And Paulette Choné tells us that Boissard's Latin emblems were used for teaching Latin in Protestant schools (*Emblèmes et pensée symbolique en Lorraine*, 687).

8 Judi Loach (Welsh School of Architecture) has discovered class notes from a French Jesuit *collège* that demonstrate the role of emblem books in secondary-school curriculum at the level of day-to-day teaching and assignments. Cf. Aldo Scaglione, *The Liberal Arts and the Jesuit College System*, 120–5.

One such group of emblems, composed by the *rhetores* of the Jesuit college in Antwerp, was published as *Typus mundi in quo eius calamitates et pericula nec non divini, humanique amoris antipathia, embelmatice proponuntur* (Antwerp: J. Cnobbaert, 1627), and reprinted in 1630, 1652 and 1697 (see Praz, *Studies*, 519).

9 On this change, see, e.g., Ernesto Grassi, *Renaissance Humanism. Studies in Philosophy and Poetics*, chap. 1.

10 Cf. d'Aubigné's description of that court in *Princes*, 1019–26:

Les filles de la cour sont galantes honnestes
Qui se font bien servir, moins chastes, plus secrettes
Qui sçavent le mieux feindre un mal pour accoucher;
On blasme celle-la qui n'a pas sçeu cacher;
Du Louvre les retraits sont hideux cimetieres
D'enfans vuidez, tuez par les apotiquaires:
Nos filles ont bien sçeu quelles receptes font
Massacre dans leur flanc des enfans qu'elles ont. (*Les Tragiques*, 120)

11 Taken from Lucian, this myth, in which eloquence and wisdom are joined with physical strength, had been associated with the French crown since the reign of François Ier. See Marc-René Jung, *Hercule dans la littérature française du XVIe siècle*, and Lecoq, 425–6.

12 Cf. Françoise Bardon, *Le Portrait mythologique à la cour de France sous Henri IV et de Louis XIII*, 133, where she discusses the *placards* 'nés de la guerre' to become 'une habitude de propagande.'

13 See Russell, *The Emblem and Device in France*, 40–3, 70–2; Josèphe Jacquiot, 'L'Allégorie aux revers de médailles et de jetons du XVe au XVIIe siècle'; and Vladimir Jurěn, 'Le Jeton français et la littérature emblématique.' The best compendium of courtly devices for *revers de médailles* is probably to be found in F. Feuardent, *Jetons et méreaux depuis Louis IX jusqu'à la fin du consulat de Bonaparte*.

14 Descriptions and transcriptions of these placards may be found in vol. 4 of L'Estoile's *Mémoires-journaux*; the album itself is to be found at the Bibliothèque Nationale, Rés. g. Fol. La [25]. 6.

15 IV, 286 (f. 29^r in the album).

16 See 89–92, and Lecoq, passim.

17 Lestoile, IV, 294 (f. 31^r in the album). Cf. Françoise Bardon, *Le Portrait mythologique*, 39–43. This motif, too, had long been associated with the French monarchy; the reverse of a medal struck for Henri II shows Perseus delivering Andromeda, with the motto (in Greek) 'Je combats par tous les moyens.' See *Trésor de numismatique et de glyptique ... médailles françaises*, pl. 13, no. 5.

18 Cf. Bouquet, f. 1ᵛ, where he uses Alciato's emblem *Foedera* (10) to exhort the new king to work at uniting the French nobility behind him.
19 *Le Portrait mythologique*, 39.
20 L'Estoile, 295–7; P. Coustau, *Pegme*, 414; J.J. Boissard, *Emblematum liber* 46–7. See, too, Arthur Henkel and Albrecht Schöne, eds., *Emblemata*, cols. 1171–3.
21 Cf. Christian Jouhaud, 'Lisibilité et persuasion. Les placards politiques,' especially 318–24.
22 Mildelbourg: Simon Molard, 1605, with several other editions issuing from Paris and Rouen until at least 1656. Here I am following Claude Le Villain's 1626 Rouen edition, to which my paginal indications refer. Unflattering proverbial characterizations were common in the 16th century and were one of the effects of growing national consciousness in Renaissance Europe. In *L'Estampe satirique en France pendant les guerres de religion*, 322, André Blum describes the links between this kind of work and the illustrated proverbs of the late 15th and early 16th centuries, and claims that the compositional technique shows a Flemish influence; some of his other examples come from the famous album of satirical prints and broadsides at the Bibiothèque Nationale, Dépt. des Estampes, Tf. 1 Rés.
23 *Studies*, 325.
24 Cf. Russell, *The Emblem and Device in France*, 89–93.
25 This opinion must have been very current if we can judge from the presentation of Spaniards in such French comedies as Odet de Turnèbes' *Les Contens*.
26 This last emblem might remind a reader really familiar with the emblem tradition of Alciato's offensive emblem 80, *Adversus naturam peccantes*, thus reinforcing the criticism by adding a resonance of unnaturalness to the Spaniard's conduct.
27 University of Glasgow SM434.
28 *Emblemata, Welche das Leben, die Thaten, Sitten und wunderbare verwandlung dess Signor Spangniols*, Nürnberg, Pol. All. 24,857 (c. 1600). See David Kunzle, *The Early Comic Strip*, 198. This example shows that such satire was less indigenously and patriotically French than Blum (320 and passim) would have it. The French version in our illustration was published in 1609 (BN Dépt des Est., Qb1. 1609).
29 A Paris, Chez les 24 & 25. Paris, 1617 (BN Dépt des Est., Hennin 1813).
30 For other examples of emblematic satire on medals and in engravings, and directed against Concini, see Bardon, *Portrait*, 131–2, 164, and 217; see too Blum, 318–20.
31 M. de Chaumelz, *Devises panegyriques pour Anne d'Autriche*.
32 L'Estoile, IV, 32–3; Henri III's famous device composed of three crowns with the motto *Ultima coelo manet* to suggest that, already possessing the crowns of

France and Poland, the last was waiting for him in heaven, was satirized by changing the word *coelo* to *claustro*, as is suggested here.

33 *Harvard College Library. Department of Printing and Graphic Arts. Catalogue of Books and Manuscripts. Part I: French Sixteenth-Century Books*, II, 471. One 17th-century example centres on the death of the duchess of Arpajon; the Bibliothèque Nationale possesses a single-sheet of in-folio size containing the device of a moon in eclipse with the motto *Cresciuta manco*. Sonnets front and back develop the theme of mourning (BN Ye. 172). Le Moyne reproduces this device, still attributed to Mme Arpajon, but with the motto *Deficio dum perficior* (*De l'art des devises*, 208–9).

34 Cf. M.R. Jung, *Etudes sur le poème allégorique*, 76–7.

35 See Russell, *The Emblem and Device in France*, 41–3. If, as seems likely (following Claudie Balavoine's argument in 'Archéologie de l'emblème littéraire'), Alciato created his first emblems as gifts for the Saturnalia, following the model of Martial's *apophoreta*, then devices would seem to be exceptionally appropriate gifts for a humanist's *étrennes*. On this question see, too, John Manning's introduction to his edition of *The Emblems of Thomas Palmer. Two Hundred Poosees. Sloane MS. 3794*, xxviii–xxxii, where Manning points out *inter alia* that 'posie' meant 'emblem' in late 16th-century England, but that Puttenham also equated the term with *apophoreta*.

36 Instead of Sully's self-serving, and somewhat biased, account, I am following Henri Estienne, *L'Art de faire les devises*, 146–50 (passage quoted from 148–9). Cf. Sully's *Mémoires* and also Jacquiot, 'L'Allégorie aux revers de médailles et de jetons du XVe au XVIIe siècle.' This kind of sparring through the medium of the device recalls too the psychological warfare between Jean Sans Peur and Louis d'Orléans two hundred years earlier (cf. Paradin, *Devises heroiques*, 222–5, and Russell, *The Emblem and Device in France*, 26).

37 Estienne, 149–50.

38 See François d'Amboise, *Discours ou traicté des devises*, 2–3. There is some reflection of these readings in Sully's *Mémoires*. See also Russell, *The Emblem and Device in France*, 41–6.

39 For a discussion of this portrait, see Françoise Bardon, 'Sur un portrait de François Ier'; and Russell, 'Emblematics and Cultural Specificity.'

For an earlier prototype, see Wolff Traut's allegorical portrait of Maximilian. Cf. A.H. Schutz, 'Ronsard's "Amours" xxxii and the Tradition of the Synthetic Lady,' for a discussion of a tradition of 'composite' women that goes back to Pindar.

40 *Pagan Mysteries in the Renaissance*, 213–4. Following Raymond Waddington in 'The Bisexual Portrait of Francis I,' Stephen Orgel revived Wind's claim about the androgynous nature of this portrait in a lecture at the symposium 'Aspects

of Renaissance and Baroque Symbol Theory (1500–1700),' University of Tennessee at Chattanooga, 1–3 May 1992, in order to stress the bisexuality thus expressed. It seems fair, though, to assume that a quasi-official portrait like this one must have been made under the assumption that the king would *not* be perceived as some androgynous creature. When Henri III was presented in clearly androgynous guise, thirty or forty years later, it was to attack and undermine his authority. See my article cited in n. 39 above.

41 Cf. W. McAllister Johnson, 'Once More the Galerie François Ier at Fontainebleau.'

42 On the psychology of such 'deifications,' see Edgar Wind, 'Studies in Allegorical Portraiture,' and Ernst Kantorowicz's classic study, *The King's Two Bodies.*

43 *Les Moeurs polies et la littérature de cour sous Henri II*, 176–7, 186–7.

44 Paolo Giovio, *Dialogue*, 26.

45 See Andrew C. Ritchie, 'Léonard Limousin's Triumph of the Faith, with Portraits of the House of Guise.' Henri II's device was composed of a crescent moon and the motto *Donec totum impleat orbem.*

46 *Diane de Poitiers et le mythe de Diane*, 50.

47 Cf. Natalie Zemon Davis, *Fiction in the Archives*, passim.

48 Pontus de Tyard, *Oeuvres poétiques complètes*, 270–1. Cf. Gisèle Mathieu-Castellani, *Emblèmes de la mort*, 111–18.

49 *Les Illustres Observations antiques du Seigneur Gabriel Symeon Florentin*, 96. On Simeoni, see Toussaint Renucci, *Un Aventurier des lettres au XVIe siècle, Gabriel Symeoni.*

This passage is reminiscent of Aneau's pretext for the creation of the emblems in his *L'Imagination poetique*: 'A lors je estimant que sans cause n'avoient esté faictes, luy promis que de muettes, & mortes, je les [Macé Bonhomme's unused woodcuts] rendroie parlantes, & vives: leur inspirant ame, par vive Poësie' (6).

50 P.-D. Roussel, *Le Château de Diane de Poitiers à Anet*, 113. Cf. E. Bourciez, *Les Moeurs polies*, 186. This device may also be found at Fontainebleau, in the Chapel of the Eglise de la Sainte Trinité; see Pierre Dan, 164.

The device was recalled by Gabriel Rollenhagen in his *Nucleus emblematum selectissimorum*, I, 24, where it is generalized to speak of the prayers of the just.

51 'Emblems and Devices on a Ceiling in the Château of Dampierre-sur-Boutonne,' see especially 222.

52 For a description of the château, see Gérard Pesme, *En flânant au château de Dampierre-sur-Boutonne*. The ceiling was first described by Louis Audiat, *Epigraphie santone et aunisienne*; François Gebelin's description of the individual devices in *Les Châteaux de la Renaissance* should be compared with that of M.A. De Angelis in the article cited in n. 6 to this chapter.

Jeanne de Vivonne passed her presumed predilection for devices on to her daughter, whose interesting album of devices was, as late as the 1960s, in the collection of Fr. Chandon de Briailles (see Jacques Lavaud, 'Note sur un recueil manuscrit d'emblèmes composé pour la Maréchale de Retz'; and Enzo Giudici, *Maurice Scève, poeta della Délie*, I, Collana di Cultura, 9, figs. 4–26.

53 See De Angelis, passim.

54 The chapel is now to be found, reconstructed, in the Metropolitan Museum in New York.

55 Giudici, figs. 1–3.

56 Cf. Paul Bonnefon, *Montaigne, l'homme et l'oeuvre*, 142.

57 See André Masson, *Le Décor des bibliothèques du moyen-âge à la Révolution*, 76–80.

58 Ibid, 110.

59 Ibid, 48–52.

60 *L'Imagination poetique*, 22.

61 'L'Ecole de Fontainebleau,' Paris, Grand Palais, 17 octobre 1972–15 janvier 1973.

62 Cf., e.g., BN ms fr. 5227, f. 3^{v}, with the famous *Candor illaesus* device of Pope Clement VII. Early in the century, however, it was more common to keep motto and figure together, perhaps in a roundel; Clement's device may be found presented this way, together with the *Suave* device of his uncle, Leo X, each in one of the roundels in the frame of a miniature representing the martyrdom of St Catherine, from Clement's missal, that was offered as lot 21 in Christie's London sale of 20 June 1990.

63 Reymond was active in Paris and Germany between 1534 and 1578. The allegories of the signs of the zodiac are in the collection of the Musée Jacquemart-André in Paris, and what are presumably 19th-century reproductions of two of the months (July and August) may be seen at the Carnegie Museum in Pittsburgh.

64 See Josèphe Chartrou, *Les Entrées solennelles*, 31–2.

65 See, e.g., Jacques Vanuxem, 'Le Carrousel de 1612 sur la Place Royale et ses devises,' and Jean Alard, *Entree du Roy a Tolose*; BN Lb^{3}5. 1784.

66 Maurice Scève, *Oeuvres complètes*, 532–4.

67 See my discussion of this composition in 'Emblematics and Cultural Specificity: Two Examples from Sixteenth-Century France.' Cf. *The Entry of Henry II into Paris, 1549*, ed. I.D. McFarlane.

68 Rouen, Biblio. Munic. ms 1268 (Y.28): *Relation de l'entrée de Henri II, roi de France, à Rouen, le 1er octobre 1550*, and Margaret McGowan's edition.

69 Masson, 48–52. See above, 213.

70 *Recueil des choses notables, qui ont esté faites à Bayonne.*

71 Cf. Alan R. Young, *Tudor and Jacobean Tournaments* and *The English Tournament Imprese.*

72 'The Lady and the Unicorn, or M. de Nemours à Coulomiers: Enigma, Device, Blazon and Emblem in *La Princesse de Clèves*.'

73 E.g., 'Pour une dame qui donna une teste de mort en devise,' *Les Epigrammes*, 154.
74 Recalling a story first told by Giovio, Brantôme shows how devices could be incorporated into clothing to make a statement, as a Pavian countess did with her dress decorated with butterflies and candles (*Les Dames galantes*, ed. M. Rat, 79–80). Cf. the drawing by Holbein the Younger representing a young lady with ALS.IN.ERN.ALS.IN. ('All in honour' or 'In all honor') embroidered on her corsage (*Les Mots dans le dessin*, 87e Exposition du Cabinet des Dessins. Musée du Louvre, 1986, no. 37).
75 As presented in BN ms fr. 894.
76 See Edgar Wind, '"Aenigma Termini": The Emblem of Erasmus,' and James McConica, 'The Riddle of Terminus.'
77 See Charles R. Beard, 'Cap Brooches of the Renaissance,' and Praz, *Studies*, 53–5.
78 Benvenuto Cellini, *Autobiography*, 72.
79 Examples may be found in Du Bellay, *Antiquitez de Rome* (son.14) and paintings of Temperance by Vermeer (see Linda Freeman Bauer, 'Seventeenth-Century Naturalism and the Emblematic Interpretation of Paintings').
80 For some sense of the place of framing in the theory of the forms, see Menestrier, *L'Art des emblemes* (1662), 84.
81 Brantôme, *Oeuvres complètes*, IX, 512–13.

9: Emblematic Structures in Renaissance Literature

1 BN ms fr. 1524. On other bindings, emblematically decorated with *memento mori* designs and mourning devices for Henri III and Catherine de Medicis, see Alfred Franklin, *Paris et les parisiens au seizième siècle*, 202–5, and Frances Yates, *The French Academies of the Sixteenth Century*, 179.
2 See Russell, *The Emblem and Device in France*, 58.
3 See Greta Dexter, 'Guillaume de La Perrière.'
4 *The Grammar of Silence. A Reading of Marguerite de Navarre's Poetry*, 234–41.
5 *L'Heptameron*, 132. See as well Russell, 'Some Ways of Structuring Character in the *Heptameron*.'
6 See Corrozet's *Hecatomgraphie*, sig. e7v, and Scève, *Délie*, diz. 159 and the preceding *emblesme*, 'Fuyant ma mort, j'haste ma fin.' Cf. Russell, 'Emblematic Structures in Sixteenth-Century French Poetry.'
7 See H. Miedema, 'The Term *Emblema* in Alciati.'
8 *The Icy Fire. Five Studies in European Petrarchism.*
9 For an idea of how this metaphoric vocabulary might be used to provide descriptive epithets in lyric poetry, see Jean de La Jessée's sonnet 'Le jeune Cerf navré,' included by Marcel Raymond in his anthology of *La Poésie française et le maniérisme*, 103.

On the Baudreuil tapestries, see Adolfo Salvatore Cavallo, *Medieval Tapestries in the Metropolitan Museum of Art*, 347–58.

10 See Russell, 'Some Ways of Structuring Character in the *Heptameron*.'

11 On the notion of allegorical space, see Walter J. Ong, 'From Allegory to Diagram in the Renaissance Mind.'

12 It reminds us of the allegory of the young man at court in d'Aubigné's *Les Tragiques*, Princes, ll. 1107ff.

13 *Pantagruel*, chap. 24. For further discussion of Rabelais' involvement with emblems and emblematics, see François Rigolot and Sandra Sider, 'Fonctions de l'écriture emblématique chez Rabelais'; Jerome Schwartz, 'Scatology and Eschatology in Gargantua's Androgyne Device'; and Russell, 'A Note on Panurge's "pusse en l'aureille"' and 'Panurge and His New Clothes.'

14 See Jerome Schwartz, 'Emblematic Structures in Yver's *Printemps*,' and Robert J. Sealy, *The Palace Academy of Henry III*. In *From Tales to Truths*, 51, Donald Stone notes that Belleforest added to his translation of Bandello a prose version of La Perrière's 18th emblem in the *Theatre*, the domestic Venus with her foot on a turtle.

15 As quoted by Peter Bayley in *French Pulpit Oratory, 1598–1650*, 75.

16 Ibid, 84; Binet's work has been reprinted by Dominique Seban, with a preface by Marc Fumaroli.

17 'Emblematic Structures in Sixteenth-Century French Poetry,' 'Montaigne's Emblems,' 'Du Bellay's Emblematic Vision of Rome,' and 'L'Emblématique et la description dans la poésie française de Du Bellay.' What follows is a continuation of the first of these articles.

18 Agrippa d'Aubigné, *Oeuvres*, 861.

19 Antoine Chandieu, *Octonaires sur la vanité et inconstance du monde*, ed. Françoise Bonali-Fiquet, 73 (no. XXX).

20 Etienne Jodelle, *Oeuvres complètes*, I, 371.

21 See Terence Cave and Michel Jeanneret, *Métamorphoses spirituelles. Anthologie de la poésie religieuse française 1570–1630*, 57.

22 Cf. François Cornilliat, 'Le commentaire a-t-il horreur du vide? L'attribution du sens chez Barthélemy Aneau.'

23 *Oeuvres complètes*, ed. A. Thibaudet and M. Rat, II, 12; 480a. See Russell, 'Montaigne's Emblems.'

24 For evidence of such construction in parts of Montaigne's text composed before 1580, see Marianne S. Meijer, 'L'Ordre des *Essais* dans les deux premiers volumes,' 17–27.

25 Cf. Jean-Jacques Boissard, 'Mundus imago dei est,' the keynote emblem in the manuscript collection of his emblems in the Institut de France in Paris (ms 623).

26 Cf. the discussion of Alciato's peach emblem (159) and Michelangelo's Ganymede drawing, 168–74 above.

27 Corrozet used a similar image in the preface to his *Hecatomgraphie*; see my discussion of it in *The Emblem and Device in France*, 175–6. Cf., as well, Germaine Warkentin, 'The Form of Dante's "Libello" and Its Challenge to Petrarch,' where she discusses the evolution of the authorial act from the Middle Ages to the Renaissance in reference to Petrarch and his followers.

28 See R.K. Angress, *The Early German Epigram. A Study in Baroque Poetry*, 20.

29 See Henkel and Schöne, *Emblemata. Handbuch zur Sinnbildkunst des XVI. und XVII. Jahrhunderts*, cols. 321–2.

30 *Works*, ed. U.T. Holmes et al. II, 364.

31 BN ms fr. 20614.

32 Cotgrave defines 'crayon' as 'Dry painting; or, a painting in, or Picture of, dry colours; also, the Table whereon a Painter mingleth (such) colours; and the first draught, or lineaments of a picture, made with any of them; hence also, a patterne, or example.' The expression 'crayon de mes vers,' then, reminds us how literally words conjured pictures in an oral culture.

33 See Zacharias Heyns, *Emblemata, Emblemes chrestiennes, et morales*, for Du Bartas; Jacob Cats, *Maechdenplicht ... Officium Puellarum, in castis Amoribus, Emblemate expressum*, for Montaigne; and for Ronsard, see Karl-Ludwig Selig, 'Notes on Ronsard in the Netherlands.'

Conclusion

1 In the introduction to his critical edition of Menestrier's *L'Art des emblemes* (1684), xii.

2 *The Gothic Idol: Ideology and Image-Making in Medieval Art*, passim.

3 Ibid, 220–41.

4 But as Etienne Binet's *Essay des merveilles de nature* shows, this material needed to be sorted, accommodated to the emerging scientific view of the world, and sanitized of its superstitions in order to provide preachers with a useful rhetorical tool.

5 'Marcus Gheeraerts and the Aesopic Connection in Seventeenth-Century Scientific Illustration,' 132–8.

6 See above, chap. 3.

7 See Russell, 'Emblematics and Cultural Specificity: Two Examples from Sixteenth-Century France.'

8 Cf. Jean Rousset, 'La Querelle de la métaphore.'

9 Cf. *Les Mots et les choses*, 112, 126–31.

Bibliography

Shelf marks are provided only for unique copies, for copies with manuscript marginalia, and for works that are difficult to locate, or to identify an edition that could be confused with another.

I. Primary Sources

Aesop. *Fabellae aliquot aesopicae in usum puerorum selectae*. Antwerp: Christopher Plantin, 1586.

– *Les Fables du tresancien Esope phrygien premierement escriptes en grec, & depuis mises en Rithme Françoise*. Trans. Gilles Corrozet. Paris: Denys Janot, 1542.

Alard, Jean. *Entree du Roy a Tolose*. Toulouse: Raim. Colomiés, 1622.

Alciato, Andrea. *Emblematum liber*. 1531; rpt. Hildesheim: Georg Olms, 1977.

– *Emblematum libri duo*. Lyons: Jean de Tournes, 1549; BN Rés. Z. 2518.

– *Emblemes*. Trans. Barthélemy Aneau. Lyons: Macé Bonhomme, 1549.

– *Emblemata, cum Claudii Minois ad eadem commentariis*. Leiden: Plantin, 1591, 8°.

– *Emblemata cum commentariis*. Padua: P.P. Tozzi, 1621.

– *Lettere*. Ed. G.L. Barni. Florence: Felice Le Monnier, 1953.

Alciatus, Andreas. *The Latin Emblems* and *Emblems in Translation*. Ed. Peter M. Daly, Virginia W. Callahan, and Simon Cuttler. 2 vols. Toronto: University of Toronto Press, 1985.

Amboise, François d'. *Discours ou traicté des devises*. Paris: Rolet Boutonne, 1620.

Aneau, Barthélemy. *Decades de la description, forme, et vertu naturelle des animaulx, tant raisonnables, que Brutz*. Lyons: Balthasar Arnoullet, 1549.

– *L'Imagination poetique*. Lyons: Macé Bonhomme, 1552.

– *Picta poesis*. Lyons: Macé Bonhomme, 1552.

Aubigné, Agrippa d'. *Oeuvres*. Ed. Henri Weber et al. Bibliothèque de la Pléiade. Paris: Gallimard, 1969.

– *Les Tragiques*. Ed. Jacques Bailbé. Paris: Garnier-Flammarion, 1968.

Baïf, Jean-Antoine de. *Evvres en rime*. Ed. C. Marty-Laveaux. 5 vols. 1881–90; rpt. Geneva: Slatkine, 1966.

Bargagli, Scipione. *Dell'imprese*. Venice: Francesco de' Franceschi Senese, 1594.

Baude, Henri. *Dictz moraulx pour faire tapisserie*. Ed. Annette Scoumanne. TLF. Geneva and Paris: Droz, 1959.

– *Les Vers de Maître Henri Baude*. Ed. Jules Quicherat. Paris, 1856.

(Baude) Lemaître, Jean-Loup. *Catalogue de l'exposition Henri Baude, Dictz moraulx pour faire tapisserie*. Ussel: Musée du pays d'Ussel; Paris: Diffusion de Boccard, 1988.

Belleau, Rémy. *Les Amours et nouveaux eschanges des pierres précieuses*. Ed. A. Van Bever. Paris: E. Sansot, 1909.

– *La Bergerie*. Ed. D. Delacourcelle. TLF. Geneva and Lille: Droz, 1954.

Berthod, F. *Emblesmes sacrez tirez de l'Escriture. Inventees et expliquees en vers Françoys avec une breve Meditation sur le mesme sujet. Pour servir à la conduite de la vie Chrestienne*. 2 vols. Paris: E. Loyson, 1657–65.

Bestiaires du moyen âge. Trans. Gabriel Bianciotto. Paris: Stock, 1980.

Bèze, Théodore de. *Icones, id est verae imagines virorum doctrina simul et pietate illustrium*. 1580; rpt. Menston: Scolar Press, 1971.

Binet, Etienne. *Essay des merveilles de nature et des plus nobles artifices*. Ed. Dominique Seban and Marc Fumaroli. Evreux: 'Des Opérations' Association du Théâtre de la Ville d'Evreux, 1987.

– *Meditations affectueuses sur la vie de la tressainte Vierge Mere de Dieu*. Antwerp: Martin Nutius, for Theodore de Galle, 1632; University of Glasgow, SM Add 227.

Boissard, Jean-Jacques. *Emblematum liber*. 1593; rpt. Hildesheim and New York: Georg Olms, 1977.

– *Theatrum vitae humanae*. Metz: Abraham Faber, 1596.

Bouhours, Dominique, S.J. *Les Entretiens d'Ariste et d'Eugene*. Paris: Sebastien Mabre-Cramoisy, 1671.

Bozon, Nicole. *Les Contes moralisées*. Ed. Lucy Toulmin Smith and Paul Meyer. SATF. Paris: Firmin Didot, 1889.

Brant, Sebastian. *Das Narrenschiff*. Ed. Manfred Lemmer. 2nd ed. Tübingen: Max Niemeyer, 1968.

– *Le Nef des folz du monde*. Trans. P. Riviere. Paris: G. de Marnef et al., 1497; BN Rés. Yh. 1.

– *The Ship of Fools*. Trans. Edwin Zeydel. New York, 1944.

Brantôme. *Les Dames galantes*. Ed. Maurice Rat. Paris: Garnier, 1967.

– *Oeuvres complètes*. Ed. L. Lalanne. 11 vols. Paris, 1864–82; rpt. New York: Johnson Reprint, 1968.

Castiglione, Baldesar. *The Book of the Courtier*. Trans. Charles S. Singleton. Garden City, NY: Doubleday/Anchor, 1959.

Cats, Jacob. *Maechdenplicht ... Officium Puellarum, in castis Amoribus, Emblemate expressum*. Middelburgh: Hans vander Hellen, 1618.

– *Silenus Alcibiades*. Middelburg: J. Hellens, 1618.

Cebes of Thebes. *Cebes' Tablet*. Ed. Sandra Sider. New York: Renaissance Society of America, 1979.

– *Le Tableau de Cebes*. Trans. Gilles Corrozet. Paris: Denys Janot, 1543.

Cellini, Benvenuto. *Autobiography*. Trans. John Addington Symonds. New York: Doubleday/Dolphin, 1961.

Chandieu, Antoine de La Roche. *Octonaires sur la vanité et inconstance du monde*. Ed. Françoise Bonali-Fiquet. TLF. Geneva: Droz, 1979.

Chassignet, Jean-Baptiste. *Sonnets franc-comtois inédits*. Ed. Théodore Courtaux. 1892; rpt. Geneva: Slatkine, 1969.

Chaumelz, M. de. *Devises panegyriques pour Anne d'Autriche*. Bordeaux: Jacques Mongiron Milanges, 1667.

Christine de Pisan. *The Epistle of Othea to Hector (Harleian manuscript 838)*. Ed. James D. Gordon. Philadelphia, 1942.

– *Les Cent Hystoires de Troye, l'epistre de Othea*. Paris: Philippe Le Noir, 1522; BN Rés. Ye. 214.

– *Epistre Othea. Remaniement de Jean Miélot. Bibl. Royale de Belgique, MS. 9392*. Ed. J. van den Gheyn. Brussels: Vromant, 1913.

Cicero, M. T. *De officiis*. Augsburg: Steyner, 1531.

Colonna, Francesco. *Le Songe de Poliphile*. Ed. Albert-Marie Schmidt. Paris: Les Libraires Associés, 1963.

Cordier, Gentil. *Anona prima, in tres partes divisa: emblematum, epigrammatum, variorum*. Paris: Delas, 1595.

Corrozet, Gilles. *Emblemes*. Paris: Denys Janot, 1543 (with his translation of the *Tabula Cebetis*).

– *Hecatomgraphie*. 1540; rpt. London: Scolar Press, 1974.

– *Hecatomgraphie*. Paris: Denys Janot, 1540.

– *Hecatomgraphie*. Ed. H. Oulmont. Paris: Champion, 1905.

– *Parnasse des poetes françois modernes contenant leurs plus riches & graves sentences, discours ...* Paris: Gilles Corrozet, 1570.

Corrozet, Jean. *Emblemes ou preceptes moraux. Tirez des escrits de feu Gilles Corrozet, non encore imprimez*. Paris: J. Corrozet, 1641; Arsenal 8° B. L. 33.034.

Cotgrave, Randle. *A Dictionarie of the French and English Tongues*. 1611; rpt. Columbia, S.C: University of South Carolina Press, 1950.

Cousin, Jean. *Le Livre de fortune*. Ed. Ludovic Lalanne. Paris and London: Librairie d'Art, J. Rouam, 1883.

Coustau, Pierre. *Petri Costalii Pegma*. Lyons: Macé Bonhomme, 1555.

– *Le Pegme*. Trans. Lanteaume de Romieu. Lyons: Macé Bonhomme, 1560.

Dan, Pierre, S.J. *Le Tresor des merveilles de la maison royale de Fontainebleau*. Paris: Sebastien Cramoisy, 1642.

La Danse macabre de Guyot Marchant. Ed. Pierre Champion. 1486; facsimile rpt. Paris: Editions des Quatre Chemins, 1925.

De Bry, J.-T. *Emblemata nobilitati*. Frankfurt: J.-T. de Bry, 1592; BN Rés. Z. 3734.

– *Emblemata saecularia. Moeurs et coutumes au XVIe siècle*. Facsimile ed. F. Warnecke. Paris: J. Welter, 1895.

– *Emblemata saecularia*. Frankfurt: J.-T. de Bry, 1596; Rouen, Bibliothèque Municipale, Leber 1394.

Devises pour les tapisseries du roy. Ed. Marianne Grivel and Marc Fumaroli. Paris: Herscher, 1988.

Du Bartas, Guillaume de Saluste, Sieur. *Die Schöpfungswoche. La Sepmaine ou creation du monde*. Ed. Kurt Reichenberger. 2 vols. Tübingen: Max Niemeyer, 1963.

– *The Works of Guillaume De Salluste Sieur Du Bartas*. Ed. U.T. Holmes et al. 3 vols. 1935–40; rpt. Geneva: Slatkine, 1977.

Du Bellay, Joachim. *La Deffence et illustration de la langue francoyse*. Ed. Henri Chamard. S.T.F.M. Paris: Marcel Didier, 1948.

Emblesmes sus les actions et perfections et meurs du Segnor Espagnol. Traduit du Castillien. Mildelbourg: Simon Molard, 1605.

L'Enfer Marot. 1544; BN Rothschild 2858.

L'Entrée de Henri II. Rouen, 1550. Ed. Margaret McGowan. Amsterdam, 1974.

The Entry of Henry II into Paris, 1549. Ed. I.D. McFarlane. Binghamton, NY: Medieval and Renaissance Texts and Studies, 1982.

Erasmus, Desiderius. *Collected Works*. Toronto: University of Toronto Press, 1974–.

– *De la declamation des louenges de follie*. Paris, 1520; BN Rés. Y^2 949.

– *Stultitiae laus*. Basel: Typis Genathianus, 1676; BN Y^2 12.450bis.

Estienne, Henri. *De l'art de faire les devises*. Paris: Jean Paslé, 1645.

Fournival, Richard de. *Li Bestiaires d'amours*. Ed. Cesare Segre. Milan-Naples: Riccardo Ricciardi, 1957.

Friedrich, Andreas. *Emblemes nouveaux*. Paris: Abraham Pacard, 1617.

Fulgentius the Mythographer. Trans. Leslie George Whitbread. Columbus: Ohio State University Press, 1971.

Giovio, Paolo. *Dialogue des devises d'armes et d'amours*. Trans. Vasquin Philieul. Lyons: Guillaume Rouille, 1561.

– *Dialogo dell'imprese militari et amorose*. Rome: Antonio Barre, 1555.

Gringore, Pierre. *Les Menus propos des amoureux*. Paris: G. Couteau, 1521.

Gueroult, Guillaume. *Figures de la Bible illustrée de huictains françoys*. Lyons: G. Rouille, 1564.

– *Le Premier Livre des emblemes*. Lyons: Balthasar Arnoullet, 1550.
– *Le Premier Livre des emblemes*. Ed. De Vaux de Lancey. Rouen: Lainé, 1937.
– *Second Livre de la description des animaux, contenant le blason des oyseaux*. Lyons: Balthasar Arnoullet, 1550.
Heyns, Zacharias. *Emblemata, Emblemes chrestiennes, et morales*. Rotterdam: Pieter van Waesberge, 1625.
Holbein, Hans. *Historiarum Veteris Testamenti Icones*. 1543; rpt. London: Paddington Press, 1976.
Horapollo. *De la signification des notes hieroglyphiques*. Paris: J. Kerver, 1543.
– *The Hieroglyphics*. Trans. George Boas. Bollingen Series, XXIII. New York: Pantheon, 1950.
Le Jardin d'Honneur. Contenant en soy plusieurs Apologies, Proverbes et Dictz moraulx: avec les hystoires et figures. Rouen, 1545.
Jodelle, Etienne. *Oeuvres complètes*. Ed. E. Balmas. 2 vols. Paris: Gallimard, 1965–8.
Junius, Hadrianus. *Emblemata*. Ed. Hester Black. Menston: Scolar Press, 1972.
La Faye, Antoine de. *Emblemata et epigrammata miscellanea*. Geneva: P. and J. Chouet, 1610.
La Jessée, Jean de. *Les Premieres Oeuvres*. Antwerp: Plantin, 1583.
La Perrière, Guillaume de. *La Morosophie*. Lyons: Macé Bonhomme, 1553.
– *Le Theatre des bons engins*. Paris: Denys Janot, 1540 ns.
– *Le Theatre des bons engins*. Ed. Greta Dexter. Gainesville, FL: Scholars' Facsimiles and Reprints, 1964.
– *Le Theatre des bons engins*. Ed. Alison Saunders. Menston: Scolar Press, 1973.
Latini, Brunetto. *Li Livres dou tresor*. Ed. Francis J. Carmody. Berkeley: University of California Press, 1948.
Le Moyne, Pierre, S.J. *De l'art des devises*. Paris: Sebastien Cramoisy, 1666.
L'Estoile, Pierre de. *Mémoires-journaux*. Ed. G. Brunet. 12 vols. Paris, 1875–96.
Lorris, Guillaume and Jean de Meung. *Le Roman de la Rose*. Ed. Clément Marot. Paris, 1526; BN Rés. Ye. 22.
Luther, Martin. *Selections from His Writings*. Ed. John Dillenberger. New York: Doubleday/Anchor, 1961.
Marguerite de Navarre. *L'Heptaméron*. Ed. Michel François. Paris: Garnier, 1960.
Marolles, Michel de. *Catalogue de livres d'estampes*. Paris: Frederic Leonard, 1666.
Marot, Clément. *Les Epigrammes*. Ed. C.A. Mayer. London: Athlone, 1970.
– *Oeuvres diverses*. Ed. C.A. Mayer. London: Athlone, 1966.
Melancthon, Philip, ed. *Epigrammata Philippi Melancthonis Selectiora*. Frankfurt: S. Feyerabend, 1583.
Menestrier, Claude-François, S.J. *L'Art des emblemes*. Lyons: Benoist Coral, 1662.
– *L'Art des emblemes*. Paris: R.J.B. de la Caille, 1684.
– *L'Art des emblemes* (1684). Ed. François Epée. Thèse pour le doctorat de 3e cycle

(Lettres et Sciences humaines) Université Lyon II, 1981.
Mignault, Claude. *De liberali adolescentum institutione*. Paris: J. Richer, 1575.
– *Oratio de re literaria, in qua de studio recte instituendo agitur*. Paris: J. Richer, 1574.
Mikrokosmos. Antwerp: Gerard de Jode, 1579.
Miroir de la redemption. Lyons: Mathieu Husz, 1478.
Montaigne, Michel de. *Oeuvres complètes*. Ed. A. Thibaudet and M. Rat. Bibliothèque de la Pléiade. Paris: Gallimard, 1962.
Montenay, Georgette de. *Emblemes ou devises chrestiennes*. Ed. C.N. Smith. Menston: Scolar Press, 1971.
Murner, Thomas. *Logica memorativa. Chartiludium logice*. Strasbourg, 1509.
Nancel. *Petri Rami vita*. Ed. Peter Sharratt. In *Humanistica Lovaniensia*, 24 (1975), 161–277.
Ovid. *La Bible des poetes de Ovide Metamorphose*. Paris: Philippe Le Noir, 1531.
– *Metamorphose ... moralisé par maistre Thomas Waleys ... translaté et compilé par Colard Mansion*. Bruges: C. Mansion, 1484.
– *Metamorphoseos libri moralizati*. Lyons: C. Davost, for Etienne Gueynard, 1510.
Palmer, Thomas. *The Emblems of Thomas Palmer. Two Hundred Poosees. Sloane MS. 3794*. Ed. John Manning. AMS Studies in the Emblem, 2. New York: AMS Press, 1988.
Papon, Loys. *Oeuvres*. Ed. N. Yemeniz and Guy de La Grye. 1857; rpt. Geneva: Slatkine, 1969.
– *Supplément aux oeuvres*. Ed. N. Yemeniz and Guy de La Grye. 1860; rpt. Geneva: Slatkine, 1969.
Paradin, Claude. *Devises heroiques*. Lyons: J. de Tournes and Guillaume Gazeau, 1551; expanded edition, 1557.
– *Quadrins historiques de la Bible*. Lyons: Jean de Tournes, 1553.
Philostratus. *Les Images, ou tableaux de platte peinture*. Trans. Blaise de Vigenere. Paris: Veuve Abel l'Angelier and Veuve M Guillemot, 1615.
Physiologus. Trans. Michael J. Curley. Austin: University of Texas Press, 1979.
Pictorii sacra et satyrica epigrammata. Basel: J. Froben, 1518; BN Rés. m. Yc. 257.
Plotinus. *The Enneads*. Trans. Stephen Mackenna. 4th ed., revised by B.S. Page. London: Faber and Faber, 1969.
– *Les Ennéades*. Trans. Emile Bréhier. 6 vols. Paris: Belles Lettres, 1956–64.
Pontus de Tyard. *Oeuvres poétiques complètes*. Ed. John C. Lapp. STFM. Paris: Champion, 1966.
Possevino, Antonio. *Tractatio de poësi & pictura*. 2nd ed. Lyons: Pillehotte, 1595.
Le Printemps de Madame poesie chanté par les vrays amantz au Theatre de magnificence. Lyons: Jacques Berion, 1551; BN Rés. Ye. 1694.
Proverbes en rime. Ed. Grace Frank and Dorothy Miner. Baltimore: Johns Hopkins University Press, 1937.

Rationarium Evangelistarum omnia in se evangelica prosa, versu, imaginibusque quam mirifice complectens. Pforzheim, 1510.

Recueil de pieces sur la querelle de Marot et de Sagon. BN Rothschild 2594.

Recueil des choses notables, qui ont esté faites à Bayonne. Paris: Vascosan, 1566; BN Rés. Lb[33].178.

Richeome, Louis. *Tableaux sacrez*. Paris: Laurent Sonnius, 1601.

Robertet, Jean. *Oeuvres*. Ed. Margaret Zsuppăn. TLF. Geneva: Droz, 1970.

Rollenhagen, Gabriel. *Nucleus emblematum selectissimorum*. Cologne: Crispin de Passe, 1611–13.

Sadeler, Johannes. *Emblemata evangelica ad XII signa coelestia sive totidem anni menses accommodata*. 1585; BN Dépt. des Est., Ec. 71b, f. 108–11.

[Sala, Pierre]. Aurelia Forni Marmocchi, 'U' opera inedita di Pierre Sala: "Fables et emblemes en vers."' *Atti della Accademia delle Scienze dell'Istituto di Bologna, Classe di Scienze Morali, Rendiconti*, 63/2 (1975), 149–87.

– 'Un nuovo manoscritto delle "Fables" di Pierre Sala (con sette favole inedite).' Ibid, 66/2 (1978), 129–63.

Scaliger, J.-C. *Poetices libri septem*. Geneva: J. Crispin, 1561.

Scève, Maurice. *Oeuvres complètes*. Ed. Pascal Quignard. Paris: Mercure de France, 1974.

Sellius, Bernard. *Emblemata sacra e praecipius utriusque Testamenti historiis concinnata a Bernardo Sellio Noviomago & a Petro vander Burgio figurae aeneis elegantissimis illustrat*. Amsterdam: Michel Colin, 1613; BN Dépt. des Est., Te. 39a.

Simeoni, Gabriello. *Figure de la biblia, illustrate de stanze tuscane*. Lyons: G. Rouille, 1574.

– *Les Illustres Observations antiques du Seigneur Gabriel Symeon Florentin*. Lyons: Jean de Tournes, 1558.

Taegio, Bartolomeo. *Il Liceo ... Libro secondo*. Milan: Paolo Gottardo Pontio, 1571.

Tasso, Torquato. *Dialogo dell'Imprese*. Naples: Stigiola, 1594.

Thaon, Philippe de. *Le Bestiaire*. Ed. E. Walberg. 1900; rpt. Geneva: Slatkine, 1970.

Thesaurus amicorum. Lyons: Jean de Tournes, 1558; BN Rés. G. 2640.

Tory, Geoffroy. *Ædiloquium ceu Disticha, partibus Aedium urbanarum & rusticarum suis quaeque locis adscribenda. Item, Epitaphia septem, de Amorum aliquot passionibus Antiquo more, & sermone veteri, vietóque conficta*. Paris: Simon Colines, 1530.

– *Champ Fleury ou l'art et science de la proportion des lettres*. Ed. Gustave Cohen. 1931; rpt. Geneva: Slatkine, 1973.

– *VII Epitaphes d'amour et emblemes*. Montanthiaume, S. et O., 1959.

Traductions de latin en françoys, imitations et inventions nouvelles, tant de Clement Marot que d'autres. Paris: Estienne Groulleau, 1550; BN Rés. pYc. 1646.

Trois traitez de la philosophie naturelle non encore imprimez ... Paris: Guillaume

Marette, 1612.

Urfé, Anne d'. *Les Oeuvres morales et spirituelles inédites*. Ed. Yves Le Hir. TLF. Geneva: Droz, 1977.

Veen, Otto van. *Les Emblemes de l'Amour humain*. Brussels: F. Foppens, 1667.

Willett, Andrew. *Sacrorum emblematum centuria una*. Cambridge: John Legate, c. 1591/2.

II. SECONDARY SOURCES

Amielle, Ghislaine. *Les Traductions françaises des Métamorphoses d'Ovide*. Paris: Jean Touzot, 1988.

Angress, R.K. *The Early German Epigram: A Study in Baroque Poetry*. Studies in the Germanic Languages and Literatures, 2. Lexington: University of Kentucky Press, 1971.

Anzelewsky, Fedja. *Dürer, His Art and Life*. Trans. Heide Grieve. New York: Alpine, 1981.

Ashworth, William B., Jr. 'Marcus Gheeraerts and the Aesopic Connection in Seventeenth-Century Scientific Illustration.' *Art Journal* (Summer 1984), 132–8.

Audiat, Louis. *Epigraphie santone et aunisienne*. Niort, 1875.

Audin, Marius. *Le Thesaurus Amicorum de Jean de Tournes*. Lyons, 1927.

Aulotte, Robert. 'D'Egypte en France par l'Italie: Horapollon au XVIe siècle.' In *Mélanges à la mémoire de Franco Simone. France et Italie dans la culture européenne*. 2 vols. Geneva: Slatkine, 1980. I, 555–72.

Balavoine, Claudie. 'Archéologie de l'emblème littéraire: La dédicace à Conrad Peutinger des *Emblemata* d'André Alciat.' In *Emblèmes et devises au temps de la Renaissance*. Ed. M.-T. Jones-Davies. Paris: Touzet, 1981. 9–21.

– 'Bouquets de fleurs et colliers de perles: Sur les recueils de formes brèves au XVIe siècle.' In *Les Formes brèves de la prose et le discours discontinu (XVIe et XVIIe siècles)*. Ed. Jean Lafond. De Pétrarque à Descartes, 46. Paris: J. Vrin, 1984. 51–71.

– 'Les *Emblemes* d'Alciat: Sens et contresens.' In *L'Emblème à la Renaissance*. Ed. Yves Giraud. Paris: SEDES/CDU, 1982. 49–59.

– 'La Mise en mot dans la *Délie* de Scève: Plaidoyer pour une anabase.' In *L'Intelligence du passé. Les faits l'écriture et le sens. Mélanges offerts à Jean Lafond* (Tours: Presses de l'Université, 1988). 73–85.

– 'Le Modèle hiéroglyphique à la Renaissance.' In *Le Modèle à la Renaissance*. Ed. Jean Lafond. Paris: Vrin, 1986. 209–225.

Bardon, Françoise. *Diane de Poitiers et le mythe de Diane*. Paris: PUF, 1963.

– *Le Portrait mythologique à la cour de France sous Henri IV et Louis XIII*. Paris: Picard, 1974.

– 'Sur un portrait de François Ier.' *Information d'Histoire de l'Art*, 8 (1963), 1–7.

Barroux, Robert. 'Catalogue d'une bibliothèque à la fin du XVIe siècle.' *RSS*, 15 (1928), 324–36.

Bath, Michael. 'Honey and Gall or: Cupid and the Bees. A Case of Iconographic Slippage.' In *Andrea Alciato and the Emblem Tradition: Essays in Honor of Virginia Woods Callahan*. Ed. Peter M. Daly. Studies in the Emblem, 4. New York: AMS Press, 1989. 59–94.

– 'Two Early English-owned Alciato Editions in Glasgow University Library.' *Emblematica*, 2 (1987), 387–8.

Bauer, Linda Freeman. 'Seventeenth-Century Naturalism and the Emblematic Interpretation of Paintings.' *Emblematica*, 3 (1988), 209–28.

Bayley, Peter. *French Pulpit Oratory, 1598–1650*. Cambridge: Cambridge University Press, 1980.

Beard, Charles R. 'Cap Brooches of the Renaissance.' *Connoisseur*, 104 (1939), 287–93.

Beaune, Colette. 'Costume et pouvoir en France à la fin du Moyen Age: Les devises royales vers 1400.' *Revue des Sciences Humaines*, 55 (1981), 125–46.

Bergal, Irene. 'Word and Picture: Erasmus' *Parabolae* in La Perrière's *Morosophie*.' *BHR*, 47 (1985), 113–23.

Bland, David. *A History of Book Illustration*. 2nd ed. Berkeley and Los Angeles: University of California Press, 1969.

Blench, J.W. *Preaching in England in the Late Fifteenth and Sixteenth Centuries*. New York: Barnes and Noble, 1964.

Bloomfield, Morton. 'A Grammatical Approach to Personification Allegory.' *Modern Philology*, 60 (1963), 161–71.

– 'Symbolism in Medieval Literature.' *Modern Philology*, 56(1958), 73–81.

Blum, André. *L'Estampe satirique en France pendant les guerres de religion*. Paris: Giard & Brière, 1927.

Bohat, A. 'Les Peintures murales de la Renaissance au Château de Busset (Allier).' *BHR*, 41 (1979), 245–53.

Bologna, Giulia. *Illuminated Manuscripts: The Book before Gutenberg*. New York: Weidenfeld and Nicolson, 1988.

Bonnardot, Alfred. *Gilles Corrozet et Germain Brice*. Paris: H. Champion, 1880.

Bonnefon, Paul. *Montaigne, l'homme et l'oeuvre*. Paris-Bordeaux: J. Rouam and G. Gounouilhou, 1893.

Bouchereaux, S.M. 'Recherches bibliographiques sur G. Corrozet.' *Bulletin du Bibliophile et du Bibliothécaire* (1948), 134–51, 204–20, 291–301, 324-36.

Bourciez, Edouard. *Les Moeurs polies et la littérature de cour sous Henri II*. 1886; rpt. Geneva: Slatkine, 1967.

Brun, Robert. *Le Livre français illustré de la Renaissance*. 2nd ed. Paris: Picard, 1969.

Brunon, Claude-Françoise. 'Signe, figure, langage: Les *Hieroglyphica* d'Horapollon.' In *L'Emblème à la Renaissance*. Ed. Yves Giraud. Paris: SEDES/CDU, 1982. 29–47.

Bullart, Isaac. *Academie des sciences et des arts*. 2 vols. Brussels: F. Foppens, 1682.

Burin, Elizabeth. 'Pierre Sala's Pre-Emblematic Manuscripts.' *Emblematica*, 3 (1988), 1–30.

Cahn, Walter. 'The Rule and the Book: Cistercian Book Illumination in Burgundy and Champagne.' In *Monasticism and the Arts*. Ed. T.G. Verdon et al. Syracuse, NY: Syracuse University Press, 1984. 139–72.

Calkins, Robert G. *Illuminated Books of the Middle Ages*. Ithaca, NY: Cornell University Press, 1983.

Callahan, Virginia W. 'Andrea Alciati's View of Erasmus: Prudent Cunctator and Bold Counselor.' In *Acta Conventus Neo-Latini Sanctandreani. Proceedings of the Fifth International Congress of Neo-Latin Studies*. Ed. I.D. McFarlane. Binghamton, NY: Medieval and Renaissance Texts and Studies, 1981. 203–10.

– 'Erasmus: An Emblematic Portrait by Andrea Alciati.' *Erasmus of Rotterdam Society Yearbook Nine* (1989), 73–90.

– 'The Erasmus-Alciati Friendship.' In *Acta Conventus Neo-Latini Lovaniensis. Proceedings of the First International Congress of Neo-Latin Studies*. Ed. J. Ijsewijn and E. Kessler. Munich: Fink, 1973. 133–41.

Camille, Michael. 'The Book of Signs: Writing and Visual Difference in Gothic Manuscript Illumination.' *Word & Image*, 1 (1985). 133–48.

– *The Gothic Idol: Ideology and Image-Making in Medieval Art*. Cambridge: Cambridge University Press, 1989.

– 'Seeing and Reading: Some Visual Implications of Medieval Literacy and Illiteracy.' *Art History*, 8 (1985), 26–50.

Campa, Pedro F. *Emblemata Hispanica: An Annotated Bibliography of Spanish Emblem Literature to the Year 1700*. Durham, NC: Duke University Press, 1990.

Campbell, Lorne. *Renaissance Portraits*. New Haven, CT: YaleUniversity Press, 1990.

Carroll, Eugene A. *Rosso Fiorentino. National Gallery of Art, Washington, 25.x.87–3.i.88*. Washington, DC, 1987.

Carruthers, Mary. *The Book of Memory: A Study of Memory in Medieval Culture*. Cambridge: Cambridge University Press, 1990.

Cavallo, Adolfo Salvatore. *Medieval Tapestries in the Metropolitan Museum of Art*. New York: Metropolitan Museum of Art/Harry N. Abrams, 1993.

Cave, Terence, and Michel Jeanneret. *Métamorphoses spirituelles. Anthologie de la poésie religieuse française 1570–1630*. Paris: José Corti, 1972.

Céard, Jean, and Jean-Claude Margolin. *Rébus de la Renaissance. Des Images qui parlent.* 2 vols. Paris: Maisonneuve and Larose, 1986.

Chartrou, Josèphe. *Les Entrées solennelles et triomphales à la Renaissance (1484-1551).* Paris: PUF, 1928.

Chenu, M.-D., O.P. *La Théologie au douzième siècle.* Paris: Vrin, 1957.

Choné, Paulette. *Emblèmes et pensée symbolique en Lorraine (1525–1633). 'Comme un jardin au coeur de la chrétienté.'* Paris: Klincksieck, 1991.

Chydenius, Johan. 'La Théorie du symbolisme médiéval.' *Poétique*, no. 23 (1975), 322–41.

Clanchy, M.T. *From Memory to Written Record. England, 1066–1307.* Cambridge, MA: Harvard University Press, 1979.

Clark, Kenneth. 'Leon Battista Alberti on Painting.' *Proceedings of the British Academy*, 30 (1944), 283–302.

Cohen, Gustave. 'Emblèmes moraux inédits du XVe siècle.' In *Mélanges ... offerts à Paul Laumonnier.* Paris: Droz, 1935. 89–96.

Connat, M. 'Mort et testament de Rémy Belleau.' *BHR*, 6 (1945), 328–56.

Cornilliat, François. 'Le commentaire a-t-il horreur du vide? L'attribution du sens chez Barthélemy Aneau.' *Poétique*, 77 (1989), 78–88.

– 'Physiologie du mariage et de l'emblème: Aneau et Alciat.' *Littérature*, no. 78 (1990), 22–45.

Cottrell, Robert. *The Grammar of Silence: A Reading of Marguerite de Navarre's Poetry.* Washington, DC: The Catholic University of America Press, 1986.

Daly, Peter M. 'The Union Catalogue of Emblem Books and the *Corpus Librorum Emblematum.*' *Emblematica*, 3 (1988), 121–33.

Davis, Natalie Zemon. *Fiction in the Archives: Pardon Tales and Their Tellers in Sixteenth-Century France.* Stanford, CA: Stanford University Press, 1987.

De Angelis, Maria Antonietta. 'Emblems and Devices on a Ceiling in the Château of Dampierre-sur-Boutonne.' *JWCI*, 46 (1983), 221–8.

De Hamel, Christopher. *A History of Illuminated Manuscripts.* Boston: David R. Godine, 1986.

Delisle, Léopold. 'Livres d'images destinés à l'instruction religieuse et aux exercices de piété des laïques.' In *Histoire littéraire de la France ... commencé par des Religieux Bénédictins.* 1893; rpt. New York: Kraus, 1971. XXXI, 213–85.

Deutsch, Babette. *Poetry Handbook: A Dictionary of Terms.* New York: Grosset & Dunlap, 1957.

Dexter, Greta. 'Guillaume de La Perrière.' *BHR*, 17 (1955), 56–73.

– 'L'Imagination poétique (à propos de B. Aneau).' *BHR*, 37 (1975), 49–62.

– '*La Morosophie* de la Perrière.' *Les Lettres Romanes*, 30 (1976), 64–75.

Dieckmann, Liselotte. *Hieroglyphics: The History of a Literary Symbol.* St. Louis, MO: Washington University Press, 1970.

Dorez, Léon. 'Etudes aldines, II: Les origines et la diffusion du "Songe de

Poliphile,"' *Revue des Bibliothèques*, 6 (1896), 237–86.

Dragonnetti, R. *La Vie de la lettre au Moyen Age*. Paris: Editions du Seuil, 1973.

Drysdall, Denis L. 'Defence and Illustration of the German Language: Wolfgang Hunger's Preface to Alciati's *Emblems* (Text and Translation).' *Emblematica*, 3 (1988), 137–60.

– 'The Hieroglyphs at Bologna.' *Emblematica*, 2 (1987), 225–47.

– 'Préhistoire de l'emblème: Commentaires et emplois du terme avant Alciat.' *Nouvelle Revue du Seizième Siècle*, no. 6 (1988), 29–44.

Duer, Leslie T. 'The Painter and the Poet: Visual Design in *The Duchess of Malfi*.' *Emblematica*, 1 (1986), 293–316.

Duplessis, Georges. *Les Emblèmes d'Alciat*. Paris: Librairie de l'Art J. Rouam, 1884.

Durand, Gilbert. *L'Imagination symbolique*. 2nd ed. Paris: PUF, 1968.

Dutschke, Dennis. *Census of Petrarch Manuscripts in the United States*. Censimento dei Codici Petrarcheschi, 9. Padua: Antenore, 1986.

Eckhardt, A. *Rémy Belleau, sa vie et sa 'Bergerie.'* 1917; rpt. Geneva: Slatkine, 1969.

L'Emblème à la Renaissance. Ed. Yves Giraud. Paris: SEDES/CDU, 1982.

Essling, Prince d', and E. Müntz. *Pétrarque, ses études d'art, son influence sur les artistes*. Paris: Gazette des Beaux-Arts, 1902.

Fabia, Pierre. *Pierre Sala, sa vie et son oeuvre*. Lyons: M. Audin, 1934.

Farmer, Norman K., Jr. 'Lady Drury's Oratory: The Painted Closet from Hawstead Hall.' In *Poets and the Visual Arts in Renaissance England*. Austin: University of Texas Press, 1984. 77–105, 116–17.

Febvre, Lucien, and Henri-Jean Martin. *L'Apparition du livre*. 1958; rpt. Paris: Albin Michel, 1971.

Feuardent, F. *Jetons et méreaux depuis Louis IX jusqu'à la fin du consulat de Bonaparte*. 6 vols. 1904–15; rpt. Maastricht: A.G. van der Dussen, 1982.

Fleming, John V. 'Obscure Images by Illustrious Hands.' In *Text and Image*. Acta, X. Ed. David W. Burchmore. Binghamton, NY: CEMERS, 1983. 1–26.

Fletcher, Angus. *Allegory: The Theory of a Symbolic Mode*. Ithaca, NY: Cornell University Press, 1964.

Forster, Leonard. *The Icy Fire: Five Studies in European Petrarchism*. Cambridge: Cambridge University Press, 1969.

Foucault, Michel. *Les Mots et les choses*. Bibliothèque des Sciences Humaines. Paris: Gallimard, 1966.

Fournoux, B. de. 'Henri Baude et les fresques du château de Busset.' *Bulletin de la Société d'Emulation du Bourbonnais*, 58 (1977), 287–95.

Fowler, Ken. 'Social Content in Mathias Holtzwart's *Emblematum Tyrocinia*.' *Emblematica*, 4 (1989), 15–38.

Franklin, Alfred. *Paris et les parisiens au seizième siècle*. Paris: Emile-Paul frères, 1921.

Frappier, Jean. 'Variations sur le thème du miroir.' *Cahiers de l'Association Internationale des Etudes Françaises*, 11 (1959), 134–59.

Friedman, Lionel J., ed. *Text and Iconography for Joinville's Credo*. Cambridge, MA: Medieval Academy of America, 1958.

Gaffiot, Félix. *Dictionnaire illustré latin-français*. Paris: Hachette, 1934.

Gebelin, François. *Les Châteaux de la Renaissance*. Paris: Les Beaux-arts, 1927.

Genette, Gérard. *Palimpsestes*. Paris: Editions du Seuil, 1982.

Gerig, L. 'Barthélemy Aneau: A Study in Humanism.' *Romanic Review*, 1 (1910), 181–207, 279–89; 2 (1911), 163–85; 4 (1913), 27–57.

Giehlow, Karl. *Die Hieroglyphenkunde des Humanismus in der Allegorie der Renaissance*. In *Jahrbuch der Kunsthistorischen Sammlungen des aller höchsten Kaiserhauses*, XXXII, 1 (1915), 1–232.

Giudici, Enzo. *Maurice Scève, poeta della Délie*. Vol. I: *La struttura e la genesi esteriore del poema*. Collana di Cultura, 9. Rome: Ateneo, 1965.

Gombrich, E.H. *Symbolic Images: Studies in the Art of the Renaissance*. London: Phaidon, 1972.

Gougaud, L. 'Muta praedicatio.' *Revue Bénédictine*, 42 (1930), 168–71.

Grassi, Ernesto. *Renaissance Humanism: Studies in Philosophy and Poetics*. Trans. Walter F. Veit. Binghamton, NY: Medieval and Renaissance Texts and Studies, 1988.

Green, Henry. *Andrea Alciati and His Books of Emblems*. 1872; rpt. New York: Burt Franklin, 1965.

Grieco, Sara F. Matthews. *Ange ou diablesse. La représentation de la femme au XVIe siècle*. Paris: Flammarion, 1991.

Hagstrum, Jean H. *The Sister Arts*. Chicago: University of Chicago Press, 1958.

Hamon, Philippe. 'Qu'est-ce qu'une description?' *Poétique*, no. 12 (1972), 465–85.

Harthan, John. *The History of the Illustrated Book*. London: Thames and Hudson, 1981.

Haussherr, Reiner, ed. *La Bible moralisée de la Bibliothèque Nationale d'Autriche. Codex Vindobonensis 2554*. Paris: Club du Livre-Philippe Lebaud, 1973.

Heckscher, William S. 'Reflections on Seeing Holbein's Portrait of Erasmus at Longford Castle.' In *Essays in the History of Art Presented to Rudolf Wittkower*. Ed. Douglas Fraser, Howard Hibbard, and Milton J. Levine. London: Phaidon, 1967. 128–48; rpt. in *Art and Literature. Studies in Relationship*. Ed. Egon Verheyen. Saecula spiritalia, 17. Baden-Baden: Valentin Koerner, 1985. 281–307.

– and Agnes B. Sherman. *Emblem Books in the Princeton University Library*. Princeton, NJ, 1984.

– and Karl-August Wirth. 'Emblem, Emblembuch.' In *Reallexikon zur deutschen Kunstgeschichte*, V (Stuttgart, 1959), cols. 85–228.

Henkel, Arthur, and Albrecht Schöne, eds. *Emblemata. Handbuch zur Sinnbild-*

kunst des XVI. und XVII. Jahrhunderts. Stuttgart: J.B. Metzler, 1967.

Henry, Avril, ed. *Biblia pauperum*. Ithaca, NY: Cornell University Press, 1987.

Hindman, Sandra. 'Authors, Artists, and Audiences.' In *Pen to Press: Illustrated Manuscripts and Printed Books in the First Century of Printing*. Ed. Sandra Hindman and J.D. Farquhar. College Park, MD: Art Dept., 1977. 157–211.

– *Christine de Pizan's 'Epistre Othéa': Painting and Politics at the Court of Charles VI*. Toronto: Pontifical Institute of Mediaeval Studies, 1986.

Hirst, Michael. *Michelangelo Draftsman. National Gallery of Art, Washington, 9 October–11 December 1988*. Milan: Olivetti, 1988.

Hocke, Gustav René. *Labyrinthe de l'art fantastique*. Trans. Cornélius Heim. Paris: Denoël/Gonthier, 1967.

Hoffmann, Konrad. 'Alciato and the Historical Situation of Emblematics.' In *Andrea Alciato and the Emblem Tradition: Essays in Honor of Virginia Woods Callahan*. Ed. Peter M. Daly. AMS Studies in the Emblem, 4. New York: AMS Press, 1989. 1–45.

Homann, Holger. *Studien zur Emblematik des 16. Jahrhunderts*. Utrecht: Haentjens, Dekker, & Gumbert, 1971.

Huizinga, Johann. *The Waning of the Middle Ages*. Trans. F. Hopman. 1924; New York: Doubleday Anchor, 1954.

Hutton, James. *The Greek Anthology in France*. Ithaca, NY: Cornell University Press, 1946.

– *The Greek Anthology in Italy to the Year 1800*. Ithaca, NY: Cornell University Press, 1935.

Iversen, Erik. *The Myth of Egypt and Its Hieroglyphics in the European Tradition*. Copenhagen: Gad, 1961.

Jacquiot, Josèphe. 'L'Allégorie aux revers de médailles et de jetons du XVe au XVIIe siècle.' *Cahiers de l'Association Internationale des Etudes Françaises*, 28 (1976), 51–63.

Jauss, Hans Robert. 'Entstehung und Strukturwandel der allegorischen Dichtungen.' In *Grundriss der romanischen Literaturen des Mittelalters*, Bd. VI/1. *La Littérature didactique, allégorique et satirique*. Heidelberg: Carl Winter, 1968. 146–244.

Jean-Richard, Pierrette. *Les Incunables de la Collection Edmond de Rothschild. La gravure en relief sur bois et sur métal*. Paris, 1974.

Johnson, W. McAllister. 'Once More the Galerie François Ier at Fontainebleau.' *Gazette des Beaux-Arts*, 103 (1984), 127–44.

Jouhaud, Christian. 'Lisibilité et persuasion. Les placards politiques.' In *Les Usages de l'imprimé*. Ed. Roger Chartier. Paris: Fayard, 1987. 309–41.

Jung, M.-R. *Etudes sur le poème allégorique en France au moyen âge*. Berne: Franke, 1971.

– *Hercule dans la littérature française du XVIe siècle. De l'Hercule courtois à l'Hercule baroque*. THR, 79. Geneva: Droz, 1966.

Jurĕn, Vladimir. 'Le Jeton français et la littérature emblématique.' *XVIIe Siècle*, no. 158 (1988), 21–40.

Kantorowicz, Ernst. *The King's Two Bodies: A Study in Medieval Political Theology*. Princeton, NJ: Princeton University Press, 1957.

Klein, Robert. 'La Théorie de l'expression figurée dans les traités italiens sur les *imprese*, 1555–1612.' In *La Forme et l'intelligible*. Ed. André Chastel. Paris: Gallimard, 1970. 125–50.

Köhler, Johannes. *Angewandte Emblematik im Fliesensaal von Wrisbergholzen bei Hildesheim*. Hildesheim: August Lax, 1988.

Kren, Thomas, ed. *Renaissance Painting in Manuscripts: Treasures from the British Library*. New York: Hudson Hills Press, 1983.

Kristeva, Julia. *Semeiotike. Recherches pour une sémanalyse (extraits)*. Coll. Points-Littérature. Paris: Editions du Seuil, 1978.

Kunzle, David. *The Early Comic Strip*. Berkeley and Los Angeles: University of California Press, 1973.

Labarre, Albert. *Le Livre dans la vie amiénoise du seizième siècle*. Louvain and Paris: Nauwelaerts, 1971.

Lachèvre, Frédéric. *Bibliographie des recueils collectifs de poésies du XVIe siècle*. Paris: Champion, 1922.

Landwehr, John. *Dutch Emblem Books*. Utrecht: Haentjens, Dekker, & Gumbert, 1962.

Langlois, Ernest. *Recueil d'arts de seconde rhétorique*. Paris: Imprimerie Nationale, 1902.

Laumonnier, Paul. 'Sur la bibliothèque de Ronsard.' *RSS*, 14 (1927), 315–35.

Laurens, Pierre. *L'Abeille dans l'ambre. Célébration de l'épigramme. Les Formes du Discours*. Paris: Belles Lettres, 1989.

– and Florence Vuillemier. 'De l'archéologie à l'emblème: La genèse du *Liber Alciat*,' *Revue de l'Art*, no. 101 (1993), 86–95.

Lavaud, Jacques. 'Note sur un recueil manuscrit d'emblèmes composé pour la Maréchale de Retz.' *HR*, 4 (1937), 421–3.

Lawall, David B. 'Notes on a Newly Acquired Manuscript Device Book.' *Princeton University Library Chronicle*, 18 (1957), 210–15.

Lebègue, Raymond. 'Note.' *RSS*, 17 (1930), 344–5.

Leber, C. *Catalogue des livres ... de M.C. Leber*. 4 vols. Paris: Techener, 1839.

Lecoq, Anne-Marie. *François Ier imaginaire. Symbolique et politique à l'aube de la Renaissance française*. Paris: Macula, 1987.

Lemoisne, P.-A. 'Note.' *Les Trésors des Bibliothèques de France*, 4 (1933), 157–9.

Leroux de Lincey. *Le Livre des proverbes français*. 2 vols. Paris, 1859.

Longeon, Claude. *Une Province française à la Renaissance. La Vie intellectuelle en Forez au 16e siècle*. St Etienne: Centre d'Etudes Foréziennes, 1975.

Lubac, Henri de. *Exégèse médiévale. Les Quatre sens de l'Ecriture*. 4 vols. Paris: Aubier, 1959–64.

McConica, James. 'The Riddle of Terminus.' *Erasmus in English*, 2 (1971), 2–7.

McCulloch, Florence. *Medieval Latin and French Bestiaries*. Studies in the Romance Languages and Literatures, 33. Chapel Hill, NC: University of North Carolina Press, 1960.

– 'Pierre Gringore's *Menus propos des amoureux* and Richard de Fournival's *Bestiaire d'amour*.' *Romance Notes*, 10 (1968), 150–9.

McLuhan, Marshall. *The Gutenberg Galaxy*. Toronto: University of Toronto Press, 1962.

MacQueen, John. *Allegory*. The Critical Idiom, 14. London: Methuen, 1970.

Mâle, Emile. *L'Art religieux de la fin du moyen âge en France*. 3rd ed. Paris: Armand Colin, 1925.

Mandowsky, Erna. 'Ricerche intorno all'Iconologia di Cesare Ripa.' *La Bibliofilia*, 41 (1939), 7–27, 111–24, 204–35, 279–326. Also available in the author's Hamburg dissertation: *Untersuchungen zur Iconologia des Cesare Ripa* (1934).

Manning, John. 'A Bibliographical Approach to the Illustrations in Sixteenth-Century Editions of Alciato's *Emblemata*.' In *Andrea Alciato and the Emblem Tradition. Essays in Honor of Virginia Woods Callahan*. Ed. Peter M. Daly. AMS Studies in the Emblem, 4. New York: AMS Press, 1989. 127–76.

– 'Continental Emblem Books in Sixteenth-Century England: The Evidence of Sloane MS. 3794.' *Emblematica*, 1 (1986), 1–12.

Marmocchi, Aurélia Forni, and Gianni Mombello. *Le Raccolte francese di favole esopiane*. Geneva: Slatkine, 1981.

Massing, Jean Michel. 'A New Work by François Du Moulin and the Problem of Pre-Emblematic Traditions.' *Emblematica*, 2 (1987), 249–71.

– 'Proverbial Wisdom and Social Criticism: Two New Pages from the Walters Art Gallery's *Proverbes en rime*.' *JWCI*, 46 (1983), 208–10.

Masson, André. *Le Décor des bibliothèques du moyen-âge à la Révolution*. Histoire des Idées et Critique Littéraire, 125. Geneva: Droz, 1972.

Mathieu-Castellani, Gisèle. *Emblèmes de la mort. Le dialogue de l'image et du texte*. Paris: Nizet, 1988.

Meijer, Marianne S. 'L'Ordre des *Essais* dans les deux premiers volumes.' In *Montaigne et les Essais. 1580–1980. Actes du Congrès de Bordeaux*. Ed. F. Moureau, R. Granderoute, and C. Blum. Geneva: Slatkine, 1983. 17–27.

Mérindol, Christian de. *Le Roi René et la seconde maison d'Anjou. Emblématique, Art, Histoire*. Paris: Léopard d'Or, 1987.

Mesnard, Jean. 'Les Traductions françaises d'Alciat.' In *Crossroads and Perspec-*

tives: French Literature of the Renaissance. Studies in Honor of V.E. Graham. Ed. C.M. Grisé and C.D.E. Tolton. THR, 211. Geneva: Droz, 1986. 101–20.

Miedema, Hessel. 'The Term *Emblema* in Alciati.' *JWCI*, 31 (1968), 234–50.

Minnis, A.J. *Medieval Theory of Authorship*. 2nd ed. Philadelphia: University of Pennsylvania Press, 1988.

Mombello, Gianni. *La Tradizione manoscritta dell' 'Epistre Othea' di Christine de Pisan. Prolegomeni all' edizione del testo.* Turin, 1967.

Montagu, Jennifer. *An Index of Emblems of the Italian Academies Based on Michele Maylender's 'Storie delle accademie d'Italia.'* London: Warburg Institute, 1988.

Morier, Henri. *Dictionnaire de poétique et de rhétorique*, 3rd ed. Paris: PUF, 1981.

Mortimer, Ruth, ed. *Harvard College Library. Department of Printing and Graphic Arts. Catalogue of Books and Manuscripts. Part I. French Sixteenth-Century Books.* 2 vols. Cambridge, MA: Harvard University Press, 1964.

Moss, Ann. *Poetry and Fable: Studies in Mythological Narrative in Sixteenth-Century France.* Cambridge: Cambridge University Press, 1984.

Muratova, Xenia. 'Workshop Methods in English Late Twelfth-Century Illumination and the Production of Luxury Bestiaries.' In *Beasts and Birds of the Middle Ages: The Bestiary and Its Legacy.* Ed. Willene B. Clark and Meradith T. McMunn. Philadelphia: University of Pennsylvania Press, 1989. 53–68.

O'Connor, Dorothy. 'Sébastien Brant en France au XVIe siècle.' *Revue de Littérature Comparée*, 8 (1928), 309–17.

Ong, Walter J., S.J. 'From Allegory to Diagram in the Renaissance Mind.' *Journal of Aesthetics and Art Criticism*, 17 (1959), 423–40.

– *Orality and Literacy: The Technologizing of the Word.* London and New York: Methuen, 1982.

– *The Presence of the Word.* 1967; rpt. Minneapolis: University of Minnesota Press, 1981.

– *Ramus, Method, and the Decay of Dialogue.* Cambridge, MA: Harvard University Press, 1958.

Orth, Myra Dickman. 'Godefroy le Batave, Illuminator to the French Royal Family, 1516–1526.' In *Manuscripts in the Fifty Years after the Invention of Printing.* Ed. J.B. Trapp. London: Warburg Institute, 1983. 50–5.

Panofsky, Erwin, ed. *Abbot Suger on the Abbey Church of Saint Denis and Its Art Treasures.* 2nd ed. Princeton, NJ: Princeton University Press, 1979.

– *Studies in Iconology: Humanistic Themes in the Art of the Renaissance.* New York and Evanston: Harper and Row, 1962.

Parent, Annie. *Les Métiers du livre à Paris au XVIe siècle (1535–1560).* Geneva: Droz, 1974.

Parry, G.A. '"Les Enigmes de l'amour" de Pierre Sala.' *Revue de Philologie*

Française, 22–3 (1908–9), 214–20.

Pastoureau, Michel. '"Arma senescunt, insignia florescunt." Notes sur les origines de l'emblème.' In *Figures et couleurs. Etude sur la symbolique et la sensibilité médiévales*. Paris: Léopard d'Or, 1986. 125–37.

– 'Couleurs, décors, emblèmes.' In *Figures et couleurs. Etude sur la symbolique et la sensibilité médiévales*. Paris: Léopard d'Or, 1986. 51–7.

– 'L'Illustration du livre: comprendre ou rêver?' In *Histoire de l'édition française. Le livre conquérant*. Ed. Henri-Jean Martin, Roger Chartier, and Jean-Pierre Vivet. Paris: Prodomis, 1982. I, 501–29.

Perdrizet, Paul. *Etude sur le Speculum humanae salvationis*. Paris, 1908.

Perrier, Simone. 'Le Corps de la sentence: Les "Emblèmes Chrestiens" de Georgette de Montenay.' *Littérature*, no. 78 (1990), 54–64.

Pesme, Gérard. *En flânant au château de Dampierre-sur-Boutonne*. Angoulême, 1953.

Picot, Emile. *Catalogue des livres composant la Bibliothèque de feu M. le Baron James de Rothschild*. 4 vols. Paris, 1884–1920; rpt. New York: B. Franklin, 1967.

– *Le Théâtre mystique de Pierre Du Val*. Paris: D. Morgand, 1882.

Pinvert, Lucien. *Jacques Grévin*. Paris: Fontemoing, 1899.

Pogue, Samuel. *Jacques Moderne*. THR, 101. Geneva: Droz, 1969.

Pope-Hennessy, John. *The Portrait in the Renaissance*. Bollingen Series, XXXV.12. New York: Pantheon, 1966.

Porcher, Jean. 'Deux tapisseries à rébus.' *HR*, 2 (1935), 57–60.

– 'Un Poème allégorique à la louange des femmes.' *Les Trésors des Bibliothèques de France*, 4 (1933), 160–9.

Porteman, Karel. 'The Earliest Reception of the "Ars Emblematica" in Dutch: An Investigation into Preliminary Matters.' In *The European Emblem: Selected Papers from the Glasgow Conference, 11–14 August, 1987*. Ed. B.F. Scholz, M. Bath, and D. Weston. Leiden: E.J. Brill, 1990. 33–53.

Pozzi, Giovanni. *Francesco Colonna et Alde Manuce*. Trans. Florenzo Monteleone. Paris: Société Monotype, 1962.

– 'Les Hiéroglyphes de l'*Hypnerotomachia Poliphili*.' In *L'Emblème à la Renaissance*. Ed. Yves Giraud. Paris: SEDES/CDU, 1982 15–27.

Praz, Mario. *Studies in Seventeen-Century Imagery*. 2nd. ed. Rome: Edizioni di Storia e Letteratura, 1964.

Princeton Encyclopedia of Poetry and Poetics. Enlarged ed. Ed. Alex Preminger et al. Princeton, NJ: Princeton University Press, 1974.

Quentin-Bauchat, Ernest. *La Bibliothèque de Fontainebleau et les livres des derniers Valois à la Bibliothèque Nationale (1515–1589)*. Paris: E. Paul, L. Huard, et Guillemen, 1891.

Rawles, Stephen. 'Corrozet's *Hecatomgraphie*: Where Did the Woodcuts come from and where Did They go?' *Emblematica*, 3 (1988), 31–64.

– 'The Earliest Editions of Guillaume de La Perrière's *Theatre des bons engins.*' *Emblematica*, 2 (1987), 381–6.

Raymond, Marcel. *La Poésie française et le maniérisme*. Philadelphia: Temple University Press, 1972.

Read, Herbert. *Icon and Idea. The Function of Art in the Development of Human Consciousness*. New York: Schocken Books, 1965.

Rechtien, John G. 'A 1520 French Translation of the Moriae Encomium.' *Ren.Q.* 27 (1974), 23–35.

Renucci, Toussaint. *Un Aventurier des lettres au XVIe siècle, Gabriel Symeoni*. Paris: Didier, 1943.

Reure, O.C. *Notice sur les emblèmes de Anne d'Urfé avec des stances de Loys Papon*. Lyons: Brun, 1904.

Rice, Howard C., Jr. 'More Emblem Books.' *Princeton University Library Chronicle*, 18 (1957), 77–83.

Rigolot, François, and Sandra Sider. 'Fonctions de l'écriture emblématique chez Rabelais.' *L'Esprit Créateur*, 28 (1988), 36–47.

Ritchie, Andrew C. 'Léonard Limousin's Triumph of the Faith, with Portraits of the House of Guise.' *AB*, 21 (1939), 238–50.

Ritter, Georges. *Les Vitraux de la Cathédrale de Rouen*. Cognac, Charente, 1926.

Rosenheim, Max. 'The *Album Amicorum*.' *Archaeologia*, 62, pt. 1 (1910), 251–308.

Rothstein, Marian. 'Disjunctive Images in Renaissance Books.' *Renaissance and Reformation*, 14, n.s. (1990), 101–20.

Roussel, P.-D. *Le Château de Diane de Poitiers à Anet*. Anet, 1882.

Rousset, Jean. 'La Querelle de la métaphore.' In *L'Intérieur et l'extérieur*. Paris: José Corti, 1968. 57–71.

Russell, Daniel. 'Alciati's Emblems in Renaissance France.' *Renaissance Quarterly*, 34 (1981), 534–54.

– 'Conception of Self, Conception of Space, and Generic Convention: An Example from the *Heptaméron*.' *Sociocriticism*, 4–5 (1986/87), 159–83.

– 'Directions in French Emblem Studies.' *Emblematica*, 5 (1991), 129–50.

– 'Du Bellay's Emblematic Vision of Rome.' *Yale French Studies*, 47 (1972), 98–109.

– 'The Emblem and Authority.' *Proceedings of the First International Conference on Word and Image. Word & Image*, 4, no.1 (1988), 81–7.

– *The Emblem and Device in France*. Lexington, KY: French Forum Publishers, 1985.

– 'Emblematic Structures in Sixteenth-Century French Poetry.' *Jahrbuch für Internationale Germanistik*, 14 (1982), 54–100.

– 'Emblematics and Cultural Specificity: Two Examples from Sixteenth-Century France.' *Emblematic Perceptions: Essays in Honor of William S. Heckscher on the*

Occasion of His Ninetieth Birthday. Ed. Peter M. Daly and Daniel S. Russell. New York: AMS Press, 1995. 135–57.

– 'Emblematics in the French Provinces: The Case of Loys Papon and Anne d'Urfé in the Forez.' In *Lapidary Inscriptions: Renaissance Essays for Donald A. Stone, Jr*. Ed. Barbara C. Bowen and Jerry C. Nash. Lexington, KY: French Forum Publishers, 1991. 123–37.

– 'L'Emblématique et la descripition dans la poésie française de Du Bellay.' In *Du Bellay. Actes du Colloque International d'Angers du 26 au 29 mai 1989*. Angers: Presses de l'Université d'Angers, 1990. 237–47.

– 'Emblème et mentalité symbolique.' *Littérature*, no. 78 (1990), 11–21.

– 'Emblems and Hieroglyphics: Some Observations on the Beginnings and the Nature of Emblematic Forms. *Emblematica*, 1 (1986), 227–43.

– 'M. de Montplaisir and His Emblems.' *Neophilologus*, 67 (1983), 503–16.

– 'Montaigne's Emblems.' *French Forum*, 9 (1984), 261–75.

– 'More French Translations of Alciato's Emblems.' *Emblematica*, 5 (1991), 121–5.

– 'The Needs of the Literary Historian.' In *An Index of Emblem Art*. Ed. Peter M. Daly. AMS Studies in the Emblem, 6. New York: AMS Press, 1990. 107–19.

– 'A Note on Panurge's "pusse en l'aureille."' *Etudes Rabelaisiennes*, 11 (1974), 83–7.

– 'Panurge and His New Clothes.' *Etudes Rabelaisiennes*, 14 (1978), 89–104.

– 'Reading Alciato in Sixteenth-Century France: Simon Bouquet's *Imitations et traductions de cent dixhuict emblemes d'Alciat*.' In *Andrea Alciato and the Emblem Tradition: Essays in Honor of Virginia Woods Callahan*. Ed. Peter M. Daly. AMS Studies in the Emblem, 4. New York: AMS Press, 1989. 205–21.

– 'Some Ways of Structuring Character in the *Heptaméron*.' In *Critical Tales: New Studies of the Heptaméron and Early Modern Culture*. Ed. John D. Lyons and Mary McKinley. Philadelphia: University of Pennsylvania Press, 1993. 203–17.

Sainéan, Lazare. 'Le Songe de Poliphile.' In *Problèmes littéraires du seizième siècle*. Paris: Boccard, 1927. 251–60.

Saulnier, V.-L. *Maurice Scève*. 1948; rpt. Geneva: Slatkine, 1981.

– 'Proverbe et paradoxe du XVe au XVIe siècle.' In *Pensée humaniste et tradition chrétienne aux XVe et XVIe siècles*. Ed. H. Bédarida. Paris: CNRS, 1950. 87–104.

Saunders, Alison. 'Alciati and the Greek Anthology.' *Journal of Medieval and Renaissance Studies*, 12 (1982), 1–18.

– *The Sixteenth-Century French Emblem Book: A Decorative and Useful Genre*. THR, 224. Geneva: Droz, 1988.

Saxl, Fritz. 'A Spiritual Encyclopedia of the Later Middle Ages.' *JWCI*, 5 (1942), 82–142.

Sayles, Hilary J.M. 'Chronological List of Emblem Books.' In Mario Praz, *Studies in Seventeenth-Century Imagery, Part II*. Rome: Edizioni di Storia e Letteratura, 1974.

Scaglione, Aldo. *The Liberal Arts and the Jesuit College System*. Amsterdam: John Benjamins, 1986.

Schapiro, Meyer. *Words and Pictures*. The Hague and Paris: Mouton, 1973.

Schleier, Reinhart. *Tabula Cebetis: Studien zur Rezeption einer antiken Bildbeschreibung im 16. und 17. Jahrhundert*. Berlin: Mann, 1974.

Scholes, Robert. *Structuralism in Literature: An Introduction*. New Haven, CT: Yale University Press, 1974.

Scholz, Bernhard F. 'From Illustrated Epigram to Emblem: The Canonization of a Typographical Arrangement.' In *New Ways of Looking at Old Texts. Papers of the Renaissance English Text Society 1985–1991*. Ed. W. Speed Hill. Medieval and Renaissance Texts and Studies, 107. Binghamton, NY: Renaissance English Text Society, 1993. 140–57.

– '"Libellum composui epigrammaton, cui titulum feci Emblemata"': Alciatus's Use of the Expression *Emblema* Once Again.' *Emblematica*, 1 (1986), 213–26.

Schutz, A.H. 'Ronsard's "Amours" xxxii and the Tradition of the Synthetic Lady.' *Romance Philology*, 1 (1947), 125–35.

– *Vernacular Books in Parisian Private Libraries of the Sixteenth Century*. Chapel Hill: University of North Carolina Press, 1955.

Schwartz, Jerome. 'Emblematic Structures in Yver's *Printemps*.' *Journal of Medieval and Renaissance Studies*, 17 (1987), 235–55.

– 'Scatology and Eschatology in Gargantua's Androgyne Device.' *Etudes Rabelaisiennes*, 14 (1978), 265–75.

– 'Some Emblematic Marriage Topoi in the French Renaissance.' *Emblematica*, 1 (1986), 245–65.

Sealy, Robert J. *The Palace Academy of Henry III*. THR, 184. Geneva: Droz, 1981.

Selig, Karl-Ludwig. 'Notes on Ronsard in the Netherlands.' *Studi Francesi*, 13 (1969), 281–4.

Seznec, Jean. *The Survival of the Pagan Gods*. Trans. Barbara F. Sessions. 1953; New York: Harper Torchbooks, 1961.

Sider, Sandra. 'Horapollo.' In *Catalogus Translationum et Commentariorum: Medieval and Renaissance Latin Translations and Commentaries*. Vol. 6. Washington, DC: Catholic University Press, 1986. 15–29.

Simone, Franco. *The French Renaissance: Medieval Tradition and Italian Influence in Shaping the Renaissance in France*. Trans. H. Gaston Hall. London: Macmillan, 1969.

Smalley, Beryl. *English Friars and Antiquity in the Early Fourteenth Century*. Oxford: B. Blackwell, 1960.

Stock, Brian. *The Implications of Literacy: Written Language and Models of Interpretation in the Eleventh and Twelfth Centuries*. Princeton, NJ: Princeton University Press, 1983.

Stone, Donald. *From Tales to Truths*. Frankfurt-am-Main: Klostermann, 1973.

Strudel, Armand. '"Allegoria in factis" et "allegoria in verbis,"' *Poétique*, no. 23 (1975), 342–57.

Tatarkiewicz, W. *Medieval Aesthetics*. The Hague: Mouton, 1970.

Tervarent, Guy de. *Attributs et symboles dans l'art profane (1450–1600)*. THR, 29. Geneva: Droz, 1958.

Tiemann, Barbara. *Fabel und Emblem: Gilles Corrozet und die französische Renaissance-Fabel*. Munich: Fink, 1974.

– 'Sebastian Brant und das frühe Emblem in Frankreich.' *Deutsche Vierteljahrsschrift für Literaturgeschichte*, 47 (1973), 598–644.

Todorov, Tzvetan. *Symbolisme et interprétation*. Paris: Editions du Seuil, 1978.

Toubert, Hélène. 'Formes et fonctions de l'enluminure.' In *Histoire de l'édition française*. Ed. Henri-Jean Martin and Roger Chartier. Paris: Prodomis, 1983. I, 87–129.

Trapp, J.B., ed. *Manuscripts in the Fifty Years after the Invention of Printing*. London: Warburg Institute, 1983.

Trésor de numismatique et de glyptique ... médailles françaises depuis le règne de Charles VII jusqu'à celui de Louis XVI. Paris: Ritter et Goupil, 1836.

Tung, Mason. 'Towards a New Census of Alciati's Editions.' *Emblematica*, 4 (1989), 135–76.

Tuve, Rosemond. *Allegorical Imagery*. Princeton, NJ: Princeton University Press, 1966.

Vanuxem, Jacques. 'Le Carrousel de 1612 sur la Place Royale et ses devises.' In *Les Fêtes de la Renaissance*. Ed. Jean Jacquot. Paris: CNRS, 1956. I, 191–203.

Viard, P.E. *André Alciat*. Paris: S.A. du 'Recueil Sirey,' 1926.

Voet, Leon. *The Plantin Press (1555–1589)*. 6 vols. Amsterdam: Van Hoewe, 1982.

Volkmann, Ludwig. *Bilderschriften der Renaissance*. Leipzig, 1923; rpt. Nieuwkoop: De Graaf, 1969.

Waddington, Raymond. 'The Bisexual Portrait of Francis I: Fontainebleau, Castiglione and the Tone of Courtly Mythology.' In *Playing with Gender: A Renaissance Pursuit*. Ed. Jean R. Brink, Maryanne Horowitz, and Allison P. Coudert. Urbana and Chicago: University of Illinois Press, 1991. 99–132.

Warkentin, Germaine. 'The Form of Dante's "Libello" and Its Challenge to Petrarch.' *Quaderni d'Italianistica*, 2 (1981), 160–70.

Weinberg, Bernard. *A History of Literary Criticism in the Italian Renaissance*. 2 vols. Chicago: University of Chicago Press, 1961.

Weinberg, Kurt. 'The Lady and the Unicorn, or M. de Nemours à Coulomiers: Enigma, Device, Blazon and Emblem in *La Princesse de Clèves*.' *Euphorion*, 71 (1977), 306–35.

Whitman, Jon. *Allegory: The Dynamics of an Ancient and Medieval Technique*. Oxford: Clarendon Press, 1987.
Wilson, Adrian, and Joyce Lancaster Wilson. *A Medieval Mirror: Speculum Humanae Salvationis*. Berkeley and Los Angeles: University of California Press, 1984.
Wind, Edgar. '"Aenigma Termini": The Emblem of Erasmus.' *JWI*, 1 (1937), 66–9.
– *Pagan Mysteries in the Renaissance*. 2nd ed. New York: Norton, 1968.
– 'Studies in Allegorical Portraiture.' *JWI*, 1 (1937), 138–62.
Woodner Collection. Master Drawings. The Metropolitan Museum of Art 1990. New York: Abaris Books, 1990.
Yates, Frances. *The Art of Memory*. Chicago: University of Chicago Press, 1966.
– *The French Academies of the Sixteenth Century*. Studies of the Warburg Institute, 15. London, 1947.
Young, Alan R. *The English Tournament Imprese*. AMS Studies in the Emblem, 3. New York: AMS Press, 1988.
– *Tudor and Jacobean Tournaments*. London: George Philip, 1987.
– 'Wenceslaus Hollar, the London Book Trade, and Two Unidentified English Emblem Books.' In *The English Emblem and the Continental Tradition*. Ed. Peter M. Daly. Studies in the Emblem, 1. New York: AMS Press, 1988. 151–202.
Zumthor, Paul. *Le Masque et la lumière*. Paris: Editions du Seuil, 1978.
– 'Récit et anti-récit: Le "Roman de la Rose."' In *Langue, texte, énigme*. Paris: Editions du Seuil, 1975. 249–64.

Index of Manuscripts

Index of Motifs

Index of Names and Key Terms

www.ingramcontent.com/pod-product-compliance
Lightning Source LLC
LaVergne TN
LVHW090804070826
844660LV00022B/1070

9781442655010